C# For Dummies®

Cheat Sheet

Operators

Precedence	Operators	Cardinality	Associativity
High	() [] .	unary	left to right
	! ~ + – ++ –– (cast)	unary	left to right
	* / %	binary	left to right
	+ –	binary	left to right
	< <= > >=	binary	left to right
	== !=	binary	left to right
	&	binary	left to right
	^	binary	left to right
	|	binary	left to right
	&&	binary	left to right
	||	binary	left to right
	?:	ternary	right to left
Low	= *= /= %= += -= &= ^= |= <<= >=	binary	right to left

Integer Variable Types

Type	Size (bytes)	Range	In Use
sbyte	2	–128 to 127	sbyte sb = –12;
byte	2	0 to 255	byte b = 12;
short	4	–32,768 to 32,767	short sn = –123;
ushort	4	0 to 65,535	ushort usn = 123;
int	8	–2,147,483,648 to 2,147,483,647	int n = 123;
uint	8	0 to 4,294,967,295	uint un = 123U;
long	16	–9,223,372,036,854,775,808 to 9,223,372,036,854,775,807 — "a whole lot"	long l = 123L;
ulong	16	0 to 18,446,744,073,709,551,615	long ul = 123UL;

Floating Point Variable Types

Type	Range	Accuracy	In Use
float	$* 10^{-45}$ to $3.4 * 10^{38}$	6–7 digits	float f = 1.2F;
double	$* 10^{-324}$ to $1.7 * 10^{308}$	15–16 digits	double d = 1.2;

For Dummies: Bestselling Book Series for Beginners

C# For Dummies®

Other Variable Types

Type	Range	In Use
decimal	up to 28 digits	decimal d = 123M;
char	N/A	char x = 'c'; char y = '\x123'; char newline = '\n';
string	N/A	string s = "my name"; string empty = "";
bool	true & false	bool b = true;

Controlling Program Flow

```
if (i < 10)
{
  // go here if i is less than 10
}
else
{
  // go here otherwise
}


while(i < 10)
{
  // keep looping through here as
  // long as i is less than 10
}


for(int i = 0; i < 10; i++)
{
    // loop 10 times
}


foreach(MyClass mc in myCollection)
{
  // ... execute once for each mc
  // object in myCollection
}
```

Defining a Class

```
[public][abstract]classMyClassName
{
    [static][access]typedataMember;
    [<static|virtual|abstract|new|
override>][access]type method
(. . . args . . .)
}
access is public|protected|
internal|private|protected
internal
```

Notes:

[feature]	feature is optional
<feature1	feature2>	either feature1 or else feature2
...	unspecified number of statements or expressions

Hungry Minds™

For Dummies: Bestselling Book Series for Beginners

by Stephen Randy Davis

Hungry Minds™

Best-Selling Books • Digital Downloads • e-Books • Answer Networks • e-Newsletters • Branded Web Sites • e-Learning

New York, NY ◆ Cleveland, OH ◆ Indianapolis, IN

C# For Dummies®

Published by
Hungry Minds, Inc.
909 Third Avenue
New York, NY 10022
www.hungryminds.com
www.dummies.com

Library of Congress Control Number: 2001092928

ISBN: 0-7645-0814-8

Printed in the United States of America

10 9 8 7 6 5 4 3 2 1

1B/RU/RR/QR/IN

Distributed in the United States by Hungry Minds, Inc.

Distributed by CDG Books Canada Inc. for Canada; by Transworld Publishers Limited in the United Kingdom; by IDG Norge Books for Norway; by IDG Sweden Books for Sweden; by IDG Books Australia Publishing Corporation Pty. Ltd. for Australia and New Zealand; by TransQuest Publishers Pte Ltd. for Singapore, Malaysia, Thailand, Indonesia, and Hong Kong; by Gotop Information Inc. for Taiwan; by ICG Muse, Inc. for Japan; by Intersoft for South Africa; by Eyrolles for France; by International Thomson Publishing for Germany, Austria and Switzerland; by Distribuidora Cuspide for Argentina; by LR International for Brazil; by Galileo Libros for Chile; by Ediciones ZETA S.C.R. Ltda. for Peru; by WS Computer Publishing Corporation, Inc., for the Philippines; by Contemporanea de Ediciones for Venezuela; by Express Computer Distributors for the Caribbean and West Indies; by Micronesia Media Distributor, Inc. for Micronesia; by Chips Computadoras S.A. de C.V. for Mexico; by Editorial Norma de Panama S.A. for Panama; by American Bookshops for Finland.

For general information on Hungry Minds' products and services please contact our Customer Care Department within the U.S. at 800-762-2974, outside the U.S. at 317-572-3993 or fax 317-572-4002.

For sales inquiries and reseller information, including discounts, premium and bulk quantity sales, and foreign-language translations, please contact our Customer Care Department at 800-434-3422, fax 317-572-4002, or write to Hungry Minds, Inc., Attn: Customer Care Department, 10475 Crosspoint Boulevard, Indianapolis, IN 46256.

For information on licensing foreign or domestic rights, please contact our Sub-Rights Customer Care Department at 212-884-5000.

For information on using Hungry Minds' products and services in the classroom or for ordering examination copies, please contact our Educational Sales Department at 800-434-2086 or fax 317-572-4005.

For press review copies, author interviews, or other publicity information, please contact our Public Relations Department at 317-572-3168 or fax 317-572-4168.

For authorization to photocopy items for corporate, personal, or educational use, please contact Copyright Clearance Center, 222 Rosewood Drive, Danvers, MA 01923, or fax 978-750-4470.

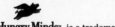

About the Author

Stephen R. Davis, who goes by the name of Randy, has been a programmer and author almost 20 years now. He is currently a Senior Consultant with Valtech, a global consulting, training, and mentoring company (`www.valtech.com`).

Randy can be reached for compliments at `www.stephendavis.com`. Send all complaints to `device NUL`.

Dedication

To Drs. Madeleine Duvic, Jennifer Cather, and Estil Vance. Go, team!

Author's Acknowledgments

I find it very strange that only a single name appears on the cover of any book, but especially a book like this. In reality, many people contribute in its creation. I would like to thank the editorial staff at Hungry Minds, especially John Pont. This book would have been a poorer work but for their involvement.

I would like to thank Valtech for the use of their equipment, time, and encouragement. I've never met a more talented group of guys.

I am indebted to my agents, Claudette Moore and Debbie McKenna. We seem to learn more about each other and more about life with every book.

Most of all, I thank my wife, Jenny, and son, Kinsey, for their patience and devotion. I hope we manage to strike a reasonable balance. Feel free to visit me at `www.stephendavis.com`.

Publisher's Acknowledgments

We're proud of this book; please send us your comments through our Hungry Minds Online Registration Form located at www.dummies.com.

Some of the people who helped bring this book to market include the following:

Acquisitions, Editorial, and Media Development

Project Editor: John W. Pont

Acquisitions Editor: Bob Woerner

Technical Editor: Greg Guntle

Editorial Manager: Constance Carlisle

Permissions Editor: Carmen Krikorian

Media Development Specialist: Marisa Pearman

Media Development Manager: Laura VanWinkle

Media Development Supervisor: Richard Graves

Editorial Assistants: Amanda Foxworth, Jean Rogers

Production

Project Coordinator: Jennifer Bingham

Layout and Graphics: Kelly Hardesty, Gabriele McCann, Jacque Schneider, Betty Schulte, Brian Torwelle, Julie Trippetti, Jeremey Unger, Erin Zeltner

Proofreaders: Andy Hollandbeck, Susan Moritz, TECHBOOKS Production Services

Indexer: TECHBOOKS Production Services

General and Administrative

Hungry Minds Technology Publishing Group: Richard Swadley, Senior Vice President and Publisher; Mary Bednarek, Vice President and Publisher, Networking; Joseph Wikert, Vice President and Publisher, Web Development Group; Mary C. Corder, Editorial Director, Dummies Technology; Andy Cummings, Publishing Director, Dummies Technology; Barry Pruett, Publishing Director, Visual/Graphic Design

Hungry Minds Manufacturing: Ivor Parker, Vice President, Manufacturing

Hungry Minds Marketing: John Helmus, Assistant Vice President, Director of Marketing

Hungry Minds Production for Branded Press: Debbie Stailey, Production Director

Hungry Minds Sales: Michael Violano, Vice President, International Sales and Sub Rights

Contents at a Glance

Cartoons at a Glance

By Rich Tennant

page 91

"Excuse me – is anyone here NOT talking about C#?"

page 33

page 387

"Before I go on to explain more advanced procedures like the 'Zap-Rowdy-Students-who-Don't-Pay-Attention' function, we'll begin with some basics."

page 9

page 197

"We're here to clean the code."

page 345

Cartoon Information:
Fax: 978-546-7747
E-Mail: richtennant@the5thwave.com
World Wide Web: www.the5thwave.com

Table of Contents

Introduction

● ●

*P*rogramming problems have changed over the years. In the early days, computer languages were difficult, and the tools clumsy. Writing a program that did anything worthwhile was difficult. As technology improved, more advanced programming languages appeared on the market. First, there was the C programming language, and later came C++ (pronounced "C plus plus"). The tools were improving as well. Pretty soon, there were integrated development environments with editors and designers and debuggers and gosh knows what all else built into a single cradle-to-grave package.

You'd think that these new languages and tools would've made programming easier, but they didn't — the problems just kept getting harder. Just when I thought that we programmers were about to catch up, along came Web development.

With the advent of the Web, the world fell into two camps: the adherents of solutions based on the Windows operating system and "everyone else." At first, "everyone else" grabbed the advantage. Their Java-based tools enabled programmers to write programs that are distributed across the Web.

In June 2000, Microsoft introduced its answer: a suite of languages and tools called .NET (pronounced "dot net") and its flagship programming language, C# (pronounced "C sharp").

The Java drinkers make their claims on superiority, while the .NETitians make their own arguments. Without seeming to take sides on this argument, a great deal of the difference can be summed up in a single sentence: Java says rewrite everything in Java and you can run it on any machine; .NET says rewrite nothing and you can run it on Windows. (In principle, .NET is not tied directly to the Windows operating system, but in practice there's very little chance that other major operating systems vendors will take up the .NET banner.)

C# works well with the .NET environment, enabling the programmer to create programs that communicate over the Web, including providing services to existing Web pages. C# can be integrated with other programming languages such as Visual Basic and Visual C++, enabling the programmer to migrate existing applications to the Web without the need to rewrite them all at once.

Even beyond that, however, C# is right on key. Visual C# together with the Microsoft Visual Studio .NET environment provide the instruments programmers need to compose harmonious applications.

About This Book

The goal of this book is to explain C# to you, but there's a problem.

Microsoft created C# as a major part of its .NET initiative. For what are probably political reasons, Microsoft turned the specifications for the C# language over to the ECMA (pronounced "ek ma") international standards committee in the summer of 2000, long before .NET was a reality. In theory, any company can come up with its own version of C# written to run on any operating system, on any machine larger than a calculator.

However, as of this writing only one vendor produces a C# compiler — Microsoft. In addition, Microsoft's Visual C# comes packaged in only one way: as part of the Visual Studio .NET suite of tools.

Thus, in describing C# to you, I can't avoid dealing with Visual C#, at least to some degree. I have tried to keep the Visual Studio portions to a reasonable minimum. I could just tell you, "Run your program any way you want," but instead I might say, "Execute your C# program from Visual Studio by pressing the F5 key." I want you to be able to focus on the C# language and not on the mechanics of getting simple things to work.

Balanced against that, I realize that many, if not most, readers will want to use C# to write Windows applications. Although this book is not about Windows programming, per se, I devote one part of this book to demonstrating how C# and Visual Studio combine to form a powerful Windows programming environment.

I also realize that some power users will be using C# to build Web-ready, distributed applications; however, publishing limitations require me to draw the line somewhere. *C# For Dummies* does not tackle the challenges of .NET and distributed programming.

Foolish Assumptions

Before you can start programming in C#, you must have a C# development environment set up on your computer. As of this writing, that means Microsoft's Visual Studio. You must have installed Visual Studio .NET to build the programs in this book.

You need the Common Language Runtime (CLR) before you can even execute the programs generated by C#. Visual Studio .NET copies the CLR onto your machine for you as part of the installation procedure. In addition, Microsoft plans to include the CLR with later versions of Windows, but has not done so as of this writing.

How to Use This Book

I've made this book as easy to use as possible. Figuring out a new language is hard enough. Why make it any more complicated than it needs to be? The book is divided into six parts. Part I introduces you to C# programming with Visual Studio. This part guides you step-by-step in the creation of two different types of programs. I strongly encourage you to start here and read these two chapters in order before branching out into the other parts of the book. Even if you've programmed before, the basic program framework created in Part I is reused throughout the book.

The chapters in Parts II through IV stand alone. I have written these chapters so you can open up the book to any one of them and start reading. If you are new to programming, however, you will have to read Part II before you can jump ahead. However, when you return to refresh your memory on some particular topic, you should have no trouble flipping to a section without the need to restart back 20 pages.

Part V returns to the hand-holding, "do it like this" style. *C# For Dummies* is about C# programming. However, C# and Visual Studio .NET really shine when creating full-blown Windows applications. Part V takes you through the steps of building a non-trivial Windows program. You won't know all there is to know about building high-powered Windows applications when you finish, but Part V will give you a jumpstart in that direction.

Of course, the Part of Tens finishes out the lineup.

How This Book Is Organized

Here's a brief rundown on what you'll find in each part of the book.

Part I — Creating Your First C# Programs

You'll create lots of programs in your C# career. What better way to start out than writing a fun little (and I mean little) Windows application? This part shows you, step by step, how to write the smallest Windows application possible using the Visual Studio .NET interface. Part I also shows you how to create the basic C# framework used in the other parts of this book.

Part II — Basic C# Programming

At the most basic level, Shakespeare's plays are just a series of words all strung together. By the same token, 90 percent of any C# program you ever write consists of creating variables, performing arithmetic operations, and controlling the execution path through a program. This part concentrates on these core operations.

Part III — Object-Based Programming

It's one thing to declare variables here or there and to add them and subtract them. It's quite another thing to write real programs for real people. Part III focuses on how to organize your data to make it easier to use in creating a program.

Part IV — Object-Oriented Programming

You can organize the parts of an airplane all you want, but until you make it do something, it's nothing more than a collection of parts. It's not until you fire up the engines and start the wings flapping that it's going anywhere.

In like fashion, Part IV explains how to turn a collection of data into a real object — an object that has internal members, sure, but an object that can mimic the properties of a real-world item. This part presents the essence of object-oriented programming.

Part V — Windows Programming with Visual Studio

Figuring out C# is one thing, but understanding how to write a full-blown Windows application with bows, tassels, buttons, and bells is quite another. Just for fun, Part V takes you step-by-step through the process of using C# together with the Visual Studio interface to create a "more than trivial" Windows application. You'll be proud of the result, even if your kid doesn't call his friends over to see it.

Part VI — The Part of Tens

C# is great at finding errors in your programs — at times, it seems a little too good at pointing out my shortcomings. However, believe it or not, C# is trying to do you a favor. Every problem it finds is another problem that you would otherwise have to find on your own.

Unfortunately, the error messages can be confusing. One chapter in this part presents the ten most common C# build error messages, what they mean, and how the heck to get rid of them.

Many readers are coming to C# from another programming language. The second chapter in The Part of Tens describes the ten major differences between C# and its progenitor, C++.

About the CD-ROM

The enclosed CD-ROM contains a host of goodies. First, there's all the source code from this book. Then there's a set of utilities. The Sharp Developer utility provides a quick C# editing capability. I don't recommend it for full-scale development, but it's useful for making a quick change without waiting for Visual Studio to boot up. The Win2000 utility is a trial version of a professional-grade software design tool meant for the serious developer.

Don't forget the ReadMe file, which has all the most up-to-date information.

Icons Used in This Book

Throughout the pages of this book, I use the following icons to highlight important information.

This icon flags technical stuff that you can skip on the first reading.

The Tip icon highlights a point that can save you a lot of time and effort.

Remember this. It's important.

Remember this, too. This one can sneak up on you when you least expect it and generate one of those really hard-to-find bugs.

This icon identifies code you can find on the CD-ROM that comes with this book. This feature is designed to save you some typing when your fingers start to cramp, but don't abuse it. You'll gain a better understanding of C# by entering the programs yourself.

Conventions Used in This Book

Throughout this book, I use several conventions to help you out. Terms that are not "real words," such as the name of some program variable, appear in this font in order to minimize the confusion factor. Program listings are offset from text as follows:

```
use System;
namespace MyNameSpace
{
  public class MyClass
  {
  }
}
```

Each listing is followed by a clever, insightful explanation. Complete programs are included on the CD-ROM for your viewing pleasure. Small code segments are not.

Finally, you'll see command arrows, as in the phrase, "Choose File⇨Open With⇨Notepad." That means choose the File menu option. Then, from the pull-down menu that appears, choose Open With. Finally, from the resulting submenu, choose Notepad.

Where to Go From Here

Obviously, the first step is to figure out the C# language, ideally using *C# For Dummies*, of course. I would give myself a few months of writing simple C# programs before taking on the next step of learning how to create Windows applications. Part V might make it look easy, but there are lots of pitfalls. Try out each of the components available in the Visual Studio toolbox. Visual Studio's extensive, approachable Help system describes all these *widgets*. Give yourself many months of Windows application experience before you branch out into writing programs intended to be distributed over the Internet.

In the meantime, you can keep up with C# goings-and-comings in several loca-tions. First, check out the official source: `msdn.microsoft.com/msdn`. In addition, various programmer Web sites have extensive material on C#, including lively discussions all the way from how to save a source file to the relative merits of deterministic versus nondeterministic garbage collection. Around my house, garbage collection is very deterministic: It's every Wednesday morning. Here are a few large C# sites, in no particular order:

- ✔ `codeguru.earthweb.com/csharp`
- ✔ `csharpindex.com`
- ✔ `www.c-sharpcorner.com`

I maintain a Web site, `www.stephendavis.com`, containing a set of Frequently Asked Questions (FAQs). If you encounter something that you can't figure out, try going there — maybe I've already answered your question. In addi-tion, I include a list of any mistakes that might have crept into the book. Finally, and I do mean finally, there's a link to my e-mail address, in case you can't find the answer to your question on the site.

Part I
Creating Your First C# Programs

The 5th Wave — By Rich Tennant

"Before I go on to explain more advanced procedures like the 'Zap-Rowdy-Students-who-Don't-Pay-Attention' function, we'll begin with some basics."

In this part . . .

Y ou have a long way to go before you've mastered C#, so have a little fun just to get your feet wet. Part I takes you through the steps for creating the most basic Windows application possible using the Visual Studio .NET interface. Part I also shows you how to create the basic C# framework for the example programs that appear throughout this book.

Chapter 1

Creating Your First C# Windows Program

*I*n this chapter, I explain a little bit about computers, computer languages, C#, and Visual Studio .NET. Then, I take you through the steps for creating a very simple Windows program written in C#.

Getting a Handle on Computer Languages, C#, and .NET

A computer is an amazingly fast, but incredibly stupid servant. Computers will do anything you ask them to (within reason) and they do it extremely fast — and getting faster all the time. As of this writing, the common PC processing chip can handle almost 1 billion instructions per second. That's *billion*, with a 'b.'

Unfortunately, computers don't understand anything that resembles a human language. Oh, you may come back at me and say something like, "Hey, my telephone lets me dial my friend by just speaking his name. I know that a tiny computer runs my telephone. So, that computer speaks English." But it's a computer program that understands English, not the computer itself.

The language that computers understand is often called *machine language*. It is possible, but extremely difficult and error prone, for humans to write machine language.

For historical reasons, machine language is also known as assembly language. In the old days, each manufacturer provided a program called an assembler that would convert special words into individual machine instructions. Thus, you might write something really cryptic like MOV AX,CX. (That's an actual Intel processor instruction, by the way.) The assembler would convert that instruction into a pattern of bits corresponding to a single machine instruction.

Humans and computers have decided to meet somewhere in the middle. Programmers create their programs in a language that is not nearly as free as human speech but a lot more flexible and easy to use than machine language. The languages that occupy this middle ground — C#, for example — are called *high-level* computer languages. (*High* is a relative term here.)

What's a program?

What is a program? In one sense, a Windows program is an executable file that you can run by double-clicking its icon in a window. For example, the version of Microsoft Word that I'm using to write this book is a program. You call that an *executable program,* or *executable* for short. The names of executable program files generally end with the extension .EXE.

But a program is something else, as well. An executable program consists of one or more *source files.* A C# program file is a text file that contains a sequence of C# commands, which fit together according to the laws of C# grammar. This file is known as a *source file,* probably because it's a source of frustration and anxiety.

What's C#?

The C# programming language is one of those intermediate languages that programmers use to create executable programs. C# fills the gap between the powerful, but complicated C++ and the easy-to-use, but limited Visual Basic. A C# program file carries the extension .CS.

Some wags have pointed out that C-sharp and B-flat are the same note, but you should not refer to this new language as B-flat within earshot of Redmond, Washington.

C# is

- ✔ **Flexible:** C# programs can execute on the current machine, or they can be transmitted over the Web and executed on some distant computer.

- ✔ **Powerful:** C# has essentially the same command set as C++, but with the rough edges filed smooth.

- ✔ **Easier to use:** C# modifies the commands responsible for most C++ errors to make them safer.

- ✔ **Visually oriented:** The C# library provides the help needed to readily create complicated display frames with drop-down menus, tabbed windows, grouped buttons, scroll bars, and background images, to name just a few.

- ✔ **Internet friendly:** C# plays a pivotal role in Microsoft's new Internet-based .NET (pronounced *dot net*) strategy.

- ✔ **Secure:** Any language intended for use on the Internet must include some type of security to protect against malevolent hackers.

Finally, C# is an integral part of .NET (pronounced DOT-NET).

What's .NET?

.NET is Microsoft's strategy to open up the Web to mere mortals like you and me. To get this one, you need a little background.

Internet programming is very difficult in older languages like C and C++. Sun Microsystems responded to that problem by creating the Java programming language. To create Java, Sun took the grammar of C++, made it a lot more user friendly, and centered it around distributed development.

When programmers say "distributed," they're describing geographically dispersed computers running programs that talk to each other — in many cases, via the Internet.

Microsoft decided to play along and licensed the source code for Java, creating its own version called Visual J++ (pronounced "jay plus plus"). In this way, Microsoft instantly gained access to the progress that Sun and many other companies had made developing Java utilities. However, problems arose when Microsoft attempted to add features to the language. Unfortunately for Microsoft, its contract licensing the Java source code prohibited that sort of thing. Even worse, the contract was too simple to read anything more into it than what was intended. Sun effectively pushed Microsoft out of the Java business.

Being forced out of Java was just as well because Java has a serious problem: You pretty much have to write your entire program in Java in order to get its full benefit. Microsoft had too many developers and too many millions of lines of existing source code, so Microsoft had to come up with some way to support multiple languages. Enter .NET.

.NET is a framework, in many ways similar to Java.

The previous generation platform was made up of tools with cryptic names like Visual C++ 6.0, COM+, ASP+, Dynamic Linked Libraries, and Windows 2000 (and earlier). .NET updates these with Visual Studio .NET, improved COM+, ASP.NET, a new version of Windows, and .NET-enabled servers. .NET supports emerging communication standards such as XML and SOAP rather than Microsoft proprietary formats. Finally, .NET supports the hottest buzz-word since *object-oriented*: Web Services.

Microsoft would claim that .NET is much superior to Sun's suite of Web tools based on Java, but that's not the point. Unlike Java, .NET does not require you to rewrite existing programs. A Visual Basic programmer can add just a few lines in order to make an existing program "Web knowledgeable" (meaning that it knows how to get data off the Internet). .NET supports all the common Microsoft languages and approximately 20 other languages written by third-party vendors. However, C# is the flagship language of the .NET fleet. Unlike most other languages, C# can access every feature of .NET.

What is Visual Studio .NET?
What about Visual C#?

You sure ask lots of questions. The first popular programming language from Microsoft was Visual C++. It was called "Visual" because it had a built-in graphical user interface (GUI — pronounced "gooey"). This GUI included everything you needed to develop nifty-giffy C++ programs.

Microsoft added other Visual languages, including Visual Basic and Visual FoxPro. Eventually, Microsoft rolled all these languages into a single environment — Visual Studio. As Visual Studio 6.0 started getting a little long in the tooth, developers anxiously awaited Version 7. Shortly before its release, however, Microsoft decided to rename it as Visual Studio .NET in order to highlight this new environment's relationship to .NET.

That sounded like a marketing ploy to me until I started delving into it. Visual Studio .NET differs quite a bit from its predecessors — enough so to warrant a new name.

Microsoft calls its implementation of the language Visual C#. In reality, Visual C# is nothing more than the C# component of Visual Studio. C# is C#, with or without the Visual Studio.

Okay, that's it. No more questions.

Creating a Windows Application with C#

To help you get your feet wet with C# and Visual Studio, this section takes you through the steps for creating a Windows program. Windows programs are commonly called Windows applications, or WinApps for short. This first WinApp serves as a pattern for Windows programs to follow.

In addition, this program serves as a test of your Visual Studio environment. This is a test; this is only a test. Had it been an actual Windows program . . . Wait, it *is* an actual Windows program. If you can successfully create, build, and execute this program, your Visual Studio environment is set up properly, and you are ready to rock.

Creating the template

Writing Windows applications from scratch is a notoriously difficult process. Numerous session handles, descriptors, contexts — creating even a simple Windows program poses innumerable challenges.

Visual Studio .NET in general and C# in particular greatly simplify the task of creating your basic WinApp. To be honest, I'm a little disappointed that you don't get to go through the thrill of doing it by hand. In fact, why not switch over to Visual C++ and . . . . Okay, bad idea.

Because the C# language is built specifically to execute under Windows, it can shield you from many of the complexities. In addition, Visual Studio .NET includes an Applications Wizard that builds template programs.

Typically, *template programs* doesn't actually do anything — at least not anything useful (sounds like most of my programs). However, they do get you beyond that initial hurdle of getting started. Some template programs are reasonably sophisticated. In fact, you'll be amazed at how much capability the App Wizard can build on its own.

To get started, crank up Visual Studio .NET.

Make sure that you've completed the Visual Studio installation.

1. **To start Visual Studio, click Start➪Programs➪Microsoft Visual Studio.NET 7.0➪Microsoft Visual Studio.NET 7.0, as shown in Figure 1-1.**

    After much gnashing of CPU teeth and thrashing of disk, the Visual Studio desktop appears. Now things are getting interesting.

2. **Choose File➪New➪Project, as shown in Figure 1-2.**

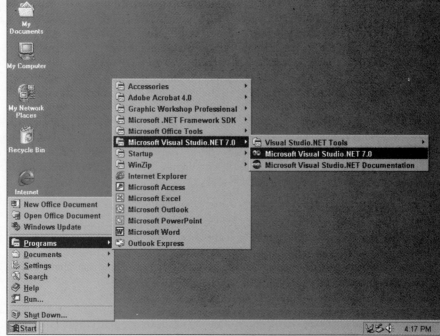

Figure 1-1:
What a
tangled web
we weave
when a C#
program
we do
conceive.

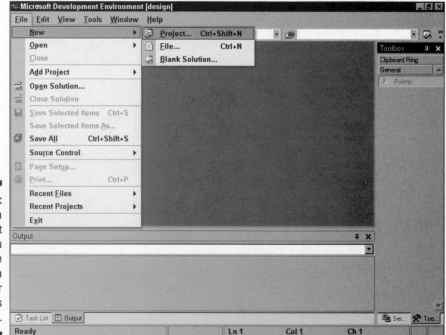

Figure 1-2:
Creating a
New Project
starts you
down the
road to a
better
Windows
application.

Visual Studio responds by opening the New Project dialog box, as shown in Figure 1-3.

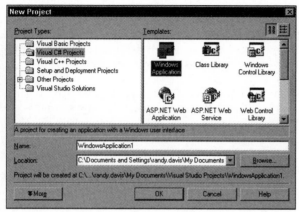

Figure 1-3: The Visual Studio Application Wizard is just waiting to create a new Windows program for you.

A *project* is a collection of files that Visual Studio builds together to make a single program. All your files will be C# source files, which carry the extension .CS. Project files use the extension .PRJ.

3. **Under Project Types, select Visual C# Projects, and under Templates, click Windows Application. If you don't see the correct application icon right away, don't panic — you may need to scroll around in the Templates pane a bit.**

   Don't click OK, yet.

4. **In the Name field, enter a name for your project, or use the default name.**

   The Application Wizard will create a folder in which it stores various files, including the project's initial C# source file. The Application Wizard uses the name you enter in the Name field as the name of that folder. The initial default name is WindowsApplication1. If you've been here before, the default name may be WindowsApplication2, WindowsApplication3, and so on.

   For this example, you can use the default name and the default location for this new folder: My Documents\Visual Studio Projects\ WindowsApplication1.

5. **Click OK.**

   The Application Wizard blinks the disk light for a few minutes before opening a blank *Frame1* in the middle of the display.

Building and running your first actual Windows program

After the Application Wizard loads the template program, Visual Studio opens the program in Design mode. You should convert this empty C# source program into a Windows Application, just to make sure that the template the Application Wizard generated doesn't have any errors.

The act of converting a C# source file into a living, breathing Windows Application is call *building*. If your source file has any errors, Visual C# will find them during the build process.

Choose Build⇨Build. An Output window pops open, and a set of messages scrolls by. The last message in the Output window should be `Build: 1 succeeded, 0 failed, 0 skipped` (or something very close to that). This is the computer equivalent of "No runs, no hits, no errors."

Figure 1-4 shows what my desktop looks like after building the default Windows program. Don't sweat the positions of the windows. You can move them around like leaves. The important parts are the Form[Design] window and the Output window.

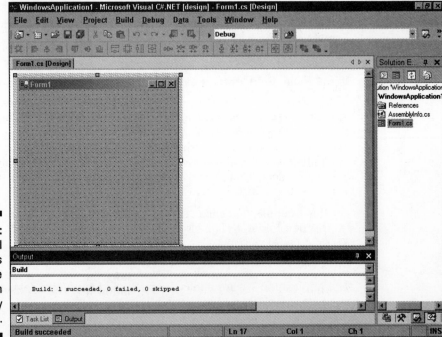

Figure 1-4: The initial Windows template program isn't very exciting.

You can now execute this program by choosing Debug➪Start Without Debugging. The program should start and open up a window that looks just like the one in the Form[Design] window but without the spots, as shown in Figure 1-5.

Figure 1-5:
The template Windows application works, but it won't convince your spouse that Visual Studio .NET is worth the price.

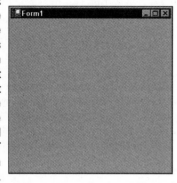

In C# terms, this window is called a *form*. A form has a border and a title bar across the top with the little Minimize, Maximize, and Close buttons.

Click the little Close button in the upper-right corner of the frame to terminate the program.

See! C# programming isn't so hard.

As much as anything, this initial program is a test of your installation. If you've gotten this far, your Visual Studio is in good shape for the programs throughout the rest of this book.

Go ahead and update your resume to note that you are officially a Windows applications programmer. Well, maybe an application (as in one) programmer, so far.

Painting pretty pictures

The default Windows program isn't very exciting, but you can jazz it up a little bit. Return to Visual Studio and select the window with the tab Form1.cs [Design]. This is the Forms Designer window.

The Forms Designer is a very powerful feature. It enables you to "paint" your program into the form. When you're done, click Build, and the Forms Designer creates the C# code necessary to make a C# application with a pretty frame just like the one you painted.

In the following sections, you build an application with two text fields and a button. The user can type into one of the text fields (the one labeled Source) but not in the other (which is labeled Target). When the user clicks a button labeled Copy, the program copies the text from the Source field into the Target field. That's it.

Putting some controls in place

The labeled windows that make up the Visual Studio user interface are called *views*. All those little doodads like buttons and text boxes are known as *controls*. (You also may hear the term *widget*.) As a Windows programmer, you use these tools to build the graphical user interface (GUI), usually the most difficult part of a Windows program. In the Forms Designer, these tools live in a view known as the Toolbox.

If your Toolbox isn't open, choose View⇨Toolbox. Figure 1-6 shows my Visual Studio desktop with the Toolbox open.

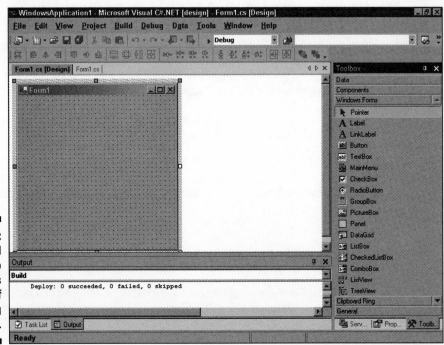

Figure 1-6:
The Visual
Studio
Toolbox is
chock-full of
interesting
controls.

Don't worry if your windows are not in the same places as mine. For example, your Toolbox may be on the left side of the screen, on the right, or in the middle. You can move any of the views anywhere on the desktop, if you want.

The Toolbox has various sections, including Data, Components, and Windows Forms. These sections simply organize the controls so you're not over-whelmed by them all. The Toolbox comes loaded with many controls, and you can make up your own.

Click the bar labeled `Windows Forms`. You use these controls to jazz up a form. The little arrows on the right enable you to scroll up and down within the Windows Forms.

You add a control to a form by dragging it and dropping it where you want. Give it a try:

1. **Grab the Textbox control, drag it over to the form labeled** `Form1`, **and let it go.**

   A textbox appears in the form. The text within the textbox says `textBox1`. This is the name the Forms Designer assigned to that particular control. You can resize the textbox by clicking and dragging its corners.

   You can only make the textbox longer. You can't make it any taller because by default these are single-line textboxes.

2. **Grab another textbox and drop it underneath the first one.**

3. **Now grab a button and drop it below the two textboxes.**

4. **Resize the form and move everything around until the form looks pretty.**

   Figure 1-7 shows my form.

Figure 1-7:
The initial layout of my form looks a lot better than yours.

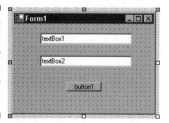

Controlling the properties

The most glaring problem with the application now is that button label. `button1` is not very descriptive. You need to fix that first.

Each control has a set of properties that determine the control's appearance and the way it works. You access these properties through the Properties view:

1. **Select the button by clicking it.**

2. **Enable the Properties view by choosing View⇨Properties Window.**

   The button control has two sets of properties: the appearance set listed at the top and the behavior properties down below. You need to change the Text property.

3. **Select the Text property in the right-hand column of the Properties view. In the left-hand column, type in** Copy **and then press Enter.**

   Figure 1-8 shows these settings in the Properties view and the resulting form.

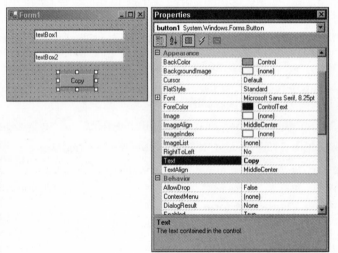

Figure 1-8:
The Properties view gives you control over your controls.

You can set the Text properties of the textbox controls to change their initial contents. I set my Text properties to "I'm typing away over here" and "Program copies text into here" so the user will know what to do when the program starts.

Similarly, changing the Text property of the Form changes the text in the title bar. Click somewhere in the Form, type in the new name in the Text property, and then press Enter. I set the title bar to "Text Copy Application."

4. Select the lower textbox and scroll through the Behavior properties until you get to one called ReadOnly. Set that to True by clicking it and selecting from the drop-down menu, as shown in Figure 1-9.

Figure 1-9:
Setting the
textbox to
read only
keeps users
from editing
the field
when the
program is
executing.

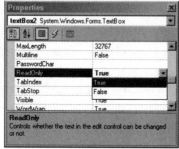

5. Click the Save button in the Visual Studio toolbar to save your work.

While you work, click the Save button every once in awhile just to make sure you don't lose too much if your dog were to trip over the power cord.

Building the application

Choose Build⇨Build to rebuild the application. This step builds a new Windows Application with the Form you've just created. The Output window should open, if it wasn't already, and you should see the stream of messages go by with a final `1 succeeded, 0 failed, 0 skipped` message.

Now execute the program by choosing Debug⇨Start Without Debugging. The resulting program opens a form that looks like the one you've been editing, as shown in Figure 1-10. You can even type into the upper textbox. You can't type into the lower textbox (unless you forgot to change the ReadOnly property).

Figure 1-10:
The
program
window
looks like
the Form
you just
built.

Make it do something, daddy

The program looks right but it doesn't do anything. Click the Copy button and nothing happens. So far, you've only set the Appearance properties — the properties that manage the appearance of the controls. Now, you need to put the smarts into the Copy button to actually copy the text from the source textbox to the target:

1. **In the Forms Designer, select the Copy button again.**

2. **Click the little lightning bolt right above the list of properties in the Properties window to open a completely new set of properties.**

   These are called the *active properties.* They manage what a control does while the program executes.

   You need to set the Click property. This property determines what the button does when the user clicks it. That makes sense.

3. **Double-click the Click property and watch all heck break loose.**

   The Design view is one of two different ways of looking at your application. The other is the Code view, which shows the C# source code the Forms Designer has been building for you behind the scenes. Visual Studio knows that you need to enter some C# code in order to make the program transfer the text.

   When you double-click the Click property, Visual Studio switches the display over to the Code view and creates a new *method.* Visual Studio gives this method the descriptive name button1_Click(). When the user clicks the Copy button, this method will perform the actual transfer of text from textBox1, the source, to textBox2, the target.

   Don't worry too much about what a method is. I describe methods in Chapter 8. Just go with the flow for now.

   This method simply copies the Text property from textBox1 to textBox2.

4. **Add the following line of code to the button1_Click() method:**

   ```
   textBox2.Text = textBox1.Text;
   ```

   Notice how C# tries to help you out as you type. Figure 1-11 shows the display as I type the last letter of the preceding line. The drop-down list of the properties for a textbox helps to jog your memory about which properties are available and how they're used. This auto-complete feature is a great help during programming.

5. **Choose Build⇨Build to add the new click method into the program.**

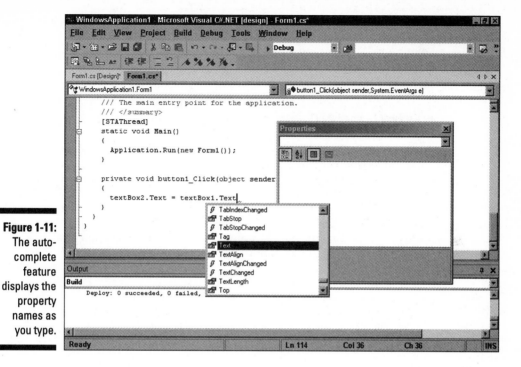

Trying out the final product

Choose Debug⇨Start Without Debugging to execute the program one last time. Type some text in the source textbox and then click the Copy button. The text is magically copied over to the target source box, as shown in Figure 1-12. Gleefully repeat the process, typing whatever you want and copying away until you get tired of it.

Figure 1-12:
It works!

Looking back on the creation process, you may be struck by how picture-oriented it all is. Grab controls, drop them around on the frame, set properties, and that's about it. You only had to write one line of C# code, and even that wasn't much.

You could argue that the program doesn't do much, but I would disagree. Look back at some of the earlier Windows programming books in the days before App Wizards, and you'll see how many hours of coding even a simple application like this would have taken.

Visual Basic programmers beware!

To those Visual Basic programmers among you, this probably seems mundane. In fact, the Forms Designer works a lot like the later versions of the Visual Basic developer. However, the C# Designer is much more powerful than its Visual Basic counterpart (at least those versions prior to Visual Basic .NET). The C# language is a more powerful language than the previous Visual Basic. The .NET library of routines is more powerful than the old Visual Basic library. And .NET supports distributed, cross-language development, which Visual Basic did not. Other than that, I would say they're about the same.

Chapter 2

Creating Your First C# Console Application

*E*ven the most basic of Windows programs can be daunting to the beginning C# programmer. Just check out Chapter 1 if you don't believe me. A so-called *console application* program — or console app (all of us in-the-know types drop off unnecessary syllables when poss) — generates significantly less C# code and is much easier to understand.

In this chapter, you use Visual Studio to create a template console app. Then, you manually simplify that template just a little more. You can use the result as a template for many of the programs I describe in this book.

The primary purpose of this book (the first several parts, anyway) is to help you understand C#. You can't create the next Starship graphics game in C# until you know the C# language.

Creating a Console Application Template

The following instructions are for Visual Studio. You have to resort to the documentation that came with your environment if you use anything other than Visual Studio. Alternatively, you can just type the source code directly into your C# environment.

Creating the source program

Complete these steps to create your C# console app template:

1. **Choose File⇨New⇨Project to create a new project.**

   Visual Studio presents you with a window of icons representing the different types of applications that you can create.

2. **From this New Project window, click the** Console Application **icon.**

   Make sure you select the Visual C# Projects folder in the New Project window; otherwise, Visual Studio might create something awful like a Visual Basic or Visual C++ application.

   Visual Studio requires that you create a project before you can start to enter your C# program. A project is like a bucket in which you throw all the files that go into making your program. When you tell your compiler to build the program, it sorts through the project to find the files it needs in order to recreate the program.

   The default name for your first application is ConsoleApplication1. The default place to store this file is somewhere deep in My Documents. Maybe because I'm difficult (or maybe because I'm writing a book), I like to put my programs where I want them, not necessarily where Visual Studio wants them.

3. **To change the default directory for your program, click the Browse button and navigate to some existing directory.**

   I chose the name C#Programs as the directory for all my programs.

4. **Type in the name field in order to change the name of the project that you're about to create. For this first program, enter** HelloWorld.

5. **Click OK.**

   After a bit of disk whirring and chattering, Visual Studio generates a file called Class1.cs. (If you look in the window labeled Solutions Explorer, you see some other files. Ignore them for now.) C# source files carry the extension .CS. The name Class1 is the default name assigned for the program file.

The contents of your first console app appear as follows:

```
using System;

namespace HelloWorld
{
  /// <summary>
  /// Summary description for Class1.
  /// </summary>
  class Class1
  {
    static void Main(string[] args)
    {
```

```
        //
        // TODO: Add code to start application here
        //
    }
  }
}
```

For the Windows executable program you create in Chapter 1, Visual Studio reverses the `using System` and `namespace HelloWorld` lines. C# accepts these commands in either order. (There is a difference, but it's subtle and way beyond the scope of this chapter.)

Taking it out for a test drive

Choose Build➪Build in order to convert your C# program into an executable program.

Visual Studio responds with the following message:

```
- Build started: Project: HelloWorld, Configuration: Debug .NET -

Preparing resources...

Build complete -- 0 errors, 0 warnings
Building satellite assemblies...

---------------------- Done ----------------------
Build: 1 succeeded, 0 failed, 0 skipped
```

The key point here is the `1 succeeded` part.

As a general rule of programming, "succeeded" is good; "failed" is bad.

To execute the program, choose Debug➪Start. The program terminates immediately. The program seemingly hasn't done anything at all. In fact, it hasn't. The template is nothing but a shell.

Creating Your First Real Console App

Edit the `Class1.cs` template file until it appears as follows.

Don't sweat the stuff following the double or triple slashes (`//` or `///`) and don't worry about whether to enter one or two spaces or one or two new lines. However, do pay attention to capitalization.

```
using System;
```

```
namespace HelloWorld
{
  public class Class1
  {
    // This is where our program starts
    static void Main(string[] args)
    {
      // prompt user to enter a name
      Console.WriteLine("Enter your name, please:");

      // now read the name entered
      string sName = Console.ReadLine();

      // greet the user with the name that was entered
      Console.WriteLine("Hello, " + sName);

      // wait for user to acknowledge the results
      Console.WriteLine("Press Enter to terminate...");
      Console.Read();
    }
  }
}
```

Choose Build⇨Build to convert this new version of `Class1.cs` into the `Class1.exe` program.

From within Visual Studio .NET, click Debug⇨Start. The program immediately prompts you for your name. Type your name and then press the Enter key. The program responds as follows:

```
Enter your name, please:
Stephen
Hello, Stephen
Press Enter to terminate...
```

The program responds with the phrase "Hello, " followed by the name you entered. It then dutifully waits for you to press Enter before the program gives up the ghost.

You can also execute the program from the DOS command line. Open up a DOS window. Enter **CD \C#Programs\HelloWorld\bin\Debug**. Now enter **Class1** to execute the program. The output should be identical. You can also navigate to the `\C#Programs\HelloWorld\bin\Debug` folder in the Windows Explorer and then double-click the `Class1.exe` file.

Reviewing the Program

In the following sections, you take this first C# console app apart one section at a time in order to understand how it works.

The program framework

The basic framework for all console applications starts with

```
using System;

namespace HelloWorld
{
  public class Class1
  {
    // This is where our program starts
    public static void Main(string[] args)
    {
        // your code goes here
    }
  }
}
```

The program starts executing right after the statement containing Main and ends at the closed brace following Main. I explain the meaning of these statements in due course. More than that I cannot say for now.

The phrase using System can come immediately before or immediately after the phrase namespace HelloWorld {. The order doesn't matter.

Comments

The template already has lots of lines, and I've added several other lines, such as the following:

```
// This is where our program starts
public static void Main(string[] args)
```

C# ignores the first line in this example. This line is known as a comment.

Any line that begins with // or /// is free text and is ignored by C#. Consider // and /// to be equivalent for now.

Why include lines in your program if the computer ignores them?

A program, even a C# program, isn't easy to understand. Remember that a programming language is a compromise between what computers understand and what humans understand. Writing comments enables you to explain your C# statements. These comments can help you while you write the code, and they're especially helpful to the poor sap who has to come along a year later and try to recreate your logic. Adding extra explanatory text makes the job much easier.

Comment early and often. It helps you and other programmers to remember what you meant when you wrote all those C# statements.

The meat of the program

The real core of this program is embedded within the block of code marked with `Main()`:

```
// prompt user to enter a name
Console.WriteLine("Enter your name, please:");

// now read the name entered
string sName = Console.ReadLine();

// greet the user with the name that was entered
Console.WriteLine("Hello, " + sName);
```

The program begins executing with the first C# statement: `Console.WriteLine`. This command writes the character string `Enter your name, please:` to the console.

The next statement reads in the user's answer and stores it in a "workbox" called `sName`. (I have more to say about these storage locations in Chapter 3.) The last line combines the string `Hello,` and the user's name and outputs the result to the console.

The final three lines wait for the user to press the Enter key before proceeding. These lines ensure that the user has time to read the output before the program proceeds:

```
// wait for user to acknowledge the results
Console.WriteLine("Press Enter to terminate...");
Console.Read();
```

This step can be important depending upon how you execute the program and depending upon the environment. Within Visual Studio, you can execute a program in either of two ways. If you use the Debug⇨Start command, Visual Studio closes the output window as soon as the program terminates. The same thing happens when you execute the program by double-clicking the executable file's icon in Windows Explorer.

No matter how you execute the program, waiting for the user to press the Enter key before quitting solves any problems.

Part II
Basic C#
Programming

The 5th Wave — By Rich Tennant

"Excuse me – is anyone here NOT talking about C#?"

In this part . . .

The newest E-commerce, B2B, DOT.COM, whiz-bang program uses the same basic building blocks as the most simple temperature conversion program. This part presents the basics of creating variables, performing arithmetic operations, and controlling the execution path through a program.

Chapter 3

Living with Variability — Declaring Value-Type Variables

- -

- -

*T*he most fundamental of all concepts in programming is that of the variable. A C# variable is like a small box in which you can store things, particularly numbers, for later use.

The term *variable* is borrowed from the world of mathematics. For example, the mathematician might say

```
n = 1
```

This statement means that from this point forward, the mathematician can use the term *n* to mean 1 — that is, until the mathematician changes it to something else (a number, an equation, a concept, or whatever).

The meaning of the term *variable* doesn't differ much in the programming world. The C# programmer may say

```
int n;
n = 1;
```

Those statements define a "thing" n and assign it the value 1. From that point forward in the program, the variable n has the value 1, until the programmer changes it to some other number.

Unfortunately for programmers, C# places several limitations on variables — limitations that mathematicians don't have to consider. (Unless, of course, you're a mathematician who just happened to pick up this book to pass the time.)

Declaring a Variable

When the mathematician says, "n is equal to 1," that means the term *n* is equivalent to 1 in some ethereal way. The mathematician is free to introduce variables in a willy-nilly fashion. For example, the mathematician might say

```
x = y² + 2y + y
if k = y + 1 then
x = k²
```

Here, the mathematician has written down some quadratic equation. Perhaps the variables *x* and *y* were previously defined somewhere. However, the program then throws down another variable *k,* sort of out of the blue. Here, *k* doesn't so much mean that *k* has the value of *y* plus 1 but that *k* takes the place of the concept of *y* plus one — a sort of shorthand. Skim through any mathematics book and you'll see what I mean. And I do mean *skim*; I wouldn't want you to get wrapped up in that book and forget about this one.

Programmers must be precise in their terminology. For example, a C# programmer may write the following code:

```
int n;
n = 1;
```

The first line means, "Carve off a small amount of storage in the computer's memory and assign it the name *n*." This step is analogous to reserving one of those storage lockers at the train station and slapping the label *n* on the side. The second line says, "Store the value 1 into the variable *n*, thereby replacing whatever that storage location already contains." The train locker equivalent is, "Open up the train locker, rip out whatever happens to be there, and shove a 1 in its place."

The = symbol is called the *assignment operator* — not the equals sign or some other vague term.

The mathematician says, "n equals 1." The C# programmer says in a more precise way, "Store the value 1 into the variable n." (Think about the train locker and you see why that is preferable.) C# operators tell the computer what you want to do. In other words, operators are verbs and not descriptors. The assignment operator takes the value on its right and stores it into the variable on the left.

What's an int?

Mathematicians deal with concepts. They can make up variables any time they want, and a single variable may have different meanings throughout the same equation. At best, mathematicians look at variables as some amorphous value — at worst, some vague concept. Don't laugh; you probably think the same way.

The mathematician might write

```
n = 1;
n = 1.1;
n = House
n = "Texas is a dump"
```

Those lines equate the variable *n* with all sorts of things, and the mathematician thinks nothing of it. I don't think about it much either except for that last line. As the bumper stickers down here say, "Don't mess with Texas."

C# is not nearly that flexible. In C#, each variable has a fixed type. When you allocate one of those train lockers, you have to pick one of the size you need. If you picked an "integer locker," you couldn't turn around and hope to stuff the entire state of Texas in it — maybe Rhode Island, but not Texas.

For the example in the preceding section of this chapter, you select a locker that's designed to handle an integer — C# calls it an int. Integers are the counting numbers 1, 2, 3, and so on, plus the negative numbers –1, –2, –3, and so on.

Before you can use a variable, you must declare it. After you declare a variable as int, it can hold and regurgitate integer values, as the following example demonstrates:

```
// declare a variable n
int n;
// declare an int variable m and initialize it
// with the value 2
int m = 2;
// assign the value stored in m to the variable n
n = m;
```

The first line after the comment is a declaration that creates a little storage area, n, designed to hold an integer value. The initial value of n is not specified until it is assigned a value. The second declaration creates an int variable m with an initial value of 2.

The term *initialize* means to assign an initial value. To initialize a variable is to assign it a value for the first time. You don't know for sure what the value of a variable is until it has been initialized.

The final statement in the program assigns the value stored in m, which is 2, to the variable n. The variable n continues to contain the value 2 until it is assigned a new value.

Rules for declaring variables

You can initialize a variable as part of the declaration:

```
// declare another int variable and give it
// the initial value of 1
int o = 1;
```

This is equivalent to sticking a 1 into that int storage locker when you first rent it, rather than opening up the locker and stuffing in the value later.

Initialize a variable when you declare it. In most, but not all cases, C# will initialize the variable for you, but don't rely on that fact.

You may declare variables anywhere (well, almost anywhere) within a program. However, you may not use a variable until you declare it and set it to some value. Thus, the following two assignments are not legal:

```
// the following is illegal because m is not assigned
// a value before it is used
int m;
n = m;
// the following is illegal because p has not been
// declared before it is used
p = 2;
int p;
```

Finally, you cannot declare the same variable twice.

Variations on a theme — different types of int

Most simple variables are of type int. However, C# provides a number of twists to the int variable type for special occasions.

All integer variable types are limited to whole numbers. The int type suffers from other limitations as well. For example, an int variable can only store values in the range from –2 billion to 2 billion.

The actual range is –2,147,483,648 to 2,147,483,647, to be exact.

A distance of 2 billion inches is greater than the circumference of the Earth.

In case 2 billion isn't quite enough for you, C# provides an integer type called `long` (short for `long int`) that can represent numbers as large as I can imagine. The only problem with a `long` is that takes a larger train locker: A `long` consumes 8 bytes (64 bits) — twice as much as a garden-variety `int`.

To be more accurate, a `long` consumes two `int`-size train lockers. This train locker analogy is getting pretty worn — I'll just say _byte_ from now on.

A `long` can represent a number up to roughly plus or minus 10^{20}. No kidding.

The exact range of a _long_ is –9,223,372,036,854,775,808 to 9,223,372,036,854,775,807.

C# provides several other integer variable types, as shown in Table 3-1.

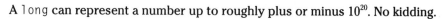

Table 3-1		The Size and Range of C# Integer Types	
Type	_Size [bytes]_	_Range_	_In Use_
sbyte	2	–128 to 127	sbyte sb = 12;
byte	2	0 to 255	byte b = 12;
short	4	–32,768 to 32,767	short sn = 123456;
ushort	4	0 to 65,535	ushort usn = 62345678;
int	8	–2 billion to 2 billion	int n = 1234567890;
uint	8	0 to 4 billion	uint un = 3234567890U
long	16	$–10^{20}$ to 10^{20} — "a whole lot"	long l = 123456789012L
ulong	16	0 to 2 times 10^{20}	long ul = 123456789012UL

As I explain in the section "Declaring Numeric Constants," later in this chapter, fixed values such as 1 also have a type. By default, a simple constant such as 1 is assumed to be an `int`. Constants other than an `int` must be marked with their variable type. For example, 123U is an unsigned integer, `uint`.

Most integer variables are called _signed_, which means they can represent negative values. Unsigned integers can only represent positive values, but you get twice the range in return. As you can see from Table 3-1, the names of most unsigned integer types start with a `u`, while the signed types generally don't have a prefix.

Representing Fractions

Integers are great for most calculations. I made it into the 6th grade before I ever found out that anything else existed. I still haven't forgiven my 6th-grade teacher for starting me down the slippery slope of fractions. Before I knew it, I was failing a Calculus class, wondering how I ever got there.

Many calculations involve fractions, which simple integers can't accurately represent. The common equation for converting from Fahrenheit to Celsius temperatures demonstrates the problem:

```
// convert the temperature 41 degrees Fahrenheit
int nFahr = 41;
int nCelsius = (nFahr - 32) * (5 / 9)
```

This equation works just fine for some values. For example, 41 degrees Fahrenheit is 5 degrees Celsius. "Correct, Mr. Davis," says my 6th-grade teacher.

Okay, try a different value: 100 degrees Fahrenheit. Working through the equation, 100 – 32 is 68; 68 times 5/9 is 37. "No," she says, "the answer is 37.78." Even that's wrong because it's really 37.777 . . . with the 7 repeating forever, but I'm not going to push the point.

An int can only represent integer numbers. The integer equivalent of 37.78 is 37. This lopping off of the fractional part of a number in order to get it to fit into an integer variable is called integer *truncation*.

Truncation is not the same thing as rounding off. Truncation lops off the fractional part. Round-off picks the closest integer value. Thus, truncating 1.9 results in 1. Rounding off 1.9 results in the value 2.

For temperatures, 37 may be good enough. It's not like I wear short-sleeve shirts at 37 degrees but pull on a sweater at 37.7 degrees. But integer truncation is unacceptable for many, if not most applications.

Actually, the problem is much worse than that. An int can't handle the ratio 5/9 either; it always yields the value 0. Consequently, the equation as written in this example calculates nCelsius as 0 for all values of nFahr. Even I will admit that's unacceptable.

This book's CD includes an int-based temperature conversion program contained in the directory ConvertTemperatureWithRoundOff. At this point, you may not understand all the details, but you can see the conversion equations and execute the program Class1.exe to see the results.

Handling Floating Point Variables

The limitations of an `int` variable are unacceptable for some applications. The range generally isn't a problem — the double-zillion range of a 64-bit integer should be enough for anyone. However, the fact that an `int` is limited to whole numbers is a bit harder to swallow.

In some cases, you need numbers that can have a nonzero fractional part. Mathematicians call these *real numbers*. I always thought that was a ridiculous name for a number. Are integer numbers somehow unreal?

Notice that I said a real number *can* have a nonzero fractional part — that is, 1.5 is a real number, but so is 1.0. For example, 1.0 + 0.1 is 1.1. Just keep that point in mind as you read the rest of this chapter.

Fortunately, C# understands real numbers. Real numbers come in two flavors: floating point and decimal. Floating point is the most common type. I describe the `decimal` type a little later in this chapter.

Declaring a floating point variable

A floating point variable carries the designation `float`, and you declare one as shown in the following example:

```
float f = 1.0;
```

After you declare it as `float`, the variable f is a `float` for the rest of its natural instructions.

Floating point numbers owe their name to the fact that the decimal point is allowed to "float" between the digits from left to right, like 10.0 to 1.00 to 0.100. Cute, but descriptive.

Table 3-2 describes the set of floating point types. All floating point variables are signed (that is to say, there's no such thing as a floating point variable that can't represent a negative value).

Table 3-2	The Size and Range of the Floating Point Variable Types			
Type	**Size [bytes]**	**Range**	**Accuracy**	**In Use**
float	8	$1.5 * 10^{-45}$ to $3.4 * 10^{38}$	6 – 7 digits	float f = 1.2F;
double	16	$5.0 * 10^{-324}$ to $1.7 * 10^{308}$	15 – 16 digits	double d = 1.2;

The default floating point variable type is the `double` and not `float`.

The Accuracy column in Table 3-2 refers to the number of significant digits that such a variable type can represent. For example, 5/9 is actually 0.555 . . . with an unending sequence of fives. However, a `float` variable is said to have six significant digits of accuracy, which means numbers after the sixth digit are ignored. Thus, 5/9 may appear as follows when expressed as a `float`:

```
0.5555551457382
```

You know that all the digits after the sixth 5 are incorrect.

A `float` actually has 6.5 significant digits. The extra half of significance stems from the fact that floating point accuracy is related to $10^{\log \text{ to the base } 2}$. Probably more than you wanted to know.

The same number 5/9 may appear as follows when expressed as a `double`:

```
0.55555555555555557823
```

The `double` packs a whopping 15 to 16 significant digits.

C# floating point numbers default to double precision, so use `double` variable types unless you have a specific reason to do otherwise. However, programs that use either `double` or `float` are still said to be floating point programs.

Converting some more temperatures

Here's the formula for converting from Fahrenheit to Celsius temperatures written using floating point variables:

```
double dCelsius = (dFahr - 32.0) * (5.0 / 9.0)
```

Your CD contains a floating point version of the temperature conversion program called `ConvertTemperatureWithFloat`.

The following example shows the result of executing the `double`-based `ConvertTemperatureWithFloat` program:

```
Enter temp in degrees Fahrenheit:100
Temperature in degrees Celsius = 37.777777777777779
Hit Enter to terminate...
```

That's better than even my 6th-grade teacher could do. Take that, Mrs. Schmekowitz!

Examining some limitations of floating point variables

You may be tempted to use floating point variables all the time because they solve the truncation problem so nicely. Sure they use up a bit more memory, but memory is cheap these days, so why not? But floating point variables also have limitations.

Counting

You can't use floating point variables as counting numbers. Some C# structures need to count (as in 1, 2, 3, and so on). You and I know that 1.0, 2.0, and 3.0 are counting just as well as 1, 2, and 3, but C# doesn't know that. For example, how does C# know that you aren't actually saying 1.000001?

Whether you find that argument convincing or not, you can't use a floating point variable when counting things.

Comparing numbers

You have to be very careful when comparing floating point numbers. For example, 12.5 may be represented as 12.500001. Most people don't care about that little extra bit (no pun intended) on the end. However, the computer takes things extremely literally. To C#, 12.500000 and 12.500001 are not the same at all.

So, if you add 1.1 to 1.1, you can't tell if the result is 2.2 or 2.200001. And if you ask, "Is dDoubleVariable equal to 2.2?," you may not get the results you expect. Generally, you have to resort to some bogus comparison like this: "Is the absolute value of the difference between dDoubleVariable and 2.2 less than .000001?"

The Pentium processor plays a trick to make this problem less troublesome than it otherwise might be: It performs floating point arithmetic in an especially long double format — that is, rather than use 64 bits, it uses a whopping 80 bits. When rounding off an 80-bit float into a 64-bit float, you (almost) always get the expected result even if the 80-bit number was off a bit or two.

Calculation speed

Processors such as the x86 varieties used in older Windows-based PCs could perform integer arithmetic much faster than arithmetic of the floating point persuasion. In those days, programmers would go out of their way to limit a program to integer arithmetic.

The difference in additional speed on my Pentium III processor for a simple (perhaps too simple) test of about 300,000,000 additions and subtractions was about 3 to 1. That is to say, for every `double` add, I could have done three `int` adds. (Computations involving multiplication and division may show different results.)

I had to write my addition and subtraction operations in such a way as to avoid cache effects. The program and the data were cached, but the compiler was not able to cache any intermediate results in CPU registers.

Not so limited range

In the past, a floating point variable could represent a considerably larger range of numbers than an integer type. It still can, but the range of the `long` is large enough to render the point moot.

Even though a simple `float` can represent a very large number, the number of significant digits is limited. For example, 123,456,789F is the same as 123,456,000F.

Using the Decimal Type — A Combination of Integers and Floats

As I explain in previous sections of this chapter, both the integer and floating point types have their problems. Floating point variables have round-off problems associated with limits to their accuracy, while `int` variables just lop off the fractional part of a variable all together. In some cases, you need a variable type that offers the best of two worlds:

- Like a floating point variable, it can store fractions.
- Like an integer, numbers of this type offer exact values for use in computations — for example, 12.5 is really 12.5 and not 12.500001.

Fortunately, C# provides such a variable type, called `decimal`. A `decimal` variable can represent any number between 10^{-28} and 10^{28} — that's a lot of zeros! And it does so without round-off problems.

Declaring a decimal

Decimal variables are declared and used like any variable type:

```
decimal m1;         // good
decimal m2 = 100;   // better
decimal m3 = 100M;  // best
```

The declaration of m1 allocates a variable m1 without initializing it to anything. Until you assign it a value, the contents of m1 are indeterminate. But that's okay, because C# won't let you use m1 for anything until you get around to assigning it a value of some sort.

The second declaration creates a variable m2 and initializes it a value of 100. What isn't obvious is that 100 is actually of type int. Thus, C# must convert the int into a decimal type before performing the initialization. Fortunately, C# understands what you meant and performs the conversion for you.

The declaration of m3 is the best. This clever declaration initializes m3 with the decimal constant 100M. The letter M at the end of the number specifies that the constant is of type decimal. (See "Declaring Numeric Constants," later in this chapter.)

Comparing decimals, integers, and floating point types

The decimal variable type seems to have all the advantages and none of the disadvantages of int or double types. Variables of this type have a very large range, they don't suffer from round-off problems, and 25.0 is 25.0 and not 25.00001.

The decimal variable type has two significant limitations, however. First, a decimal is not considered a counting number because it may contain a fractional value. Consequently, you can't use them in flow control loops, which I explain in Chapter 5.

The second problem with decimal variables is equally as serious or even more so. Computations involving decimal values are significantly slower than those involving either simple integer or floating point values — and I do mean significant. On my crude benchmark test of 300,000,000 adds and subtracts, the operations involving decimal variables were approximately 50 times slower than those involving simple int variables. I suspect that the relative computational speed gets even worse for more complex operations. In addition, most computational functions, such as calculating sines or exponents, are not available for the decimal number type.

Clearly, the decimal variable type is most appropriate for applications such as banking, in which accuracy is extremely important but the number of calculations is relatively small.

Examining the bool Type — Is it Logical?

Finally, a logical variable type. Except in this case, I really mean a type logical. The Boolean type bool can have two values: true or false. I kid thee not — a whole variable type for just two values.

Former C and C++ programmers are accustomed to using the int value 0 (zero) to mean false and non-zero to mean true. That doesn't work in C#.

You declare a bool variable as follows:

```
bool thisIsABool = true;
```

No conversion path exists between bool variables and any other types. In other words, you can't convert a bool directly into something else. (Even if you could, you shouldn't because it doesn't make any sense.) In particular, you can't cast a bool into an int (such as false becomes zero) nor a string (such as false becomes "false").

However, the bool variable type plays an important role in forcing C# program execution down different paths, as I describe in Chapter 5.

Checking out Character Types

A program that can do nothing more than spit out numbers may be fine for mathematicians, accountants, insurance agents with their mortality figures, and folks calculating cannon shell trajectories. (Don't laugh. The original computers were built to generate tables of cannon shell trajectories to help artillery gunners.) However, for most applications, programs must deal with letters as well as numbers.

C# treats letters in two distinctly different ways: individual characters of type char and strings of characters called, cleverly enough, string.

Char variable type

The char variable is a box capable of holding a single character. Character constants appear as a character surrounded by a pair of single quotation marks, as in this example:

```
char c = 'a';
```

You can store any single character from the Roman, Hebrew, Arab, Cyrillic, and most other alphabets. You can also store Japanese katakana characters and many Japanese and Chinese kanjis.

In addition, char is considered a counting type. That means you can use a char type to control the looping structures that I describe in Chapter 5. Character variables do not suffer from any type of round-off problems.

The character variable does not include any font information. So, you may store into a char variable what you think is a perfectly good kanji (and it might well be, I can't tell); however, when you look at the character, it will look like garbage if you are not looking at it through the eyes of the proper font.

Special char types

Some characters within a given font are not printable in the sense that you don't see anything when you look at them on the computer screen or printer. The most obvious example of this is the space, which is represented by the character ' ' — see what I mean? Other characters have no letter equivalent — for example, the tab character. C# uses the backslash to flag these characters, as shown in Table 3-3.

Table 3-3	Special Characters
Character Constant	*Value*
'\n'	new line
'\t'	tab
'\0'	a null character
'\r'	a carriage return
'\\'	a backslash

The string type

Another common variable type is the string. The following examples show how you declare and initialize string variables:

```
// declare and initialize later
string someString1;
someString1 = "this is a string";
// or initialize when declared
string someString2 = "this is a string";
```

Naming conventions

Programming is hard enough without programmers making it harder. To make your C# source code easier to wade through, adopt a naming convention and stick to it. As much as possible, your naming convention should follow those adopted by other C# programmers.

The main rule is that the names of things other than variables start with a capital letter. Make these names as descriptive as possible, which often means that a name consists of multiple words. These words should be capitalized but butted up against each other with no underscore between them — for example, thisIsALongVariableName.

I have adopted the further rule that the first letter of the variable name indicates the type of the variable. Most of these letters are straightforward: f for float, d for double, s for

string, and so on. The only one that's even the slightest bit different is n for int. There's one exception to this rule: For reasons that stretch way back into the Fortran programming language in the 60s, the single letters i, j, and k are also used as common names for an int.

Notice that I said that I "adopted" this naming convention. I didn't make it up. It was invented by some guy at Microsoft during the days of C programming. Because he was of Hungarian extraction, this notation came to be called Hungarian notation.

Hungarian notation seems to have fallen out of favor. I still prefer it, however, because it enables me to know in a flash the type of each variable in a program without referring back to the declaration.

A string constant is a set of characters surrounded by double quotes. The characters in a string include the special characters shown in Table 3-3. A string cannot be written across a line in the C# source file but it can contain the new-line character, as the following examples show:

```
// the following is not legal
string someString = "This is a line
and so is this";
// however, the following is legal
string someString = "This is a line\nand so is this";
```

When written out, the last line in this example places the two phrases on separate lines:

```
This is a line
and so is this
```

A string is not a counting type. A string also is not a value-type — no "string" exists that's intrinsic to the processor. Only one of the common operators works on string objects: The + operator concatenates two strings into one. For example:

```
string s = "this is a phrase"
         + " and so is this";
```

This code sets the `string` variable s equal to the following string:

```
"this is a phrase and so is this"
```

One other thing: The string with no characters, written "", is a valid string.

Comparing `string` *and* `char`

Although strings deal with characters, the `string` type is amazingly different from the `char`. Of course, certain trivial differences exist. You enclose a character with single quotes as in the following example:

```
'a'
```

On the other hand, you put double quotes around a string:

```
"this is a string"
```

The rules concerning strings are not the same as those concerning characters. For one thing, you know right up front that a `char` is a single character, and that's it. For example, the following code makes no sense:

```
char c1 = 'a';
char c2 = 'b';
char c3 = c1 + c2
```

Actually, this code almost compiles but with a completely different meaning than intended. These statements convert c1 into an `int` consisting of the numeric value of c1. C# also converts c2 into an `int` and then adds the two integers. The error occurs when trying to store the results back into c3 — numeric data may be lost storing an `int` into the smaller `char`. In any case, the operation makes no sense.

A string, on the other hand, can be any length. So, concatenating two strings does make sense:

```
string s1 = "a";
string s2 = "b";
string s3 = s1 + s2;  // result is "ab"
```

As part of its library, C# defines an entire suite of string operations. I describe them in Chapter 9.

What's a Value-Type?

All C# instructions have to be implemented in the machine instructions of the native CPU — an Intel class processor in the case of PCs. These CPUs also have the concept of variables. For example, the Intel processor has eight internal locations known as *registers*, each of which can store a single int. Without getting into the details of the CPU, however, I'll just say that the types described in this chapter, with the exception of decimal and string, are intrinsic to the processor. Thus, a CPU instruction exists that says, "Add one int to another int." A similar instruction exists for adding a double to a double. Because these types of variables are built into the processor, they are known as *intrinsic* variable types.

In addition, the variable types that I describe in this chapter are of fixed length — again with the exception of string. A fixed length variable type always occupies the same amount of memory. So, if I assign a = b, C# can transfer the value of b into a without taking extra measures designed to handle variable length types. This characteristic gives these types of variables the name *value-types*.

The types int, double, and bool, and their close derivatives, like unsigned int, are intrinsic variable types. The intrinsic variable types plus decimal are also known as value-types. The string type is neither.

The programmer-defined types that I explain in Chapter 6 are neither value types nor intrinsic.

Declaring Numeric Constants

There are very few absolutes in life; however, I'm about to give you a C# absolute:

Every expression has a value and a type.

In a declaration such as int n, you can easily see that the variable n is an int. Further, you can reasonably assume that the type of a calculation n + 1 is an int. However, what type is the constant 1?

The type of a constant depends on two things: its value and the presence of an optional descriptor letter at the end of the constant. Any integer type less than 2 billion is assumed to be an int. Numbers larger than 2 billion are assumed to be long. Any floating pointing number is assumed to be a double.

Table 3-4 demonstrates constants that have been declared to be of a particular type. The case of these descriptors is not important. Thus, 1U and 1u are equivalent.

Table 3-4	Common Constants Declared Along With Their Type
Constant	*Type*
1	int
1U	unsigned int
1L	long int
1.0	double
1.0F	float
1M	decimal
true	bool
false	bool
'a'	char
'\n'	char (the character newline)
'\x123'	char (the characters whose numeric value is hex 123)
"a string"	string
" "	string (an empty string)

Changing Types — The Cast

Humans don't treat different types of counting numbers any differently. For example, a normal person (as distinguished from a C# programmer like yourself) doesn't think about the number 1 as being signed, unsigned, short, or long.

Even though C# does consider these types to be different, even C# realizes that a relationship exists between them. For example, the following code converts an int into a long:

```
int nValue = 10;
long lValue;
lValue = nValue;  // this is OK
```

An int variable can be converted into a long because any value of an int can be stored in a long and because they are both counting numbers. C# makes the conversion for you automatically without comment.

A conversion in the opposite direction can cause problems, however. For example, the following is illegal:

```
int lValue = 10;
int nValue;
nValue = lValue;  // this is illegal
```

Some values that you can store in a long do not fit in an int (4 billion, for example). C# generates an error in this case because data may be lost during the conversion process. This type of bug is very difficult to catch.

But what if you know that the conversion is okay? For example, even though lValue is a long, maybe you know that its value can't exceed 100 in this particular program. In that case, converting the long variable lValue into the int variable nValue would be perfectly okay.

You can tell C# that you know what you're doing by means of a *cast*:

```
int lValue = 10;
int nValue;
nValue = (int)lValue;  // this is now OK
```

In a cast, you place the name of the type you want in parentheses and put it immediately in front of the value you want to convert. This cast says, "Go ahead and convert the long lValue into an int — I know what I'm doing." In retrospect, I admit the assertion that I know what I'm doing seems overly confident.

A counting number can be converted into a floating point automatically, but a cast from a floating point into a counting number requires a cast:

```
double dValue = 10.0;
long lValue = (long)dValue;
```

All conversions to and from the decimal require a cast. In fact, all numeric types can be converted into all other numeric types through the application of a cast.

Neither bool nor string can be converted directly into any other type.

Built-in C# functions can convert a number, character, or boolean into its string "equivalent." For example, you can convert the bool value true into the string "true"; however, you cannot consider this a direct conversion. The bool true and "true" are completely different things.

Chapter 4

Smooth Operators

- -

- -

Mathematicians create variables and manipulate them in various ways, adding them together, multiplying them, and — here's a toughie — even integrating them. Chapter 2 describes how to declare and define variables. However, it says nothing about how to use variables to get anything done after you've declared them. This chapter looks at the operations you can perform on variables to actually get something done.

Writing programs that get things done is good. You'll never make it as a C# programmer if your programs don't actually do anything. Unless, of course, you're a consultant, like me.

Performing Arithmetic

The set of arithmetic operators breaks down into several groups: the simple arithmetic operators, the assignment operators, and a set of special operators unique to programming. After you've digested these, you also need to digest a separate set of logical operators.

Simple operators

You learned all the simple operators in elementary school. Table 4-1 lists them.

Table 4-1	The Simple Operators
Operator	*What It Means*
– (unary)	take the negative of
*	multiply
/	divide
+	add
– (binary)	subtract
%	modulo

Most of these operators are called *binary operators* because they operate on two values: one on the left side of the operator and one on the right side. The one exception is the unary negative. However, this one is just as straightforward as the others:

```
int n1 = 5;
int n2 = -n1;  // n2 now has the value -5
```

The value of –n is the negative of the value of n.

The modulo operator may not be quite as familiar. Modulo is similar to the remainder after division. Thus, 5 % 3 is 2, and 25 % 3 is 1 (25 – 3 * 8).

The strict definition of % is "the operator such that: x = (x / y) + x % y."

The arithmetic operators other than modulo are defined for all the numeric types. The modulo operator is not defined for floating point because you have no remainder after division of floating point values.

Operating orders

The value of some expressions may not be clear. Consider, for example, the following expression:

```
int n = 5 * 3 + 2;
```

Does the programmer mean "multiply 5 times 3 and then add 2," which is 17, or does this line mean "multiply 5 times the sum of 3 and 2," which gives you 25?

C# executes common operators from left to right. So, the preceding example assigns the value 17 to the variable n.

C# determines the value of n in the following example by first dividing 24 by 6 and then dividing the result of that operation by 2 (as opposed to dividing 24 by the ratio 6 over 2):

```
int n = 24 / 6 / 2
```

The various operators have a hierarchy, or order of precedence. C# scans an expression and performs the operations of higher precedence before those of lower precedence. In previous books, I take great pains to explain the order of precedence, but I have since decided that was a complete waste of time (and brain cells). You should always compel the order of precedence by using parentheses.

The value of the following expression is clear, regardless of the operators' order of precedence:

```
int n = (7 % 3) * (4 + (6 / 3));
```

C# looks for the innermost parentheses for the first expression to evaluate:

```
int n = (7 % 3) * (4 + 2);
```

Having done that, C# works its way outward, evaluating each set of parentheses in turn:

```
int n = 1 * 6;
```

And here's the final result:

```
int n = 7
```

This rule has perhaps one exception. I don't condone this behavior, but many programmers omit parentheses in examples like the following one, because everyone knows that multiplication has higher precedence than addition:

```
int n = 7 + 2 * 3;
```

The value here is 13 (not 27).

The assignment operator

C# has inherited an interesting concept from C and C++: Assignment is itself a binary operator. The assignment operator has the value of the argument to the right. The assignment has the same type as both arguments, which must match.

This new view of the assignment operator has no effect on the expressions you've seen so far:

```
n = 5 * 3;
```

In this example, 5 * 3 is 15 and an `int`. The assignment operator stores the `int` on the right into the `int` on the left and returns the value 15. However, this new view of the assignment operator does allow the following:

```
m = n = 5 * 3;
```

Operators are evaluated in series from right to left. The right-hand assignment stores the value 15 into n and returns 15. The left-hand assignment stores 15 into m and returns a 15, which is then dropped on the floor.

This strange definition for assignment makes the following rather bizarre expressions legal:

```
int n;
int m;
n = m = 2;
```

C# extends the simple operators with a set of operators constructed from other binary operators. For example:

```
n += 1;
```

This expression is equivalent to

```
n = n + 1;
```

An assignment operator exists for just about every binary operator. I'm really not sure how these various assignment operators came to be, but there they are.

The increment operator

Of all the additions that you may perform in programming, adding 1 to a variable is the most common:

```
n = n + 1;
```

C# defines the assignment operator shorthand:

```
n += 1;
```

Even that's not good enough. C# provides an even shorter version:

```
++n; // increment n by 1
```

Why have an increment operator, and why two of them?

The reason for the increment operator lies in the obscure fact that the PDP-8 computer of the 1970s had an increment instruction. This would be of little interest today were it not for the fact that the C language, the original precursor to C#, was originally written for the PDP-8. Because that machine had an increment instruction, n++ generated fewer machine instructions than n = n + 1. As slow as those machines were, saving a few machine instructions was a big deal.

Today, compilers are smarter and there's no difference in the execution time for n++ and

n = n + 1 so the need for the increment operator has gone away. However, programmers are creatures of habit, and the operator remains to this day. You almost never see a C++ programmer increment a value using the longer but more intuitive n = n + 1. Instead, you see the increment operator.

Further, when standing by itself (that is, not part of a larger expression), the post-increment operator almost always appears instead of the pre-increment. There's no reason other than habit and the fact that it looks cooler.

All three of the preceding statements are equivalent — they all increment n by 1.

The increment operator is strange enough, but, believe it or not, C# actually has two increment operators: ++n and n++. The first one, ++n, is called the *preincrement operator*, while n++ is the *postincrement operator*. The difference is subtle but important.

Remember that every expression has a type and a value. In the following segment, both ++n and n++ are of type int:

```
int n;
n = 1;
int o = ++n;
n = 1;
int m = n++;
```

But what are the resulting values of m and o? (Hint: The choices are 1 or 2.)

The value of o is 2, and the value of m is 1. That is, the value of the expression ++n is the value of n after being incremented, while the value of the expression n++ is the value of n before it is incremented. Either way, the resulting value of n is 2.

Equivalent decrement operators — that is, n-- and --n — exist to replace n = n - 1. These work in exactly the same way as the increment operators.

Performing Logical Comparisons — Is That Logical?

C# also provides a set of logical comparison operators, as shown in Table 4-2.

Table 4-2	The Logical Comparison Operators
Operator	*Operator Is True If . . .*
a == b	a has the same value as b
a > b	a is greater than b
a >= b	a is greater than or equal to b
a < b	a is less than b
a <= b	a is less than or equal to b
a != b	a is not equal to b

These operators are called *logical comparisons* because they return either a true or a false of type bool.

Here's an example that involves a logical comparison:

```
int m = 5;
int n = 6;
bool b = m > n;
```

This example assigns the value false to the variable b because 5 is not greater than 6.

The logical comparisons are defined for all numeric types, including float, double, decimal, and char. All of the following are legal:

```
bool b;
b = 3 > 2;
b = 3.0 > 2.0;
b = 'a' > 'b';
b = 10M > 12M;
```

The comparison operators always produce results of type bool. The comparison operators are not valid for variables of type string. (Not to worry; C# offers other ways to compare strings.)

Comparing floating point numbers: Is your float bigger than mine?

Comparing two floating values can get dicey, and you need to be very careful with these comparisons. Consider the following comparison:

```
float f1;
float f2;
f1 = 10;
f2 = f1 / 3;
bool b1 = (3 * f2) == f1;
f1 = 9;
f2 = f1 / 3;
bool b2 = (3 * f2) == f1;
```

The only difference between the calculations of b1 and b2 is the original value of f1. So, what are the values of b1 and b2? The value of b2 is clearly true: 9/3 is 3; 3 * 3 is 9; and 9 equals 9. Voila.

The value of b1 is not so obvious: 10/3 is 3.333.... 3.333... * 3 is 9.999.... Is 9.999... equal to 10? That depends upon how clever your processor and compiler are. On a Pentium processor or later, C# is not smart enough to realize that b1 should be true if the calculations are moved away from the comparison.

To jump ahead just a little bit, you can use the system absolute value function to compare f1 and f2 as follows:

```
Math.Abs(d1 - 3.0 * d2) < .00001; // use whatever level of accuracy
```

This function returns true for both cases. You can use the constant Double.Epsilon instead of .00001 to get the absolute maximum level of accuracy. Epsilon is the smallest possible difference between two non-equal double variables.

Just compounding the confusion with compound logical operations

The bool variables have another set of operators defined just for them, as shown in Table 4-3.

Table 4-3	The Compound Logical Operators
Operator	*Operator Is True If . . .*
!a	a is false
a & b	a and b are true
a | b	either a or b or else both are true (also known as a and/or b)
a ^ b	a is true or b is true but not both (also known as a xor b)
a && b	a is true and b is true with short-circuit evaluation
a || b	a is true or b is true with short-circuit evaluation

The ! operator is the logical equivalent of the minus sign. For example, !a is true if a is false, and false if a is true. Can that be true?

The next two operators are straightforward enough. First, a & b is only true if both a and b are true. And a | b is true if either a or b is true. The ^ (also known as *exclusive or*) is sort of an odd beast. An exclusive or is true if either a or b is true but not if both a and b are true.

All three operators produce a logical bool value as their result.

The &, |, and ^ operators have what's known as a *bitwise operator* version. When applied to int variables, they perform their magic on a bit-by-bit basis. Thus, 6 & 3 is 2 (0110_2 & 0011_2 is 0010_2), 6 | 3 is 7 (0110_2 | 0011_2 is 0111_2), and 6 ^ 3 is 5 (0110_2 ^ 0011_2 is 0101_2). Binary arithmetic is really cool but beyond the scope of this book.

The remaining two logical operators are similar to, but subtly different from the first three. Consider the following example:

```
bool b = (boolExpression1) & (boolExpression2);
```

In this case, C# evaluates boolExpression1 and boolExpression2. It then looks to see if they are both true before deciding the value of b. However, this may be a wasted effort. If one expression is false, there's no reason to perform the other. Regardless of the value of the second expression, the result will be false.

The && operator enables you to avoid evaluating both expressions unnecessarily:

```
bool b = (boolExpression1) && (boolExpression2);
```

In this case, C# evaluates boolExpression1. If it's false, b is set to false, and the program continues on its merry way. On the other hand, if boolExpression1 is true, C# evaluates boolExpression2 and stores the result in b.

The && operator uses what's called *short-circuit evaluation* because it short-circuits around the second boolean expression, if necessary.

The || operator works the same way:

```
bool b = (boolExpression1) || (boolExpression2);
```

If boolExpression1 is true, there's no point in evaluating boolExpression2 because the result is true no matter what.

Finding the Perfect Date — Matching Expression Types

In calculations, an expression's type is just as important as its value. Consider the following expression:

```
int n;
n = 5 * 5 + 7;
```

My calculator says the resulting value of n is 32. However, that expression also has a type.

Written in "type language," the preceding expression becomes

```
int [=] int * int + int;
```

To evaluate the type of an expression, follow the same pattern you use to evaluate the expression's value. Multiplication takes precedence over addition. An int times an int is an int. Addition comes next. An int plus an int is an int. In this way, you can reduce the preceding expression as follows:

```
+
int * int + int
int + int
int
```

Calculating the type of an operation

The matching of types actually burrows down to the *subexpression*. Each expression has a type, and the type of the left- and right-hand sides of an operator must match what is expected of that operator:

```
type1 <op> type2 ⇨ type3
```

(The arrow means "produces.") Both type1 and type2 must be compatible with the operator op.

Most operators come in various flavors. For example, the multiplication operator comes in the following forms:

```
int     * int     ➪ int
uint    * uint    ➪ uint
long    * long    ➪ long
float   * float   ➪ float
decimal * decimal ➪ decimal
double  * double  ➪ double
```

Thus, 2 * 3 uses the int * int version of the * operator to produce the int 6.

Implicit type conversion

Okay, that's great for multiplying two ints or two floats. But what happens when the left- and right-hand arguments are not of the same type? For example, what happens in the following case?

```
int n1 = 10;
double d2 = 5.0;
double dResult = n1 * d2;
```

First, C# doesn't have an int * double operation. C# could just generate an error message and leave it at that; however, it tries to make sense out of what the programmer intended. C# does have int * int and double * double versions of multiplication. C# could convert d2 into its int equivalent, but that would involve losing any fractional part of the number (digits to the right of the decimal point). Instead, C# converts the int n1 into a double and uses the double * double operator. This is known as an *implicit promotion*.

An implicit promotion is *implicit* because C# does it automatically, and it's a *promotion* because it involves some natural concept of uphill and downhill. The list of multiplication operators is in promotion order from int to double or from int to decimal. No implicit conversion exists between the floating point types and decimal. Converting from the more capable type such as double to a less capable type such as int is known as a *demotion*.

A promotion is also known as an *up conversion* and a demotion is also known as a *down conversion*.

Implicit demotions, or down conversions, are not allowed. C# generates an error message in such cases.

Explicit type conversion — the cast

What if C# was wrong? What if the programmer really did want to perform integer multiplication?

You can change the type of any value-type variable through the use of the cast operator. A *cast* consists of the desired type contained in parentheses and placed immediately in front of the variable or expression in question.

Thus, the following expression uses the `int * int` operator:

```
int n1 = 10;
double d2 = 5.0;
int nResult = n1 * (int)d2;
```

The cast of `d2` to an `int` is known as an *explicit demotion*. The conversion is explicit because the programmer explicitly declared her intent — duh.

You can make an explicit conversion between any two value types, whether up or down the promotion ladder.

Avoid implicit type conversion. Make any changes in value-type explicit through the use of a cast.

Leave logical alone

C# offers no type conversion path to or from the `bool` type.

Assigning types

The same matching of types applies to the assignment operator.

Inadvertent type mismatches that generate compiler error messages usually occur in the assignment operator, not at the point of the actual mismatch.

Consider the following multiplication example:

```
int n1 = 10;
int n2 = 5.0 * n1;
```

The second line in this example generates an error message due to a type mismatch , but the error occurs at the assignment — not at the multiplication. Here's the horrible tale: In order to perform the multiplication, C# implicitly converts `n1` to a `double`. C# can then perform `double` multiplication, the result of which is the all-powerful `double`.

However, the type of the right-hand and left-hand operators of the assignment operator must match, but the type of the left-hand operator cannot change. Because C# refuses to demote an expression implicitly, the compiler generates the following error message: `Cannot implicitly convert type double to int`.

C# allows this expression with an explicit cast:

```
int n1 = 10;
int n2 = (int)(5.0 * n1);
```

(The parentheses are necessary because the cast operator has very high precedence.) This works. The `n1` is promoted to a `double`, the multiplication is performed, and the `double` result is demoted to an `int`. However, you have to worry about the sanity of the programmer because 5 * n1 is so much easier for both the programmer and the C# compiler.

The Ternary Operator — I Wish it Were a Bird and Would Fly Away

Most operators take two arguments — a few take one. Only one operator takes three arguments — the ternary operator. This operator is maligned and for good reason. It has the following format:

```
bool expression ? expression1 : expression2
```

I'll confuse you even more with an example:

```
int a = 1;
int b = 2;
int nMax = (a > b) ? a : b;
```

If the condition a is greater than b, the value of the expression is a. If a is not greater than b, the value of the expression is b.

Expressions 1 and 2 can be as complicated as you like but they must be true expressions; they cannot contain any declarations or other non-expression type statements.

The ternary operator is unpopular for several reasons. First, it isn't necessary. Using the type of if statements described in Chapter 5 has the same effect and is easier to understand. Second, the ternary is a true expression no matter how much it may look like some type of if statement. For example, expressions 1 and 2 must be of the same type. This leads to the following:

```
int a = 1;
double b = 0.0;
int nMax = (a > b) ? a : b;
```

This statement doesn't compile even though nMax would've ended up with the value of a. Because a and b must be of the same type, a is promoted to a double to match b. The resulting type of ?: is now double, which must be demoted to an int before the assignment is allowed:

```
int a = 1;
double b = 0.0;
int nMax;
// this works
nMax = (int)((a > b) ? a : b);
// so does this
nMax = (a > b) ? a : (int)b;
```

You will rarely see the ternary operator in use.

Chapter 5

Controlling Program Flow

● ●

In This Chapter

▶ Making decisions if you can

▶ Deciding what else to do

▶ Looping without going in a circle

▶ Using the while loop

▶ Using the for loop

● ●

*C*onsider the following very simple program:

```
using System;
namespace HelloWorld
{
  public class Class1
  {
    // This is where the program starts
    static void Main(string[] args)
    {
      // prompt user to enter a name
      Console.WriteLine("Enter your name, please:");
      // now read the name entered
      string sName = Console.ReadLine();
      // greet the user with the entered name
      Console.WriteLine("Hello, " + sName);
      // wait for user to acknowledge the results
      Console.WriteLine("Press Enter to terminate...");
      Console.Read();
    }
  }
}
```

Besides introducing you to a few fundamentals of C# programming, this program is almost worthless. It simply spits back out whatever you typed in. You can imagine more complicated example programs that take in input, perform some type of calculations, generate some type of output (otherwise, why do the calculations?) and then exit at the bottom. However, even a program such as that can be of only limited use.

One of the key elements of any computer processor is its ability to make decisions. When I say "make decisions," I mean the processor sends the flow of execution down one path of instructions if a condition is true, or another path if the condition is not true. Any programming language must offer this fundamental capability to control the flow of execution.

There are three basic types of flow control: the if statement, the loop, and the jump.

I describe one of the looping controls, the foreach, in Chapter 6.

Controlling Program Flow

The basis of all C# decision-making capability is the if statement (the basis of all my decisions is the maybe):

```
if (bool expression)
{
    // control passes here if the expression is true
}
// control passes to this statement whether the expression is true or not
```

A pair of parentheses immediately following the keyword if contains some conditional expression of type bool. (See Chapter 4 for a discussion of bool expressions.) Immediately following the expression is a block of code set off by a pair of braces. If the expression is true, the program executes the code within the braces. If the expression is not true, the program skips over the code in the braces.

The if statement is easier to understand with a concrete example:

```
// make sure that a is not negative:
// if a is less than 0 . . .
if (a < 0)
{
    //  . . .then assign 0 to a
    a = 0;
}
```

This segment of code makes sure that the variable a is greater than or equal to zero. The if statement says, "If a is less than 0, assign 0 to a."

The braces are not required. C# treats if(bool expression) statement; exactly as if it had been written if(bool expression) {statement;}. General consensus (and my preference) is to always use braces. In other words, don't ask — just do it.

What if *I need an example?*

Consider a small program that calculates interest. The user enters the principal and the interest rate, and the program spits out the resulting value at the end of the year. (This is not a sophisticated program.) The simplistic calculation appears as follows in C#:

```
// calculate the value of the principal
// plus interest
decimal mInterestPaid;
mInterestPaid = mPrincipal * (mInterest / 100);
// now calculate the total
decimal mTotal = mPrincipal + mInterestPaid;
```

The first equation multiplies the principal `mPrincipal` times the interest `mInterest` to get the interest to be paid `mInterestPaid`. (I divide by 100 because interest is usually input in "per cent.") The interest to be paid is then added back into the principal, resulting in a new principal, which is stored in the variable `mTotal`.

The program must anticipate almost anything when dealing with human input. For example, you don't want to accept a negative principal or interest (even if you do end up paying negative interest). The following `CalculateInterest` program includes checks to make sure that neither of these happen:

```
// CalculateInterest -
//              calculate the interest amount
//              paid on a given principal. If either
//              the principal or the interest rate is
//              negative, then generate an error message.
using System;
namespace CalculateInterest
{
  public class Class1
  {
    public static int Main(string[] args)
    {
      // prompt user to enter source principal
      Console.Write("Enter principal:");
      string sPrincipal = Console.ReadLine();
      decimal mPrincipal = Convert.ToDecimal(sPrincipal);
      // make sure that the principal is not negative
      if (mPrincipal < 0)
      {
        Console.WriteLine("Principal cannot be negative");
        mPrincipal = 0;
      }
      // enter the interest rate
      Console.Write("Enter interest:");
      string sInterest = Console.ReadLine();
      decimal mInterest = Convert.ToDecimal(sInterest);
      // make sure that the interest is not negative either
      if (mInterest < 0)
      {
        Console.WriteLine("Interest cannot be negative");
        mInterest = 0;
```

```
        }
        // calculate the value of the principal
        // plus interest
        decimal mInterestPaid;
        mInterestPaid = mPrincipal * (mInterest / 100);
        // now calculate the total
        decimal mTotal = mPrincipal + mInterestPaid;
        // output the result
        Console.WriteLine();  // skip a line
        Console.WriteLine("Principal    = " + mPrincipal);
        Console.WriteLine("Interest     = " + mInterest + "%");
        Console.WriteLine();
        Console.WriteLine("Interest paid = " + mInterestPaid);
        Console.WriteLine("Total         = " + mTotal);
        // wait for user to acknowledge the results
        Console.WriteLine("Press Enter to terminate...");
        Console.Read();
        return 0;
    }
  }
}
```

The CalculateInterest program begins by prompting the user for his name using the WriteLine() to write a string out to the console.

Tell the user exactly what you want. If possible, specify the format you want as well. Users don't respond well to uninformative prompts like >.

The example program uses the ReadLine() command to read in whatever the user types up to the Enter key in the form of a string. Because the program is looking for the principal in the form of a decimal, the input string must be converted using the Convert.ToDecimal() command. The result is stored in mPrincipal.

The ReadLine(), WriteLine(), and ToDecimal() commands are all examples of *function calls*. I describe function calls in detail in Chapter 6; however, these function calls are straightforward. You should be able to get at least the gist of the meaning using my extraordinarily insightful explanatory narrative. If that doesn't work, ignore my narrative. If that still doesn't work, skim through the beginning of Chapter 6.

The next line checks mPrincipal. If it is negative, the program outputs a nasty-gram, indicating that the user has fouled up. The program does the same thing for the interest rate. That done, the program performs the simplistic interest calculation outlined earlier and spits out the result using a series of WriteLine() commands.

The program generates the following output with a legitimate principal and a usurious interest rate that is legal in most states:

```
Enter principal:1234
Enter interest:21

Principal    = 1234
Interest     = 21%

Interest paid = 259.14
Total        = 1493.14
Press Enter to terminate...
```

Executing the program with illegal input generates the following output:

```
Enter principal:1234
Enter interest:-12.5
Interest cannot be negative

Principal    = 1234
Interest     = 0%

Interest paid = 0
Total        = 1234
Press Enter to terminate...
```

Indent the lines within an if clause in order to enhance readability. C# completely ignores such indentation. Most programming editors support auto indenting whereby the editor automatically indents as soon as you enter the if command. To set auto indenting in Visual Studio, choose Tools⇨Options. Then, select the Text Editor folder. From there, select C#. Finally, click Tabs. On this page, enable Smart Indenting and set the number of spaces per indent to whatever you prefer. I use two spaces per indent for this book. Set the Tab Size to the same value.

What else *can I do?*

Some functions must check for mutually exclusive conditions. For example, the following code segment stores the maximum of two numbers, a and b in the variable max:

```
// store the maximum of a and b into the variable max
int max;
// if a is greater than b . . .
if (a > b)
{
    // . . .save off a as the maximum
    max = a;
}
// if a is less than or equal to b . . .
if (a <= b)
{
    // . . .save off b as the maximum
    max = b;
}
```

The second if statement is needless processing because the two conditions are mutually exclusive. If a is greater than b, then it can't possibly be less than or equal to b. C# defines an else clause for just this case.

The else keyword defines a block of code that's executed if the if block is not.

The code segment to calculate the maximum now appears as follows:

```
// store the maximum of a and b into the variable max
int max;
// if a is greater than b . . .
if (a > b)
{
    //  . . .save off a as the maximum; otherwise . . .
    max = a;
}
else
{
    //  . . .save off b as the maximum
    max = b;
}
```

If a is greater than b, the first block is executed; otherwise, the second block is executed. In the end, max contains the greater of a or b.

Avoiding even the else

Sequences of else clauses can get confusing. Some programmers, me included, like to avoid them when doing so won't cause even more confusion. You could write the maximum calculation like this:

```
// store the maximum of a and b into the variable max
int max;
// assume that a is greater than b
max = a;
// if it is not . . .
if (b > a)
{
  // ...then you can change your mind
  max = b;
}
```

Some programmers avoid this style like the plague, and I can sympathize. That doesn't mean I'm going to change; it just means I sympathize. You see both this style and the "else style" in common use.

Embedded if statements

The CalculateInterest program warns the user of illegal input; however, continuing with the interest calculation even if one of the values is illogical doesn't seem quite right. It causes no real harm here because the interest calculation takes little or no time and the user can ignore the results, but some calculations aren't nearly so quick. In addition, why ask the user for an interest rate after she has already entered an invalid value for the principal? The user knows that the results of the calculation will be invalid no matter what she enters next.

The program should only ask the user for an interest rate if the principal is reasonable and only perform the interest calculation if both values are valid. To accomplish this, you need two if statements, one within the other.

An if statement found within the body of another if statement is called an *embedded* statement.

The following program, CalculateInterestWithEmbeddedTest, uses embedded if statements to avoid stupid questions if a problem with the input is detected:

```
// CalculateInterestWithEmbeddedTest -
//              calculate the interest amount
//              paid on a given principal. If either
//              the principal or the interest rate is
//              negative, then generate an error message
//              and don't proceed with the calculation.
using System;
namespace CalculateInterestWithEmbeddedTest
{
  public class Class1
  {
    public static void Main(string[] args)
    {
      // define a maximum interest rate
      int nMaximumInterest = 50;
      // prompt user to enter source principal
      Console.Write("Enter principal:");
      string sPrincipal = Console.ReadLine();
      decimal mPrincipal = Convert.ToDecimal(sPrincipal);
      // if the principal is negative . . .
      if (mPrincipal < 0)
      {
        // . . .generate an error message . . .
        Console.WriteLine("Principal cannot be negative");
      }
      else
      {
        // . . .otherwise, enter the interest rate
        Console.Write("Enter interest:");
        string sInterest = Console.ReadLine();
        decimal mInterest = Convert.ToDecimal(sInterest);
        // if the interest is negative or too large . . .
        if (mInterest < 0 || mInterest > nMaximumInterest)
        {
          // . . .generate an error message as well
          Console.WriteLine("Interest cannot be negative " +
                            "or greater than " + nMaximumInterest);
          mInterest = 0;
        }
        else
```

```
    {
        // both the principal and the interest appear to be
        // legal; calculate the value of the principal
        // plus interest
        decimal mInterestPaid;
        mInterestPaid = mPrincipal * (mInterest / 100);
        // now calculate the total
        decimal mTotal = mPrincipal + mInterestPaid;
        // output the result
        Console.WriteLine();  // skip a line
        Console.WriteLine("Principal    = " + mPrincipal);
        Console.WriteLine("Interest     = " + mInterest + "%");
        Console.WriteLine();
        Console.WriteLine("Interest paid = " + mInterestPaid);
        Console.WriteLine("Total        = " + mTotal);
    }
}
// wait for user to acknowledge the results
Console.WriteLine("Press Enter to terminate...");
Console.Read();
    }
  }
}
```

The program first reads the principal from the user. If the principal is negative, the program outputs an error message and quits. If the principal is not negative, control passes to the else clause, where the program continues executing.

The interest rate test has been improved in this sample. Here, the program requires an interest rate that's non-negative (a mathematical law) and less than some maximum (a judiciary law — we can only wish that credit cards had an interest rate limit). This if statement uses a compound test:

```
if (mInterest < 0 || mInterest > nMaximumInterest)
```

This statement is true if mInterest is less than zero or mInterest is greater than nMaximumInterest. Notice that I declare nMaximumInterest at the top of the program rather than *hard code* it as a constant here.

Define important constants at the top of your program.

Encoding constants in variables at the top of your program serves several purposes. First, it gives each constant a name. nMaximumInterest is much more descriptive than 50. Second, it makes the constant easy to find in the event that you need to change it. Finally, it makes the constant easier to change. Notice that the same nMaximumInterest appears in the error message. Changing nMaximumInterest to 60, for example, changes not only the test but also the error message.

Entering a correct principal but a negative interest rate generates the following:

```
Enter principal:1234
Enter interest:-12.5
Interest cannot be negative or greater than 50.
Press Enter to terminate...
```

Only by entering both a legal principal and a legal interest rate does the program generate the desired calculation:

```
Enter principal:1234
Enter interest:12.5

Principal    = 1234
Interest     = 12.5%

Interest paid = 154.25
Total        = 1388.25
Press Enter to terminate...
```

Looping Commands

The if statement enables a program to take a different path through the code being executed depending upon the results of a bool expression. This statement makes for drastically more interesting programs than a program without decision-making capability. Adding the ability to execute a set of instructions in an iterative manner adds another quantum jump in capability.

Consider the CalculateInterest program from earlier in this chapter. Performing this simple interest calculation with a calculator or by hand with a piece of paper would be much easier than writing and executing a program.

What if you could calculate the amount of principal for each of several succeeding years? That would be a lot more useful. A simple macro in a Microsoft Excel spreadsheet would still be easier, but at least you're getting closer.

What you need is a way for the computer to execute the same short sequence of instructions multiple times. This is known as a *loop*.

Start with the basic loop while *you're at it*

The C# keyword while introduces the most basic form of execution loop:

```
while(bool expression)
{
    // . . .repeatedly executed as long as the expression is true
}
```

When the while loop is first encountered, the bool expression is evaluated. If the expression is true, the code within the block is executed. When the block of code reaches the closed brace, control returns back to the top, and the whole process starts over again. (Kind of the way I feel when I'm walking the dog. He and I loop around and around the yard until he . . . well, until we're finished.) Control passes beyond the closed brace the first time the `bool` expression is evaluated and turns out to be false.

If the condition is not true the first time the `while` loop is encountered, the set of commands within the braces is never executed.

Programmers often get sloppy in their speech. (Programmers are sloppy most of the time.) A programmer might say that a loop is executed until some condition is false. To me, that implies that control passes outside the loop no matter where the program happens to be executing as soon as the condition becomes false. This is most definitely not the case. The program does not check whether the condition is true or not until control specifically passes back to the top of the loop.

You can use the `while` loop to create the program `CalculateInterest Table`, a looping version of the `CalculateInterest` program. `Calculate InterestTable` calculates a table of principals showing accumulated annual payments:

```
// CalculateInterestTable - calculate the interest
//            paid on a given principle over a period
//            of years
using System;
namespace CalculateInterestTable
{
  using System;
  public class Class1
    {
    public static void Main(string[] args)
    {
      // prompt user to enter source principal
      Console.Write("Enter principal:");
      string sPrincipal = Console.ReadLine();
      decimal mPrincipal = Convert.ToDecimal(sPrincipal);
      // if the principal is negative . . .
      if (mPrincipal < 0)
      {
        // . . .generate an error message . . .
        Console.WriteLine("Principal cannot be negative");
      }
      else
      {
        // . . .otherwise, enter the interest rate
        Console.Write("Enter interest:");
        string sInterest = Console.ReadLine();
        decimal mInterest = Convert.ToDecimal(sInterest);
        // if the interest is negative . . .
        if (mInterest < 0)
        {
          // . . .generate an error message as well
          Console.WriteLine("Interest cannot be negative");
          mInterest = 0;
        }
        else
        {
          // both the principal and the interest appear to be
          // legal; finally, input the number of years
          Console.Write("Enter number of years:");
```

```
        string sDuration = Console.ReadLine();
        int nDuration = Convert.ToInt32(sDuration);
        // verify the input
        Console.WriteLine();  // skip a line
        Console.WriteLine("Principal    = " + mPrincipal);
        Console.WriteLine("Interest     = " + mInterest + "%");
        Console.WriteLine("Duration     = " + nDuration + "years");
        Console.WriteLine();
        // now loop through the specified number of years
        int nYear = 1;
        while(nYear <= nDuration)
        {
            // calculate the value of the principal
            // plus interest
            decimal mInterestPaid;
            mInterestPaid = mPrincipal * (mInterest / 100);
            // now calculate the new principal by adding
            // the interest to the previous principal
            mPrincipal = mPrincipal + mInterestPaid;
            // round off the principal to the nearest cent
            mPrincipal = decimal.Round(mPrincipal, 2);
            // output the result
            Console.WriteLine(nYear + "-" + mPrincipal);
            // skip over to next year
            nYear = nYear + 1;
        }
    }
    }
    // wait for user to acknowledge the results
    Console.WriteLine("Press Enter to terminate...");
    Console.Read();
    }
    }
}
```

The output from a trial run of `CalculateInterestTable` appears as follows:

```
Enter principal:1234
Enter interest:12.5
Enter number of years:10

Principal    = 1234
Interest     = 12.5%
Duration     = 10years

1-1388.25
2-1561.78
3-1757
4-1976.62
5-2223.7
6-2501.66
7-2814.37
8-3166.17
9-3561.94
10-4007.18
Press Enter to terminate...
```

Each value represents the total principal after the number of years elapsed assuming simple interest compounded annually. For example, the value of $1,234 at 12.5 percent is $3,561.94 after 9 years.

Most of the values show two decimal places for the cents in the amount. Because trailing zeros are not displayed, some values show only a single or even no digit after the decimal point. Thus, $12.70 is displayed as 12.7. You can fix this using the special formatting characters described in Chapter 9.

The `CalculateInterestTable` program begins by reading the principal and interest values from the user and checking to make sure they're valid. `CalculateInterestTable` then reads the number of years over which to iterate and stores this value in the variable nDuration.

Before entering the `while` loop, the program declares a variable nYear, which it initializes to 1. This will be the "current year" — that is, this number will change "each year" as the program loops. If the year number contained in nYear is less than the total duration contained in nDuration, the principal for "this year" is recalculated by calculating the interest based on the "previous year." The calculated principal is output along with the current year offset.

The statement `decimal.Round()` rounds off the calculated value to the nearest fraction of a cent.

The key to the program lies in the last line within the block. The statement `nYear = nYear + 1;` increments nYear by 1. If nYear begins with the value 3, its value will be 4 after this expression. This incrementing moves the calculations along from one year to the next.

After the year has been incremented, control returns to the top of the loop, where the value nYear is compared to the requested duration. In the example run, if the current year is less than 10, the calculation continues. After being incremented 10 times, the value of nYear becomes 11, which is greater than 10 (even I knew that), and program control passes to the first statement after the `while` loop. That is to say, the program stops looping.

Most looping commands follow this same basic principle of incrementing a counter until it exceeds a previously defined value.

The counting variable nYear in `CalculateInterestTable` must be declared and initialized before the `while` loop in which it is used. In addition, the nYear variable must be incremented, usually as the last statement within the loop. As this example demonstrates, you have to look ahead to see what variables you will need. This pattern is easier after you've written a few thousand `while` loops, like I have.

When writing `while` loops don't forget to increment the counting variable, as I have in this example:

```
int nYear = 1;
while (nYear < 10)
{
    // . . . .whatever . . .
}
```

(I left off the `nYear = nYear + 1;`.) Without the increment, nYear is always 1, and the program loops forever. This is called an infinite loop. The only way to exit an infinite loop is to terminate the program (or reboot). (I guess nothing is truly infinite, with the possible exception of a particle passing through the event window of a black hole.)

Make sure the terminating condition can be satisfied. Usually, this means your counting variable is being incremented properly. Otherwise, you're looking at an infinite loop, an angry user, bad press, and 50 years of poor harvest.

Infinite loops are a common mistake, so don't get embarrassed when you get caught in one.

Do *loop* while *you can*

A variation of the `while` loop is the `do...while` loop. In this case, the condition is not checked until the end of the loop:

```
int nYear = 1;
do
{
    //  . . .some calculation . . .
    nYear = nYear + 1;
} while (nYear < nDuration);
```

In contrast to the `while` loop, the `do...while` loop is executed at least once no matter what the value of nDuration is. However, the `do...while` loop is fairly uncommon in practice.

Breaking up is easy to do

You can use two special controls within a loop: `break` and `continue`. Executing the `break` command causes control to pass to the first expression immediately following the inner-most loop. The similar `continue` command passes control straight back up to the conditional expression at the top of the loop in order to start over and get it right this time.

I have rarely used `continue` in my programming career and I doubt that many programmers even remember that it exists. Don't forget about it completely because it might be a trick question in an interview or crossword puzzle.

For example, suppose you want to take your money out of the bank as soon as the principal exceeds a certain number of times the original amount, irrespective of how many years duration. (After all, how much money do you really need?) You could easily accommodate this by adding the following within the loop:

```
if (mPrincipal > (maxPower * mOriginalPrincipal))
{
  break;
}
```

Anyone who watches "The Simpsons" as much as I do knows who `maxPower` is. (Hint: Doh!)

The `break` clause is not executed until the condition within the `if` comparison is true — in this case, until the calculated principal is `maxPower` times the original principal or more. Executing the `break` statement passes control outside of the `while(nYear <= nDuration)`, and the program continues on to its untimely death.

For a version of the interest table program with this addition, see `Calculate InterestTableWithBreak` on the CD. (I don't include the listing here, for brevity's sake.)

An example output from this program appears as follows:

```
Enter principal:100
Enter interest:25
Enter number of years:100

Principal   = 100
Interest    = 25%
Duration    = 100 years
Quit if a multiplier of 10 is reached

1-125
2-156.25
3-195.31
4-244.14
5-305.18
6-381.48
7-476.85
8-596.06
9-745.08
10-931.35
11-1164.19
Press Enter to terminate...
```

The program terminates as soon as the calculated principal exceeds $1,000 — thank goodness, you didn't have to wait 100 years!

Looping until you get it right

The `CalculateInterestTable` program is smart enough to terminate in the event that the user enters an invalid balance or interest amount. However, jumping immediately out of the program just because the user mistypes seems a little harsh. Even my user-unfriendly accounting program gives me three chances to get my password right before it gives up.

A combination of the `while` and `break` enable the program to be a little more flexible. The `CalculateInterestTableMoreForgiving` program demonstrates the principle:

```
// CalculateInterestTableMoreForgiving - calculate the interest
//           paid on a given principle over a period
//           of years. This version gives the user 3 chances
//           to input the legal principle and interest.
using System;
namespace CalculateInterestTableMoreForgiving
{
  using System;
  public class Class1
  {
    public static void Main(string[] args)
    {
      // define a maximum interest rate
      int nMaximumInterest = 50;
      // prompt user to enter source principal; keep prompting
      // until you get the correct value
      decimal mPrincipal;
      while(true)
      {
        Console.Write("Enter principal:");
        string sPrincipal = Console.ReadLine();
        mPrincipal = Convert.ToDecimal(sPrincipal);
        // exit if the value entered is correct
        if (mPrincipal >= 0)
        {
          break;
        }
        // generate an error on incorrect input
        Console.WriteLine("Principal cannot be negative");
        Console.WriteLine("Try again");
        Console.WriteLine();
      }
      // now enter the interest rate
      decimal mInterest;
      while(true)
      {
        Console.Write("Enter interest:");
        string sInterest = Console.ReadLine();
        mInterest = Convert.ToDecimal(sInterest);
        // don't accept interest that is negative or too large . . .
        if (mInterest >= 0 && mInterest <= nMaximumInterest)
        {
          break;
        }
        //  . . .generate an error message as well
        Console.WriteLine("Interest cannot be negative " +
                          "or greater than " + nMaximumInterest);
        Console.WriteLine("Try again");
        Console.WriteLine();
      }
      // both the principal and the interest appear to be
      // legal; finally, input the number of years
      Console.Write("Enter number of years:");
      string sDuration = Console.ReadLine();
      int nDuration = Convert.ToInt32(sDuration);
      // verify the input
      Console.WriteLine();  // skip a line
      Console.WriteLine("Principal     = " + mPrincipal);
```

```
        Console.WriteLine("Interest    = " + mInterest + "%");
        Console.WriteLine("Duration    = " + nDuration + " years");
        Console.WriteLine();
        // now loop through the specified number of years
        int nYear = 1;
        while(nYear <= nDuration)
        {
          // calculate the value of the principal
          // plus interest
          decimal mInterestPaid;
          mInterestPaid = mPrincipal * (mInterest / 100);
          // now calculate the new principal by adding
          // the interest to the previous principal
          mPrincipal = mPrincipal + mInterestPaid;
          // round off the principal to the nearest cent
          mPrincipal = decimal.Round(mPrincipal, 2);
          // output the result
          Console.WriteLine(nYear + "-" + mPrincipal);
          // skip over to next year
          nYear = nYear + 1;
        }
        // wait for user to acknowledge the results
        Console.WriteLine("Press Enter to terminate...");
        Console.Read();
      }
   }
}
```

This program works largely the same as previous examples, except in the area of the user input. In this case, a `while` loop replaces the `if` statement used in previous examples to detect invalid input. For example:

```
decimal mPrincipal;
while(true)
{
  Console.Write("Enter principal:");
  string sPrincipal = Console.ReadLine();
  mPrincipal = Convert.ToDecimal(sPrincipal);
  // exit if the value entered is correct
  if (mPrincipal >= 0)
  {
    break;
  }
  // generate an error on incorrect input
  Console.WriteLine("Principal cannot be negative");
  Console.WriteLine("Try again");
  Console.WriteLine();
}
```

This section of code inputs a value from the user within a loop. If the value of the text is okay, the program exits the loop and continues on. However, if the input has an error, the user is presented with an error message, and control passes back to start over.

Think about it this way: "The program continues to loop until the user gets it right."

Notice that the conditionals have been reversed because the question is no longer whether illegal input should generate an error message, but whether the correct input should exit the loop. In the interest section, for example, the test `mPrincipal < 0 || mPrincipal > nMaximumInterest` changes to `mInterest >= 0 && mInterest <= nMaximumInterest`. Clearly, `mInterest >= 0` is the opposite of `mInterest < 0`. What may not be so obvious is that the OR `||` is replaced with an AND `&&`. "Exit the loop if interest is greater than zero AND less than the maximum amount."

One last point to note: The `mPrincipal` variable must be declared outside of the loop due to scope rules, which I explain in the next section of this chapter.

It may sound obvious to say, but the expression `true` evaluates to `true`. Therefore, `while(true)` is your archetypical infinite loop. It is the embedded `break` command that exits the loop. Therefore, if you use the `while(true)` loop, make doubly sure that your break condition can occur.

The output from an example execution of this program showing my ignorance appears as follows:

```
Enter principal:-1000
Principal cannot be negative
Try again

Enter principal:1000
Enter interest:-10
Interest cannot be negative or greater than 50
Try again

Enter interest:10
Enter number of years:5

Principal    = 1000
Interest     = 10%
Duration     = 5 years

1-1100
2-1210
3-1331
4-1464.1
5-1610.51
Press Enter to terminate...
```

The program refuses to accept my negative principal or interest, patiently explaining my mistake on each loop.

Explain exactly what the user did wrong before looping back for further input.

Focusing on scope rules

A variable declared within the body of a loop is only defined within that loop. Consider the following code snippet:

```
int nDays = 1;
while(nDays < nDuration)
{
    int nAverage = nValue / nDays;
    //  . . .some series of commands . . .
    nDays = nDays + 1;
}
```

The variable `nAverage` is not defined outside of the `while` loop. There are various reasons for this, but consider this one: The first time the loop executes, the program encounters the declaration `int nAverage`, and the variable is defined. On the second loop, the program again encounters the declaration for `nAverage` — were it not for the scope rules, this would be an error because the variable is already defined.

There are other, more convincing reasons than this one, but it will do for now.

Suffice to say that the variable `nAverage` goes away, as far as C# is concerned, as soon as the program reaches the closed brace.

Experienced programmers say that the scope of the variable `nAverage` is limited to the `while` loop.

Understanding the Most Common Control for Looping

The `while` loop is the simplest and second most commonly used looping structure in C#. However, the `while` loop is used about as often as metric tools in Detroit compared to the `for` loop.

The `for` loop has the following structure:

```
for(initExpression; condition; incrementExpression)
{
    // . . .body of code . . .
}
```

When the `for` loop is encountered, the program first executes the `initExpression` expression. It then executes the `condition`. If the condition expression is true, the program executes the body of the loop, which is surrounded by the braces immediately following the `for` command. Upon reaching the closed brace, control passes to `incrementExpression` and then back to `condition`, where the loop starts over again.

In fact, the definition of a `for` loop can be converted into the following `while` loop:

```
initExpression;
while(condition)
{
    // . . .body of code . . .
    incrementExpression;
}
```

An example

You can better see how the `for` loop works with an example:

```
// here is some C# expression
a = 1;
// now loop for awhile
for(int nYear = 1; nYear < nDuration; nYear = nYear + 1)
{
    // . . .body of code . . .
}
// the program continues here
a = 2;
```

Assume that the program has just executed the `a = 1;` expression. Next, the program declares the variable `nYear` and initializes it to 1. That done, the program compares `nYear` to `nDuration`. If `nYear` is less than `nDuration` the body of code within the braces is executed. Upon encountering the closed brace, the program jumps back up to the top and executes the `nYear = nYear + 1` clause before sliding back over to the `nYear < nDuration` comparison.

What do you need another loop for?

Why do you need the `for` loop if C# has an equivalent `while` loop? The short answer is that you don't — the `for` loop doesn't bring anything to the table that the `while` loop can't already do.

However, the sections of the `for` loop exist for convenience and to clearly establish the three parts that every loop should have: the setup, the exit criteria, and the increment. Not only is this easier to read, but it's also easier to get right. (Remember that the most common mistakes in a `while` loop are forgetting to increment the counting variable and failing to provide the proper exit criteria.)

Beyond any sort of song-and-dance justification that I might make, the most important reason for understanding the `for` loop is because that's the loop that everyone uses and that's the one you'll see 90 percent of the time when reading other people's code.

The for loop is designed so that the first expression initializes a counting variable and the last section increments it; however, the C# language does not enforce any such rule. You can do anything you want in these two sections — you would be ill-advised to do anything but initialize and increment the counting variable, however.

The increment operator is particularly popular when writing for loops. (I describe the increment operator along with other operators in Chapter 4.) The previous for loop is usually written as follows:

```
for(int nYear = 1; nYear < nDuration; nYear++)
{
    // . . .body of code . . .
}
```

You'll almost always see the post-increment operator used in a for loop instead of the pre-increment, though the effect in this case is the same. There's no reason other than habit and the fact that it looks cooler. (Next time you want to break the ice, just haul out your C# listing full of post-increment operators to show how cool you really are. It almost never works but it's worth a try.)

The for loop has one variation that I really can't claim to understand. If the logical condition expression is missing, it is assumed to be true. Thus, for(;;) is an infinite loop.

You will actually see for(;;) used as an infinite loop more often than while(true). Why, I can't even start to understand.

Nested Loops

One loop can appear within an outer loop:

```
for( . . .some condition . . .)
{
  for( . . .some other condition . . .)
  {
    // . . .do whatever . . .
  }
}
```

The inner loop is executed to completion upon each pass through the outer loop.

A loop contained within another loop is called a *nested* loop.

Nested loops cannot "cross." For example, the following is not possible:

```
do                  // start a do loop
{
  for( . . .)       // start some for loop
  {
  } while( . . .)   // end do..while loop
}                   // end for loop
```

I'm not even sure what that would mean, but that doesn't matter because it's not legal anyway.

A `break` statement within a nested loop breaks out of the inner loop only.

In the following example, the `break` statement exits out of loop B and back into loop A:

```
// for loop A
for( . . .some condition . . .)
{
  // for loop B
  for( . . .some other condition . . .)
  {
    //  . . .do whatever . . .
    if (something is true)
    {
      break;         // breaks out of loop B and not A
    }
  }
}
```

C# doesn't have a `break` command that exits both loops simultaneously.

That's not as big a limitation as it sounds. In practice, the often-complex logic contained within such nested loops is better encapsulated in a function. Executing a `return` from within any of the loops exits the function, thereby bailing out of all loops no matter how nested they might be. I describe functions in Chapter 7.

The following whimsical `DisplayXWithNestedLoops` program uses a pair of nested loops to display a large X down the application console:

```
// DisplayXWithNestedLoops - use a pair of nested loops to
//                           create an X pattern
using System;
namespace DisplayXWithNestedLoops
{
  public class Class1
  {
    public static void Main(string[] args)
    {
      int nConsoleWidth = 40;
      // iterate through the rows of the "box"
      for(int nRowNum = 0;
          nRowNum < nConsoleWidth;
          nRowNum += 2)
      {
        // now iterate through the columns
        for (int nColumnNum = 0;
```

```
                nColumnNum < nConsoleWidth;
                nColumnNum++)
        {
            // the default character is a space
            char c = ' ';
            // if the column number and row number are the same . . .
            if (nColumnNum == nRowNum)
            {
                // . . .replace the space with a backslash
                c = '\\';
            }
            // if the column is on the opposite side of the row . . .
            int nMirrorColumn = nConsoleWidth - nRowNum;
            if (nColumnNum == nMirrorColumn)
            {
                // . . .replace the space with a slash
                c = '/';
            }
            // output whatever character at the current
            // row and column
            Console.Write(c);
        }
        Console.WriteLine();
    }
    // wait for user to acknowledge the results
    Console.WriteLine("Press Enter to terminate...");
    Console.Read();
    }
  }
}
```

The `DisplayXWithNestedLoops` program begins by defining an arbitrary number of rows and columns representing the size of the X to be drawn. Make this number larger, and the X stretches off the bottom of the application window.

The program uses a `for` loop to iterate through the rows of the X. The program then enters a second `for` loop, which iterates across the columns of the display. This draws a matrix on the display. The only problem left is to decide which cells within the matrix get spaces, thereby making them invisible, and which get characters. Fill in the proper cells, and you get an X.

The program first defines a `char c`, which it initializes to the default value of space. The program then compares the row and column number. If they are equal, the program replaces the space with a backward slash.

Remember that a backslash is used to mark special characters. For example, '\n' is a newline. The special character '\\' is the backslash.

By itself, replacing the space when the rows and columns are equal would draw a line from the upper left of the matrix to the bottom right. In order to get a mirrored slash, the program places a forward slash '/' when the number of the column on the opposite side is equal to the row number.

The result from this program is as follows:

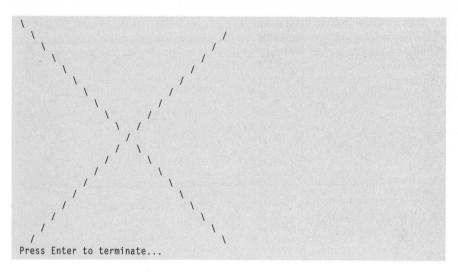

```
  \                               /
    \                           /
      \                       /
        \                   /
          \               /
            \           /
              \       /
                \   /
                / \
              /     \
            /         \
          /             \
        /                 \
      /                     \
    /                         \
  /                             \
Press Enter to terminate...
```

Not much to it, but I thought it was cute.

If you want to get serious, check out DisplaySin, which uses the same type of logic to display a sine wave vertically down the application display. I may be a nerd (actually there's no doubt about it), but I think that program is really cool. I cut my programming teeth on programs like that.

The switch *Control*

Often, you want to test a variable for numerous different values. For example, nMaritalStatus might be 0 for unmarried, 1 for married, 2 for divorced, 3 for widowed (I think I got them all — oh, wait), or 4 for none of your business. To differentiate between these values, you could use a series of if statements:

```
if (nMaritalStatus == 0)
{
  // must be unmarried
  //  . . .do something . . .
}
else
{
  if (nMaritalStatus == 1)
  {
    // must be married
    //  . . .do something else . . .
```

And so on.

You can see that these repetitive if statements get old quickly. Testing for multiple cases is such a common occurrence that C# provides a special construct to decide between a set of mutually exclusive conditions. This control is called the switch and it works as follows:

```
switch(nMaritalStatus)
{
  case 0:
          // . . .do the unmarried stuff . . .
          break;
  case 1:
          // . . .do the married stuff . . .
          break;
  case 2:
          // . . .do the divorced stuff . . .
          break;
  case 3:
          // . . .do the widowed stuff . . .
          break;
  case 4:
          // . . .get out of my face . . .
          break;
  default:
          // goes here if doesn't pass any of the cases;
          // this is probably an error condition
          break;
  break;
}
```

The expression at the top of the switch statement is evaluated. In this case, the expression is simply the variable nMaritalStatus. The value of that expression is then compared against the value of each of the cases. Control passes to the default clause if no match is found.

The argument to the switch statement can also be a string:

```
string s = "Davis";
switch(s)
{
  case "Davis":
          // . . .control will actually pass here . . .
          break;
  case "Smith":
          // . . .do the married stuff . . .
          break;
  case "Jones":
          // . . .do the divorced stuff . . .
          break;
  case "Hvidsten":
          // . . .do the widowed stuff . . .
          break;
  default:
          // goes here if doesn't pass any of the cases
          break;
}
```

Using the switch statement involves some severe restrictions:

✔ The argument to the switch() must be one of the counting types or a string.

✔ Floating point values are excluded.

✔ The various `case` values must refer to a value of the same type as the `switch` expression.

✔ The `case` values must be constant in the sense that their value must be known at compile time. (A statement such as `case x` is not legal unless x is some type of constant.)

✔ Each clause must end in a `break` statement (or some other exit command that you haven't seen yet, like `return`). The `break` passes control out of the `switch`.

This rule has one exception: A single `case` clause may have more than one `case` label, as in the following case:

```
string s = "Davis";
switch(s)
{
  case "Davis":
  case "Hvidsten":
        // do the same thing whether s is Davis or Hvidsten
        // since they're related
        break;
  case "Smith":
        // . . .do the married stuff . . .
        break;
  default:
        // goes here if doesn't pass any of the cases
        break;
}
```

This approach enables the program to perform the same operation whether the input is "Davis" or "Hvidsten."

The Lowly goto

You can transfer control in an unstructured fashion using the `goto` statement. The `goto` is followed by one of the following:

✔ A label

✔ A `case` from a `switch` statement

✔ The keyword `default`, meaning the default clause of a `switch` statement

The following snippet demonstrates how the `goto` is used:

```
// if the condition is true . . .
if (a > b)
{
  // . . .control passes unconditionally from the goto to the label
  goto exitLabel;
}
```

```
//  . . .what ever other code goes here . . .
exitLabel:
  // control continues here
```

The goto is unpopular for the very reason that makes it such a powerful control command: It is almost completely unstructured. Tracking the flow of control through anything larger than a trivial piece of code can be very difficult if you use goto.

Religious wars have sprung up over the use of the goto. In fact, the C# language itself has been criticized for the very inclusion of the control. In actual fact, goto is neither all that horrible nor necessary. Because you can almost always avoid using goto, I recommend staying away from it.

Part III
Object-Based Programming

The 5th Wave   By Rich Tennant

THAT IT! TARZAN TAKE NO MORE! KEEP GET BAD MESSAGE! WHAT MEAN?! TARZAN TRY EVERYTHING! MAKE TARZAN MAD LIKE CHEETAH! WANT PUT ROLODEX THROUGH SCREEN!

SYNTAX ERROR!

In this part . . .

It's one thing to declare a variable here or there and to add them and subtract them. It's quite another thing to write real programs that people can use — simple people, but people nonetheless. In this part, you discover how to group data and how to operate on that data. These skills form the basis of all programming jobs you'll find in the classifieds.

Chapter 6

Collecting Data — The Class and the Array

In This Chapter

▶ Introducing the C# class

▶ Storing data in an object

▶ Assigning and using object references

▶ Creating and building arrays of objects

*Y*ou can freely declare and use all the intrinsic types — such as `int`, `double`, and `bool` — to store the information necessary to make your program the best that it can be. For some programs, these simple variables are enough. However, most programs need a means to bundle related data together in a neat package.

Some programs need to bundle up pieces of data that logically belong together but aren't of the same type. For example, a college enrollment application handles students, each with its own name, rank (grade point average), and serial number. Logically, the student's name may be a `string`, the grade point average could be a `double`, and the serial number a `long`. That type of program needs some way to bundle these three different types of variables into a single structure called `Student`. Fortunately, C# provides a structure known as the *class* for accommodating groupings of unlike-typed variables.

In other cases, programs need to collect up a series of like-typed objects. Take, for example, a program designed to average grades. A `double` does a good job of representing an individual grade. However, you need some type of collection of `double` variables to contain all the many grades that a student collects during his career. C# provides the *array* for just this purpose.

Finally, a real program to process student records would need to graduate groups of students before they can set out on a life of riches and fame. This type of program needs both the class and the array concept rolled into one: arrays of students. Through the magic of C# programming, you can do this as well.

Showing Some Class

A *class* is a bundling of unlike data and functions that logically belong together into one tidy little package. C# gives you the freedom to foul up your classes any way you want, but classes are designed to represent *concepts*.

Analysts say that "a class maps concepts from the problem into the program." For example, suppose your problem is to build a traffic simulator. This traffic simulator will model traffic patterns for the purpose of building streets, intersections, and highways. I would really like you to build a traffic simulator that could fix the intersection in front of my house.

Any description of a problem concerning traffic would include the term *vehicle* in its solution. Vehicles have a top speed that must be figured into the equation. They also have a weight, and some of them are clunkers. In addition, vehicles stop, vehicles go, and go, vehicles, go! Thus, *vehicle* is part of the problem domain.

A good C# traffic simulator program would necessarily include the class `Vehicle`, which describes the relevant properties of a vehicle. The C# `Vehicle` class would have properties like `dTopSpeed`, `nWeight`, and `bClunker`. I address the `stop` and `go` part in Chapter 7.

Defining a class

An example of the class `Vehicle` might appear as follows:

```
public class Vehicle
{
    public string sModel;          // name of the model
    public string sManufacturer;   // ditto
    public int nNumOfDoors;        // the number of doors on the vehicle
    public int nNumOfWheels;       // you get the idea
}
```

A class definition begins with the words `public class`, followed by the name of the class — in this case, `Vehicle`.

Like all names in C#, the name of the class is case-sensitive. C# doesn't enforce any rules concerning class names, but an unofficial rule holds that the name of a class starts with a capital letter.

The class name is followed by a pair of open and closed braces. Within the braces, you have zero or more *members*. The members of a class are variables that make up the parts of the class. In this example, class `Vehicle` starts with the member `string sModel`, which contains the name of the model of the vehicle. Were this a car, the model name might be "Trouper II."

You know, I don't think I've ever seen or heard of a "Trouper I." The second member of this example `Vehicle` class is the `string sManufacturer`. The final two properties are the number of doors and the number of wheels on the vehicle.

As with any variable, make the names of the members as descriptive as possible. Although I've added comments to the data members, that really isn't necessary. The name of each variable says it all.

The `public` attribute in front of the class name makes the class universally accessible throughout the program. Similarly, the `public` attribute in front of the member names makes them accessible to everything else in the program. Other attributes are possible. Chapter 11 covers the topic of accessibility in more detail.

The class definition should describe the properties of the object that are salient to the problem at hand. That's a little hard to do right now because you don't know what the problem is, but you can see where I'm headed here.

What's the object?

Defining a `Vehicle` design is not the same thing as building a car. Someone has to build some sheet metal and turn some bolts before anyone can drive an actual vehicle. A class object is declared in a similar but not identical fashion to an intrinsic object.

The term *object* is used universally to mean a "thing." Okay, that isn't too helpful. An `int` variable is an `int` object. A vehicle is a `Vehicle` object. You are a reader object. I am an author . . . Okay, forget that last one.

The following code segment creates a `car` of class `Vehicle`:

```
Vehicle myCar;
myCar = new Vehicle();
```

The first line declares a variable `myCar` of type `Vehicle`, just like you might declare a `nSomethingOrOther` of class `int`. The `new Vehicle()` command creates an object of type `Vehicle` and stores the location into the variable `myCar`. The `new` has nothing to do with the age of `myCar`. My car could qualify for an Antique license plate if it weren't so ugly. The `new` creates a new block of memory in which your program can store the properties of `myCar`.

In C# terms, you say that `myCar` is an object of class `Vehicle`. You also say that `myCar` is an instance of `Vehicle`. In this context, *instance* means "an example of" or "one of." You can also use the word *instance* as a verb, as in instantiating a `Vehicle`.

Compare the declaration of myCar with that of an int variable num:

```
int num;
num = 1;
```

The first line declares the variable num and the second line assigns an already created constant of type int into the location of the variable num.

There's actually a difference in how the intrinsic num and the object myCar are stored in memory. The constant 1 does not occupy memory because both the CPU and the C# compiler already know what a "1" is. Your CPU doesn't have the concept of a Vehicle. The new Vehicle expression allocates the memory necessary to describe a vehicle to the CPU, to C#, to the world, and, yes, to the universe!

Accessing the members of an object

Each object of class Vehicle has its own set of members. The following expression stores the number 1 into the nNumberOfDoors member of the object referenced by myCar:

```
myCar.nNumberOfDoors = 1;
```

Every C# operation must be evaluated by type as well as by value. The object myCar is an object of type Vehicle. The variable Vehicle.nNumberOfDoors is of type int (look again at the definition of the Vehicle class). The constant 5 is also of type int, so the type of the variable on the right side of the assignment operator matches the type of the variable on the left.

Similarly, the following code stores a reference to the strings describing the model and manufacturer name of myCar:

```
myCar.sManufacturer = "BMW";       // don't get your hopes up
myCar.sModel = "Izeta";            // the Urkle-mobile
```

(The Izeta was a small car built during the 1950s with a single door that opened up the entire front of the car.)

An example object-based program

The following simple VehicleDataOnly program

- ✔ Defines the class Vehicle.
- ✔ Creates an object myCar.
- ✔ Assigns properties to myCar.
- ✔ Retrieves those values back out of the object for display.

Just be a clod — Why bother with class?

The class construct has grown in importance in programming languages over time. If you look at the chain of major languages, along with their approximate dates of maximum popularity, you can see the pattern:

✔ **Fortran (pre-1960 through early 80s):** No concept of a class

✔ **C (late 70s until mid 90s):** Classes used for organization only; possible to write programs that do not make use of classes

✔ **C++ (mid 80s until present):** A much more evolved class concept; still possible to write programs that don't make use of classes, but only by limiting yourself to a subset of the language

✔ **Java (mid 90s until present):** The class is a fundamental concept; impossible to write code without making use of classes

✔ **C# (today):** Same as Java

The class concept has grown in importance because programmers discovered that classes were very good at describing real-world objects. Suppose, for example, that I'm writing a banking program that deals with bank accounts. A bank account has features like an accountholder's name, account number, balance, and bank name. In my heart, I know that these properties belong together in a single structure because they all describe the same object: an account at my local bank. Holding a balance separate from the bank account number, for example, just doesn't make sense.

In C#, I might create a BankAccount class, complete with a string describing the holder's name, an int with the account number, a double or a decimal variable containing the balance, a string with the bank name, and so on. A single BankAccount variable describes all the relevant properties of a given bank account in my problem.

```
// VehicleDataOnly - create a Vehicle object, populate its
//                   members from the keyboard and then write it
//                   back out
using System;
namespace VehicleDataOnly
{
  public class Vehicle
  {
    public string sModel;        // name of the model
    public string sManufacturer; // ditto
    public int nNumOfDoors;      // the number of doors on the vehicle
    public int nNumOfWheels;     // you get the idea
  }
  public class Class1
  {
    // This is where the program starts
    static void Main(string[] args)
    {
      // prompt user to enter her name
      Console.WriteLine("Enter the properties of your vehicle");
      // create an instance of Vehicle
      Vehicle myCar = new Vehicle();
      // populate a data member via a second-party variable
      Console.Write("Model name = ");
      string s = Console.ReadLine();
```

```
        myCar.sModel = s;
        // or you can populate the data member directly
        Console.Write("Manufacturer name = ");
        myCar.sManufacturer = Console.ReadLine();
        // enter the remainder of the data
        Console.Write("Number of doors = ");
        s = Console.ReadLine();
        myCar.nNumOfDoors = Convert.ToInt32(s);
        Console.Write("Number of wheels = ");
        s = Console.ReadLine();
        myCar.nNumOfWheels = Convert.ToInt32(s);
        // now display the results
        Console.WriteLine("\nYour vehicle is a ");
        Console.WriteLine(myCar.sManufacturer + " " + myCar.sModel);
        Console.WriteLine("with " + myCar.nNumOfDoors + " doors, "
                         + "riding on " + myCar.nNumOfWheels
                         + " wheels");
        // wait for user to acknowledge the results
        Console.WriteLine("Press Enter to terminate...");
        Console.Read();
    }
  }
}
```

The program listing begins with a definition of the `Vehicle` class.

The definition of a class can appear either before or after `Class1` — it doesn't really matter. However, adopt a style and stick with it.

The program creates an object `myCar` of class `Vehicle` and then populates each of the fields by reading the appropriate data from the keyboard. The input data isn't checked for legality. The program then spits out the information just entered in a slightly different format.

The output from executing this program appears as follows:

```
Enter the properties of your vehicle
Model name = Metropolitan
Manufacturer name = Nash
Number of doors = 2
Number of wheels = 4

Your vehicle is a
Nash Metropolitan
with 2 doors, riding on 4 wheels
Press Enter to terminate...
```

The calls to `Read()` as opposed to `ReadLine()` leave the cursor right after the output string. This makes the user's input appear on the same line as the prompt. In addition, the addition of the new-line character '\n' generates a blank line without the need to execute `WriteLine()`.

Discriminating between objects

Detroit tracks each car it makes without getting them confused. Similarly, a program can create numerous objects of the same class:

```
Vehicle car1 = new Vehicle();
car1.sManufacturer = "Studebaker";
car1.sModel = "Avanti";
// the following has no effect on car1
Vehicle car2 = new Vehicle();
car2.sManufacturer = "Hudson";
car2.nVehicleNamePart = "Hornet";
```

Creating an object `car2` and assigning it the manufacturer name "Hudson" has no effect on the `car1` Studebaker.

In part, the ability to discriminate between objects is the real power of the class construct. The object associated with the Hudson Hornet can be created, manipulated, and dispensed with as a single entity, separate from other objects, including the Avanti. (These are both classic automobiles, especially the latter.)

Can you give me references?

The dot operator and the assignment operator are the only two operators defined on reference types:

```
// create a null reference
Vehicle yourCar;
// assign the reference a value
yourCar = new Vehicle();
yourCar.sManufacturer = "Rambler";
// create a new reference and point it to the same object
Vehicle yourSpousalCar = yourCar;
```

The first line creates an object `yourCar` without assigning it a value. A reference that has not been initialized is said to point to the *null object*. Any attempt to use an uninitialized reference generates an immediate error that terminates the program.

The C# compiler can catch most attempts to use an uninitialized reference and generate a warning at build time. If you somehow slip one past the compiler, accessing an uninitialized reference terminates the program immediately.

The second statement creates a new `Vehicle` object and assigns it to `yourCar`. The last statement in this code snippet assigns the reference `yourSpousalCar` to the reference `yourCar`. As shown in Figure 6-1, this has the effect of causing `yourSpousalCar` to refer to the same object as `yourCar`.

The following two calls have the same effect:

```
// build your car
Vehicle yourCar = new Vehicle();
yourCar.sModel = "Kaiser";
// it also belongs to your spouse
Vehicle yourSpousalCar = yourCar;
```

```
// changing one changes the other
yourSpousalCar.sModel = "Henry J";
Console.WriteLine("your car is a " + yourCar.sModel);
```

Executing this program would output "Henry J" and not "Kaiser." Notice that yourSpousalCar does not point to yourCar; rather, both yourCar and yourSpousalCar refer to the same vehicle.

Figure 6 -1:
The relationship between two references to the same object.

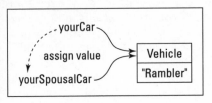

In addition, the reference yourSpousalCar would still be valid even if the variable yourCar were somehow "lost" (went out of scope, for example):

```
// build your car
Vehicle yourCar = new Vehicle();
yourCar.sModel = "Kaiser";
// it also belongs to your spouse
Vehicle yourSpousalCar = yourCar;
// when she takes your car away . . .
yourCar = null;               // yourCar now references the "null object"
//  . . .yourSpousalCar still references the same vehicle
Console.WriteLine("your car was a " + yourSpousalCar.sModel);
```

Executing this program generates the output "your car was a Kaiser" even though the reference yourCar is no longer valid.

The object is no longer *reachable* from the reference yourCar. The object does not become completely unreachable until both yourCar and yourSpousalCar are "lost" or nulled out.

Classes that contain classes are the happiest classes in the world

The members of a class can themselves be references to other classes. For example, vehicles have motors, which have power and efficiency factors. (I suppose a bicycle doesn't have a displacement.) You could throw these factors directly into the class as follows:

```
public class Vehicle
{
  public string sModel;          // name of the model
  public string sManufacturer;   // ditto
  public int nNumOfDoors;        // the number of doors on the vehicle
  public int nNumOfWheels;       // you get the idea
  public int nPower;             // power of the motor [HP]
  public double displacement;    // engine displacement [liter]
}
```

However, power and engine displacement are not properties of the car. For example, my son's Jeep comes with two different motor options with drastically different horsepower. The 2.4-liter Jeep is a snail while the same car outfitted with the 4.0-liter engine is quite peppy.

The motor is a concept of its own and deserves its own class:

```
class Motor
{
  public int nPower;             // power [horse power]
  public double displacement;    // engine displacement [liter]
}
```

You can combine this class into the Vehicle as follows:

```
public class Vehicle
{
  public string sModel;          // name of the model
  public string sManufacturer;   // ditto
  public int nNumOfDoors;        // the number of doors on the vehicle
  public int nNumOfWheels;       // you get the idea
  public Motor motor;
}
```

Creating myCar now appears as follows:

```
// first create a Motor
Motor largerMotor = new Motor();
largerMotor.nPower = 230;
largerMotor.displacement = 4.0;
// now create the car
Vehicle sonsCar = new Vehicle();
sonsCar.sModel = "Cherokee Sport";
sonsCar.sManfacturer = "Jeep";
sonsCar.nNumberofDoors = 2;
sonsCar.numberOfWheels = 4;
// attach the motor to the car
sonsCar.motor = largerMotor;
```

From the Vehicle, you can access the motor displacement in two stages. You can either take one step at a time:

```
Motor m = sonsCar.motor;
Console.WriteLine("The motor displacement is " + m.displacement);
```

Or, you can access it directly:

```
Console.Writeline("The motor displacement is " + sonsCar.motor.displacement);
```

Either way, you can only access the `displacement` from the `Motor`.

This example is bundled up in the simple program `VehicleAndMotor` on your CD.

Generating static in class members

Most data members of a class describe each object. Consider the `Car` class:

```
public class Car
{
    public string sLicensePlate;      // the license plate ID
}
```

The license plate ID is an *object property*, meaning that it describes each object of class `Car` uniquely. For example, thank goodness for you that my car has a different license plate from yours; otherwise, you might not make it out of your driveway:

```
Car myCar = new Car();
myCar.sLicensePlate = "XYZ123";

Car yourCar = new Car();
yourCar.sLicensePlate = "ABC789";
```

However, some properties exist that all cars share. For example, the number of cars built is a property of the class `Car` but not of any one object. These are called *class properties* and are flagged in C# with the keyword `static`:

```
public class Car
{
    public static int nNumberOfCars; // the number of cars built
    public string sLicensePlate;     // the license plate ID
}
```

Static members are not accessed through the object. Instead, you access them via the class itself, as the following code snippet demonstrates:

```
// create a new object of class Car
Car newCar = new Car();
newCar.sLicensePlate = "ABC123";
// now increment the count of cars to reflect the new one
Car.nNumberOfCars++;
```

The object member `newCar.sLicensePlate` is accessed through the object `newCar`, while the class (static) member `Car.nNumberOfCars` is accessed through the class `Car`.

Defining const *data members*

One special type of static is the `const` data member. You must establish the value of a `const` variable in the declaration, and you may not change it anywhere within the program:

```
class Class1
{
  // number of days in the year (including leap day)
  public const int nDaysInYear = 366;
  public static void Main(string[] args)
  {
    int[] nMaxTemperatures = new int[nDaysInYear];
    for(int index = 0; index < nDaysInYear; index++)
    {
      // . . .accumulate the maximum temperature for each
      // day of the year . . .
    }
  }
}
```

You can use the constant `nDaysInYear` in place of the value 366 anywhere within your program. The `const` variable is useful because it can replace a meaningless constant such as 366 with the descriptive name `nDaysInYear` to enhance the readability of your program.

The C# Array

Variables containing single values are all well and good. Even class structures that can describe compound objects like a vehicle are critical. But you also need a construct for holding a set of objects. The built-in class `Array` is a structure that can contain a series of elements of the same type (all `int` values, all `double` values, and so on, or all `Vehicle` objects, `Motor` objects, and so on).

The argument for the array

Consider the problem of averaging a set of 10 floating point numbers. Each of the 10 numbers requires its own `double` storage (averaging `int` variables could result in rounding errors, as described in Chapter 3):

```
double d0 = 5;
double d1 = 2;
double d2 = 7;
double d3 = 3.5;
double d4 = 6.5;
double d5 = 8;
double d6 = 1;
double d7 = 9;
double d8 = 1;
double d9 = 3;
```

Now, you need to accumulate each of these values into a common sum, which you would then divide by 10 (the number of values):

```
double dSum = d0 + d1 + d2 + d3 + d4 + d5 + d6 + d7 + d8 + d9;
double dAverage = dSum / 10;
```

Listing each element by name is tedious. Okay, maybe not so tedious when you have only 10 numbers to average, but imagine averaging 100 or even 1,000 floating point values.

The fixed value array

Fortunately, you don't need to name each element separately. C# provides a structure, known as an array, that can store a sequence of values. Using an array, you can rewrite the preceding code segment as follows:

```
double[] dArray = {5, 2, 7, 3.5, 6.5, 8, 1, 9, 1, 3};
```

The Array class provides a special syntax that makes it more convenient to use. The double brackets [] refer to the way you access individual elements in the array:

```
dArray[0] corresponds to d0
dArray[1] corresponds to d1
. . .
```

The 0th element of the array corresponds to d0, the 1th element to d1, and so on.

The array's element numbers — 0, 1, 2, and so on — are known as the *index*.

The array index starts at 0 and not at 1. Therefore, you typically don't refer to the element at index 1 as the first element but the "one-th element" or the "element at index 1." The first element is the zero-th element. If you insist on using normal speech, just be aware that the first element is at index 0 and the second element is at index 1.

dArray wouldn't be much of an improvement were it not for the fact that the index of the array can be a variable. Using a for loop is easier than writing each element out by hand, as the following program demonstrates:

```
// FixedArrayAverage - average a fixed array of
//                     numbers using a loop
namespace FixedArrayAverage
{
  using System;
  public class Class1
  {
    public static int Main(string[] args)
    {
      double[] dArray =
```

```
            {5, 2, 7, 3.5, 6.5, 8, 1, 9, 1, 3};
      // accumulate the values in the array
      // in the variable dSum
      double dSum = 0;
      for (int i = 0; i < 11; i++)
      {
        dSum = dSum + dArray[i];
      }
      // now calculate the average
      double dAverage = dSum / 10;
      Console.WriteLine(dAverage);
      // wait for user to acknowledge the results
      Console.WriteLine("Press Enter to terminate...");
      Console.Read();
      return 0;
    }
  }
}
```

Array bounds checking

The FixedArrayAverage program loops through an array of 10 elements. Fortunately, the loop iterates through all 10 elements. But what if I had made a mistake and didn't iterate through the loop properly? There are two cases to consider.

What if I had only iterated through nine elements? C# would not have considered this an error: If you want to read nine elements of a 10-element array, who is C# to say any different? Of course, the average would be incorrect, but the program wouldn't know.

What if I had iterated through 11 (or more) elements? Now, C# cares a lot. C# will not allow you to index beyond the end of an array, for fear that you will overwrite some important value in memory. To test this, I changed the comparison in the for loop to the following: for(int i = 0; i < 11; i++), replacing the value 10 with 11 in the comparison. When I executed the program, I got the following error:

```
Exception occurred: System.IndexOutOfRangeException:
        An exception of type System.IndexOutOfRangeException
        was thrown at
        FixedArrayAverage.Class1.Main(String[] args)
        in c:\c#programs\fixedarrayaverage\class1.cs:line 19
```

(I have added newlines to enhance the readability.)

At first glance, this error message seems imposing. However, you can get the gist rather quickly: An IndexOutOfRangeException was reported. Clearly, C# is telling me that the program tried to access an array beyond the end of its range — accessing element 11 in a 10-element array. (The message goes on to indicate the exact line from which the access was made, but you haven't progressed far enough in the book to understand the entire message completely.)

The program begins by initializing a variable dSum to 0. The program then loops through the values stored in dArray, adding each one to dSum. By the end of the loop, dSum has accumulated the sum of all the values in the array. The resulting sum is divided by the number of elements to create the average. The output from executing this program is the expected 4.6. (I checked it with my calculator — I think).

The variable length array

The array used in the example program FixedArrayAverage suffers from two serious problems. The size of the array is fixed at 10 elements. Worse yet, the value of those 10 elements is specified directly in the program.

A program that could read in a variable number of values, perhaps determined by the user during execution, would be much more flexible. It would work not only for the 10 values specified in FixedArrayAverage, but also for any other set of values.

The format for declaring a variable sized array differs slightly from that of a fixed size, fixed value array:

```
double[] dArray = new double[N];
```

N represents the number of elements to allocate.

The updated program VariableArrayAverage enables the user to specify the number of values to enter. Because the program retains the values entered, not only does it calculate the average, but it also displays the results in a pleasant format:

```
// VariableArrayAverage - average an array whose size is
//                        determined by the user at run time.
//                        Accumulating the values in an array
//                        allows them to be referenced as often
//                        as desired. In this case, the array
//                        creates an attractive output.
namespace VariableArrayAverage
{
  using System;
  public class Class1
  {
    public static int Main(string[] args)
    {
      // first read in the number of doubles
      // the user intends to enter
      Console.Write("Enter the number of values to average:");
      string sNumElements = Console.ReadLine();
      int numElements = Convert.ToInt32(sNumElements);
      Console.WriteLine();
      // now declare an array of that size
      double[] dArray = new double[numElements];
      // accumulate the values into an array
      for (int i = 0; i < numElements; i++)
```

```
    {
        // prompt the user for another double
        Console.Write("enter double #" + (i + 1) + ": ");
        string sVal = Console.ReadLine();
        double dValue = Convert.ToDouble(sVal);
        // add this to the array
        dArray[i] = dValue;
    }
    // accumulate 'numElements' values from
    // the array in the variable dSum
    double dSum = 0;
    for (int i = 0; i < numElements; i++)
    {
        dSum = dSum + dArray[i];
    }
    // now calculate the average
    double dAverage = dSum / numElements;
    // output the results in an attractive format
    Console.WriteLine();
    Console.Write(dAverage
                + " is the average of ("
                + dArray[0]);
    for (int i = 1; i < numElements; i++)
    {
        Console.Write(" + " + dArray[i]);
    }
    Console.WriteLine(") / " + numElements);
    // wait for user to acknowledge the results
    Console.WriteLine("Press Enter to terminate...");
    Console.Read();
    return 0;
    }
  }
}
```

Look at the output of a sample run in which I enter five sequential values, 1 through 5, and the program calculates the average to be 3:

```
Enter the number of values to average:5

enter double #1: 1
enter double #2: 2
enter double #3: 3
enter double #4: 4
enter double #5: 5

3 is the average of (1 + 2 + 3 + 4 + 5) / 5
Press Enter to terminate...
```

The VariableArrayAverage program begins by prompting the user for the number of values she intends to average. The result is stored in the int variable numElements. In the example, the number entered is 5.

The program continues by allocating an array dArray with the specified number of elements. In this case, the program allocates an array with five elements. The program loops the number of times specified by numElements, reading a new value from the user each time.

After the user enters the values, the program applies the same algorithm used in the `FixedArrayAverage` program to calculate the average of the sequence.

The final section generates the output of the average along with the numbers entered in an attractive format (attractive to me — beauty is in the eye of the beholder).

Getting console output just right is a little tricky. Follow each statement in the `FixedArrayAverage` carefully as the program outputs open parentheses, equal signs, plus signs, and each of the numbers in the sequence, and compare this with the output.

The `VariableArrayAverage` program doesn't completely satisfy my thirst for flexibility. I don't want to have to tell the program how many numbers I want to average. What I'd really like is to enter numbers to average as long as I want and then tell the program to average whatever I've entered. C# provides other types of *containers*, some of which can grow and shrink as necessary. Chapter 16 describes these containers.

The Length property

The `for` loop used to populate the array in the `VariableArrayAverage` program begins as follows:

```
// now declare an array of that size
double[] dArray = new double[numElements];
// accumulate the values into an array
for (int i = 0; i < numElements; i++)
{
  // prompt the user for another double
  Console.Write("enter double #" + (i + 1) + ": ");
  string sVal = Console.ReadLine();
  double dValue = Double.FromString(sVal);
  // add this to the array
  dArray[i] = dValue;
}
```

The `dArray` is declared to be `numElements` in length. Thus, the clever programmer (me) used a `for` loop to iterate through `numElements` of the array.

It would be a shame and a crime to have to schlep the variable `numElements` around with `dArray` everywhere it goes just so you know how long it is. Fortunately, that isn't necessary. An array has a property called `Length` that contains its length. `dArray.Length` has the same value as `numElements`.

The following `for` loop would have been preferable:

```
// accumulate the values into an array
for (int i = 0; i < dArray.Length; i++)
{
```

Why do the formats of fixed and variable length arrays differ so much?

On the surface, the syntax of fixed and variable length arrays look quite a bit different:

```
double[] dFixedLengthArray = {5, 2, 7, 3.5, 6.5, 8, 1, 9, 1, 3};
double[] dVariableLengthArray = new double[10];
```

The difference is that C# is trying to save you some work. C# allocates the memory for you in the case of the fixed length array `dFixedLengthArray`. I could have done it myself:

```
double[] dFixedLengthArray = new double[10] {5, 2, 7, 3.5, 6.5, 8, 1, 9, 1, 3};
```

Here, I have specifically allocated the memory using `new` and then followed that declaration with the initial values for the members of the array.

Lining Up Arrays of Objects

Programmers often must deal with sets of user-defined objects. For example, a university needs some type of structure to describe the students attending the fine institution of higher learning. Pfft!

A simplified `Student` class appears as follows:

```
public class Student
{
  public string sName;
  public double dGPA;          // grade point average
}
```

This class contains nothing more than the student's name and grade point average.

The following line declares an array of `num` references to `Student` objects:

```
Student[] students = new Student[num];
```

`new Student[num]` does *not* declare an array of `Student` objects. This line declares an array of references to `Student` objects.

So far, each element `students[i]` references the `null` object. You can also say that none of the elements in the array points to a `Student` object. First, you must populate the array as follows:

```
for (int i = 0; i < students.Length; i++)
{
    students[i] = new Students();
}
```

Now the program can enter the properties of the individual students:

```
students[i] = new Student();
students[i].sName = "My Name";
students[i].dGPA = dMyGPA;
```

You can see this wonder in the following `AverageStudentGPA` program, which inputs information on a number of students and spits out the average of their GPAs:

```
// AverageStudentGPA - calculate the average GPAs (grade point
//                     averages) of a number of students.
using System;
namespace AverageStudentGPA
{
  public class Student
  {
    public string sName;
    public double dGPA;         // grade point average
  }
  public class Class1
  {
    public static void Main(string[] args)
    {
      // find out how many students
      Console.WriteLine("Enter the number of students");
      string s = Console.ReadLine();
      int nNumberOfStudents = Convert.ToInt32(s);
      // allocate an array of Student objects
      Student[] students = new Student[nNumberOfStudents];
      // now populate the array
      for (int i = 0; i < students.Length; i++)
      {
        // prompt the user for the name - add one to
        // the index because people are 1-oriented while
        // C# arrays are 0-oriented
        Console.Write("Enter the name of student "
                      + (i + 1) + ": ");
        string sName = Console.ReadLine();
        Console.Write("Enter grade point average: ");
        string sAvg = Console.ReadLine();
        double dGPA = Convert.ToDouble(sAvg);
        // create a Student from that data
        Student thisStudent = new Student();
        thisStudent.sName = sName;
        thisStudent.dGPA  = dGPA;
        // add the student object to the array
        students[i] = thisStudent;
      }
      // now average the students that you have
      double dSum = 0.0;
      for (int i = 0; i < students.Length; i++)
      {
        dSum += students[i].dGPA;
      }
      double dAvg = dSum/students.Length;
      // output the average
      Console.WriteLine();
      Console.WriteLine("The average of the "
                        + students.Length
                        + " students is " + dAvg);
```

```
     // wait for user to acknowledge
     Console.WriteLine("Press Enter to terminate...");
     Console.Read();
    }
  }
}
```

The program prompts the user for the number of students to consider. It then creates the properly sized array of references to Student objects.

The program now enters an initial for loop in which it populates the array. The user is prompted for the name and GPA of each student in turn. This data is used to create a Student object, which is promptly stuffed into the next element in the array.

After all the Student references are snuggled fast in their beds, the program enters a second loop. In this loop, the GPA of each student is read using the statement students[i].GPA. The GPAs are rounded up, summed together, and averaged. The average is then output to the user.

Here's the output from a typical run from this program:

```
Enter the number of students
3
Enter the name of student 1: Randy
Enter grade point average: 3.0
Enter the name of student 2: Jeff
Enter grade point average: 3.5
Enter the name of student 3: Carrie
Enter grade point average: 4.0

The average of the 3 students is 3.5
Press Enter to terminate...
```

The name of an object reference variable should always be singular, as in student. The name of the variable should somehow include the name of the class, as in badStudent or goodStudent or sexyCoedStudent. The name of an array (or any other collection, for that matter) should be plural, as in students or phoneNumbers or phoneNumbersInMyPalmPilot. As always, this tip reflects the opinion of the author and not this book's publisher nor any of its shareholders — C# doesn't care how you name your variables.

A Flow Control Command Made foreach Array

Given an array of objects of class Student, the following loop averages their grade point averages:

```
public class Student
{
  public string sName;
  public double dGPA;         // grade point average
}
public class Class1
{
  public static void Main(string[] args)
  {
    //  . . .create the array . . .
    // now average that students that you have
    double dSum = 0.0;
    for (int i = 0; i < students.Length; i++)
    {
      dSum += students[i].dGPA;
    }
    double dAvg = dSum/students.Length;
    //  . . .do something with that array . . .
  }
}
```

The for loop iterates through the members of the array.

students.Length contains the number of elements in the array.

C# provides yet another control called the foreach designed specifically for iterating through containers such as the array. It works as follows:

```
// now average that students that you have
double dSum = 0.0;
foreach (Student stud in students)
{
  dSum += stud.dGPA;
}
double dAvg = dSum/students.Length;
```

The first time through the loop, the foreach fetches the first Student object in the array and stores it in the variable stud. On each subsequent pass, the foreach retrieves the next element. Control passes out of the foreach when all the elements in the array have been processed.

Notice that no index appears in the foreach statement. This greatly reduces the chance of error.

Former C, C++, and Java programmers find the foreach a little uncomfortable at first because it is unique to C#; however, the foreach sort of grows on you. It is the easiest of all the looping commands for accessing arrays.

The foreach is actually more powerful than it would seem from this example. The foreach works on other collection types in addition to arrays. (Bonus Chapter 1 discusses collections.) In addition, the example foreach would skip elements of the array that were not of type Student.

Sorting Through Arrays of Objects

A common programming challenge is the need to sort the elements within an array. Just because an array cannot grow or shrink in size does not mean that the elements within the array cannot be moved, removed, or added. For example, the following code snippet swaps the location of two Student elements within the array students:

```
Student temp = students[i]; // save off the i'th student
students[i] = students[j];
students[j] = temp;
```

Here, the object reference in the ith location in the students array is saved off so that it is not lost when the second statement copies its value. Finally, the temp variable is saved back into the jth location. Pictorially, this looks like Figure 6-2.

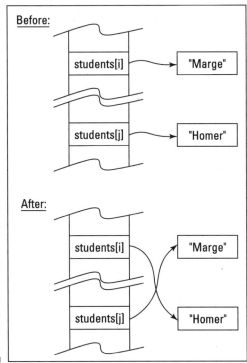

Figure 6-2: "Swapping two objects" actually means "swapping two references to the same object."

The following program demonstrates how to use the ability to manipulate elements within an array as part of a sort. This particular sorting algorithm is called the *bubble sort*. It's not so great on large arrays with thousands of entries but it's simple and effective on small arrays:

```
// SortStudents - this program demonstrates how to sort
//                an array of objects
using System;
namespace SortStudents
{
  class Class1
  {
    public static void Main(string[] args)
    {
      // create an array of students
      Student[] students = new Student[5];
      students[0] = Student.NewStudent("Homer", 0);
      students[1] = Student.NewStudent("Lisa", 4.0);
      students[2] = Student.NewStudent("Bart", 2.0);
      students[3] = Student.NewStudent("Marge", 3.0);
      students[4] = Student.NewStudent("Maggie", 3.5);
      // output the list as is:
      Console.WriteLine("Before sorting:");
      OutputStudentArray(students);
      // now sort the list of students by grade (best
      // grade first)
      Console.WriteLine("\nSorting the list\n");
      Student.Sort(students);
      // display the resulting list
      Console.WriteLine("The students sorted by grade:");
      OutputStudentArray(students);
      // wait for user to acknowledge the results
      Console.WriteLine("Press Enter to terminate...");
      Console.Read();
    }
    // OutputStudentArray - display all the students in the array
    public static void OutputStudentArray(Student[] students)
    {
      foreach(Student s in students)
      {
        Console.WriteLine(s.GetString());
      }
    }
  }
  // Student - description of a student with name and grade
  class Student
  {
    public string sName;
    public double dGrade = 0.0;
    // NewStudent - return a new and initialized student object
    public static Student NewStudent(string sName, double dGrade)
    {
      Student student = new Student();
      student.sName = sName;
      student.dGrade = dGrade;
      return student;
    }
    // GetString - convert the current Student object into
    //             a string
    public string GetString()
    {
```

```
        string s = "";
        s += dGrade;
        s += " - ";
        s += sName;
        return s;
    }
    // Sort - sort an array of students in decreasing order
    //        of grade - use the bubble sort algorithm
    public static void Sort(Student[] students)
    {
        bool bRepeatLoop;
        // keep looping until the list is sorted
        do
        {
            // this flag is reset to true if an object is found
            // out of order
            bRepeatLoop = false;
            // loop through the list of students
            for(int index = 0; index < (students.Length - 1); index++)
            {
                // if two of the students are in the wrong order . . .
                if (students[index].dGrade <
                                    students[index + 1].dGrade)
                {
                    //  . . .then swap them . . .
                    Student to = students[index];
                    Student from = students[index + 1];
                    students[index]     = from;
                    students[index + 1] = to;
                    //  . . .and flag the fact that you'll need to make
                    // another pass through the list of students
                    // (keep iterating through the loop checking
                    // until all the objects are in order)
                    bRepeatLoop = true;
                }
            }
        } while (bRepeatLoop);
    }
}
```

Let's start by examining the output of the program just to get an idea:

```
Before sorting:
0 - Homer
4 - Lisa
2 - Bart
3 - Marge
3.5 - Maggie

Sorting the list

The students sorted by grade:
4 - Lisa
3.5 - Maggie
3 - Marge
2 - Bart
0 - Homer
Press Enter to terminate...
```

In the interest of saving time, both yours and mine, I hard coded the program to create five students. The NewStudent() method allocates a new Student object, initializes its name and grade, and returns the result. Homer gets his usual failing grade, while Lisa makes her A+. The program uses the OutputStudentArray() function to display the elements in the student array before it is sorted.

The program then invokes the Sort() function.

After sorting, the program repeats the output process just to amaze you with the now sorted result.

Of course, the key novelty to the SortStudents program is the Sort() method. This algorithm works by continuously looping through the list of students until the list is sorted. On each pass through the student array, the program checks each student to its neighbor. If the two are found to be out of order, the function swaps them and then flags the fact that the list was not found to be completely sorted. Figures 6-3 through 6-6 show the student list after each pass.

Figure 6-3:
Before starting the bubble sort.

Homer	Ø
Lisa	4
Bart	2
Marge	3
Maggie	3.5

Figure 6-4:
After pass 1 of the bubble sort.

Lisa	4	
Bart	2	
Marge	3	
Maggie	3.5	
Homer	Ø	◄── Homer works his way to the bottom.

Figure 6-5:
After pass 2 of the bubble sort.

Lisa	4	◄── Lisa stays at the top.
Marge	3	
Maggie	3.5	
Bart	2	◄── Bart drops down, too, but not below Homer.
Homer	Ø	

Figure 6-6:
The next-to-last pass results in a sorted list. The final pass terminates the sort because nothing changes.

Lisa   4
Maggie   3.5 ⟩ swapping Maggie and Marge.
Marge   3
Bart   2
Homer   Ø

Eventually, the best students, such as Lisa and Maggie, "bubble" their way to the top, while the worst students, like Homer, fall to the bottom. Hence the name bubble sort.

The key to this or any other sort function is that the elements within the array can be reordered by assigning the reference value of one element in the array to that of another. Note that this assignment of references does not make a copy of the object and is, hence, a very quick operation.

Chapter 7

Putting on Some High-Class Functions

*P*rogrammers need the ability to break large programs up into smaller chunks that are easier to handle. For example, the programs contained in previous chapters are reaching the limit of what a person can digest at one time.

C# lets you divide your code up into chunks known as *functions*. Properly designed and implemented functions can greatly simplify the job of writing complex programs.

Defining and Using a Function

Consider the following example:

```
class Example
{
  public int nInt;
  public static int nStaticInt
  public void MemberFunction()
  {
    Console.WriteLine("this is a member function");
  }
  public static void ClassFunction()
  {
    Console.WriteLine("this is a class function");
  }
}
```

The element `nInt` is a data member, just like those in Chapter 6. However, the element `MemberFunction()` is new. `MemberFunction()` is known as a *member function*. A member function is a set of C# code that you can execute by referencing the function's name. This is best explained by example — even I'm confused right now.

The following code snippet assigns a value to the object data member `nInt` and the class, or static, member:

```
Example example = new Example(); // create an object
example.nInt = 1;                // initialize the data member through object
Example.nStaticInt = 2;          // initialize class member through class
```

The following snippet defines and accesses `MemberFunction()` and `ClassFunction()` in almost the same way:

```
Example example = new Example(); // create an object
example.MemberFunction();        // invoke the member function
                                 // with that object
Example.ClassFunction();         // invoke the class function with the class
```

The expression `example.MemberFunction()` passes control to the code contained within the function. C# follows an almost identical process for `Example.ClassFunction()`. Executing this simple code snippet generates the output from the `WriteLine()` contained within each function:

```
this is a member function
this is a class function
```

After a function completes execution, it returns control to the point where it was called.

I include the parentheses when describing functions in order to make them a little easier to follow. Otherwise, I get confused trying to understand what I'm saying.

The bit of C# code within the two example functions does nothing more than write a silly string to the console, but functions generally perform useful and sometimes complex operations like calculating the sine of something, or concatenating two strings, or surreptitiously e-mailing your URL to Microsoft. A function can be as large and complex as you want it to be.

An Example Function for Your Files

In this section, I take the monolithic `CalculateInterestTable` programs from Chapter 5 and divide them up into several reasonable functions as a demonstration of how the proper definition of functions can help make the program easier to write and understand.

I explain the exact details of the function definitions and function calls in later sections of this chapter. This example simply gives an overview.

By reading the comments with the actual C# code removed, you should be able to get a good idea of what a program does. If you cannot, you aren't commenting properly.

In outline form, the `CalculateInterestTable` program appears as follows:

```
public static void Main(string[] args)
{
  // prompt user to enter source principal
  // if the principal is negative
  // generate an error message
  // prompt user to enter the interest rate
  // if the interest is negative, generate an error message as well
  // finally, prompt user to input the number of years
  // display the input back to the user
  // now loop through the specified number of years
  while(nYear <= nDuration)
  {
    // calculate the value of the principal
    // plus interest
    // output the result
  }
}
```

If you stand back and study the program from a distance, you can see that it divides up into the following three sections:

✔ An initial input section in which the user inputs the principal, interest, and duration information

✔ A section that mirrors back the input data so the user can verify that the correct data was entered

✔ A final section that creates and outputs the table

These are good places to start looking for ways to divide the program. In fact, if you further examine the input section of that program, you can see that the same basic set of code is used to input

✔ The principal

✔ The interest

✔ The duration

That observation gives you another good place to look.

I have used this information to create the following `CalculateInterest TableWithFunctions` program:

```
// CalculateInterestTableWithFunctions - generate an interest table
//                                much like the other interest table
//                                programs, but this time using a
//                                reasonable division of labor among
//                                several functions.
using System;
namespace CalculateInterestTableWithFunctions
{
  public class Class1
  {
    public static void Main(string[] args)
    {
      // Section 1 - input the data you will need to create the table
      decimal mPrincipal = 0;
      decimal mInterest = 0;
      decimal mDuration = 0;
      InputInterestData(ref mPrincipal,
                        ref mInterest,
                        ref mDuration);
      // Section 2 - verify the data by mirroring it back to the user
      Console.WriteLine();  // skip a line
      Console.WriteLine("Principal    = " + mPrincipal);
      Console.WriteLine("Interest     = " + mInterest + "%");
      Console.WriteLine("Duration     = " + mDuration + " years");
      Console.WriteLine();
      // Section 3 - finally, output the interest table
      OutputInterestTable(mPrincipal, mInterest, mDuration);
      // wait for user to acknowledge the results
      Console.WriteLine("Press Enter to terminate...");
      Console.Read();
    }
    // InputInterestData - retrieve from the keyboard the
    //                     principal, interest, and duration
    //                     information needed to create the
    //                     future value table
    // (This function implements Section 1 by breaking it down into
    // its three components)
    public static void InputInterestData(ref decimal mPrincipal,
                                         ref decimal mInterest,
                                         ref decimal mDuration)
    {
      // 1a - retrieve the principal
      mPrincipal = InputPositiveDecimal("principal");
      // 1b - now enter the interest rate
      mInterest = InputPositiveDecimal("interest");
      // 1c - finally, the duration
      mDuration = InputPositiveDecimal("duration");
    }
    // InputPositiveDecimal - return a positive decimal number from
    //                        the keyboard.
    // (Inputting any one of principal, interest rate, or duration
    // is just a matter of inputting a decimal number and making
    // sure that it's positive)
    public static decimal InputPositiveDecimal(string sPrompt)
    {
      // keep trying until the user gets it right
      while(true)
      {
        // prompt the user for input
        Console.Write("Enter " + sPrompt + ":");
        // retrieve a decimal value from the keyboard
        string sInput = Console.ReadLine();
```

```
        decimal mValue = Convert.ToDecimal(sInput);
        // exit the loop if the value entered is correct
        if (mValue >= 0)
        {
            // return the valid decimal value entered by the user
          return mValue;
        }
        // otherwise, generate an error on incorrect input
        Console.WriteLine(sPrompt + " cannot be negative");
        Console.WriteLine("Try again");
        Console.WriteLine();
    }
}
// OutputInterestTable - given the principal and interest
//                       generate a future value table for
//                       the number of periods indicated in
//                       mDuration.
// (this implements section 3 of the program)
public static void OutputInterestTable(decimal mPrincipal,
                                       decimal mInterest,
                                       decimal mDuration)
{
    for (int nYear = 1; nYear <= mDuration; nYear++)
    {
        // calculate the value of the principal
        // plus interest
        decimal mInterestPaid;
        mInterestPaid = mPrincipal * (mInterest / 100);
        // now calculate the new principal by adding
        // the interest to the previous principal
        mPrincipal = mPrincipal + mInterestPaid;
        // round off the principal to the nearest cent
        mPrincipal = decimal.Round(mPrincipal, 2);
        // output the result
        Console.WriteLine(nYear + "-" + mPrincipal);
    }
}
}
```

I have divided the Main() section into three clearly distinguishable parts, each marked with bolded comments. I further divide the first section into 1a, 1b, and 1c.

Normally, you wouldn't include the bolded comments. The listings would get rather complicated with all the numbers and letters if you did. In practice, those types of comments aren't necessary if the functions are well thought out.

Part 1 calls the function InputInterestData() to input the three variables the program needs in order to create the table: mPrincipal, mInterest, and mDuration. Part 2 displays these three values just as the earlier versions of the program do. The final part outputs the table via the function Output InterestTable().

Starting at the bottom and working up, the OutputInterestTable() function contains an output loop with the interest rate calculations. This is the same loop used in the in-line, non-function CalculateInterestTable program in Chapter 5. The advantage of this version, however, is that when writing this section of code, you don't need to concern yourself with any of the details of inputting or verifying the data. In writing this function, you need to think, "Given the three numbers, principal, interest, and duration, output an interest table," and that's it. After you're done, you can return to the line that called the OutputInterestTable() function and continue from there.

The same divide-and-conquer logic holds for InputInterestData(). You can focus solely on inputting the three decimal values. However, in this case, you realize that inputting each decimal involves the same operations. The InputPositiveDecimal() function bundles these operations into a set of code that you can apply to principal, interest, and duration alike.

This InputPositiveDecimal() function displays the prompt it was given and awaits input from the user. The function returns the value to the caller if it is not negative. If the value is negative, the function outputs an error message and loops back to try again.

From the user's standpoint, this program acts exactly the same as the in-line version in Chapter 5, which is just the point:

```
Enter principal:100
Enter interest:-10
interest cannot be negative
Try again

Enter interest:10
Enter duration:10

Principal    = 100
Interest     = 10%
Duration     = 10 years

1-110
2-121
3-133.1
4-146.41
5-161.05
6-177.16
7-194.88
8-214.37
9-235.81
10-259.39
Press Enter to terminate...
```

I have taken a lengthy, somewhat difficult program and broken it up into smaller, more understandable pieces while reducing some duplication. As we say in Texas, "You can't beat that with a stick."

Why bother with functions?

When Fortran introduced the function concept during the 1950s, the sole purpose was to avoid duplication of code by combining similar sections into a common element. Suppose you were to write a program that needed to calculate and display ratios in multiple places. Your program could call the `DisplayRatio()` function when needed, more or less for the sole purpose of avoiding duplicating code. The savings may not seem so important for a function as small as `DisplayRatio()`, but functions can grow to be much larger. Besides, a common function like `WriteLine()` may be invoked in hundreds of different places.

Quickly, a second advantage became obvious: It is easier to code a single function correctly. The `DisplayRatio()` function includes a check to make sure that the denominator is not zero. If you repeat the calculation code throughout your program, you could easily forget this test occasionally — in some cases, you might remember to include the check, and in other places forget.

Not so obvious is a third advantage: A carefully crafted function reduces the complexity of the program. A well-defined function should stand for some concept. You should be able to describe the purpose of the function without using the words *and* or *or*.

A function like `calculateSin()` is an ideal example. The programmer that has been tasked with this assignment can implement this complex operation without worrying about how it might be used. The applications programmer can use `calculateSin()` without worrying about how this operation is performed internally. This greatly reduces the number of things that the applications programmer has to worry about. By reducing the number of "variables," a large job gets accomplished by implementing two smaller, easier jobs.

Large programs such as a word processor are built up from layers and layers of functions at ever-increasing levels of abstraction. For example, a `RedisplayDocument()` function would undoubtedly call a `Reparagraph()` function to redisplay the paragraphs within the document. `Reparagraph()` would need to invoke a `CalculateWordWrap()` function to decide where to wrap the lines that make up the paragraph. `CalculateWordWrap()` would have to call a `LookUpWordBreak()` function in order to decide where to break a word at the end of the line, in order to make the sentences wrap more naturally. Each of these functions was described in a single, simple sentence.

Without the ability to abstract complex concepts, writing programs of even moderate complexity would become almost impossible, much less creating an operating system such as Windows XP, a utility such as WinZip, a word processor like WordPerfect, or a game such as StarFighter, to name a few examples.

Having Arguments with Functions

A method such as the following example is about as useful as my hair brush because no data passes into or out of the function:

```
public static void Output()
{
   Console.WriteLine("this is a function");
}
```

Compare this example to real-world functions that actually do something. For example, the sine operation requires some type of input — after all, you have to take the sine of something. Similarly, to concatenate two strings into one, you need two strings. So, the Concatenate() function requires at least two strings as input. "Gee, Wally, that sounds logical." You need some way to get data into and out of a function.

Passing an argument to a function

The values input to a function are called the *function arguments*. Most functions require some type of arguments if they're going to do something. In this way, functions remind me of my son: We need to have an argument before he'll do anything. You pass arguments to a function by listing them in the parentheses that follow the function name. Consider the small addition to the earlier Example class:

```
public class Example
{
  public static void Output(string funcString)
  {
    Console.WriteLine("Output() was passed the argument: "
                      + funcString);
  }
}
```

I could invoke this function from within the same class as follows:

```
Output("Hello");
```

I would get the following not too exciting output:

```
Output() was passed the argument: Hello
```

The program passes a reference to the string "Hello" to the function Output(). The function receives the reference and assigns it the name funcString. The Output() function can use funcString within the function just as it would any other string variable.

I'll change the example in one minor way:

```
string upperString = "Hello";
Output(upperString);
```

This code snippet assigns the variable upperString to reference the string "Hello". The call Output(upperString) passes the object referenced by upperString, which is your good old friend "Hello". Figure 7-1 depicts this process. From there, the effect is the same.

Figure 7-1:
The call
Output
(upper
String)
copies the
value of
upper
String to
func
String.

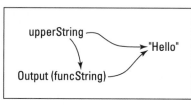

Passing multiple arguments to functions

When I ask my daughter to wash the car, she usually gives me more than just a single argument. Because she has lots of time on the couch to think about it, she can keep several at the ready.

You can define a function with multiple arguments of varying types. Consider the following example function AverageAndDisplay():

```
// AverageAndDisplay
using System;
namespace Example
{
  public class Class1
  {
    public static void Main(string[] args)
    {
      // access the member function
      AverageAndDisplay("grade 1", 3.5, "grade 2", 4.0);
      // wait for user to acknowledge
      Console.WriteLine("Press Enter to terminate...");
      Console.Read();
    }
    // AverageAndDisplay - average two numbers with their
    //                     labels and display the results
    public static void AverageAndDisplay(string s1, double d1,
                                         string s2, double d2)
    {
      double dAverage = (d1 + d2) / 2;
      Console.WriteLine("The average of "  + s1
                   + " whose value is " + d1
                   + " and "             + s2
                   + " whose value is " + d2
                   + " is " + dAverage);
    }
  }
}
```

Executing this simple program generates the following output:

```
The average of grade 1 whose value is 3.5 and grade 2 whose value is 4 is 3.75
Press Enter to terminate...
```

The function `AverageAndDisplay()` is declared with several arguments in the order in which they are to be passed.

As usual, execution of the example program begins with the first statement after `Main()`. The first non-comment line in `Main()` invokes the function `AverageAndDisplay()`, passing the two strings "grade 1" and "grade 2" and the two `double` values 3.5 and 4.0.

The function `AverageAndDisplay()` calculates the average of the two `double` values, d1 and d2, passed to it along with their names contained in s1 and s2, and the calculated average is stored in `dAverage`.

Matching argument definitions with usage

Each argument in a function call must match the function definition in both type and order. The following is illegal and generates a build-time error:

```
// AverageWithCompilerError - this version does not compile!

using System;
namespace AverageWithCompilerError
{
  public class Class1
  {
    public static void Main(string[] args)
    {
      // access the member function
      AverageAndDisplay("grade 1", "grade 2", 3.5, 4.0);
      // wait for user to acknowledge
      Console.WriteLine("Press Enter to terminate...");
      Console.Read();
    }
    // AverageAndDisplay - average two numbers with their
    //                     labels and display the results
    public static void AverageAndDisplay(string s1, double d1,
                                         string s2, double d2)
    {
      double dAverage = (d1 + d2) / 2;
      Console.WriteLine("The average of " + s1
                + " whose value is " + d1
                + " and "            + s2
                + " whose value is " + d2
                + " is " + dAverage);
    }
  }
}
```

C# can't match the type of each argument in the call to `AverageAndDisplay()` with the corresponding argument in the function definition. The string "grade 1" matches the first string in the function definition; however, the function definition calls for a `double` as its second argument rather than the `string` that's passed.

You can easily see that I simply transposed the second and third arguments. That's what I hate about computers — they take me too literally. I know what I said, but it's obvious what I meant!

Overloading a function does not mean giving it too much to do

You can give two functions within a given class the same name *as long as* their arguments differ. This is called *overloading* the function name.

The following example demonstrates overloading:

```
// AverageAndDisplayOverloaded - this version demonstrates that
//                               the average and display function
//                               can be overloaded
using System;
namespace AverageAndDisplayOverloaded
{
  public class Class1
  {
    public static void Main(string[] args)
    {
      // access the first member function
      AverageAndDisplay("my GPA", 3.5, "your GPA", 4.0);
      Console.WriteLine();
      // access the second member function
      AverageAndDisplay(3.5, 4.0);
      // wait for user to acknowledge
      Console.WriteLine("Press Enter to terminate...");
      Console.Read();
    }
    // AverageAndDisplay - average two numbers with their
    //                     labels and display the results
    public static void AverageAndDisplay(string s1, double d1,
                                         string s2, double d2)
    {
      double dAverage = (d1 + d2) / 2;
      Console.WriteLine("The average of " + s1
                      + " whose value is " + d1);
      Console.WriteLine("and "            + s2
                      + " whose value is " + d2
                      + " is " + dAverage);
    }
    public static void AverageAndDisplay(double d1, double d2)
    {
```

```
        double dAverage = (d1 + d2) / 2;
        Console.WriteLine("The average of " + d1
                        + " and "           + d2
                        + " is " + dAverage);
    }
  }
}
```

This program defines two versions of `AverageAndDisplay()`. The program invokes one and then the other by passing the proper arguments. C# can tell which function the program wants by comparing the call with the definition. The program compiles properly and generates the following output when executed:

```
The average of my GPA whose value is 3.5
and your GPA whose value is 4 is 3.75

The average of 3.5 and 4 is 3.75
Press Enter to terminate..
```

In general, C# does not allow two functions in the same program to have the same name. After all, how could C# tell which function you intended to call? However, C# includes the number and type of the function's arguments as part of its name. Normally, you might call a function `AverageAndDisplay()`. However, C# differentiates between two functions `AverageAndDisplay (string, double, string, double)` and `AverageAndDisplay(double, double)`. When you say it that way, it's clear that the two functions are different.

Implementing default arguments

Often, you want to supply two (or more) versions of a function. One version would be the complicated version that provides complete flexibility but requires numerous arguments from the calling routine, several of which the user may not even understand.

In practice, references to the "user" of a function often mean the programmer who is making use of the function. *User* does not always refer to the ultimate user of the program.

A second version of the function would provide acceptable, if somewhat bland, performance by assuming default values for some of the arguments.

You can easily implement default arguments using function overloading.

Consider the following pair of `DisplayRoundedDecimal()` functions:

```
// FunctionsWithDefaultArguments - provide variations of the same
//                       function, some with default arguments, by
//                       overloading the function name
using System;
```

```
namespace FunctionsWithDefaultArguments
{
  public class Class1
  {
    public static void Main(string[] args)
    {
      // access the member function
      Console.WriteLine("{0}", DisplayRoundedDecimal(12.345678M, 3));
      // wait for user to acknowledge
      Console.WriteLine("Press Enter to terminate...");
      Console.Read();
    }
    // DisplayRoundedDecimal - convert a decimal value into a string
    //                         with the specified number of significant
    //                         digits
    public static string DisplayRoundedDecimal(decimal mValue,
                                     int nNumberOfSignificantDigits)
    {
      // first round the number off to the specified number
      // of significant digits
      decimal mRoundedValue =
                   decimal.Round(mValue,
                               nNumberOfSignificantDigits);
      // convert that to a string
      string s = Convert.ToString(mRoundedValue);
      return s;
    }
    public static string DisplayRoundedDecimal(decimal mValue)
    {
      // invoke DisplayRoundedDecimal(decimal, int) specifying
      // the default number of digits
      string s = DisplayRoundedDecimal(mValue, 2);
      return s;
    }
  }
}
```

The `DisplayRoundedDecimal(decimal, int)` function converts the
`decimal` value provided into a string with the specified number of digits
after the decimal point. Because decimals are very often used to display mon-
etary values, the most common choice is two digits after the decimal point.
Therefore, the `DisplayRoundedDecimal(decimal)` function provides the
same conversion service but defaults the number of significant digits to two,
thereby saving the user from even worrying about the meaning of the second
argument.

Notice that the generic (`decimal`) version of the function actually calls the
more specific (`decimal, int`) version to perform its magic. This is more
common than not. The generic functions simply provide arguments that the
programmer doesn't have the inclination to look up in the documentation.

Providing default arguments is more than just saving a lazy programmer a
tiny bit of effort. Programming requires lots of concentration. Unnecessary
trips to the reference documentation to look up the meaning of normally
defaulted arguments distract the programmer from the main job at hand,
thereby making the job more difficult, wasting time, and increasing the like-
lihood of mistakes. The author of the function understands the relationship

between the arguments and therefore bears the onus of providing friendlier, overloaded versions of functions.

Passing value-type arguments

The basic variable types such as int, double, and decimal are known as *value-type* variables. You can pass value-type variables to a function in one of two ways. The default form is to *pass by value*. An alternate form is the *pass by reference*.

Programmers can get sloppy in their speech. In referring to value-types, when a programmer says "passing a variable to a function," that usually means "pass the value of a variable to a function."

Passing value-type arguments by value

Unlike object references, value-type variables like an int or a double are normally *passed by value*, which means the value contained within the variable is passed to the function and not the variable itself.

Pass by value has the effect that changing the value of a value-type variable within a function does not change the value of that variable in the calling program:

```
// PassByValue - demonstrate pass by value semantics
using System;
namespace PassByValue
{
  public class Class1
  {
    // Update - try to modify the values of the arguments
    //          passed to it
    public static void Update(int i, double d)
    {
      i = 10;
      d = 20.0;
    }
    public static void Main(string[] args)
    {
      // declare two variables and initialize them
      int i = 1;
      double d = 2.0;
      Console.WriteLine("Before the call to Update(int, double):");
      Console.WriteLine("i = " + i + ", d = " + d);
      // invoke the function
      Update(i, d);
      // notice that the values 1 and 2.0 have not changed
      Console.WriteLine("After the call to Update(int, double):");
      Console.WriteLine("i = " + i + ", d = " + d);
      // wait for user to acknowledge
      Console.WriteLine("Press Enter to terminate...");
      Console.Read();
    }
  }
}
```

Executing this program generates the following output:

```
Before the call to Update(int, double):
i = 1, d = 2
After the call to Update(int, double):
i = 1, d = 2
Press Enter to terminate...
```

The call to Update() passes the values 1 and 2.0 and not a reference to the variables i and d. Thus, changing their value within the function has no more effect on the value of the variables back in the calling routine than asking for water with ice at an English pub.

Passing value-type arguments by reference

Passing a value-type argument to a function by reference is advantageous — in particular, when the caller wants to give the function the ability to change the value of the variable. The following PassByReference program demonstrates this capability.

C# gives the programmer the pass by reference capability via the ref and out keywords. A slight modification to the example PassByValue program snippet from the previous section demonstrates the point:

```
// PassByReference - demonstrate pass by reference semantics

using System;
namespace PassByReference
{
  public class Class1
  {
    // Update - try to modify the values of the arguments
    //          passed to it
    public static void Update(ref int i, out double d)
    {
      i = 10;
      d = 20.0;
    }
    public static void Main(string[] args)
    {
      // declare two variables and initialize them
      int i = 1;
      double d;
      Console.WriteLine("Before the call to Update(ref int, out double):");
      Console.WriteLine("i = " + i + ", d is not initialized");
      // invoke the function
      Update(ref i, out d);
      // notice that the values 1 and 2.0 have not changed
      Console.WriteLine("After the call to Update(ref int, out double):");
      Console.WriteLine("i = " + i + ", d = " + d);
      // wait for user to acknowledge
      Console.WriteLine("Press Enter to terminate...");
      Console.Read();
    }
  }
}
```

The ref keyword indicates that C# should pass a reference to i and not just the value contained within this variable. Consequently, changes made within the function are exported back out of the calling routine.

In a similar vein, the out keyword says, "Pass back by reference, but I don't care what the initial value is because I'm going to overwrite it anyway." (Man, that's a lot to pack into three words!) The out keyword is applicable when the function is only returning a value to the caller.

Executing the program generates the following output:

```
Before the call to Update(ref int, out double):
i = 1, d is not initialized
After the call to Update(ref int, out double):
i = 10, d = 20
Press Enter to terminate...
```

An out argument is always ref.

Notice that the initial values of i and d are overwritten in the function Update(). Once back in Main(), these variables retain their modified values. Compare this to the PassByValue() function in which the variables do not retain their modified values.

Don't pass a variable to a function by reference twice simultaneously

Do not, under any but the most dire circumstance, pass the same variable by reference twice in the same function call. This is more difficult to describe than it is to demonstrate. Consider the following Update() function:

```
// PassByReferenceError - demonstrate a potential error situation
//                          when calling a function using reference
//                          arguments
using System;
namespace PassByReferenceError
{
  public class Class1
  {
    // Update - try to modify the values of the arguments
    //          passed to it
    public static void DisplayAndUpdate(ref int nVar1, ref int nVar2)
    {
      Console.WriteLine("The initial value of nVar1 is " + nVar1);
      nVar1 = 10;
      Console.WriteLine("The initial value of nVar2 is " + nVar2);
      nVar2 = 20;
    }
    public static void Main(string[] args)
    {
      // declare two variables and initialize them
      int n = 1;
      Console.WriteLine("Before the call to Update(ref n, ref n):");
      Console.WriteLine("n = " + n);
      Console.WriteLine();
      // invoke the function
```

```
        DisplayAndUpdate(ref n, ref n);
        // notice that the values 1 and 2.0 have not changed
        Console.WriteLine();
        Console.WriteLine("After the call to Update(ref n, ref n):");
        Console.WriteLine("n = " + n);
        // wait for user to acknowledge
        Console.WriteLine("Press Enter to terminate...");
        Console.Read();
      }
    }
  }
```

`Update(ref int, ref int)` is now declared to accept two `int` arguments by reference, which, in and of itself, is not a problem. The problem arises when the `Main()` function invokes `Update()` passing the same variable in

Why do some arguments come out but they don't go in?

C# is very careful about keeping the programmer from doing something stupid. One of the stupid things that programmers do is forget to initialize a variable before they use it for the first time. (This is particularly true of counting variables.) C# generates an error when you try to use a variable that you've declared but not initialized:

```
int nVariable;
Console.WriteLine("this is an
   error " + nVariable);
nVariable = 1;
Console.WriteLine("but this is
   not " + nVariable);
```

However, C# cannot keep track of variables from within a function:

```
void SomeFunction(ref int
   nVariable)
{
   Console.WriteLine("is this an
      error or not? " +
      nVariable);
}
```

How can `SomeFunction()` know whether `nVariable` was initialized before being passed in the call? It can't. Instead, C# tracks the variable in the call — for example, the following call generates a compiler error:

```
int nUninitializedVariable;
SomeFunction(ref
   nUninitializedVariable);
```

If C# were to allow this call, `SomeFunction()` would have been passed a reference to an uninitialized (that is, *garbage*) variable. The `out` keyword lets both sides agree that the variable has not yet been assigned a value. The following example compiles fine:

```
int nUninitializedVariable;
SomeFunction(out
   nUninitializedVariable);
```

By the way, passing an initialized variable as an `out` argument is legal:

```
int nInitializedVariable = 1;
SomeFunction(out
   nInitializedVariable);
```

The value in `nInitializedVariable` will get blown away within `SomeFunction()`, but there's no danger of garbage being passed about.

both arguments. Within the function, Update() modifies nVar1, which references back to n from its initial value of 1 to the new value of 10. By the time Update() gets around to modifying nVar2, the value of n to which it refers has already been modified from its initial value of 1 to the new value of 10.

This is shown in the following example:

```
Before the call to Update(ref n, ref n):
n = 1

The initial value of nVar1 is 1
The initial value of nVar2 is 10

After the call to Update(ref n, ref n):
n = 20
Press Enter to terminate...
```

Exactly what's going on in this interplay between n, nVar1, and nVar2 is about as obvious as an exotic bird's mating dance. Neither the user programmer nor the Update() function author will anticipate this bizarre result. In other words, don't do it.

There's no problem with passing a single value as more than one argument in a single function call if all variables are passed by value.

Returning Values after Christmas

Many real-world operations create values to return to the caller. For example, sin() accepts an argument and returns the trigonometric sine. A function can return a value to the caller in two ways. The most common is via the return field; however, a second method uses the *call by reference* feature.

Returning a value via return postage

The following code snippet demonstrates a small function that returns the average of its input arguments:

```
public class Example
{
  public static double Average(double d1, double d2)
  {
    double dAverage = (d1 + d2) / 2;
    return dAverage;
  }
  public static void Test()
  {
    double v1 = 1.0;
    double v2 = 3.0;
    double dAverageValue = Average(v1, v2);
    Console.WriteLine("The average of " + v1
```

```
                    + " and " + v2 + " is "
                    + dAverageValue);
    // this also works
    Console.WriteLine("The average of " + v1
                    + " and " + v2 " + is "
                    + Average(v1, v2));
  }
}
```

Notice first that I declare the function as `public double Average()` — the `double` in front of the name refers to the fact that the `Average()` function returns a double precision value to the caller.

The `Average()` function applies the names d1 and d2 to the double precision values passed to it. It creates a variable dAverage to which it assigns the average of d1 and d2. It then returns the value contained in dAverage to the caller.

People sometimes say that "the function returns dAverage." This is a careless but common shorthand. Saying that dAverage or any other variable is passed or returned anywhere makes no sense. In this case, the value contained within dAverage is returned to the caller.

The call to `Average()` from the `Test()` function appears the same as any other function call; however, the `double` value returned by `Average()` is stored into the variable dAverageValue.

A function that returns a value, such as `Average()`, cannot return to the caller by encountering the closed brace of the function. If it did, how would C# know what value to return?

Returning a value using pass by reference

A function can also return one or more values to the calling routine via the `ref` and `out` keywords. Consider the `Update()` example described in the section "Passing value-type arguments by reference," earlier in this chapter:

```
// Update - try to modify the values of the arguments
//          passed to it
public static void Update(ref int i, out double d)
{
  i = 10;
  d = 20.0;
}
```

The function is declared `void` as if it does not return a value to the caller; however, because the variable i is declared `ref` and the variable d is declared `out`, any changes made to those variables within `Update()` retain their values in the calling function.

When do I return *and when do I* out?

You may be thinking, "A function can return a value to the caller, or it can use the out, or ref for that matter, to return a value to the caller. When do I use return and when do I use out?" After all, I could have written the Average() function as follows:

```
public class Example
{
  public static void Average(out double dResults, double d1, double d2)
  {
    dResults = (d1 + d2) / 2;
  }
  public static void Test()
  {
    double v1 = 1.0;
    double v2 = 3.0;
    double dAverageValue;
    Average(dAverageValue, v1, v2);
    Console.WriteLine("The average of " + v1
                    + " and " + v2 + " is "
                    + dAverageValue;
  }
}
```

Typically, you return a value to the caller via the return statement rather than via the out directive, even though it's hard to argue with the results.

Outing a value-type variable like a double requires an extra process known as *boxing*, which I describe in Chapter 14. However, efficiency should not be a driving factor in your decision.

Typically, you use the out directive when a function returns more than one value to the caller — for example:

```
public class Example
{
  public static void AverageAndProduct(out double dAverage,
                                       out double dProduct,
                                       double d1, double d2)
  {
    dAverage = (d1 + d2) / 2;
    dProduct = d1 * d2;
  }
}
```

Returning multiple values from a single function doesn't happen as often as you might think. A function that returns multiple values often does so encapsulated in a single class object or in an array of values.

Defining a function with no value at all

The declaration `public double Average(double, double)` declares a function `Average()` that returns the average of its arguments as a `double`. The number returned better be the average of the input values or someone has some serious explaining to do.

Some functions don't return a value to the caller. An earlier example function `AverageAndDisplay()` displays the average of its input arguments but doesn't return that average to the caller. That may not be such a good idea, but mine is not to question. Rather than leave the return type blank, a function like `AverageAndDisplay()` is declared as follows:

```
public void AverageAndDisplay(double, double)
```

The keyword `void` where the return type would normally go means the *non-type*. That is, the declaration `void` indicates that the `AverageAndDisplay()` function returns no value to the caller.

A function that returns no value is referred to as a *void function*. That doesn't mean the function is empty or that it's used for some medical purposes. It simply refers to the initial keyword. By comparison, a function that returns some value is known as a *non-void function*.

A non-void function must pass control back to the caller by executing a `return` followed by the value to return to the caller. A `void` function has no value to return. A void function returns when it encounters a `return` with no value attached. By default, a void function exits automatically when control reaches the closing brace of the function.

Consider the following `DisplayRatio()` function:

```
public class Example
{
  public static void DisplayRatio(double dNumerator,
                                  double dDenominator)
  {
    // if the denominator is zero . . .
    if (dDenominator == 0.0)
    {
      // . . .output an error message and . . .
      Console.WriteLine(
               "The denominator of a ratio cannot be 0");
      // . . .return to the caller
      return;
    }
    // this is only executed if dDenominator is non-zero
    double dRatio = dNumerator / dDenominator;
    Console.WriteLine("The ratio of " + dNumerator
               + " over " + dDenominator
               + " is " + dRatio);
  }
}
```

The `DisplayRatio()` function first checks to make sure that the `dDenominator` value is zero. If it is zero, the program displays an error message and returns to the caller without attempting to calculate a ratio. Doing so would divide the numerator value by zero and cause a CPU processor fault, also known by the more descriptive name *processor upchuck*.

If the `dDenomiator` is nonzero, the program displays the ratio. The closed brace immediately following the `WriteLine()` is the closed brace of the `DisplayRatio()` function and, therefore, acts as the return point for the program.

Null and zero references

A reference variable is assigned the default value `null` when created. However, a null reference is not the same thing as a reference to zero. For example, the following two references are completely different:

```
class Example
{
    int nValue;
}


// create a null reference ref1
Example ref1;


// now create a reference to a
   zero object
Example ref2 = new Example();
ref2.nValue = 0;
```

The variable `ref1` is about as empty as my wallet. That variable points to the null object — that is, it points to no object. By comparison, `ref2` points to an object whose value is zero.

This difference is much less clear in the following example:

```
string s1;
string s2 = "";
```

This is essentially the same case: `s1` points to the null object, while `s2` points to an empty string. The difference is significant, as the following function shows:

```
// Test - test modules to uti-
   lize the TestLibrary
namespace Test
{
    using System;


    public class Class1
    {
        public static int
        Main(string[] strings)
        {
            Console.WriteLine("This
program exercises the " +
                            "func-
tion TestString()");
            Console.WriteLine();
            Example exampleObject =
new Example();


            Console.WriteLine("Pass a
null object:");
            string s = null;


exampleObject.TestString(s)
;
            Console.WriteLine();
```

```
    // now pass the function
a null string
    Console.WriteLine("Pass
an empty string:");

exampleObject.TestString(""
);
    Console.WriteLine();

    // finally, pass a real
string
    Console.WriteLine("Pass a
real string:");

exampleObject.TestString("t
est string");
    Console.WriteLine();

    // wait for user to
acknowledge the results
    Console.WriteLine("Press
Enter to terminate...");
    Console.Read();
    return 0;
  }
}


class Example
{
  public void
TestString(string sTest)
  {
    // first test for a null
string
    if (sTest == null)
    {

Console.WriteLine("sTest is
null");
      return;
    }
```

```
    // check to see if sTest
points to a null string
    if (String.Compare(sTest,
"") == 0)
    {

Console.WriteLine("sTest
references an empty
string");
      return;
    }


    // Okay, output the
string
    Console.WriteLine("sTest
refers to: '" + sTest +
"'");
    }
  }
}
```

The function `TestString()` uses the comparison `sTest == null` to test for a null string. `TestString()` must use the `Compare()` function to test for an empty string. (`Compare()` returns a 0 if the two strings passed to it are equal.)

The output from this program is as follows:

```
This program exercises the
    function TestString()


Pass a null object:
sTest is null


Pass an empty string:
sTest references an empty
    string


Pass a real string:
sTest refers to: 'test string'


Press Enter to terminate...
```

The Main() Deal — Passing Arguments to a Program

Look at any console application in this book. In every case, execution begins with Main(). You can see clearly from the way that Main() is declared:

```
public static void Main(string[] args)
{
  // . . .your program goes here . . .
}
```

Main() is a static or class function of the class Class1 defined by the Visual Studio AppWizard. Main() returns no value and accepts as its arguments an array of string objects. What are these strings?

The user enters the name of the program to execute a console application. The user has the option of adding arguments after the program name. You see this all the time in commands like copy myfile C:\myDirectory, which copies the file myfile into the mydirectory folder in the root directory of the C: drive.

As demonstrated in the following DisplayArguments example, the array of string values passed to Main() are the arguments to the current program:

```
// DisplayArguments - display the arguments passed to the
//                    program
using System;
namespace DisplayArguments
{
  public class Test
  {
    public static int Main(string[] args)
    {
      // count the number of arguments
      Console.WriteLine("There are {0} program arguments",
                        args.Length);
      // the arguments are:
      int nCount = 0;
      foreach(string arg in args)
      {
        Console.WriteLine("Argument {0} is {1}",
                          nCount++, arg);
      }
      // wait for user to acknowledge the results
      Console.WriteLine("Press Enter to terminate...");
      Console.Read();
      return 0;
    }
  }
}
```

This program begins by displaying the length of the args array. This value corresponds to the number of arguments passed to the function. The program then loops through the elements of args, outputting each element to the console.

An example execution of this program generates the following results:

```
DisplayArguments /c arg1 arg2
There are 3 program arguments
Argument 0 is /c
Argument 1 is arg1
Argument 2 is arg2
Press Enter to terminate...
```

You can see that the name of the program itself does not appear in the argument list. (Another function exists by which the program can find out its own name dynamically.) In addition, the switch /c is not handled differently from other arguments — the program itself handles the parsing of arguments to the program.

Most console applications allow for switches that control some details of the way the program operates.

Passing arguments from a DOS prompt

Execute the following steps to run the `DisplayArguments` program from a DOS prompt:

1. **Click Start⇨Programs⇨Accessories⇨Command Prompt.**

   You should be looking at a black window with a blinking cursor next to a silly C:\> prompt.

2. **Navigate to the directory containing the** `DisplayArguments` **project by entering** cd \C#Programs\DisplayArguments. **(The default root folder for the example programs in this book is** C#Programs. **User the root folder that you chose if it differs from the default.)**

   The prompt changes to C:\C#Programs\DisplayArguments>.

   If all else fails, just use Windows to search for it. From the Windows Explorer, right-click the root folder C:\ and then choose Search, as shown in Figure 7-2.

   In the dialog box that's displayed, enter **DisplayArguments.exe** and click Search Now — what? as opposed to Search Later? The filename appears in the right-hand window of the Search Results, as shown in Figure 7-3. Ignore the `DisplayArguments.exe` in the `obj` directory — and the man behind the curtain, while you're at it. You may have to scroll around using the horizontal scroll bar to find the full path name, depending upon how deep in the folder hierarchy you find it. This is especially true if you store things in `MyDocuments`.

   Visual Studio.NET normally places the executables it generates in a `bin\Debug` subdirectory; however, it could be `bin\release` or another directory, if you've changed the configuration.

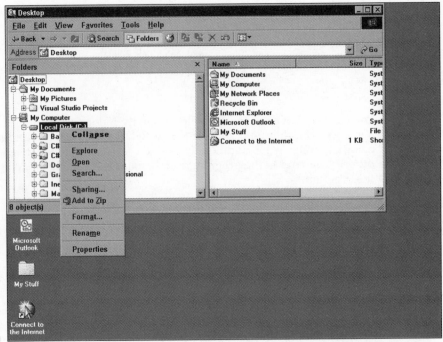

Figure 7-2:
The search facility is great for tracking down files.

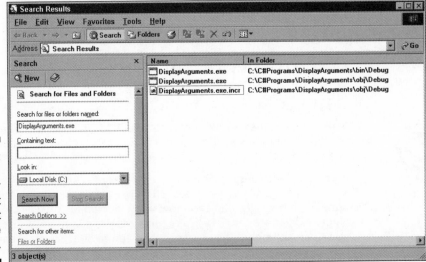

Figure 7-3:
There it is! The folder name is just to the right of the filename.

3. **Change to the subdirectory that contains the executables by entering** cd debug\bin.

Now the prompt changes to `C:\C#Programs\DisplayArguments\bin\Debug>`.

Windows has no problem with naming a file or directory with spaces included; however, DOS can get confused. You must put quotes around a file or directory name with spaces. For example, I would navigate to a file in My Stuff by using a command like this one:

```
cd \"My Stuff"
```

4. **From the command prompt, execute the DisplayArguments.exe file found there by entering** DisplayArguments /c arg1 arg2.

   The program should respond with the output shown in Figure 7-4.

Figure 7-4:
Executing
DisplayArguments
from the
DOS prompt
displays
arguments
of the
program
right back
at you.

Passing arguments from a window

You can execute a program like DisplayArguments by typing its name on the command line of the Command Prompt window. You also can execute it from the Windows interface by double-clicking the name of the program either within a window or from the Windows Explorer.

As shown in Figure 7-5, double-clicking DisplayArguments executes the program as if you had entered the program name on the command line with no arguments:

```
There are 0 program arguments
Press Enter to terminate...
```

Press Enter to terminate the program and close the window.

Dragging and dropping one or more files onto DisplayArguments.exe executes the program as if you had entered **DisplayArguments** *filenames* on the command line. (To drag and drop more than one file, select filea.txt in the list, hold down the Shift key and then select whatever files you want, as shown in Figure 7-6. Now click and drag the set of files over and drop it on

DisplayArguments.) Simultaneously dragging and dropping the files arg1.txt and arg2.txt onto DisplayArguments executes the program with multiple arguments, as shown in Figure 7-5:

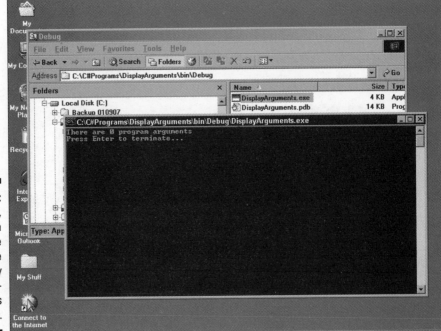

Figure 7-5:
In Windows, you can execute the console program by double-clicking its name.

The output from dropping the files arg1.txt and arg2.txt is shown in Figure 7-7.

Notice that Windows passes the files to DisplayArguments in no particular order.

Passing arguments From Visual Studio .NET

To execute a program from Visual Studio .NET, make sure that the program builds without errors. Choose Build⇨Build and check the Output window that appears for errors. The proper answer is Build: 1 succeeded, 0 failed, 0 skipped. Anything else and your program will not start.

Executing your program without passing it any arguments is but a click away. After you have a successful build, choose Debug⇨Start (or press F5), or Debug⇨Start Without Debugging (Ctrl+F5), and you're off to the races.

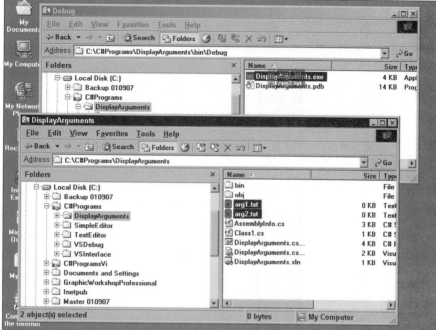

Figure 7-6:
You can
drop a file
onto a
console
program
using
Windows
drag and
drop.

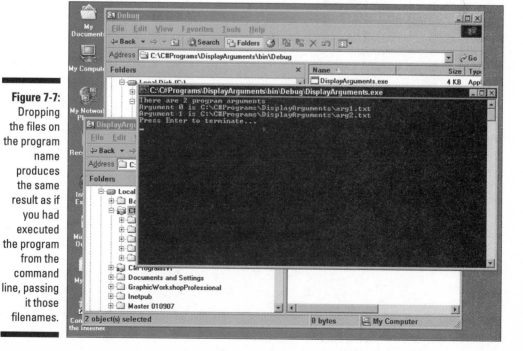

Figure 7-7:
Dropping
the files on
the program
name
produces
the same
result as if
you had
executed
the program
from the
command
line, passing
it those
filenames.

By default, Visual Studio executes a program without any arguments. If that's not what you want, you'll have to tell Visual Studio what arguments to use:

1. **Open the Solution Explorer by choosing View⇨Solution Explorer.**

   The Solution Explorer window provides a description of your *solution*. The solution consists of one or more projects. Each project describes a program. For example, the DisplayArguments project says that Class1.cs is one of the files in your program and that your program is a Console application. The project also contains other properties such as the arguments to use when executing DisplayArguments with Visual Studio.

   I cover the solution file in Bonus Chapter 20.

2. **Right-click DisplayArguments and choose Properties from pop-up menu, as shown in Figure 7-8.**

   A window like that shown in Figure 7-9 appears, showing a lot of project variables that you can meddle with — please don't.

3. **Under the Configuration Properties folder, select Debugging.**

   Right there under the Start Options is a field labeled Command Line Arguments.

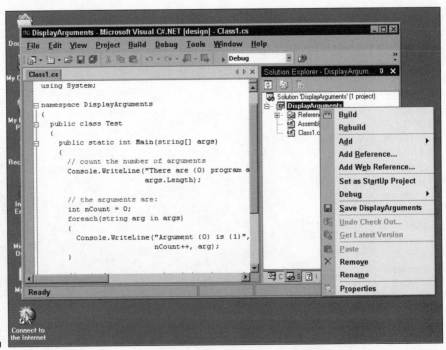

Figure 7-8: Access the project properties by right-clicking the name of the project, Display Arguments.

4. Type in the arguments that you want to pass to your program when Visual Studio starts it.

Figure 7-9 shows the arguments `/c arg1 arg2` being entered.

5. Click OK and then execute the program normally by choosing Debug⇨Start.

As shown in Figure 7-10, Visual Studio opens a DOS window with the expected results:

```
There are 3 program arguments
Argument 0 is /c
Argument 1 is arg1
Argument 2 is arg2
Press Enter to terminate...
```

The only difference between the output from executing the program from Visual Studio.NET and from the command line is the absence of the program name in the display.

The `WriteLine()` function

You may have noticed that the `WriteLine()` construct that you've been using in the programs so far is nothing more than a function call that's invoked with something called a `Console` class:

```
Console.WriteLine("this is a
    function call");
```

`WriteLine()` is one of many predefined functions provided by the C# environment. `Console` is a predefined class that refers to the application console.

The argument to the `WriteLine()` that you've been using in previous examples is a single `string`. The "+" operator enables the programmer to combine strings, or to combine a string and an intrinsic variable before the sum is passed to `WriteLine()`:

```
string s = "Sarah"
Console.WriteLine("My name is "
    + s + " and my age is " +
    3);
```

All `WriteLine()` sees in this case is "My name is Sarah and my age is 3".

A second form of `WriteLine()` provides a more flexible set of arguments:

```
Console.WriteLine("My name is
    {0} and my age is {1}.",
                     "Sarah", 3);
```

Here, the string "Sarah" is inserted where the symbol {0} appears — zero refers to the first argument after the string itself. The integer 3 is inserted at the position marked by {1}. This form is more efficient than the previous example because concatenating strings is not as easy as it sounds. It's a time-consuming business but someone has to do it.

It wouldn't be much to write home about if that were the only difference. However, this second form of `WriteLine()` also provides for a number of controls on the output format. I describe these format controls in Chapter 9.

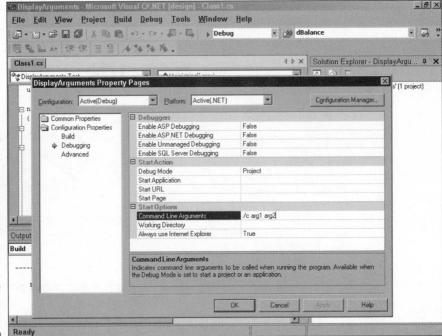

Figure 7-9:
Enter the
program
arguments
into the
Command
Line
Arguments
field of the
Property
Pages
window.

Figure 7-10:
Visual
Studio can
pass
arguments
to its
Console
Application
programs.

Chapter 8

Class Methods

*T*he function control described in Chapter 7 is a great way of dividing a programming problem up into smaller, more manageable chunks. The ability to pass integer and floating point values to and from the function gives application code the ability to communicate with the function.

There's just so much information that a few variables can communicate. An object-oriented program is based upon grouping information into objects. For this reason, C# provides a convenient, seamless means for communicating class objects to functions.

Passing an Object to a Function

You pass object references as arguments to functions in the same way as you pass value-type variables, with one difference: You always pass objects by reference.

The following small program demonstrates how you pass objects — to functions, that is:

```
// PassObject - demonstrate how to pass an object
//              to a function.
using System;
namespace PassObject
{
  public class Student
  {
    public string sName;
  }
  public class Class1
  {
```

```
public static void Main(string[] args)
{
    Student student = new Student();
    // set the name by accessing it directly
    Console.WriteLine("The first time:");
    student.sName = "Madeleine";
    OutputName(student);
    // change the name using a function
    Console.WriteLine("After being modified:");
    SetName(student, "Willa");
    OutputName(student);
    // wait for user to acknowledge
    Console.WriteLine("Press Enter to terminate...");
    Console.Read();
}
// OutputName - output the student's name
public static void OutputName(Student student)
{
    // output current student's name
    Console.WriteLine("Student's name is {0}", student.sName);
}
// SetName - modify the student object's name
public static void SetName(Student student, string sName)
{
    student.sName = sName;
}
}
}
```

The program creates a student object consisting of nothing but a name. We like to keep 'em simple down here. The program first sets the name of the student directly and passes it to the output function OutputName(). OutputName() displays the name of any Student it receives.

The program then updates the name of the student by calling SetName(). Because all objects are passed by reference in C#, the changes made to student are retained back in the calling function. When Main() outputs the student object again, the name has changed:

```
The first time:
Student's name is Madeleine
After being modified:
Student's name is Willa
Press Enter to terminate...
```

The SetName() function can change the name within the Student object and make it stick.

Defining Object Functions and Methods

A class is supposed to collect together the elements that describe a real-world object or concept. For example, a Vehicle class might contain data elements for maximum velocity, weight, carrying capacity, and so on. However, a Vehicle has active properties as well: the ability to start, to stop, and so on.

These are described by the functions that go with that vehicular data. These functions are just as much a part of the Vehicle class as the data elements.

Defining a static member function

For example, you could rewrite the program from the previous section in a slightly better way:

```
// PassObjectToMemberFunction - rely upon static member functions
//                              to manipulate fields within
//                              the object
using System;
namespace PassObjectToMemberFunction
{
  public class Student
  {
    public string sName;
    // OutputName - output the student's name
    public static void OutputName(Student student)
    {
      // output current student's name
      Console.WriteLine("Student's name is {0}", student.sName);
    }
    // SetName - modify the student object's name
    public static void SetName(Student student, string sName)
    {
      student.sName = sName;
    }
  }
  public class Class1
  {
    public static void Main(string[] args)
    {
      Student student = new Student();
      // set the name by accessing it directly
      Console.WriteLine("The first time:");
      student.sName = "Madeleine";
      Student.OutputName(student);
      // change the name using a function
      Console.WriteLine("After being modified:");
      Student.SetName(student, "Willa");
      Student.OutputName(student);
      // wait for user to acknowledge
      Console.WriteLine("Press Enter to terminate...");
      Console.Read();
    }
  }
}
```

This program has only one significant change from the PassObject program in the previous section: I put the OutputName() and SetName() functions in the Student class.

Because of that change, Main() must reference the Student class in the calls to SetName() and OutputName(). The functions are now members of the class Student and not Class1, the function in which Main() resides.

This is a small but significant step. Placing `OutputName()` within the class leads to a higher level of reuse: Outside functions that need to display the object will find the `OutputName()` along with other output functions right there as part of the class.

This is also a better solution on a philosophical level. `Class1` shouldn't need to worry about how to initialize the name of a `Student` object nor about how to output important material. The `Student` class should contain that information.

In fact, `Main()` should not initialize the name to "Madeleine" in the first place. It should call `SetName()` instead.

From within `Student`, one member function can invoke another without explicitly applying the class name. `SetName()` could invoke `OutputName()` without the need for referencing the class name. If you leave off the class name, C# assumes that the function being accessed is in the same class.

Defining a method

The data members of an object are accessed with the object and not with the class. Thus, you might say

```
Student student = new Student();
student.sName = "Madeleine";
```

C# enables you to invoke non-static member functions in the same way:

```
student.SetName("Madeleine");
```

The following example demonstrates this technique:

```
// InvokeMethod - invoke a member function through the object
using System;
namespace InvokeMethod
{
  class Student
  {
    // the name information to describe a student
    public string sFirstName;
    public string sLastName;
    // SetName - save off name information
    public void SetName(string sFName, string sLName)
    {
      sFirstName = sFName;
      sLastName  = sLName;
    }
    // ToNameString - convert the student object into a
    //                string for display
    public string ToNameString()
    {
      string s = sFirstName + " " + sLastName;
```

```
        return s;
    }
}
public class Class1
{
    public static void Main()
    {
        Student student = new Student();
        student.SetName("Stephen", "Davis");
        Console.WriteLine("Student's name is "
                            + student.ToNameString());
        // wait for user to acknowledge
        Console.WriteLine("Press Enter to terminate...");
        Console.Read();
    }
}
}
```

The output from this program is this simple line:

```
Student's name is Stephen Davis
```

Other than having a much shorter name, this program is very similar to the earlier `PassObjectToMemberFunction` program. This version uses non-static functions to manipulate both a first and a last name.

The program begins by creating a new `Student` object, `student`. The program then invokes the `SetName()` function, which stores the two strings "Stephen" and "Davis" into the data members `sFirstName` and `sLastName`. Finally, the program calls the member function `ToNameString()`, which returns the name of the `student` by concatenating the two strings.

For historical reasons that have nothing to do with C#, a non-static member function is commonly known as a *method*. I use the term *method* for non-static member functions, and I use *function* for all other types.

Look again at the `SetName()` function that updates the first and last name fields in the `Student` object. Which object does `SetName()` modify? Consider the following example to see the problem:

```
Student christa = new Student();
Student sarah = new Student();
christa.SetName("Christa", "Smith");
sarah.SetName("Sarah", "Jones");
```

The first call to `SetName()` updates the first and last name of the `christa` object. The second call updates the `sarah` object.

Thus, C# programmers say that a method operates on the *current* object. In the first call, the current object is `christa`; in the second, it's `sarah`.

Why bother with methods?

Why bother with methods? Why aren't simple functions good enough? Methods play two different but important roles.

The `SetName()` method hides the details of how the names are being stored within the `Student` class — information that external functions shouldn't need to know. This is similar to the way we use appliances such as microwave ovens. Buttons with names like `Start` and `Reset` hide the internal circuitry of the oven.

The second role of a method is to represent real properties of the class. An airplane accelerates, banks, takes off, and lands (among other things). A thorough `Airplane` class should have `Accelerate()`, `Bank()`, `TakeOff()`, and `Land()` methods that mimic these properties. Matching a class representation to the real thing enables you to think of your program in terms that are native to the problem and not of some artificial vocabulary dictated by the programming language.

Expanding a method's full name

There's a subtle but important problem with my description of method names. To see the problem, consider the following example code snippet:

```
public class Person
{
  public void Address()
  {
    Console.WriteLine("Hi");
  }
}
public class Letter
{
  string sAddress;
  // save off the address
  public void Address(string sNewAddress)
  {
    sAddress = sNewAddress;
  }
}
```

Any subsequent discussion of the `Address()` method is now ambiguous. The `Address()` method within `Person` has nothing to do with the `Address()` method in `Letter`. If my programmer friend tells me to access the `Address()` method, which `Address()` does he mean?

The problem lies not with the methods themselves, but with my description. In fact, there is no `Address()` method — only a `Person.Address()` and a `Letter.Address()` method. Attaching the class name onto the beginning of the method name clearly indicates which method is intended.

This description is very similar to people's names. Within my family, I am known as Stephen. (Actually, within my family, I am known by my middle name, but you get the point.) There are no other Stephens within my family (at least not within my close family). However, there are two other Stephens where I work.

If I'm at lunch with some co-workers and the other two Stephens aren't present, the name *Stephen* clearly refers to me. Back in the trenches (or cubicles), yelling out "Stephen" is ambiguous because it could refer to any one of us. In that context, you need to yell out "Stephen Davis" as opposed to "Stephen Williams" or "Stephen Leija."

Thus, you can actually consider `Address()` to be the first name or nickname of a method.

The class name is yet another differentiator between overloaded method names, the others being the name and number of the function arguments.

Accessing the Current Object

Consider the following `Student.SetName()` method:

```
class Student
{
    // the name information to describe a student
    public string sFirstName;
    public string sLastName;
    // SetName - save off name information
    public void SetName(string sFName, string sLName)
    {
        sFirstName = sFName;
        sLastName  = sLName;
    }
}
public class Class1
{
    public static void Main()
    {
        Student student1 = new Student();
        student1.SetName("Joseph", "Smith");
        Student student2 = new Student();
        student2.SetName("John", "Davis");
    }
}
```

The function `Main()` uses the `SetName()` method to update first `student1` and then `student2`. But you don't see a reference to either `Student` object within `SetName()` itself. In fact, there isn't a reference to a `Student` object at all. A method is said to operate on "the current object." How does a method know which one is the current object? Will the real current object please stand up?

The answer is simple. The current object is passed as an implicit argument in the call to a method — for example:

```
student1.SetName("Joseph", "Smith");
```

This call is equivalent to

```
Student.SetName(student1, "Joseph", "Smith"); // equivalent call
                                              // (but this won't
                                              // build properly)
```

I'm not saying you can invoke SetName() in two different ways, just that the two calls are semantically equivalent. The object just to the left of the "." — the hidden first argument — is passed to the function just like other arguments.

Passing an object implicitly is pretty easy to swallow, but what about a reference from one method to another?

```
public class Student
{
  public string sFirstName;
  public string sLastName;
  public void SetName(string sFirstName, string sLastName)
  {
    SetFirstName(sFirstName);
    SetLastName(sLastName);
  }
  public void SetFirstName(string sName)
  {
    sFirstName = sName;
  }
  public void SetLastName(string sName)
  {
    sLastName = sName;
  }
}
```

No object appears in the call to SetFirstName(). The current object continues to be passed along silently from one method call to the next. An access to any member from within an object method is assumed to be with respect to the current object.

What is this?

Unlike most arguments, however, the current object does not appear in the function argument list and so it is not assigned a name by the programmer. Instead, C# assigns this object the not-very-imaginative name this.

this is a keyword, and it may not be used for any other purpose, at least not without the expressed written permission of the National Football League.

Thus, you could write the previous example as follows:

```
public class Student
{
  public string sFirstName;
  public string sLastName;
  public void SetName(string sFirstName, string sLastName)
  {
    // explicitly reference the "current object" referenced by this
    this.SetFirstName(sFirstName);
    this.SetLastName(sLastName);
  }
  public void SetFirstName(string sName)
  {
    this.sFirstName = sName;
  }
  public void SetLastName(string sName)
  {
    this.sLastName = sName;
  }
}
```

Notice the explicit addition of the keyword this. Adding this to the member references doesn't add anything because this is assumed. However, when Main() makes the following call, this references student1 throughout SetName() and any other method that it might call:

```
student1.SetName("John", "Smith");
```

When is it this explicit?

You don't normally need to refer to this explicitly because it is understood where necessary by the compiler. However, two common cases require this. You need it when initializing data members:

```
// Address - define a "floor plan" for a US address
class Person
{
  public string sName;
  public int nID;
  public void Init(string sName, int nID)
  {
    this.sName = sName;
    this.nID = nID;
  }
}
```

The arguments to the Init() method are named sName and nID, which match the names of the corresponding data members. This makes the function easy to read because you know immediately which argument is stored where. The only problem is that the name sName in the argument list obscures the name of the data member.

The addition of `this` clarifies which `sName` is intended. Within `Init()`, the name `sName` refers to the function argument, but `this.sName` refers to the data member.

You also need `this` when storing off the current object for use later or by some other function. Consider the following example program `ReferencingThisExplicitly`:

```
// ReferencingThisExplicitly - this program demonstrates
//                how to explicitly use the reference to this
using System;
namespace ReferencingThisExplicitly
{
  public class Class1
  {
    public static int Main(string[] strings)
    {
      // create a student
      Student student = new Student();
      student.Init("Stephen Davis", 1234);
      // now enroll the student in a course
      Console.WriteLine
              ("Enrolling Stephen Davis in Biology 101");
      student.Enroll("Biology 101");
      // display student course
      Console.WriteLine("Resulting student record:");
      student.DisplayCourse();
      // wait for user to acknowledge the results
      Console.WriteLine("Press Enter to terminate...");
      Console.Read();
      return 0;
    }
  }
  // Student - our class university student
  public class Student
  {
    // all students have a name and id
    public string sName;
    public int    nID;
    // the course in which the student is enrolled
    CourseInstance courseInstance;
    // Init - initialize the student object
    public void Init(string sName, int nID)
    {
      this.sName = sName;
      this.nID = nID;
      courseInstance = null;
    }
    // Enroll - enroll the current student in a course
    public void Enroll(string sCourseID)
    {
      courseInstance = new CourseInstance();
      courseInstance.Init(this, sCourseID);
    }
    // Display the name of the student
    // and the course
    public void DisplayCourse()
    {
      Console.WriteLine(sName);
      courseInstance.Display();
    }
```

```
   }
   // CourseInstance - a combination of a student with
   //                  university course
   public class CourseInstance
   {
     public Student student;
     public string sCourseID;
     // Init - tie the student to the course
     public void Init(Student student, string sCourseID)
     {
       this.student = student;
       this.sCourseID = sCourseID;
     }
     // Display - output the name of the course
     public void Display()
     {
       Console.WriteLine(sCourseID);
     }
   }
} }
```

This program is fairly mundane. The Student object has room for a name, an id, and a single instance of a university course (not a very industrious student). Main() creates the student and then invokes Init() to initialize the Student object. At this point, the courseInstance reference is set to null because the student is not yet enrolled in a class.

The Enroll() method enrolls the student by initializing courseInstance with a new object. However, the CourseInstance.Init() method takes a student as its first argument along with the course id as the second argument. Which student should you pass? Clearly, you need to pass the current student — the student referred to by this. (Thus, you can say that Enroll() enrolls this student in the CourseInstance.) The Display() methods output the student and course names.

What about when I don't have this?

Mixing class function and object methods is like mixing cowboys and ranchers. Fortunately, C# gives you some ways around the problems between the two. Sort of reminds me of the song from *Oklahoma!* "Oh, the function and the method can be friends . . ."

To see the problem, consider the following program snippet MixingFunctions AndMethods:

```
// MixingFunctionsAndMethods - mixing class functions and object
//                             methods can cause problems
using System;
namespace MixingFunctionsAndMethods
{
  public class Student
  {
    public string sFirstName;
```

```
    public string sLastName;
    // InitStudent - initialize the student object
    public void InitStudent(string sFirstName, string sLastName)
    {
      this.sFirstName = sFirstName;
      this.sLastName = sLastName;
    }
    // OutputBanner - output the introduction
    public static void OutputBanner()
    {
      Console.WriteLine("Aren't we clever:");
      // Console.WriteLine(? what student do we use ?);
    }
    public void OutputBannerAndName()
    {
      // the class Student is implied but no this
      // object is passed to the static method
      OutputBanner();
      // no this object is passed, but the current
      // Student object is passed explicitly
      OutputName(this);
    }
    // OutputName - output the student's name
    public static void OutputName(Student student)
    {
      // here the Student object is referenced explicitly
      Console.WriteLine("Student's name is {0}",
                        student.ToNameString());
    }
    // ToNameString - fetch the student's name
    public string ToNameString()
    {
      // here the current object is implicit -
      // this could have been written:
      // return this.sFirstName + " " + this.sLastName;
      return sFirstName + " " + sLastName;
    }
  }
  public class Class1
  {
    public static void Main(string[] args)
    {
      Student student = new Student();
      student.InitStudent("Madeleine", "Cather");
      // output the banner and name
      Student.OutputBanner();
      Student.OutputName(student);
      Console.WriteLine();
      // output the banner and name again
      student.OutputBannerAndName();
      // wait for user to acknowledge
      Console.WriteLine("Press Enter to terminate...");
      Console.Read();
    }
  }
}
```

Start at the bottom of the program with Main() so you can better see the problems. The program begins by creating a Student object and initializing its name. The simpleton program now wants to do nothing more than output the name preceded by a short message and banner.

Main() first outputs the banner and message using the class or static function approach. The program invokes the OutputBanner() function for the banner line and the OutputName() function to output the message and the student name. The function OutputBanner() outputs a simple message to the console. Main() passes the student object as an argument to OutputName() so it can display the student's name.

Next, Main() uses the object function or method approach to outputting the banner and message by calling student.OutputBannerAndName().

OutputBannerAndName() first invokes the static function OutputBanner(). The class Student is assumed. No object is passed because the static function does not need one. Next, OutputBannerAndName() calls the OutputName() function. OutputName() is also a static function, but it takes a Student object as its argument. OutputBannerAndName() passes this.

A more interesting case is the call from ToNameString() from within OutputName(). The latter function is declared static and therefore has no this. It does have an explicit Student object, which it uses to make the call.

The OutputBanner() function would probably like to call ToNameString() as well; however, it has no Student object to use. It has no this pointer because it is a static function and it was not passed an object explicitly.

A static function cannot call a non-static method without explicitly providing an object. No object, no call.

Getting Help from Visual Studio — Auto Complete

Visual Studio .NET adds an extremely powerful programming auto-complete feature known as a *code comment report*. When you're typing in the name of a class or object in your source code, Visual Studio tries to anticipate the name of the class or method that you're trying to enter.

Describing the Visual Studio auto-complete help is easiest by example. To show you how it works, I'll use the following section of code from the program MixingFunctionsAndMethods:

```
// output the banner and name
Student.OutputBanner();
Student.OutputName(student);
Console.WriteLine();
// output the banner and name again
student.OutputBannerAndName();
```

Getting help on built-in functions from the System Library

Using `MixingFunctionsAndMethods` as an example, as I begin typing **Console.**, Visual Studio responds with a list of all the methods of `Console`. When I enter the W, Visual Studio moves the display down to the first method that begins with a *W*, which is `Write()`. Moving the selection down one by pressing the down-arrow key highlights `WriteLine()`. Immediately off to the right appears an explanation of the `WriteLine()` method, as shown in Figure 8-1. It also notes the 18 overloaded versions of the `WriteLine()` method — each with a different argument set, of course.

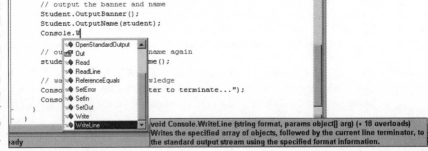

I complete the name of the function `WriteLine`. As soon as I enter the open parenthesis, Visual Studio changes the window to show the possible arguments as shown in Figure 8-2.

You don't actually have to type the name of the function. Suppose you had entered **WriteL** to uniquely identify the method you want. As soon as you enter the open parenthesis, Visual Studio completes the name for you.

Click the small arrows on the left side of the pop-up box to find the overloaded version of `WriteLine()` that you're looking for. Below the description of the function, you see the description of the first argument. In Figure 8-2, it's looking for a "format string."

As soon as I enter the string "some string" (what do you want? it's late) followed by a comma, Visual Studio responds with a description of the second argument, as shown in Figure 8-3.

Visual Studio provides help with each subsequent argument as you move down the line. Of course, this help is available for every built-in method your program uses from the standard C# library.

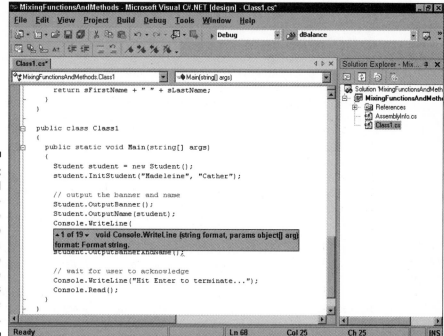

Figure 8-2:
The Visual
Studio auto-
complete
feature also
displays a
list of the
possible
arguments
for Write
Line().

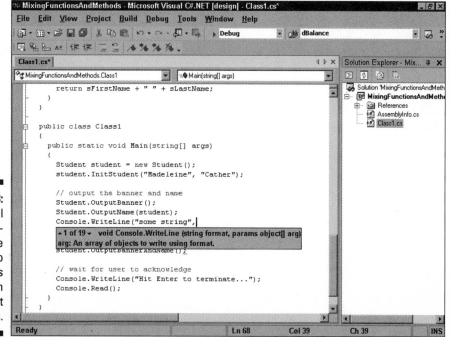

Figure 8-3:
The Visual
Studio auto-
complete
feature also
provides
help with
the different
arguments.

Getting help with your own functions and methods

Some help is available for your own functions, as well.

Continuing the example from the preceding section, I erase the very original "some string" and replace it with the intended empty string: `Console.WriteLine()`. On the very next line I enter **"student."** As soon as I type the period, Visual Studio opens a list of the members of the `student` object, as shown in Figure 8-4.

The objects with the little boxes that slant from the lower left to the upper right denote data members. The little bricks that slant from upper left to lower right denote methods.

They're easier to discriminate in practice. The data member bricks are sort of an aqua color, and the method bricks are purple with little racing stripes.

Some of the methods I don't recognize. These are basic methods that all objects get for free. Among this standard group of methods is our very own `OutputBannerAndName()`. Typing the O highlights my function and displays the declaration of the method so I know how to use the method.

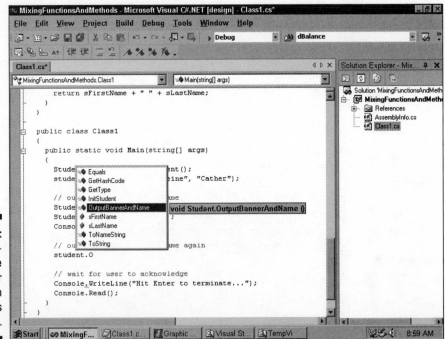

Figure 8-4:
Auto-complete works for your own methods, as well.

Once again, entering an open parenthesis at this point will auto-complete the name of the method.

The same feature works for functions, as well. As I enter the class name `Student` followed by the period, Visual Studio opens up a list of the members of `Student`. As soon as I type **"OutputN"**, Visual Studio responds with a list of the arguments for the `OutputName()` method, as shown in Figure 8-5.

Adding to the help

The Visual Studio auto-complete feature gives you considerable help by anticipating the members you may want to access as soon you enter the class or object name.

Visual Studio can provide only limited help for user-created functions and classes. For example, Visual Studio doesn't know what the method `OutputName()` does. You would have to be dreaming about how nice it will be when you can finish this book to not get some idea since the name is reasonably descriptive. Fortunately, Visual Studio gives you a sneaky way to tell the auto-complete feature what the function does, and more.

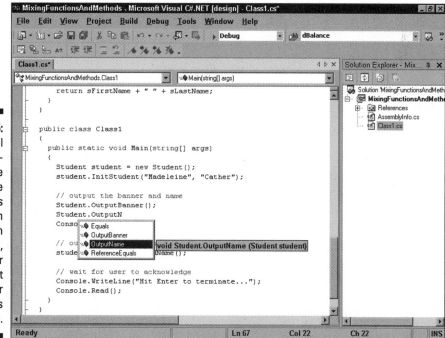

Figure 8-5:
The Visual Studio auto-complete feature gives as much information as it can, whether for object methods or class functions.

You mark a normal comment line with two slashes: //. However, Visual Studio understands a special comment of three slashes in a row: ///. This type of *documentation comment* can provide Visual Studio with extra information to be used by the auto-complete feature.

To be fair, the Java language first introduced this concept. Java provides an extra program that can pull these three-slash comments out into a separate documentation file. C# adds an improvement with its dynamic, edit-time help.

The documentation comment can contain any combination of the commands shown in Table 8-1.

Table 8-1   The Common Documentation Comment Instructions

Instruction	What It Means
<param></param>	Describes an argument to the function. Displays after you type in the function name and the open parenthesis, prompting you about what you should enter next.
<summary></summary>	Describes the function itself. Displays when you enter the name of the function during editing.
<returns></returns>	Describes the value returned by the function.

Documentation comments follow XML/HTML rules: A command starts with a <command> and ends with a </command>. In fact, they are normally known as *XML tags* due to their relationship to XML.

Numerous other XML tags are available. For more information, access the Visual Studio help (more formally known as MSDN for Visual Studio) by choosing Help➪Index and then look under "Tags for documentation comments."

The following example is a commented version of the MixingFunctionsAndMethods program:

```
// MixingFunctionsAndMethods - mixing class functions and object
//                             methods can cause problems
using System;
namespace MixingFunctionsAndMethods
{
  /// <summary>
  /// Simple description of a student
  /// </summary>
  public class Student
  {
    /// <summary>
    /// Student's given name
```

```
/// </summary>
public string sFirstName;
/// <summary>
/// Student's family name
/// </summary>
public string sLastName;

// InitStudent - initialize the student object
/// <summary>
/// Initializes the student object before it can be used.
/// </summary>
/// <param name="sFirstName">Student's given name</param>
/// <param name="sLastName">Student's family name</param>
public void InitStudent(string sFirstName, string sLastName)
{
  this.sFirstName = sFirstName;
  this.sLastName = sLastName;
}
// OutputBanner - output the introduction
/// <summary>
/// Output a banner before displaying student names
/// </summary>
public static void OutputBanner()
{
  Console.WriteLine("Aren't we clever:");
  // Console.WriteLine(? what student do we use ?);
}


// OutputBannerAndName
/// <summary>
/// Output a banner followed by the current student's name
/// </summary>
public void OutputBannerAndName()
{
  // the class Student is implied but no this
  // object is passed to the static method
  OutputBanner();

  // no this object is passed, but the current
  // Student object is passed explicitly
  OutputName(this, 5);
}


// OutputName - output the student's name
/// <summary>
4 String(' ', nIndent);
  s += String.Format("Student's name is {0}",
                     student.ToNameString());
  Console.WriteLine(s);
  return s;
}

// ToNameString - fetch the student's name
/// <summary>
/// Convert the student's name into a string for display
/// </summary>
/// <returns>The stringified student name</returns>
public string ToNameString()
```

```
    {
        // here the current object is implicit -
        // this could have been written:
        // return this.sFirstName + " " + this.sLastName;
        return sFirstName + " " + sLastName;
    }
}

/// <summary>
/// Exercise class
/// </summary>
public class Class1
{
    /// <summary>
    /// The program starts here.
    /// </summary>
    /// <param name="args"></param>
    public static void Main(string[] args)
    {
        Student student = new Student();
        student.InitStudent("Madeleine", "Cather");

        // output the banner and name
        Student.OutputBanner();
        string s = Student.OutputName(student, 5);
        Console.WriteLine();

        // output the banner and name again
        student.OutputBannerAndName();

        // wait for user to acknowledge
        Console.WriteLine("Press Enter to terminate...");
        Console.Read();
    }
}
}
```

The comments explain the purpose of the function, the purpose of each argument, the type of data returned, and a reference to a related function.

In practice, the following steps describe the display as I add the function `Student.OutputName()` to `Main()`:

1. Visual Studio offers me a list of functions. After I select the one I'm looking for, `OutputName()`, Visual Studio gives me the short description from the `<summary></summary>`, as shown in Figure 8-6.

2. After I select or type in the name of the function, Visual Studio displays a description of the first parameter taken from the `<param></param>` field along with its type.

3. Visual Studio repeats the process for the second argument, `nIndent`.

Although they're a little tedious to enter, documentation comments make methods considerably easier to use.

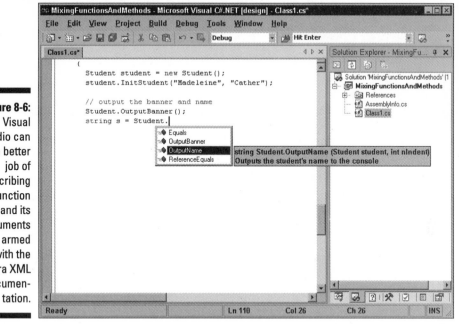

Figure 8-6:
Visual
Studio can
do a better
job of
describing
the function
and its
arguments
when armed
with the
extra XML
documen-
tation.

Generating XML documentation

You can easily persuade Visual Studio to output all the documentation you
have provided in the form of an XML file.

This entire section is very technical stuff. If you do not know what an XML file
is, this material won't mean much to you. However, if you do understand XML
files, you'll want to know about this feature.

Choose Project⇨Properties. In the Build section of the Configuration
Properties folder, find an Output property called XML Documentation File.
Fill in a name. I chose the name xmloutput.xml just because I didn't know
any better. Click OK to apply the change and close the properties window.

You can also access the project properties by right-clicking the project name
in the Solution Explorer.

Now choose Build⇨Rebuild All just to make sure you get everything rebuilt,
whether it needs rebuilding or not.

Look in the same directory as your Class1.cs source file (the project file is
in this same directory). The new file xmloutput.xml describes all the functions documented with XML tags.

Chapter 9

Stringing in the Key of C#

For many applications, you can treat a `string` like one of the built-in variable types such as `int` or `char`. Certain operations otherwise reserved for these intrinsic types are available to strings:

```
int i = 1;          // declare and initialize an int
string s = "abc";   // declare and initialize a string
```

In other respects, a `string` is treated like a user-defined class:

```
string s1 = new String();
string s2 = "abcd";
int nLengthOfString = s2.Length;
```

Which is it — a variable type or a class? In fact, `String` is a class for which C# offers special treatment. For example, the keyword `string` is synonymous with the class name `String`:

```
String s1 = "abcd"; // assign a string literal to a String obj
string s2 = s1;     // assign a String obj to a string variable
```

In this example, s1 is declared to be an object of class `String` (spelled with an uppercase *S*), while s2 is declared as a simple `string` (spelled with a lowercase *s*). However, the two assignments demonstrate that `string` and `String` are of the same (or compatible) types.

In fact, this same property is true of the other variable types, to a more limited extent. Even the lowly `int` type has a corresponding class `Int32`, `double` has the class `Double`, and so on. The distinction here is that `string` and `String` really are the same thing.

Performing Common Operations on a String

C# programmers perform more operations on strings than Beverly Hills plastic surgeons do on Hollywood hopefuls. There's hardly a program that doesn't employ the addition operator used on strings:

```
string sName = "Randy";
Console.WriteLine("His name is " + sName);
```

The String class provides this special operator. However, the String class also provides other, more direct methods for manipulating strings.

The union is indivisible, and so are strings

There's at least one thing you need to know that you didn't learn before the 6th grade: You can't change a string object itself after it has been created. Even though I might speak of modifying a string, C# doesn't have an operation that modifies the actual string object. Plenty of operations appear to modify the string that you're working with, but they always return the modified string as a new object, instead.

For example, the operation "His name is " + "Randy" changes neither of the two strings, but generates a third string, "His name is Randy". One side effect of this behavior is that you don't have to worry about someone modifying a string "out from under you."

Consider the following simplistic example program:

```
// ModifyString - the methods provided by the
//                class String do not modify the object
//                itself (s.ToUpper() does not modify
//                s; rather, it returns a new string that
//                has been converted)
using System;
namespace Example
{
  class Class1
  {
    public static void Main(string[] args)
    {
      // create a student object
      Student s1 = new Student();
      s1.sName = "Jenny";
      // now make a new object with the same name
      Student s2 = new Student();
      s2.sName = s1.sName;
      // "changing" the name in the s1 object does not
      // change the object itself because ToUpper() returns
      // a new string without modifying the original
```

```
      s2.sName = s1.sName.ToUpper();
      Console.WriteLine("s1 - {0}, s2 - {1}",
                          s1.sName,
                          s2.sName);
      // wait for user to acknowledge the results
      Console.WriteLine("Press Enter to terminate...");
      Console.Read();
    }
    // Student - we just need a class with a string in it
    class Student
    {
      public String sName;
    }
  }
}
```

The Student objects s1 and s2 are set up so that their sName data member points to the same string. The call to the ToUpper() method converts the string s1.sName to all uppercase. Normally, this would be a problem because both s1 and s2 point to the same object. However, ToUpper() does not change sName — it creates a new uppercase string.

The output of the program is simple:

```
s1 - Jenny, s2 - JENNY
Press Enter to terminate...
```

The immutability of strings also is important for string constants. A string such as "this is a string" is a form of string constant, just like 1 is an int constant. In the same way that I reuse my shirts to reduce the size of my wardrobe, a compiler might choose to combine all accesses to the single constant "this is a string". Reusing string constants can reduce the footprint of the resulting program but would be impossible if a string could be modified.

Equality for all strings: The Compare() *method*

Numerous operations treat a string as a single object — for example, the Compare() method. Compare() compares two strings as if they were numbers:

- If the left-hand string is greater than the right string, Compare() returns a 1.
- If the left-hand string is less than the right string, it returns a –1.
- If the two strings are equal, it returns a 0.

The algorithm works as follows when written in "notational C#" (C# without all the details):

```
compare(string s1, string s2)
{
  // loop through each character of the strings until
  // a character in one string is greater than the
  // corresponding character in the other string
  foreach character in the shorter string
    if (s1's character > s2's character when treated as a number)
      return 1
    if (s2's character < s1's character)
      return -1
  // Okay, every letter matches, but if the string s1 is longer
  // then it's greater
  if s1 has more characters left
    return 1
  // if s2 is longer, it's greater
  if s2 has more characters left
    return -1
  // if every character matches and the two strings are the same
  // length, then they are "equal"
  return 0
}
```

Thus, "abcd" is greater than "abbd", and "abcde" is greater than "abcd". More often than not, you don't care whether one string is greater than the other, but only whether the two strings are equal.

You do want to know which string is bigger when performing a sort.

The Compare() operation returns a 0 when two strings are identical. The following test program uses the equality feature of Compare() to perform a certain operation when the program encounters a particular string or strings.

BuildASentence prompts the user to enter lines of text. Each line is concatenated to the previous line to build a single sentence. The program exits if the user enters the word *EXIT*, *exit*, *QUIT*, or *quit*:

```
// BuildASentence - the following program constructs
//                  sentences by concatenating user
//                  input until the user enters
//                  one of the termination characters -
//                  this program shows when
//                  you need to look for string equality
using System;
namespace BuildASentence
{
  public class Class1
  {
    public static void Main(string[] args)
    {
      Console.WriteLine("Each line you entered will be "
                     + "added to a sentence until you "
                     + "enter EXIT or QUIT");
      // ask the user for input; continue concatenating
      // the phrases input until the user enters exit or
      // quit (start with a null sentence)
      string sSentence = "";
      for(;;)
```

```
                {
                    // get the next line
                    Console.WriteLine("Enter a string");
                    string sLine = Console.ReadLine();
                    // exit the loop if it's a terminator
                    if (IsTerminateString(sLine))
                    {
                        break;
                    }
                    // otherwise, add it to the sentence
                    sSentence = String.Concat(sSentence, sLine);
                    // let the user know how she's doing
                    Console.WriteLine("\nYou've entered: {0}", sSentence);
                }
                Console.WriteLine("\nTotal sentence:\n{0}", sSentence);

                // wait for user to acknowledge the results
                Console.WriteLine("Press Enter to terminate...");
                Console.Read();
            }
            // IsTerminateString - return a true if the source
            // string is equal to any of the termination strings
            public static bool IsTerminateString(string source)
            {
                string[] sTerms = {"EXIT",
                                   "exit",
                                   "QUIT",
                                   "quit"};
                // compare the string entered to each of the
                // legal exit commands
                foreach(string sTerm in sTerms)
                {
                    // return a true if you have a match
                    if (String.Compare(source, sTerm) == 0)
                    {
                        return true;
                    }
                }
                return false;
            }
        }
    }
```

After prompting the user as to what the program expects, the program creates an empty initial sentence string sSentence. From there, the program enters an "infinite" loop.

The controls while(true) and for(;;) loop forever, or at least long enough for some internal break or return to break you out. The two loops are equivalent, and in practice you'll see them both.

BuildASentence prompts the user to enter a line of text, which it reads using the ReadLine() method. Having read the line, the program checks to see if it is a terminator by using the locally created IsTerminateString(). This function returns true if sLine is one of the terminator phrases and false otherwise.

By convention, the name of a function that checks a property and returns a true or false must start with Is. In this case, the name of the function IsTerminateString() implies the question, "Is sLine a terminate string?" Of course, this is a human convention only — C# doesn't care.

If sLine is not one of the terminate strings, it is concatenated onto the end of the sentence using the String.Concat() function. The program outputs the immediate result just so the user can see what's going on.

The IsTerminateString() method defines an array of strings sTerms. Each member of this array is one of the strings you're looking for. Any of these strings cause the program to return a true, which causes the program to quit faster than a programmer forced to write COBOL.

The program must include both "EXIT" and "exit" because Compare() considers the two strings different by default. (The way the program is written, these are the only two ways to spell *exit*. Strings such as "Exit" and "eXit" would not be recognized as terminators.)

The IsTerminateString() function loops through each of the strings in the array of target strings. If Compare() reports a match to any one of the terminate phrases, the function returns a true. If the function reaches the end of the loop without a match, the function returns a false.

Iterating through an array is a great way to look for one of various possible values.

Here's an example run of the BuildASentence program:

```
Each line you entered will be added to a
sentence until you enter EXIT or QUIT
Enter a string
Programming with

You've entered: Programming with
Enter a string
 C# is fun

You've entered: Programming with C# is fun
Enter a string
 (more or less)

You've entered: Programming with C# is fun (more or less)
Enter a string
EXIT

Total sentence:
Programming with C# is fun (more or less)
Press Enter to terminate...
```

I have flagged my input in bold to make the output easier to read.

Would you like your compares with or without case?

The Compare() method used within IsTerminateString() considers "EXIT" and "exit" to be different strings. However, the Compare() function is overloaded with a second version that includes a third argument. This argument indicates whether the comparison should ignore the letter case. A true indicates "ignore."

The following version of IsTerminateString() returns a true if the string passed is uppercase, lowercase, or any combination of the two:

```
// IsTerminateString - return a true if the source string is equal
// to any of the termination characters
public static bool IsTerminateString(string source)
{
    // indicate true if passed either exit or quit,
    // irrespective of case
    return (String.Compare("exit", source, true) == 0) ||
           (String.Compare("quit", source, true) == 0);
}
```

This version of IsTerminateString() is simpler than the previous looping version. The function doesn't need to worry with case, and it can use a single conditional expression because it now has only two options to consider.

This IsTerminateString doesn't even use an if statement. The bool expression returns the value calculated directly to the user — it gets the if out.

What if *1 want to* switch *case?*

I almost hate to bring it up, but you can use the switch() control to look for a particular string.

Usually, you use the switch() control to compare a counting number to some set of possible values; however, the switch() does work on strings, as well.

The following version of IsTerminateString() uses the switch() control:

```
// IsTerminateString - return a true if the source
// string is equal to any of the termination strings
public static bool IsTerminateString(string source)
{
    switch(source)
    {
        case "EXIT":
        case "exit":
        case "QUIT":
        case "quit":
```

```
              return true;
      }
    return false;
  }
}
```

This approach works because you're comparing only a limited number of strings. The `for()` loop offers a much more flexible approach for searching for string values. Using the case-less `Compare()` gives the program greater flexibility in understanding the user.

Reading character input

A program can read from the keyboard one character at a time, but this approach can get problematic, what with worrying about newlines and the like. An easier approach reads a string and then parses the characters out of the string.

Parsing characters out of a string is another topic I don't like to mention for fear that programmers will abuse this technique. In some cases, programmers are too quick to jump down into the middle of a string and start pulling out what they find there. This is particularly true of C++ programmers because that's the only way they could deal with strings, until the addition of a string class.

Your programs can read strings as if they were arrays of characters using either the `foreach` control or the index operator `[]`.

A `string` isn't simply an array of characters — of course, you knew that. And you can only read a `string` one character at a time — you can't write.

The following simple `StringToCharAccess` program demonstrates this technique:

```
// StringToCharAccess - access the characters in a string
//                      as if the string were an array
using System;
namespace StringToCharAccess
{
  public class Class1
  {
    public static void Main(string[] args)
    {
      // read a string in from the keyboard
      Console.WriteLine("Input some random character string."
                   + "Make sure it's completely random");
      string sRandom = Console.ReadLine();
      // first output as a string
      Console.WriteLine("When output as a string:" + sRandom);
      Console.WriteLine();
      // now output as a series of characters
      Console.Write("When output using the foreach:");
```

```
    foreach(char c in sRandom)
    {
      Console.Write(c);
    }
    Console.WriteLine(); // terminate the line
    // put a blank line divider
    Console.WriteLine();
    // now output as a series of characters
    Console.Write("When output using the for:");
    for(int i = 0; i < sRandom.Length; i++)
    {
      Console.Write(sRandom[i]);
    }
    Console.WriteLine(); // terminate the line
    // wait for user to acknowledge the results
    Console.WriteLine("Press Enter to terminate...");
    Console.Read();
  }
}
```

This program first outputs some string picked totally at random. In fact, I might've read it somewhere or heard it at the office. The program first outputs the string using the conventional `WriteLine(string)` method. It follows this up by using the `foreach` to fetch each character in the string, one at a time. Finally, it uses the array brackets `[]` to do the same thing.

The results are as follows:

```
Input some random character string. Make sure it's completely random
Stephen Davis is one handsome individual

When output as a string:Stephen Davis is one handsome individual

When output using the foreach:Stephen Davis is one handsome individual

When output using the for:Stephen Davis is one handsome individual
Press Enter to terminate...
```

You can't get enough of a good thing.

In some cases, you don't want to mess with any whitespace on either end of the string.

The term *whitespace* refers to the characters that don't normally display on the screen: space, newline, tab, and vertical tab.

You can use the `Trim()` method to trim off the edges of the string:

```
// get rid of any extra spaces on either end of the string
sRandom = sRandom.Trim();
```

Even though it's a member function, `String.Trim()` returns a new string. The previous version of the string with the extra whitespace is lost and no longer usable.

Parsing numeric input

The ReadLine() function used for reading from the console returns a string. A program that expects numeric input must convert this string. C# provides just the conversion tool you need in the Convert class. This class provides a conversion method from string to each variable type. Thus, the following code segment reads a number from the keyboard and stores it into an int variable:

```
string s = Console.ReadLine();
int n = Convert.Int32(s);
```

The other conversion methods are a bit more obvious: ToDouble(), ToFloat(), and ToBoolean().

ToInt32() refers to a 32-bit, signed integer (32-bits is the size of a normal int). ToInt64() is the size of a long.

When Convert() encounters an unexpected character type, it can generate unexpected results. Thus, you must know for sure what type of data you're processing.

The following function returns a true if the string passed to it consists of only digits. You can call this function prior to converting into a type of integer, assuming that a sequence of nothing but digits is probably a legal number.

You would need to include the decimal point for floating point variables and include a leading minus sign for negative numbers, but, hey, you get the idea:

```
// IsAllDigits - return a true if all the characters
//               in the string are digits
public static bool IsAllDigits(string sRaw)
{
  // first get rid of any benign characters
  // at either end; if there's nothing left
  // then we don't have a number
  string s = sRaw.Trim();  // ignore whitespace on either side
  if (s.Length == 0)
  {
    return false;
  }
  // loop through the string
  for(int index = 0; index < s.Length; index++)
  {
    // a non-digit indicates that the string
    // probably is not a number
    if (Char.IsDigit(s[index]) == false)
    {
      return false;
    }
  }
  // no non-digits found; it's probably OK
  return true;
}
```

The function `IsAllDigits()` first removes any harmless whitespace at either end of the string. If nothing is left, the string was blank and could not be an integer. The function then loops through each character in the string. If any of these characters turns out to be a non-digit, the function returns a `false`, indicating that the string probably is not a number. If this function returns a `true`, the probability is very high that the string can be converted into an integer successfully.

The following code sample inputs a number from the keyboard and prints it back out to the console. (I omitted the `IsAllDigits()` function from the listing to save space.)

```
// IsAllDigits - demonstrate the IsAllDigits method
using System;
namespace Example
{
  class Class1
  {
    public static int Main(string[] args)
    {
      // input a string from the keyboard
      Console.WriteLine("Enter an integer number");
      string s = Console.ReadLine();
      // first check to see if this could be a number
      if (!IsAllDigits(s))
      {
        Console.WriteLine("Hey! That isn't a number");
      }
      else
      {
        // convert the string into an integer
        int n = Int32.Parse(s);
        // now write out the number times 2
        Console.WriteLine("2 * {0} = {1}", n, 2 * n);
      }
      // wait for user to acknowledge the results
      Console.WriteLine("Press Enter to terminate...");
      Console.Read();
      return 0;
    }
  }
}
```

The program reads a line of input from the console keyboard. If `IsAllDigits()` returns a `false`, the program criticizes the user. If not, the program converts the string into a number using the `Convert.ToInt32()` call. Finally, the program outputs both the number and two times the number (the latter to prove that the program did, in fact, convert the string as advertised).

The output from a sample run of the program appears as follows:

```
Enter an integer number
1A3
Hey! That isn't a number
Press Enter to terminate...
```

A better approach might be to go ahead and let Convert try to convert garbage and handle any exception it might decide to throw. However, a better-than-even chance exists that it won't throw an exception at all, but just return incorrect results — for example, returning 1 when presented with "1A3."

Handling a series of numbers

Often, a program receives a series of numbers in a single line from the keyboard. Using the String.Split() method, you can easily break the string into a number of substrings, one for each number, and parse them separately.

The Split() function chops up a single string into an array of smaller strings using some delimiter. For example, if you tell Split() to divide a string using comma as the delimiter, "1,2,3" becomes three strings, "1", "2", and "3".

The following program uses the Split() method to input a sequence of numbers to be summed:

```
// ParseSequenceWithSplit - input a series of numbers
//                          separated by commas, parse them into
//                          integers, and output the sum
namespace ParseSequenceWithSplit
{
  using System;
  class Class1
  {
    public static int Main(string[] args)
    {
      // prompt the user to input a sequence of numbers
      Console.WriteLine(
          "Input a series of numbers separated by commas:"
                        );
      // read a line of text
      string input = Console.ReadLine();
      Console.WriteLine();
      // now convert the line into individual segments
      // based upon either commas or spaces
      char[] cDividers = {',', ' '};
      string[] segments = input.Split(cDividers);
      // convert each segment into a number
      int nSum = 0;
      foreach(string s in segments)
      {
        // (skip any empty segments)
        if (s.Length > 0)
        {
          // skip strings that aren't numbers
          if (IsAllDigits(s))
          {
            // convert the string into a 32-bit int
            int num = Int32.Parse(s);
            Console.WriteLine("Next number = {0}", num);
            // add this number into the sum
            nSum += num;
          }
        }
      }
    }
```

```
        // output the sum
        Console.WriteLine("Sum = {0}", nSum);
        // wait for user to acknowledge the results
        Console.WriteLine("Press Enter to terminate...");
        Console.Read();
        return 0;
    }
    // IsAllDigits - return a true if all of the characters
    //               in the string are digits
    public static bool IsAllDigits(string sRaw)
    {
        // first get rid of any benign characters
        // at either end; if there's nothing left
        // then we don't have a number
        string s = sRaw.Trim();
        if (s.Length == 0)
        {
            return false;
        }
        // loop through the string
        for(int index = 0; index < s.Length; index++)
        {
            // a non-digit indicates that the string
            // probably is not a number
            if (Char.IsDigit(s[index]) == false)
            {
                return false;
            }
        }
        // no non-digit found; it's probably OK
        return true;
    }
}
}
```

The `ParseSequenceWithSplit` program begins by reading a string from the keyboard. The program passes the `cDividers` array to the `Split()` method to indicate that the comma and the space are the characters used to divide between individual numbers.

The program iterates through each of the smaller "subarrays" created by `Split()` using the `foreach` control. The program skips any zero-length subarrays (this would result from two dividers in a row). The program next checks to make sure the string actually contains a number by using the `IsAllDigits()` method. Valid numbers are converted into integers and then added to an accumulator, nSum. Invalid numbers are ignored. (I chose not to generate an error message.)

Here's the output of a typical run:

```
Input a series of numbers separated by commas:
1,2, a, 3 4

Next number = 1
Next number = 2
Next number = 3
Next number = 4
Sum = 10
Press Enter to terminate...
```

The program skips through the list, accepting either commas, spaces, or both as separators. It successfully skips over the *a* to generate the result of 10.

In a real-world program, you probably don't want to skip over incorrect input without comment. You almost always want to draw the user's attention to garbage in the input stream.

Controlling Output Manually

Controlling the output from programs is a very important aspect of string manipulation. Face it: The output from the program is what the user sees. No matter how elegant the internal logic of the program might be, the user probably won't be impressed if the output is shabby in appearance.

The `String` class provides help in directly formatting string data for output. The following sections examine the `Trim()`, `Pad()`, `PadRight()`, `PadLeft()`, `Substring()`, and `Concat()` methods.

Using the `Trim()` and `Pad()` methods

You can use the `Trim()` method to remove unwanted characters from either end of a string. Typically, you use this method to remove spaces so that output strings line up correctly.

Another common method for formatting output is the `Pad` functions, which add characters to either end of a string to expand the string to some predetermined length. For example, you may add spaces to the left or right of a string in order to left or right justify it, or add "*" characters to the left of a currency number.

The following small `AlignOutput` program uses both of these functions to trim up and justify a series of names:

```
// AlignOutput - left justify and align a set of strings
//               to improve the appearance of program output
namespace AlignOutput
{
  using System;
  class Class1
  {
    public static int Main(string[] args)
    {
      string[] names = {"Christa   ",
                        "  Sarah",
                        "Jonathan",
                        "Sam",
                        "  Schmekowitz "};
      // first output the names as they start out
      // (keep track of the longest string while you're at it)
      Console.WriteLine("The following names are of "
                        + "different lengths");
```

```
    foreach(string s in names)
    {
      Console.WriteLine("This is the name '{0}' before", s);
    }
    Console.WriteLine();

    // this time, fix the strings so they are
    // left justified and all the same length
    string[] sAlignedNames = TrimAndPad(names);
    // finally output the resulting padded,
    // justified strings
    Console.WriteLine("The following are the same names "
                  + "rationalized to the same length");
    foreach(string s in sAlignedNames)
    {
      Console.WriteLine(
                "This is the name '{0}' afterwards", s);
    }
    // wait for user to acknowledge
    Console.WriteLine("Press Enter to terminate...");
    Console.Read();
    return 0;
  }
  // TrimAndPad - given an array of strings, trim
  //              whitespace from both ends and then
  //              repad the strings to align them
  //              with the longest member
  public static string[] TrimAndPad(string[] strings)
  {
    // copy the source array into an array that you can
    // manipulate
    string[] stringsToAlign = new String[strings.Length];

    // first remove any unnecessary spaces from either
    // end of the names
    for(int i = 0; i < stringsToAlign.Length; i++)
    {
      stringsToAlign[i] = strings[i].Trim();
    }

    // now find the length of the longest string so that
    // all other strings line up with that string
    int nMaxLength = 0;
    foreach(string s in stringsToAlign)
    {
      if (s.Length > nMaxLength)
      {
        nMaxLength = s.Length;
      }
    }
    // finally justify all the strings to the length
    // of the maximum string
    for(int i = 0; i < stringsToAlign.Length; i++)
    {
      stringsToAlign[i] =
          stringsToAlign[i].PadRight(nMaxLength + 1);
    }
    // return the result to the caller
    return stringsToAlign;
  }
}
}
```

`AlignOutput` defines an array of names of uneven alignment and length. (You could just as easily write the program to read these names from the console or from a file.) The `Main()` function first displays the names as is. `Main()` then aligns the names using the `TrimAndPad()` method before redisplaying the resulting trimmed up strings:

```
The following names are of different lengths
This is the name 'Christa  ' before
This is the name '  Sarah' before
This is the name 'Jonathan' before
This is the name 'Sam' before
This is the name ' Schmekowitz ' before

The following are the same names rationalized to the same length
This is the name 'Christa    ' afterwards
This is the name 'Sarah      ' afterwards
This is the name 'Jonathan   ' afterwards
This is the name 'Sam        ' afterwards
This is the name 'Schmekowitz ' afterwards
```

The `TrimAndPad()` method begins by making a copy of the input `strings` array. In general, a function that operates on arrays should return a new modified array rather than modify the array passed. This is sort of like when I borrow my brother-in-law's pickup: He expects to get it back looking the same as when it left.

`TrimAndPad()` first loops through the array, calling `Trim()` on each element to remove unneeded whitespace on either end. The function loops again through the array to find the longest member. The function loops one final time, calling `PadRight()` to expand each array to match the length of the longest member in the array.

`PadRight(10)` expands an array to be at least 10 characters long. For example, `PadRight(10)` would add four spaces to the right of a six-character string.

`TrimAndPad()` returns the array of trimmed and padded strings for output. `Main()` iterates through this list, displaying each of the now gussied-up strings that you see. Voila.

Putting back together what software has cast asunder: Using the Concatenate function

You often face the problem of breaking up a string or inserting some substring into the middle of another. Replacing one character with another is most easily handled with the `Replace()` method:

```
string s = "Danger NoSmoking";
a.Replace(s, ' ', '!')
```

This example converts the string into "Danger!NoSmoking".

Replacing all appearances of one character (in this case, a space) with another (an exclamation mark) is especially useful when generating comma-separated strings for easier parsing. However, the more common and more difficult case involves breaking a single string into substrings, manipulating them separately, and then recombining them into a single, modified string.

For example, consider the following RemoveSpecialChars() function, which removes all instances of a set of special characters from a given string. This example RemoveWhiteSpace program uses this function to remove white-space (spaces, tabs, and newlines) from a string:

```
// RemoveWhiteSpace - define a RemoveSpecialChars() function
//                    which can remove any of a set of chars
//                    from a given string. Use this function
//                    to remove whitespace from a sample
//                    string.
namespace RemoveWhiteSpace
{
 using System;
  public class Class1
  {
    public static int Main(string[] strings)
    {
      // define the whitespace characters
      char[] cWhiteSpace = {' ', '\n', '\t'};
      // start with a string embedded with whitespace
      string s = " this is a\nstring";
      Console.WriteLine("before:" + s);
      // output the string with the whitespace missing
      Console.WriteLine("after:" +
                  RemoveSpecialChars(s, cWhiteSpace));
      // wait for user to acknowledge the results
      Console.WriteLine("Press Enter to terminate...");
      Console.Read();
      return 0;
    }
    // RemoveSpecialChars - remove every occurrence of
    //                      the specified character from
    //                      the string
    public static string RemoveSpecialChars(string sInput,
                                        char[] cTargets)
    {
      string sOutput = sInput;
      for(;;)
      {
        // find the offset of the character; exit the loop
        // if there are no more
        int nOffset = sOutput.IndexOf(cTargets);
        if (nOffset == -1)
        {
          break;
        }
        // break the string into the part prior to the
        // character and the part after the character
        string sBefore = sOutput.Substring(0, nOffset);
        string sAfter  = sOutput.Substring(nOffset + 1);
        // now put the two substrings back together with the
```

```
            // character in the middle missing
            sOutput = String.Concat(sBefore, sAfter);
        }
        return sOutput;
    }
}
}
```

The key to this program is the `RemoveSpecialChars()` function. This function returns a string consisting of the input string, `sInput`, with every one of a set of characters contained in the array `cTargets` removed. To better understand this function, assume that the string was "ab,cd,e" and that the array of special characters was the single character ','.

The `RemoveSpecialChars()` function enters a loop from which it will not return until every comma has been removed. The `IndexOfAny()` function returns the index within the array of the first comma that it can find. A return value of –1 indicates that no comma was found.

After the first call, `IndexOfAny()` returns a 2 ('a' is 0, 'b' is 1, and ',' is 2). The next two functions break the string apart at the index. `Substring(0, 2)` creates a substring consisting of two characters starting with offset 0: "ab". The second call to `Substring(3)` creates a string consisting of the characters starting at offset 3 and continuing to the end of the string: "cd,e". (It's the "+ 1" that skips over the comma.) The `Concat()` functions puts the two substrings back together to create "abcd,e".

Control passes back up to the top of the loop. The next iteration finds the comma at offset 4. The concatenated string is "abcde". Because no comma is left, the index returned on the final pass is –1.

The `RemoveWhiteSpace` program prints out a string containing several forms of whitespace. The program then uses the `RemoveSpecialChars()` function to strip off whitespace characters. The output from this program appears as follows:

```
before: this is a
string
after:thisisastring
Press Enter to terminate...
```

Let's `Split()` *that concatenate program*

The `RemoveWhiteSpace` program demonstrates the use of the `Concat()` and `IndexOf()` methods; however, it doesn't use the most efficient approach. As usual, a little examination reveals a more efficient approach using our old friend `Split()`. You can find this program on the enclosed CD-ROM under `RemoveWhiteSpaceWithSplit`:

```
// RemoveSpecialChars - remove every occurrence of
//                      the specified character from
//                      the string
public static string RemoveSpecialChars(string sInput,
                                        char[] cTargets)
{
   // split the input string up using the target
   // characters as the delimiters
   string[] sSubStrings = sInput.Split(cTargets);
   // sOutput will contain the eventual output information
   string sOutput = "";
   // loop through the substrings originating from the split
   foreach(string subString in sSubStrings)
   {
      sOutput = String.Concat(sOutput, subString);
   }
   return sOutput;
}
```

This version uses the Split() function to break up the input string into a set of substrings using the characters to be removed as delimiters. The delimiter is not included in the substrings created, which has the effect of removing the character(s).

The foreach loop in the second half of the program puts the pieces back together again. The output from the program is unchanged.

Controlling String.Format()

The String class also provides the Format() method for formatting output, especially the output of numbers. In its simplest form, Format() provides for the insertion of string, numeric, or boolean input in the middle of a control string. For example, consider the following call:

```
String.Format("{0} times {1} equals {2}", 2, 3, 2*3);
```

The first argument to Format() is known as the *control string*. The {n} in the middle of the control string indicates that the nth argument following the control string is to be inserted at that point. *Zero* refers to the first argument (in this case, 2), *one* refers to the next (3), and so on.

The resulting string is

```
"2 time 3 equals 6"
```

Unless otherwise directed, Format() uses a default output format for each argument type. Format() enables you to affect the output format by including modifiers in the place holders. See Table 9-1 for a listing of some of these controls. For example, {0:E6} says, "Output the number in exponential form, using six spaces for the mantissa."

Table 9-1	Format Controls Using the `String.Format()`		
Control	*Example*	*Result*	*Notes*
C — currency	{0:C} of 123.456	$123.45	The currency sign depends upon the localization setting.
	{0:C} of −123.456	($123.45)	
D — decimal	{0:D5} of 123	00123	Integers only
E — exponential	{0:E} of 123.45	1.2345E+02	Also known as scientific notation
F — fixed	{0:F2} of 123.4567	123.45	The number after the F indicates the number of digits after the decimal point.
N — number	{0:N} 123456.789	123,456.79	Adds commas and rounds off to nearest 100th
	{0:N1} 123456.789	123,456.8	Controls the number of digits after the decimal points
	{0:N0} 123456.789	123,457	
X — hexadecimal	{0:X}	0xFF	0xFF is equal to 255
{0:0...}	{0:000.00} 12.3	012.30	Forces a 0 if a digit is not already present
{0:#...}	{0:###.##} 12.3	12.3	Forces the space to be left blank; no other field can encroach on the three digits to the left and two digits after the decimal point (useful for maintaining decimal point alignment)
	{0:##0.0#} 0	0.0	Combining the # and zeros forces the space to be allocated by the #s and forces at least one digit to appear, even if the number is 0
{0:# or 0%}	{0:#00.#%} .1234	12.3%	The % displays the number as a percentage (multiplies by 100 and adds the % sign).
	{0:#00.#%} .0234	02.3%	

These format controls can seem a bit bewildering. (I didn't even mention the detailed currency and date controls.) To help you wade through these options, the following `OutputFormatControls` program enables you to enter a floating point number followed by a control sequence. The program then displays the number using the specified `Format()` control:

```
// OutputFormatControls - allow the user to reformat input
//                        numbers using a variety of format
//                        controls input at run time
namespace OutputFormatControls
{
  using System;
  public class Class1
  {
    public static int Main(string[] args)
    {
      // keep looping - inputing numbers until
      // the user enters a blank line rather than
      // a number
      for(;;)
      {
        // first input a number -
        //   terminate when the user inputs nothing
        //   but a blank line
        Console.WriteLine("Enter a double number");
        string sNumber = Console.ReadLine();
        if (sNumber.Length == 0)
        {
          break;
        }
        double dNumber = Double.Parse(sNumber);
        // now input the control codes; split them
        // using spaces as dividers
        Console.WriteLine("Enter the control codes"
                            + " separated by a blank");
        char[] separator = {' '};
        string sFormatString = Console.ReadLine();
        string[] sFormats =
                   sFormatString.Split(separator);
        // loop through the individual format controls
        foreach(string s in sFormats)
        {
          if (s.Length != 0)
          {
            // create a complete format control
            // from the control letters entered earlier
            string sFormatCommand = "{0:" + s + "}";
            // output the number entered using the
            // reconstructed format control
            Console.Write(
                "The format control {0} results in ",
                sFormatCommand);
            try
            {
              Console.WriteLine(sFormatCommand, dNumber);
            }
            catch(Exception)
            {
              Console.WriteLine("<illegal control>");
            }
```

```
            Console.WriteLine();
        }
        }
    }
// wait for user to acknowledge
        Console.WriteLine("Press Enter to terminate...");
        Console.Read();
        return 0;
    }
  }
}
```

The `OutputFormatControls` program continues to read floating point numbers into a variable `dNumber` until the user enters a blank line. Notice that the program does not include any tests to determine whether the input is a legal floating point number. Let's just assume that the user is smart enough to know what a number looks like.

The program then reads a series of control strings separated by spaces. Each control is combined with a "{0}" string into the variable `sFormatCommand`. For example, if you entered **N4**, the program would store the control "{0:N4}". The following statement writes out the number `dNumber` using the newly constructed `sFormatCommand`:

```
Console.WriteLine(sFormatCommand, dNumber);
```

In the case of our lowly N4, the command would be rendered as follows:

```
Console.WriteLine("{0:N4}", dNumber);
```

Typical output from the program appears as follows (I have bolded my input):

```
Enter a double number
12345.6789
Enter the control codes separated by a blank
C E F1 N0 0000000.00000
The format control {0:C} results in $12,345.68

The format control {0:E} results in 1.234568E+004

The format control {0:F1} results in 12345.7

The format control {0:N0} results in 12,346

The format control {0:0000000.00000} results in 0012345.67890

Enter a double number
.12345
Enter the control codes separated by a blank
00.0%
```

```
The format control {0:00.0%} results in 12.3%
Enter a double number

Press Enter to terminate...
```

When applied to the number 12345.6789, the control N0 adds commas in the proper place (the 'N' part) and lops off everything after the decimal point (the '0' portion) to render 12,346 (the last digit was rounded off, not truncated).

Similarly, when applied to 0.12345, the control 00.0% outputs 12.3%. The % sign multiplies the number by 100 and adds the % sign. The 00.0 indicates that the output should include at least two digits to the left of the decimal point and only one digit after the decimal point. The number 0.01 is displayed as 01.0% using the same 00.0% control.

The mysterious `try...catch` catches any errors that spew forth in the event you enter an illegal format command such as a 'D,' which stands for decimal. I cover exceptions in Chapter 15.

Part IV
Object-Oriented Programming

In this part . . .

Object-oriented programming is the most hyped term in the programming language — *.com* and business-to-business e-commerce eclipsed it for a year or two, but you can forget about them since the .com Crash of 2001.

C++ claims to be object-oriented — that's what differentiated it from C. Java is definitely object-oriented, as are a hundred or so other languages invented during the last ten years. But what is *object-oriented*? Do I have it? Can I get it?

Part IV demonstrates the features of C# that make it object-oriented to the core.

Chapter 10

Object-Oriented Programming — What's It All About?

. . . .

In This Chapter

▶ Making nachos

▶ Reviewing the basics of object-oriented programming

▶ Getting a handle on abstraction and classification

▶ Understanding why object-oriented programming is important

. . . .

*T*his chapter answers the musical question, "What are the concepts behind object-oriented programming and how do they differ from the functional concepts that you saw in Part II of this book?"

Object-Oriented Concept #1 — Abstraction

Sometimes when my son and I are watching football, I whip up a terribly unhealthy batch of nachos. I dump some chips on a plate, throw on some beans, cheese, and lots of jalapeños, and nuke the whole mess in the microwave oven for a few minutes.

To use my microwave, I open the door, throw the stuff in, and punch a few buttons on the front. After a few minutes, the nachos are done. (I try not to stand in front of the microwave while it's working lest my eyes start glowing in the dark.)

Now think for a minute about all the things I don't do to use my microwave:

✔ I don't rewire or change anything inside the microwave to get it to work. The microwave has an interface — the front panel with all the buttons and the little time display — that lets me do everything I need.

✔ I don't have to reprogram the software used to drive the little processor inside my microwave, even if I cooked a different dish the last time I used the microwave.

✔ I don't look inside my microwave's case.

✔ Even if I were a microwave designer and knew all about the inner workings of a microwave, including its software, I still wouldn't think about all that stuff while I was using it to heat my nachos.

These are not profound observations. You can deal with only so much stress in your life. To reduce the number of things that you deal with, you work at a certain level of detail. In object-oriented (OO) computerese, the level of detail at which you are working is called the *level of abstraction*. To introduce another OO term while I have the chance, I *abstract away* the details of the microwave's innards.

When I'm working on nachos, I view my microwave oven as a box. (As I'm trying to knock out a snack, I can't worry about the innards of the microwave oven and still follow the Cowboys on the tube.) As long as I use the microwave only through its interface (the keypad), nothing I can do should cause the microwave to enter an inconsistent state and crash or, worse, turn my nachos into a blackened, flaming mass.

Preparing functional nachos

Suppose I were to ask my son to write an algorithm for how Dad makes nachos. After he understood what I wanted, he would probably write, "Open a can of beans, grate some cheese, cut the jalapeños," and so on. When he came to the part about microwaving the concoction, he would write something like, "Cook in the microwave for five minutes" (on a good day).

That description is straightforward and complete. But it's not the way a functional programmer would code a program to make nachos. Functional programmers live in a world devoid of objects such as microwave ovens and other appliances. They tend to worry about flow charts with their myriad functional paths. In a functional solution to the nachos problem, the flow of control would pass through my finger to the front panel and then to the internals of the microwave. Pretty soon, flow would be wiggling around through complex logic paths about how long to turn on the microwave tube and whether to sound the "come and get it" tone.

In that world of functional programming, you can't easily think in terms of levels of abstraction. There are no objects and no abstractions behind which to hide inherent complexity.

Preparing object-oriented nachos

In an object-oriented approach to making nachos, I would first identify the types of objects in the problem: chips, beans, cheese, and an oven. Then, I would begin the task of modeling those objects in software, without regard for the details of how they will be used in the final program.

While I do that, I'm said to be working (and thinking) at the level of the basic objects. I need to think about making a useful oven, but I don't have to think about the logical process of making nachos, yet. After all, the microwave designers didn't think about the specific problem of my making a snack. Rather, they set about solving the problem of designing and building a useful microwave.

After I have successfully coded and tested the objects I need, I can ratchet up to the next level of abstraction. I can start thinking at the nacho-making level, rather than the microwave-making level. At this point, I can pretty much translate my son's instructions directly into C# code.

Object-Oriented Concept #2 — Classification

Critical to the concept of abstraction is that of classification. If I were to ask my son, "What's a microwave?" he would probably say, "It's an oven that . . . ." If I then asked, "What's an oven?" he might reply, "It's a kitchen appliance that . . . ." If I then asked "What's a kitchen appliance?" he would probably say, "Why are you asking so many stupid questions?"

The answers my son gave in my example questioning stem from his understanding of our particular microwave as an example of the type of things called microwave ovens. In addition, my son sees microwave ovens as just a special type of oven, which itself is just a special type of kitchen appliance.

In object-oriented computerese, my microwave is an *instance* of the class microwave. The class microwave is a subclass of the class oven, and the class oven is a subclass of the class kitchen appliances.

Humans classify. Everything about our world is ordered into taxonomies. We do this to reduce the number of things we have to remember. Take, for example, the first time you saw an SUV. The advertisement probably called the SUV "revolutionary, the likes of which have never been seen." But you and I know that just isn't so. I like the looks of some SUVs (others need to go back to take another crack at it), but hey, an SUV is a car. As such, it shares all (or at least most of) the properties of other cars. It has a steering wheel, seats, a motor, brakes, and so on. I bet I could even drive one without reading the user's manual first.

I don't have to clutter my limited storage with all the things that an SUV has in common with other cars. All I have to remember is "an SUV is a car that . . ." and tack on those few things that are unique to an SUV (like the price tag). I can go further. Cars are a subclass of wheeled vehicles along with other members, such as trucks and pickups. Maybe wheeled vehicles are a subclass of vehicles, which include boats and planes. And on, and on and on.

Why Classify?

Why should you classify? It sounds like a lot of trouble. Besides, people have been using the functional approach for so long, why change now?

Designing and building a microwave oven specifically for this one problem may seem easier than building a separate, more generic oven object. Suppose, for example, that I want to build a microwave to cook nachos and nachos only. I would not need to put a front panel on it, other than a START button. I always cook nachos the same amount of time. I could dispense with all that DEFROST and TEMP COOK nonsense. It only needs to hold one flat little plate. Three cubic feet of space would be wasted on nachos.

For that matter, I can dispense with the concept of "microwave oven" altogether. All I really need is the guts of the oven. Then, in the recipe, I put the instructions to make it work: "Put nachos in the box. Connect the red wire to the black wire. Bring the radar tube up to about 3,000 volts. Notice a slight hum. Try not to stand too close if you intend to have children." Stuff like that.

But the functional approach has some problems:

- **Too complex:** I don't want the details of oven building mixed into the details of nacho building. If I can't define the objects and pull them out of the morass of details to deal with separately, I must deal with all the complexities of the problem at the same time.

- **Not flexible:** Someday, I may need to replace the microwave oven with some other type of oven. I should be able to do so as long as they have the same interface. Without being clearly delineated and developed separately, one object type can't be cleanly removed and replaced with another.

> ✔ **Not reusable:** Ovens are used to make lots of different dishes. I don't want to create a new oven every time I encounter a new recipe. Having solved a problem once, I'd like to be able to reuse the solution in other places within my program. If I'm really lucky, I may be able to reuse it in future programs as well.

Object-Oriented Concept #3 — Usable Interfaces

An object must be able to project an external interface that is sufficient but as simple as possible. This is sort of the reverse of Concept #4. If the device interface is insufficient, users may start ripping the top off the device, in direct violation of the laws of God and Society — or at least the liability laws of the Great State of Texas. And believe me, you do not want to violate the laws of the great state of Texas. On the flip side, if the device interface is too complex, no one will buy the device, or, at least, no one will use all of its features.

People complain constantly that their VCRs are too complex (this is less of a problem with today's on-screen controls). These devices have too many buttons with too many different functions. Often, the same button has different functions, depending upon the state of the machine. In addition, no two VCRs seem to have the same interface. For whatever reason, the VCR projects an interface that is too difficult and too nonstandard for most people to use.

Compare this with an automobile. It would be difficult to argue that a car is less complicated than a VCR. However, people don't seem to have much trouble driving them. I can think of at least three significant differences between automobiles and VCRs.

All automobiles offer more or less the same controls in more or less the same place. For example, true story, my sister once had a car — need I say, a French car — with the light control on the left-hand side of the steering wheel, where the turn signal handle normally would be. You pushed down on the light lever to turn off the lights, and you raised the lever to turn them on. This may seem like a small difference, but I never did learn to turn left in that car at night without turning off the lights.

Well-designed autos do not use the same control to perform more than one operation depending upon the state of the car. I can think of only one exception to this rule: Some buttons on most cruise controls are overloaded with multiple functions.

Object-Oriented Concept #4 — Access Control

A microwave oven must be built so that no combination of keystrokes that I can enter on the front keypad will cause the oven to hurt me. Certainly, some combinations don't do anything. However, no sequence of keystrokes should

- ✔ **Break the device.** You may be able to put the device into some sort of strange state in which it won't do anything until you reset it, like throwing an internal breaker. However, you shouldn't be able to break the device from the front panel — unless, of course, you throw it to the ground in frustration. The manufacturer of such a device would probably have to send out some type of fix for a device like that.

- ✔ **Cause the device to catch fire and burn down the house.** Now, as bad as it might be for the device to break itself, catching fire is much worse. We live in a litigious society. The corporate officers of the manufacturer would likely end up in jail, especially if I have anything to say about it.

However, in order to enforce these two rules, you have to take some responsibility. You can't make any modifications to the inside of the device.

Almost all kitchen devices of any complexity, including microwave ovens, have a small seal to keep consumers from reaching inside the device. If that seal is broken, indicating that the cover of the device has been removed, the manufacturer no longer bears any responsibility. If I modify the internals of an oven, I am responsible if it subsequently catches fire and burns down the house.

Similarly, a class must be able to control access to its data members. No sequence of calls to class members should cause my program to crash. The class cannot possibly ensure this if external elements have access to the internal state of the class. The class must be able to keep critical data members inaccessible to the outside world.

How Does C# Support Object-Oriented Concepts?

Okay, how does C# implement object-oriented programming? In a sense, this is the wrong question. C# is an object-oriented language; however, it doesn't implement object-oriented programming — the programmer does. You can certainly write a non-object-oriented program in C# or any other language. Something like "you can lead a horse to water" comes to mind. But you can easily write an object-oriented program in C#.

C# provides the features necessary for writing object-oriented programs:

- ✔ **Controlled access:** C# controls the way in which members can be accessed. C# keywords enable you to declare some members wide open to the `public` while `internal` members are `protected` from view and some secrets are kept `private`. Notice the little hints. Access control secrets are let out in Chapter 11.

- ✔ **Specialization:** C# supports specialization through a mechanism known as *class inheritance*. One class inherits the members of another class. For example, you can create a `Car` class as a particular type of `Vehicle`. Chapter 12 specializes in specialization.

- ✔ **Polymorphism:** This feature enables an object to perform an operation the way it wants to. The `Rocket` type of `Vehicle` may implement the `Start` operation much differently from the way my `Car` type of `Vehicle` does. At least, I hope it does every time I turn the key in my car — with my car you never know. Chapters 13 and 14 find their own way of describing polymorphism.

Chapter 11

Holding a Class Responsible

A class must be held responsible for its actions. Just as a microwave oven shouldn't burst into flames if I press the wrong key, a class shouldn't allow itself to roll over and die when presented with incorrect data.

To be held responsible for its actions, a class must ensure that its initial state is correct, and control its subsequent state so it remains valid. C# provides both of these capabilities.

Restricting Access to Class Members

Simple classes define all their members as `public`. Consider a `BankAccount` program that maintains a `balance` data member to retain the balance in each account. Making that data member `public` puts everyone on the honor system.

I don't know about your bank, but my bank is not nearly so forthcoming as to leave a pile of money and a register for me to mark down every time I add money to or take money away from the pile. After all, I might forget to mark my withdrawals in the register. I'm not as young as I used to be — my memory is beginning to fade.

Controlling access avoids little mistakes like forgetting to mark a withdrawal here or there. It also manages to avoid some really big mistakes with withdrawals.

I know exactly what you functional types out there are thinking: "Just make a rule that other classes can't access the balance data member directly, and that's that." That approach may work in theory, but in practice it never does. People start out with good intentions (like my intentions to work out every day), but those good intentions get crushed under the weight of schedule pressures to get the product out the door. Speaking of weight . . . .

A public example of public BankAccount

The following example BankAccount class declares all of its methods public but declares the two data members nNextAccount and dBalance to be private:

```
// BankAccount - create a bank account using a double
//               variable to store the account balance;
//               (keep the balance in a private variable
//               to hide its implementation from the
//               outside world)
using System;
namespace DoubleBankAccount
{
  public class Class1
  {
    public static void Main(string[] args)
    {
      // open a bank account
      Console.WriteLine("Create a bank account object");
      BankAccount ba = new BankAccount();
      ba.InitBankAccount();
      // accessing the balance via the Deposit()
      // method is OK - Deposit() has access to all
      // the data members
      ba.Deposit(10);
      // accessing the data member directly is a compile
      // time error
      Console.WriteLine("Just in case you get this far"
                    + "\nThe following is supposed to "
                    + "generate a compile error");
      ba.dBalance += 10;
      // wait for user to acknowledge the results
      Console.WriteLine("Press Enter to terminate...");
      Console.Read();
    }
  }
  // BankAccount - define a class that represents a simple account
  public class BankAccount
  {
    private static int nNextAccountNumber = 1000;
    private int nAccountNumber;
    // maintain the balance as a single double variable
    private double dBalance;
    // Init - initialize a bank account with the next
    //        account id and a balance of 0
    public void InitBankAccount()
```

```
        {
            nAccountNumber = ++nNextAccountNumber;
            dBalance = 0.0;
        }
        // GetBalance — return the current balance
        public double GetBalance()
        {
            return dBalance;
        }
        // AccountNumber
        public int GetAccountNumber()
        {
            return nAccountNumber;
        }
        public void SetAccountNumber(int nAccountNumber)
        {
            this.nAccountNumber = nAccountNumber;
        }
        // Deposit — any positive deposit is allowed
        public void Deposit(double dAmount)
        {
            if (dAmount > 0.0)
            {
                dBalance += dAmount;
            }
        }
        // Withdraw — you can withdraw any amount up to the
        //           balance; return the amount withdrawn
        public double Withdraw(double dWithdrawal)
        {
            if (dBalance <= dWithdrawal)
            {
                dWithdrawal = dBalance;
            }
            dBalance -= dWithdrawal;
            return dWithdrawal;
        }
        // GetString — return the account data as a string
        public string GetString()
        {
            string s = String.Format("#{0} = {1:C}",
                                GetAccountNumber(),
                                GetBalance());
            return s;
        }
    }
}
```

Remember that in this code `dBalance -= dWithdrawal` is the same as `dBalance = dBalance - dWithdrawal`. C# programmers tend to use the shortest notation available.

Marking a member `public` makes that member available to any other code within your program.

The `BankAccount` class provides a method `InitBankAccount()` to initialize the members of the class, a `Deposit()` method to handle deposits, and a `Withdraw()` method to perform withdrawals. The `Deposit()` and `Withdraw()`

methods even provide some rudimentary rules like "you can't deposit a negative number" and "you can't withdraw more than you have in your account" — both good rules for a bank, I'm sure you'll agree. However, everyone's on the honor system as long as dBalance is accessible to external methods. (In this context, *external* means "external to the class but within the same program.")

Before you get too excited, however, notice that the program doesn't build. Attempts to do so generate the following error message:

```
'DoubleBankAccount.BankAccount.dBalance' is inaccessible due to its protection
                level.
```

I don't know why it doesn't just come out and say, "Hey, this is private so keep your mitts off," but that's essentially what it means. The statement ba.dBalance += 10; is illegal because dBalance is not accessible to Main(). Replacing this line with ba.Deposit(10) solves the problem.

The default access type is private. Forgetting to declare a member specifically is the same as declaring it private. However, you should include the private keyword to remove any doubt.

Jumping ahead — other levels of security

This section depends upon some knowledge of inheritance (Chapter 12) and namespaces (Chapter 16). You can skip it for now if you want but just know it's here when you need it.

C# provides other levels of security besides just public and private:

- ✔ A public member is accessible to any class in the program.
- ✔ A private member is accessible only from the current class.
- ✔ A protected member is accessible from the current class and any subclass.
- ✔ An internal member is accessible from any class within the current namespace (essentially, from any group of C# modules that you want to specify, which might mean all the modules that you write for the program but not those that your buddy writes).
- ✔ An internal protected member is accessible from the current class and any subclass and from classes within the same module.

Keeping a member hidden by declaring it private offers the maximum amount of security. However, in many cases, you don't need that level of security. After all, the members of a subclass already depend upon the members of the base class, so protected offers a nice, comfortable level of security.

If you declare each module to be a different namespace, declaring a member internal makes it available only from within the module. If, on the other hand, you use a single namespace for all your modules, not much difference exists between internal or internal protected and public.

Why Worry About Access Control?

Declaring the internal members of a class public is a bad idea for at least these reasons:

- ✔ **With all data members public, you can't easily determine when and how data members are getting modified.** Why bother building checks into the Deposit() and Withdraw() methods? In fact, why bother with these methods at all? Any method of any class can modify these elements at any time. If other functions can access these data members, they almost certainly will.

  My BankAccount program may execute for an hour or so before I notice that one of the accounts has a negative balance. The Withdraw() method would have made sure this didn't happen. Obviously, some other function accessed the balance without going through Withdraw(). Figuring out which function is responsible and under what conditions is a very difficult problem.

- ✔ **Exposing all the data members of the class makes the interface too complicated.** As a programmer using the BankAccount class, I don't want to know about the internals of the class. I just need to know that I can deposit and withdraw funds.

- ✔ **Exposing internal elements leads to a distribution of the class rules.** For example, my BankAccount class will not allow the balance to go negative under any circumstances. That's a business rule that should be isolated within the Withdraw() method. Otherwise, I have to add this check everywhere the balance is updated.

What happens when the bank decides to change the rules so that "valued customers" are allowed to carry a slightly negative balance for a short period in order to avoid unintended overdrafts? I now have to search through the program to update every section of code that accesses the balance to make sure the checks — not the bank checks — are changed.

Accessor methods

If you look more carefully at the BankAccount class, you will notice a few other methods. One, GetString(), returns a string version of the account fit for presentation to any Console.WriteLine() for display. However, displaying the contents of a `BankAccount` object may be difficult if the contents are inaccessible. In addition, using the "Render unto Caesar" policy, the class should have the right to decide how it gets displayed.

In addition, you will notice one method, `GetBalance()`, and a set of methods: `GetAccountNumber()` and `SetAccountNumber()`. You may wonder why I would bother to declare a data member like `dBalance` `private` but provide a method `GetBalance()` to return its value. I actually have two reasons. First, `GetBalance()` does not provide a means for modifying `dBalance` — it merely returns its value. This makes the balance read-only. To use the analogy of an actual bank, I can look at my balance any time I want; I just can't take money out of it without going through the bank's withdrawal mechanism.

Second, `GetBalance()` hides the internal format of the class from external methods. It's entirely possible that `GetBalance()` goes through an extensive calculation regarding the reading of receipts, the addition of account charges, and whatever else my bank may want to subtract from my balance. External functions don't know and don't care. Of course, I care what fees are being charged. I just can't do anything about it, short of changing banks.

Finally, `GetBalance()` provides a mechanism for making internal changes to the class without the need to change the users of `BankAccount`. If the FDIC mandates that my bank store deposits differently, that shouldn't change the way I access my account.

Access control to the rescue — an example

The following `DoubleBankAccount` program demonstrates a potential flaw in the `BankAccount` program. The entire program is on your CD-ROM; however, the following listing only shows `Main()` — the only portion of the program that differs from the earlier `BankAccount` program:

```
// DoubleBankAccount - create a bank account using a double
//                     variable to store the account balance;
//                     (keep the balance in a private variable
//                     to hide its implementation from the
//                     outside world)
namespace Test
{
  using System;
  public class Class1
  {
    public static int Main(string[] strings)
    {
      // open a bank account
      Console.WriteLine("Create a bank account object");
      BankAccount ba = new BankAccount();
      ba.InitBankAccount();
      // make a deposit
```

```
        double dDeposit = 123.454;
        Console.WriteLine("Depositing {0:C}", dDeposit);
        ba.Deposit(dDeposit);
        // account balance
        Console.WriteLine("Account = {0}",
                          ba.GetString());
 \
        // here's the problem
        double dAddition = 0.002;
        Console.WriteLine("Adding {0:C}", dAddition);
        ba.Deposit(dAddition);
        // resulting balance
        Console.WriteLine("Resulting account = {0}",
                          ba.GetString());
        // wait for user to acknowledge the results
        Console.WriteLine("Press Enter to terminate...");
        Console.Read();
        return 0;
      }
    }
```

The `Main()` function creates a bank account and then deposits $123.454, an amount that contains a fractional number of cents. `Main()` then deposits a small fraction of a cent to the balance and displays the resulting balance.

The output from this program appears as follows:

```
Create a bank account object
Depositing $123.45
Account = #1001 = $123.45
Adding $0.00
Resulting account = #1001 = $123.46
Press Enter to terminate...
```

Users start to complain. I just can't reconcile my checkbook with my bank statement. Personally, I'm happy if I can get to the nearest $100, but some people insist that their account match to the penny. Apparently, the program has a bug.

The problem, of course, is that $123.454 shows up as $123.45. To avoid the problem, my bank decides to round off deposits and withdrawals to the nearest cent. Deposit $123.454, and the bank takes that extra 0.4 cents. On the other side, the bank gives up enough 0.4 cents that everything balances out in the long run.

The easiest way to do this is by converting the bank accounts over to `decimal` and using the `RoundOff()` method, as shown in the `DecimalBankAccount` program:

```
// DecimalBankAccount - create a bank account using decimal
//                      variable to store the account balance;
using System;
namespace DecimalBankAccount
{
  public class Class1
  {
```

```csharp
public static void Main(string[] args)
{
  // open a bank account
  Console.WriteLine("Create a bank account object");
  BankAccount ba = new BankAccount();
  ba.InitBankAccount();
  // make a deposit
  double dDeposit = 123.454;
  Console.WriteLine("Depositing {0:C}", dDeposit);
  ba.Deposit(dDeposit);
  // account balance
  Console.WriteLine("Account = {0}",
                    ba.GetString());
  // now add in a very small amount
  double dAddition = 0.002;
  Console.WriteLine("Adding {0:C}", dAddition);
  ba.Deposit(dAddition);
  // resulting balance
  Console.WriteLine("Resulting account = {0}",
                    ba.GetString());
  // wait for user to acknowledge the results
  Console.WriteLine("Press Enter to terminate...");
  Console.Read();
}
}
// BankAccount - define a class that represents a simple account
public class BankAccount
{
  private static int nNextAccountNumber = 1000;
  private int nAccountNumber;
  // maintain the balance as a single decimal variable
  private decimal mBalance;
  // Init - initialize a bank account with the next
  //        account id and a balance of 0
  public void InitBankAccount()
  {
    nAccountNumber = ++nNextAccountNumber;
    mBalance = 0;
  }
  // GetBalance - return the current balance
  public double GetBalance()
  {
    return (double)mBalance;
  }
  // AccountNumber
  public int GetAccountNumber()
  {
    return nAccountNumber;
  }
  public void SetAccountNumber(int nAccountNumber)
  {
    this.nAccountNumber = nAccountNumber;
  }
  // Deposit - any positive deposit is allowed
  public void Deposit(double dAmount)
  {
    if (dAmount > 0.0)
    {
      // round off the double to the nearest cent before
      // depositing
      decimal mTemp = (decimal)dAmount;
      mTemp = Decimal.Round(mTemp, 2);
```

```
        mBalance += mTemp;
    }
}
// Withdraw - you can withdraw any amount up to the
//           balance; return the amount withdrawn
public decimal Withdraw(decimal dWithdrawal)
{
    if (mBalance <= dWithdrawal)
    {
        dWithdrawal = mBalance;
    }
    mBalance -= dWithdrawal;
    return dWithdrawal;
}
// GetString - return the account data as a string
public string GetString()
{
    string s = String.Format("#{0} = {1:C}",
                        GetAccountNumber(),
                        GetBalance());
    return s;
}
}
}
```

I've converted all the internal representations to decimal values, a type
better adapted to handling bank account balances than double in any case.
The Deposit() method now uses the Decimal.Round() function to round
off the deposit amount to the nearest cent before making the deposit. The
output from the program is now as expected:

```
Create a bank account object
Depositing $123.45
Account = #1001 = $123.45
Adding $0.00
Resulting account = #1001 = $123.45
Press Enter to terminate...
```

So what?

You could argue that I should have written the BankAccount program using
decimal input arguments to begin with, and I would probably agree. But the
point is that it wasn't. Other applications were written using double as the
form of storage. A problem arose. The BankAccount class was able to fix the
problem internally with no changes to the application software.

In this case, the only function affected was Main(), but the effects could have
extended to dozens of functions that accessed bank accounts, and those
functions could have been spread over hundreds of modules. None of those
functions would have to change because the fix was within the confines of
the BankAccount class. This would not have been possible if the internal
members of the class had been exposed to external functions.

Internal changes to a class will still require some retesting of other code, even though you didn't have to modify that code.

Defining class properties

The `GetX()` and `SetX()` methods demonstrated in the `BankAccount` programs are called *access functions* or simply *accessors*. Although they signify good programming habit in theory, access functions can get clumsy in practice. For example, the following code is necessary to increment `nAccountNumber` by 1.

```
SetAccountNumber(GetAccountNumber() + 1);
```

C# defines a construct called a *property* which makes using access functions much easier. The following code snippet defines a read-write property, `AccountNumber`:

```
public int AccountNumber
{
  get{return nAccountNumber;}
  set{nAccountNumber = value;}
}
```

The `get` section is implemented whenever the property is read, while the `set` section is invoked on the write. The following `Balance` property is read-only because only the `set` section is defined:

```
public double Balance
{
  get
  {
    return (double)mBalance;
  }
}
```

In use, these properties appear as follows:

```
BankAccount ba = new BankAccount();
// write the account number property
ba.AccountNumber = 1001;
// read both properties
Console.WriteLine("#{0} = {1:C}",
                  ba.AccountNumber, ba.Balance);
```

The properties `AccountNumber` and `Balance` look very much like public data members, both in appearance and in use. However, properties enable the class to protect internal members (`Balance` is a read-only property) and hide their implementation. Notice that `Balance` performs a conversion — it could have performed any number of calculations.

By convention, the names of properties begin with a capital letter.

Properties are not necessarily inefficient. The C# compiler can optimize a simple accessor to the point that it generates no more machine code than accessing the data member directly. This is important not only to an application program, but also to C# itself. The C# library uses properties throughout.

Static properties

A static (class) data member may be exposed through a static property, as shown in the following simplistic example:

```
public class BankAccount
{
  private static int nNextAccountNumber = 1000;
  public static int NextAccountNumber
  {
    get{return nNextAccountNumber;}
  }
  // . . .
}
```

The `NextAccountNumber` property is accessed through the class because it isn't a property of any single object:

```
// read the account number property
int nValue = BankAccount.NextAccountNumber;
```

Properties with side-effects

A `get` operation can perform extra work other than simply retrieving the associated property:

```
public static int AccountNumber
{
  // retrieve the property and set it up for the
  // next retrieval
  get{return ++nNextAccountNumber;}
}
```

This property increments the static account number member before returning the result. This probably is not a good idea, however, because the user of the property gets no clue that anything is happening other than the actual reading of the property.

Like the accessor functions that they mimic, properties should not change the state of the class.

Getting Your Objects Off to a Good Start — Constructors

Controlling class access is only half the problem. An object needs a good start in life if it is to grow. A class can supply an initialization method that the application calls to get things started, but what if the application forgets to call the function? The class starts out with garbage, and the situation doesn't get any better after that. If you're to hold the class accountable, you have to make sure it gets a chance to start out correctly.

C# solves that problem by calling the initialization function for you — for example:

```
MyObject mo = new MyObject();
```

In other words, this statement not only grabs an object out of a special memory area, but it also initializes that object by calling an initialization function.

Don't confuse the terms *class* and *object*. Dog is a class. My dog Scooter is an object of class Dog.

The C# Provided Constructor

C# is pretty good at keeping track of whether a variable has been initialized. C# will not allow you to use an uninitialized variable. For example, the following code generates a compile time error:

```
public static void Main(string[] args)
{
   int n;
   double d;
   double  dCalculatedValue = n + d;
}
```

C# tracks the fact that neither n nor d have been assigned a value and doesn't allow them to be used in the expression. Compiling this tiny program generates the following compiler errors:

```
Use of unassigned local variable 'n'
Use of unassigned local variable 'd'
```

By comparison, C# provides a default constructor that initializes the contents of an object to 0 for intrinsic variables, false for Booleans, and null for object references. Consider the following simple example program:

```
using System;
namespace DecimalBankAccount
{
   public class Class1
   {
      public static void Main(string[] args)
      {
         // first create an object
         MyObject localObject =  new MyObject();
         Console.WriteLine("localObject.n is {0}", localObject.n);
         if (localObject.nextObject == null)
```

```
      {
        Console.WriteLine("localObject.nextObject is null");
      }
      // wait for user to acknowledge the results
      Console.WriteLine("Press Enter to terminate...");
      Console.Read();
    }
  }
  public class MyObject
  {
    internal int n;
    internal MyObject nextObject;
  }
}
```

This program defines a class MyObject, which contains both a simple variable n of type int and a reference to an object, nextObject. The Main() function creates a MyObject and then displays the initial contents of n and nextObject.

The output from executing the program appears as follows:

```
localObject.n is 0
localObject.nextObject is null
Press Enter to terminate...
```

C# executes some small piece of code when the object is created to initialize the object and its members. Left to their own devices, the data members localObject.n and nextObject would contain random, garbage values.

The code that initializes values when they are created is called the *constructor*.

The Default Constructor

C# ensures that an object starts life in a known state: all zeroes. However, for many classes (probably most classes), all zeroes is not a valid state. Consider the BankAccount class from earlier in this chapter:

```
public class BankAccount
{
  int nAccountNumber;
  double dBalance;
  // . . .other members
}
```

Although an initial balance of zero is probably okay, an account number of 0 definitely is not the hallmark of a valid bank account.

The BankAccount class includes the InitBankAccount() method to initialize the object. However, this approach puts too much responsibility on the application software. If the application fails to invoke the InitBankAccount() function, the bank account methods may not work through no fault of their own. A class should not rely upon external functions to start the object in a legal state.

To get around this problem, the class can provide a special function that C# calls automatically when the object is created: the *class constructor*. The constructor could have been called Init(), Start(), or Create(), just as long as we all agree on the name. Instead, the constructor carries the name of the class. Thus, a constructor for the BankAccount class appears as follows:

```
public int Main(string[] args)
{
  BankAccount ba = new BankAccount();
}
public class BankAccount
{
  // bank accounts start at 1000 and increase sequentially
  // from there
  static int nNextAccountNumber = 1000;
  // maintain the account number and balance for each object
  int nAccountNumber;
  double dBalance;
  // BankAccount constructor
  public BankAccount()
  {
    nAccountNumber = ++nNextAccountNumber;
    dBalance = 0.0;
  }
  // . . . other members . . .
}
```

The contents of the BankAccount constructor are the same as those of the original Init...() method. However, the way you declare and use the method differs:

✔ The constructor carries the same name as the class.

✔ The constructor has no return type, not even void.

✔ Main() does not need to invoke any extra function in order to initialize the object when it is created.

Let's construct something

Try one of these constructor thingees out. Consider the following program, DemonstrateDefaultConstructor:

```
// DemonstrateDefaultConstructor - demonstrate how default
//                                 constructors work; create a class
//                                 with a constructor and then step
//                                 through a few scenarios
using System;
namespace DemonstrateDefaultConstructor
{
  // MyObject - create a class with a noisy constructor
  //            and an internal object
  public class MyObject
  {
    // this member is a property of the class
    static MyOtherObject staticObj = new MyOtherObject();
    // this member is a property of the object
    MyOtherObject dynamicObj;
    public MyObject()
    {
      Console.WriteLine("MyObject constructor starting");
      dynamicObj = new MyOtherObject();
      Console.WriteLine("MyObject constructor ending");
    }
  }
  // MyOtherObject- this class also has a noisy constructor
  //                but no internal members
  public class MyOtherObject
  {
    public MyOtherObject()
    {
      Console.WriteLine("MyOtherObject constructing");
    }
  }
  public class Class1
  {
    public static void Main(string[] args)
    {
      Console.WriteLine("Main() starting");
      // create an object
      MyObject localObject = new MyObject();
      // wait for user to acknowledge the results
      Console.WriteLine("Press Enter to terminate...");
      Console.Read();
    }
  }
}
```

Executing this program generates the following output:

```
Main() starting
MyOtherObject constructing
MyObject constructor starting
MyOtherObject constructing
MyObject constructor ending
Press Enter to terminate...
```

I'll reconstruct what just happened here:

1. The program starts, and `Main()` outputs the initial message.

2. `Main()` creates a *localObject* of type `MyObject`.

3. MyObject contains a static member staticObj of class MyOtherObject. All static data members are created before the first MyObject is constructed. In this case, C# populates staticObj with a newly created MyOtherObject before passing control on to the MyObject constructor. This step accounts for the second message.

4. The constructor for MyObject is given control. It outputs the initial message, MyObject constructor starting.

5. The MyObject constructor creates an object of class MyOtherObject using the new operator, creating the second message from the MyOtherObject constructor.

6. Control returns back to the MyObject constructor, which returns to Main().

7. Job well done!

Extra credit — Executing the constructor from the debugger

Just for extra credit, execute the same program from the debugger this time:

1. **Rebuild the program: Choose Build⇨Build.**

2. **Before you start executing the program from the debugger, set a break point at the Console.WriteLine() call in the MyOtherObject constructor.**

   To set a break point, click in the trough on the left-hand side of the display, next to the line at which you want to stop.

   Figure 11-1 shows my display with the breakpoint set.

3. **Rather that choosing Debug⇨Start, choose Debug⇨Step Into (or, better yet, press the F11 key).**

   Your menus should change up a bit and then a bright yellow bar appears across the Console.WriteLine() call.

4. **Press the F11 key again.**

   Your display should now look like that shown in Figure 11-2.

5. **Choose Debug⇨Run or press F5 and the program executes up to the breakpoint in MyOtherObject, as shown by the bar in Figure 11-3.**

6. **Press the F11 key twice more and you're back at the beginning of the MyObject constructor, as shown in Figure 11-4.**

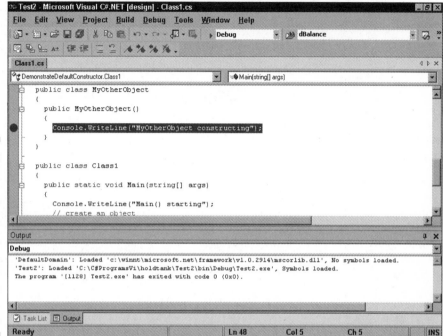

Figure 11-1:
The red highlighting in the MyOther Object constructor indicates the presence of a breakpoint.

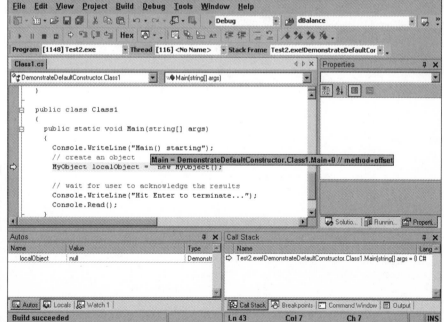

Figure 11-2:
The Visual Studio debugger display, right before jumping into constructor-ville.

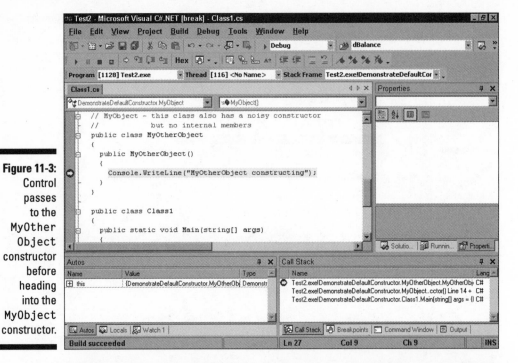

Figure 11-3:
Control passes to the MyOther Object constructor before heading into the MyObject constructor.

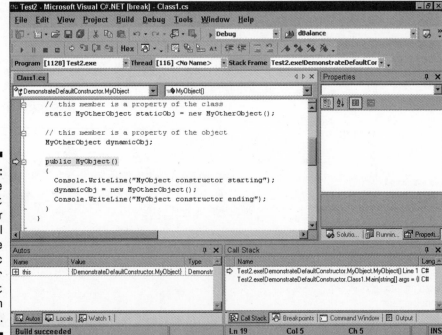

Figure 11-4:
The MyObject constructor gets control after the static MyOther Object has been constructed.

7. Continue pressing the F11 key as you walk through the program.

Don't forget to continue through the `Console.Read()` command. You'll need to press Enter in the program window before you can continue single-stepping back in the Visual Studio debugger window.

Initializing an object directly — the default constructor

You might think that almost every class would have a default constructor of some type, and in a way, you are correct. However, C# enables you to initialize data members directly using initialization statements.

Thus, I could have written the `BankAccount` class as follows:

```
public class BankAccount
{
  // bank accounts start at 1000 and increase sequentially
  // from there
  static int nNextAccountNumber = 1000;
  // maintain the account number and balance for each object
  int nAccountNumber = ++nNextAccountNumber;
  double dBalance = 0.0;
  // . . . other members . . .
}
```

Both `nAccountNumber` and `dBalance` are assigned a value as part of their declaration. This has the same effect as a constructor.

Be very clear about exactly what's happening. You might think that this statement sets `dBalance` to 0.0 directly. However, `dBalance` exists only as a part of an object. Thus, the assignment is not executed until a `BankAccount` object is created. In fact, this assignment is executed every time an object is created.

C# takes any initializers that appear in the class declaration and gathers them into an initial constructor.

Initializers are executed in the order of their appearance in the class declaration. If C# encounters both initializers and a constructor, the initializers are executed before the body of the constructor.

Let's see that construction stuff with initializers

Move the call `new MyOtherObject()` from the `MyObject` constructor to the declaration itself, as follows, and then rerun the program:

```
public class MyObject
{
  // this member is a property of the class
  static MyOtherObject staticObj = new MyOtherObject();
  // this member is a property of the object
  MyOtherObject dynamicObj = new MyOtherObject();
  public MyObject()
  {
    Console.WriteLine("MyObject constructor starting");
    Console.WriteLine("MyObject constructor ending");
  }
}
```

The output from this modified program appears as follows:

```
Main() starting
MyOtherObject constructing
MyOtherObject constructing
MyObject constructor starting
MyObject constructor ending
Press Enter to terminate...
```

You can find the entire program on the CD, under the illustrious name of `DemonstrateConstructorWithInitializer`.

Overloading the Constructor (Is That Like Overtaxing a Carpenter?)

You can overload constructors, just as you can overload any other method.

Overloading a function means defining two functions with the same short name but with different types of arguments. See Chapter 7 for details.

Suppose you wanted to provide two ways to create a `BankAccount`: one with a zero balance like mine most of the time, and another bank account with some initial value:

```
// BankAccountWithMultipleConstructors -
//                 provide our trusty bank account
//                 with a number of constructors, one
//                 for every occasion
using System;
namespace BankAccountWithMultipleConstructors
{
  using System;
  public class Class1
  {
    public static int Main(string[] args)
    {
      // create a bank account with valid initial values
      BankAccount ba1 = new BankAccount();
```

```
      Console.WriteLine(ba1.GetString());
      BankAccount ba2 = new BankAccount(100);
      Console.WriteLine(ba2.GetString());
      BankAccount ba3 = new BankAccount(1234, 200);
      Console.WriteLine(ba3.GetString());
      // wait for user to acknowledge
      Console.WriteLine("Press Enter to terminate...");
      Console.Read();
      return 0;
    }
  }
  // BankAccount - simulate a simple bank account
  public class BankAccount
  {
    // bank accounts start at 1000 and increase sequentially
    // from there
    static int nNextAccountNumber = 1000;
    // maintain the account number and balance
    int nAccountNumber;
    double dBalance;
    // provide a series of constructors depending upon the need
    public BankAccount()
    {
      nAccountNumber = ++nNextAccountNumber;
      dBalance = 0.0;
    }

    public BankAccount(double dInitialBalance)
    {
      // repeat some of the code from the default constructor
      nAccountNumber = ++nNextAccountNumber;
      // now the code unique to this constructor
      // start with an initial balance as long as it's positive
      if (dInitialBalance < 0)
      {
        dInitialBalance = 0;
      }
      dBalance = dInitialBalance;
    }
    public BankAccount(int nInitialAccountNumber,
                       double dInitialBalance)
    {
      // ignore negative account numbers
      if (nInitialAccountNumber <= 0)
      {
        nInitialAccountNumber = ++nNextAccountNumber;
      }
      nAccountNumber = nInitialAccountNumber;
      // start with an initial balance as long as it's positive
      if (dInitialBalance < 0)
      {
        dInitialBalance = 0;
      }
      dBalance = dInitialBalance;
    }
    public string GetString()
    {
      return String.Format("#{0} = {1:N}",
                           nAccountNumber, dBalance);
    }
  }
}
```

C# no longer provides a default constructor for you if you define your own constructor, no matter what type it might be.

This version of the program named `BankAccountWithMultipleConstructors` provides three constructors:

- ✔ The first constructor assigns an account ID and sets a balance of 0.
- ✔ The second constructor assigns an account ID but initializes the account with a positive balance. Negative balances are ignored.
- ✔ The third constructor allows the user to specify a positive account number and a positive balance.

`Main()` creates a different bank account using each of the three constructors and then outputs the objects created. The output from executing the program is as follows:

```
#1001 = 0.00
#1002 = 100.00
#1234 = 200.00
Press Enter to terminate...
```

A real-world class would perform a good deal more testing of the input parameters to the constructor, to make sure they're legal.

You differentiate constructors using the same rules that apply to functions. The first object to be constructed in `Main()`, `ba1`, is created with no arguments and thus is vectored to the default constructor to receive the default account ID and a balance of 0. The second account, `ba2`, is sent to the `BankAccount(double)` constructor to get the next bank account id, but is created with an initial value of 100. The third little piggie, `ba3`, goes for the full-meal deal, `BankAccount(int, double)`, and gets his own bank account id and an initial balance.

Avoiding Duplication Among Constructors

Like a typical soap opera script, the three `BankAccount` constructors have significant amounts of duplication. As you can imagine, the situation would get much worse in real-world classes that may have many constructors and even more data elements to initialize. In addition, the tests on input data can get more involved in a real-world class than on a Yahoo! Web page. Duplicating these business rules is both tedious and error prone. The checks can easily get out of synch. For example, through a coding error, two constructors might apply different sets of rules against the balance. Such errors are very difficult to find.

You would like to have one constructor call the other, but constructors are not functions — you can't just call them. However, you can create some alternative function that does the actual construction and pass control to it, as demonstrated in this BankAccountConstructorsAndFunction program:

```
// BankAccountContructorsAndFunction -
//                   provide our trusty bank account
//                   with a number of constructors, one
//                   for every occasion
using System;
namespace BankAccountContructorsAndFunction
{
  using System;
  public class Class1
  {
    public static int Main(string[] args)
    {
      // create a bank account with valid initial values
      BankAccount ba1 = new BankAccount();
      Console.WriteLine(ba1.GetString());
      BankAccount ba2 = new BankAccount(100);
      Console.WriteLine(ba2.GetString());
      BankAccount ba3 = new BankAccount(1234, 200);
      Console.WriteLine(ba3.GetString());
      // wait for user to acknowledge
      Console.WriteLine("Press Enter to terminate...");
      Console.Read();
      return 0;
    }
  }
  // BankAccount - simulate a simple bank account
  public class BankAccount
  {
    // bank accounts start at 1000 and increase sequentially
    // from there
    static int nNextAccountNumber = 1000;
    // maintain the account number and balance
    int nAccountNumber;
    double dBalance;
    // place all the real initialization code
    // in a separate, conventional function
    public BankAccount()
    {
      Init(++nAccountNumber, 0.0);
    }
    public BankAccount(double dInitialBalance)
    {
      Init(++nAccountNumber, dInitialBalance);
    }
    // the most specific constructor does all the
    // real work
    public BankAccount(int nInitialAccountNumber,
                       double dInitialBalance)
    {
      Init(nInitialAccountNumber, dInitialBalance);
    }
    private void Init(int nInitialAccountNumber,
                      double dInitialBalance)
    {
      nAccountNumber = nInitialAccountNumber;
      // start with an initial balance as long as it's positive
      if (dInitialBalance < 0)
```

```
        {
            dInitialBalance = 0;
        }
        dBalance = dInitialBalance;
    }
    public string GetString()
    {
        return String.Format("#{0} = {1:N}",
                             nAccountNumber, dBalance);
    }
  }
}
```

Here, an Init() method does the actual work of construction. However, this approach isn't exactly kosher for several reasons — not the least of which is the fact that you are now calling a method of the object before the object has been fully constructed. That's a very dangerous thing to do.

Fortunately, it isn't necessary. One constructor can refer to another, using a variation of the this keyword:

```
// BankAccountContructorsAndThis -
//                   provide our trusty bank account
//                   with a number of constructors, one
//                   for every occasion
using System;
namespace BankAccountContructorsAndThis
{
  using System;
  public class Class1
  {
    public static int Main(string[] args)
    {
      // create a bank account with valid initial values
      BankAccount ba1 = new BankAccount();
      Console.WriteLine(ba1.GetString());
      BankAccount ba2 = new BankAccount(100);
      Console.WriteLine(ba2.GetString());
      BankAccount ba3 = new BankAccount(1234, 200);
      Console.WriteLine(ba3.GetString());
      // wait for user to acknowledge
      Console.WriteLine("Press Enter to terminate...");
      Console.Read();
      return 0;
    }
  }
  // BankAccount — simulate a simple bank account
  public class BankAccount
  {
    // bank accounts start at 1000 and increase sequentially
    // from there
    static int nNextAccountNumber = 1000;
    // maintain the account number and balance
    int nAccountNumber;
    double dBalance;
    // invoke the more specific constructor by providing
    // default values for the missing arguments
    public BankAccount() : this(0, 0) {}
    public BankAccount(double dInitialBalance) :
                        this(0, dInitialBalance) {}
```

```
// the most specific constructor does all the
// real work
public BankAccount(int nInitialAccountNumber,
                   double dInitialBalance)
{
  // ignore negative account numbers; a zero account
  // number indicates that we should use the next available
  if (nInitialAccountNumber <= 0)
  {
    nInitialAccountNumber = ++nNextAccountNumber;
  }
  nAccountNumber = nInitialAccountNumber;
  // start with an initial balance as long as it's positive
  if (dInitialBalance < 0)
  {
    dInitialBalance = 0;
  }
  dBalance = dInitialBalance;
}
public string GetString()
{
  return String.Format("#{0} = {1:N}",
                       nAccountNumber, dBalance);
}
  }
}
```

This version of `BankAccount` provides the same three constructors as the previous version; however, rather than repeat the same tests in each constructor, both of the simpler constructors invoke the most flexible constructor, providing defaults for the missing arguments.

Creating an object using the default constructor invokes the `BankAccount()` constructor:

```
BankAccount bal = new BankAccount();
```

The `BankAccount()` constructor immediately passes control off to the `BankAccount(int, double)` constructor, passing it the default values 0 and 0.0:

```
public BankAccount() : this(0, 0) {}
```

The all-powerful third constructor has been updated to look for a zero bank account id and to supply a valid one instead.

Control returns to the default constructor after the invoked constructor has completed. The body of the default constructor is empty in this case.

Creating a bank account with a balance but default account id goes down the following path:

```
public BankAccount(double d) : this(0, d) {}
```

Being Object Stingy

You can't construct an object without a constructor of some sort. If you define your own constructor, C# takes its constructor away. Combining these two facts, you can create a class that can only be instantiated locally.

For example, only methods that are defined within the same namespace as BankAccount can create a BankAccount object with the constructor declared internal (see Chapter 16 for more on namespaces):

```
// BankAccount — simulate a simple bank account
public class BankAccount
{
  // bank accounts start at 1000 and increase sequentially
  // from there
  static int nNextAccountNumber = 1000;
  // maintain the account number and balance
  int nAccountNumber;
  double dBalance;
  // invoke the more specific constructor by providing
  // default values for the missing arguments
  internal BankAccount()
  {
    nAccountNumber = ++nNextAccountNumber;
    dBalance = 0;
  }
  public string GetString()
  {
    return String.Format("#{0} = {1:N}",
                         nAccountNumber, dBalance);
  }
}
```

Chapter 12

Inheritance — Is That All I Get?

*O*bject-oriented programming is based on three principles: the ability to control access (encapsulation), the ability to inherit from other classes, and the ability to respond appropriately (polymorphism).

Inheritance is a common concept. I am a human, except when I first wake up. I inherit certain properties from the class Human, such as my ability to converse, more or less, and my dependence upon air, food, and carbohydrate-based beverages with lots of caffeine. The class Human inherits its dependencies on air, water, and nourishment from the class Mammal, which inherits from the class Animal.

The capability of passing down properties is a powerful one. It enables you to describe things in an economical way. For example, if my son asks, "What's a duck?" I can say, "It's a bird that goes quack." Despite what you may think, that answer conveys a considerable amount of information. My son knows what a bird is, and now he knows all those same things about a duck plus the duck's additional property of "quackness."

Object-oriented languages express this inheritance relationship by allowing one class to inherit from another. This feature enables OO languages to generate a model that's closer to the real world than the model generated by languages that don't support inheritance.

Inheriting a Class

In the following `InheritanceExample` program, the class `SubClass` inherits from the class `BaseClass`:

```
// InheritanceExample - provide the simplest possible
//                      demonstration of inheritance
using System;
namespace InheritanceExample
{
  public class BaseClass
  {
    public int nDataMember;
    public void SomeMethod()
    {
      Console.WriteLine("SomeMethod()");
    }
  }
  public class SubClass : BaseClass
  {
    public void SomeOtherMethod()
    {
      Console.WriteLine("SomeOtherMethod()");
    }
  }
  public class Test
  {
    public static int Main(string[] args)
    {
      // create a base class object
      Console.WriteLine("Exercising a base class object:");
      BaseClass bc = new BaseClass();
      bc.nDataMember = 1;
      bc.SomeMethod();
      // now create a subclass element
      Console.WriteLine("Exercising a subclass object:");
      SubClass sc = new SubClass();
      sc.nDataMember = 2;
      sc.SomeMethod();
      sc.SomeOtherMethod();
      // wait for user to acknowledge the results
      Console.WriteLine("Press Enter to terminate...");
      Console.Read();
      return 0;
    }
  }
}
```

The class `BaseClass` is defined with a data member and a simple member function, `SomeMethod()`. The `BaseClass` object `bc` is created and exercised in `Main()`.

The class `SubClass` inherits from that class by placing the name of the class, `BaseClass`, after a colon in the class definition. `SubClass` gets all the members of `BaseClass` as its own, plus any members that it might add to the pile. `Main()` demonstrates that `SubClass` now has a data member, `nDataMember`, and a member function, `SomeMethod()`, to join the brand-new member of the family, little method `SomeOtherClass()` — and what a joy it is, too.

This is amazing

To make sense of our surroundings, humans build extensive taxonomies. For example, Fido is a special case of dog, which is a special case of canine, which is a special case of mammal, and so it goes. This ability to classify things shapes our understanding of the world.

In an object-oriented language like C#, we say that the class Student inherits from the class Person. We also say that Person is a base class of Student, and Student is a subclass of Person. Finally, we say that a Student **IS_A** Person. (Using all caps is a common way of expressing this unique relationship — I didn't make this up.)

Notice that the IS_A property is not reflexive: Although Student IS_A Person, the reverse

is not true. A Person IS_NOT_A Student. A statement like this always refers to the general case. It could be that a particular Person is, in fact, a Student. — lots of people who are members of class Person are not members of class Student. In addition, class Student has properties it does not share with class Person. For example, Student has a grade point average, but the ordinary Person does not.

The inheritance property is transitive. For example, if I define a new class GraduateStudent as a subclass of Student, then Graduate-Student is also Person. It must be that way: If a GraduateStudent IS_A Student and a Student IS_A Person, then a Graduate-Student IS_A Person. Q.E.D.

The program produces the expected output — actually, I'm sort of surprised whenever one of my programs works as expected:

```
Exercising a base class object:
SomeMethod()
Exercising a subclass object:
SomeMethod()
SomeOtherMethod()
Press Enter to terminate...
```

Why Do I Need Inheritance?

Inheritance serves several important functions. You might think that inheritance reduces the amount of typing. In a way it does — I don't need to repeat the properties of a Person when I'm describing a Student class. A more important, related issue is that major buzzword, *reuse*. Software scientists have known for some time that starting from scratch with each new project and rebuilding the same software components doesn't make much sense.

Compare the situation in software development to that of other industries. How many car manufacturers start by building their own wrenches and screwdrivers before they construct a car? And even if they did, how many would start over completely, building all new tools for the next model? Practitioners in other industries have found that starting with existing screws, bolts, nuts, and even larger off-the-shelf components such as motors and compressors makes more sense than starting from scratch.

Inheritance enables you to tweak existing software components. You can adapt existing classes to new applications without making internal modifications. The existing class is inherited into a new subclass that contains the necessary additions and modifications.

This capability carries with it a third benefit of inheritance. Suppose you inherit from some existing class. Later, you find that the base class has a bug you must correct. If you've modified the class to reuse it, you must manually check for, correct, and retest the bug in each application separately. If you've inherited the class without changes, you can generally stick the updated class into the other application without much hassle.

But the biggest benefit of inheritance is that it describes the way life is. Things inherit properties from each other. There's no getting around it. Basta! as my Italian grandmother would say.

A More Involved Example — Inheriting from a BankAccount Class

My bank maintains several types of bank accounts. One type, the savings account, has all the properties of a simple bank account plus the ability to accumulate interest. The following example `SimpleSavingsAccount` program models this relationship in C#.

To those faint of heart, you may want to steady yourself: This listing is a little on the long side; however, the pieces are fairly well divided.

```
// SimpleSavingsAccount - implement a SavingsAccount as a form of
//                        BankAccount; don't use any virtual methods
using System;
namespace SimpleSavingsAccount
{
    // BankAccount - simulate a bank account each of which
    //               carries an account id (which is assigned
    //               upon creation) and a balance
    public class BankAccount
    {
        // bank accounts start at 1000 and increase sequentially
        // from there
        public static int nNextAccountNumber = 1000;
        // maintain the account number and balance for each object
        public int nAccountNumber;
        public decimal mBalance;
        // Init - initialize a bank account with the next
        //        account id and the specified initial balance
        //        (default to zero)
```

```csharp
  public void InitBankAccount()
  {
    InitBankAccount(0);
  }
  public void InitBankAccount(decimal mInitialBalance)
  {
    nAccountNumber = ++nNextAccountNumber;
    mBalance = mInitialBalance;
  }
  // Balance
  public decimal Balance
  {
    get { return mBalance;}
  }
  // Deposit — any positive deposit is allowed
  public void Deposit(decimal mAmount)
  {
    if (mAmount > 0)
    {
      mBalance += mAmount;
    }
  }
  // Withdraw — you can withdraw any amount up to the
  //            balance; return the amount withdrawn
  public decimal Withdraw(decimal mWithdrawal)
  {
    if (mBalance <= mWithdrawal)
    {
      mWithdrawal = mBalance;
    }
    mBalance -= mWithdrawal;
    return mWithdrawal;
  }
  // ToString — stringify the account
  public string ToBankAccountString()
  {
    return String.Format("{0} - {1:C}",
      nAccountNumber, mBalance);
  }
}
// SavingsAccount — a bank account that draws interest
public class SavingsAccount : BankAccount
{
  public decimal mInterestRate;
  // InitSavingsAccount — input the rate expressed as a
  //                      rate between 0 and 100
  public void InitSavingsAccount(decimal mInterestRate)
  {
    InitSavingsAccount(0, mInterestRate);
  }
  public void InitSavingsAccount(decimal mInitial,
                                 decimal mInterestRate)
  {
    InitBankAccount(mInitial);
    this.mInterestRate = mInterestRate / 100;
  }
  // AccumulateInterest — invoke once per period
  public void AccumulateInterest()
  {
    mBalance = mBalance + (decimal)(mBalance * mInterestRate);
  }
  // ToString — stringify the account
  public string ToSavingsAccountString()
```

```
    {
      return String.Format("{0} ({1}%)",
         ToBankAccountString(), mInterestRate * 100);
    }
  }
  public class Class1
  {
    public static int Main(string[] args)
    {
      // create a bank account and display it
      BankAccount ba = new BankAccount();
      ba.InitBankAccount(100);
      ba.Deposit(100);
      Console.WriteLine("Account {0}", ba.ToBankAccountString());
      // now a savings account
      SavingsAccount sa = new SavingsAccount();
      sa.InitSavingsAccount(100, 12.5M);
      sa.AccumulateInterest();
      Console.WriteLine("Account {0}", sa.ToSavingsAccountString());
      // wait for user to acknowledge the results
      Console.WriteLine("Press Enter to terminate...");
      Console.Read();
      return 0;
    }
  }
}
```

The BankAccount class is not unlike those appearing in other chapters of this book. It begins with an overloaded initialization function InitBankAccount(): one for accounts starting out with an initial balance, and another for which zero will just have to do.

The Balance property allows others to read the balance without giving them the ability to modify it. The Deposit() method accepts any positive deposit. Withdraw()lets you take out as much as you want, as long as you have it in your account — my bank's nice, but it's not that nice. ToBankAccountString() creates a string that describes the account.

The SavingsAccount class inherits all that good stuff from BankAccount. To that, it adds an interest rate and the ability to accumulate interest at regular intervals.

Main() does about as little as it can. It creates a BankAccount, displays the account, creates a SavingsAccount, accumulates one period of interest, and displays the result:

```
Account 1001 - $200.00
Account 1002 - $112.50 (12.5%)
Press Enter to terminate...
```

Notice that the InitSavingsAccount() method invokes InitBankAccount(). This initializes the bank account-specific data members. The InitSavings Account() method could have initialized these members directly; however, it is better practice to allow the BankAccount to initialize its own members.

IS_A versus HAS_A — I'm So Confused

The relationship between SavingsAccount and BankAccount is the fundamental IS_A relationship. First, I show you why. Then, I show you what the HAS_A relationship would look like.

The IS_A relationship

The IS_A relationship between SavingsAccount and BankAccount is demonstrated by the following modification to Class1 in the SimpleSavingsAccount program from the preceding section:

```
public class Class1
{
  // DirectDeposit - deposit my paycheck automatically
  public static void DirectDeposit(BankAccount ba,
                                   decimal mPay)
  {
    ba.Deposit(mPay);
  }
  public static int Main(string[] args)
  {
    // create a bank account and display it
    BankAccount ba = new BankAccount();
    ba.InitBankAccount(100);
    DirectDeposit(ba, 100);
    Console.WriteLine("Account {0}", ba.ToBankAccountString());
    // now a savings account
    SavingsAccount sa = new SavingsAccount();
    sa.InitSavingsAccount(12.5M);
    DirectDeposit(sa, 100);
    sa.AccumulateInterest();
    Console.WriteLine("Account {0}", sa.ToSavingsAccountString());
    // wait for user to acknowledge the results
    Console.WriteLine("Press Enter to terminate...");
    Console.Read();
    return 0;
  }
}
```

In effect, nothing's changed. The only real difference is that all deposits are now being made through the local function DirectDeposit(). The arguments to this function are the bank account and the amount to deposit.

Notice (here comes the good part), Main() could pass either a bank account or a savings account to DirectDeposit() because a SavingsAccount IS_A BankAccount and is accorded all the rights and privileges thereto.

Gaining access to BankAccount *through containment*

The class SavingsAccount could have gained access to the members of BankAccount in a different way:

```
// SavingsAccount — a bank account that draws interest
public class SavingsAccount_
{
  public BankAccount bankAccount;
  public decimal mInterestRate;
  // InitSavingsAccount — input the rate expressed as a
  //                      rate between 0 and 100
  public void InitSavingsAccount(BankAccount bankAccount,
                                 decimal mInterestRate)
  {
    this.bankAccount = bankAccount;
    this.mInterestRate = mInterestRate / 100;
  }
  // AccumulateInterest — invoke once per period
  public void AccumulateInterest()
  {
    bankAccount.mBalance = bankAccount.mBalance
                  + (bankAccount.mBalance * mInterestRate);
  }
  // Deposit — any positive deposit is allowed
  public void Deposit(decimal mAmount)
  {
    bankAccount.Deposit(mAmount);
  }
  // Withdraw — you can withdraw any amount up to the
  //            balance; return the amount withdrawn
  public double Withdraw(decimal mWithdrawal)
  {
    return bankAccount.Withdraw(mWithdrawal);
  }
}
```

In this case, the class SavingsAccount_ contains a data member bankAccount (as opposed to inheriting from BankAccount). The bankAccount object contains the balance and account number information needed by the savings account. The SavingsAccount_ class retains the data unique to a savings account.

In this case, we say that the SavingsAccount_ HAS_A BankAccount.

The HAS_A relationship

The HAS_A relationship is fundamentally different from the IS_A relationship. This difference doesn't seem so bad in the following example application code segment:

```
// create a new savings account
BankAccount ba = new BankAccount()
SavingsAccount_ sa = new SavingsAccount_();
sa.InitSavingsAccount(ba, 5);
// and deposit 100 dollars into it
sa.Deposit(100);
// now accumulate interest
sa.AccumulateInterest();
```

The problem is that a `SavingsAccount_` cannot be used as a `BankAccount`.
For example, the following code example fails:

```
// DirectDeposit - deposit my paycheck automatically
void DirectDeposit(BankAccount ba, int nPay)
{
  ba.Deposit(nPay);
}
void SomeFunction()
{
  // the following example fails
  SavingsAccount_ sa = new SavingsAccount_();
  DirectDeposit(sa, 100);
  // . . . continue . . .
}
```

`DirectDeposit()` can't accept a `SavingsAccount_` in lieu of a
`BankAccount`. There's no obvious relationship between the two as far as C#
is concerned.

When to IS_A and When to HAS_A?

The distinction between the IS_A and HAS_A relationships is more than just a
matter of software convenience. This relationship has a corollary in the real
world.

For example, a Ford Explorer IS_A car (when it's upright, that is). An Explorer
HAS_A motor. If my friend says, "Come on over in your car," and I show up in
an Explorer, he has no grounds for complaint (Okay, he has grounds for complaint, but not because an Explorer isn't a car). He may have a complaint if I
show up carrying my Explorer's engine in my arms, however.

The class `Explorer` should extend the class `Car`, not only to give `Explorer`
access to the methods of a `Car`, but also to express the fundamental relationship between the two.

Unfortunately, the beginning programmer may have `Car` inherit from `Motor`,
giving the `Car` class access to the members of `Motor`, which the `Car` needs
to operate. For example, `Car` can inherit the method `Motor.Go()`. However,
this example highlights one of the problems with this approach. Even though

humans get sloppy in their speech, making a car go is not the same thing as making a motor go. The car's go operation certainly relies upon that of the motor, but they aren't the same thing — you also have to put the transmission in gear, let off the brake, and so on.

Perhaps even more than that, inheriting from `Motor` misstates the facts. A car simply is not a type of motor.

Elegance in software is a goal worth achieving in its own right. It enhances understandability, reliability, and maintainability, plus it cures indigestion and gout.

Other Considerations

C# implements a set of features designed to support inheritance.

Changing class

A program can change the class of an object. In fact, you've already seen this in one example. `SomeFunction()` can pass a `SavingsAccount` object to a method that's expecting a `BankAccount` object.

You can make this conversion more explicit:

```
BankAccount ba;
SavingsAccount sa = new SavingsAccout();
                          // OK:
ba = sa;                  // an implicit down conversion is allowed
ba = (BankAccount)sa;     // the explicit cast is preferred
                          // No!
sa = ba;                  // implicit up conversion not allowed
                          // this is OK
sa = (SavingsAccount)ba;
```

The first line stores a `SavingsAccount` object into a `BankAccount` variable. C# converts the object for you. The second line uses the cast operator to explicitly convert the object.

The final two lines convert the `BankAccount` object back into a `SavingsAccount`.

The IS_A property is not reflexive. That is, even though an Explorer is a car, a car is not necessarily an Explorer. Similarly, a `BankAccount` is not necessarily a `SavingsAccount` and so the implicit conversion is not allowed. The final line is allowed because the programmer has indicated her willingness to "chance it."

Invalid casts at run time

Generally, casting an object from `BankAccount` to `SavingsAccount` is a dangerous operation. Consider the following example:

```
public static void ProcessAmount(BankAccount bankAccount)
{
  // deposit a large sum to the account
  bankAccount.Deposit(10000.00);
  // if the object is a SavingsAccount
  // then collect interest now
  SavingsAccount savingsAccount = (SavingsAccount)bankAccount;
  savingsAccount.AccumulateInterest();
}
public static void TestCast()
{
  SavingsAccount sa = new SavingsAccount();
  ProcessAmount(sa);
  BankAccount ba = new BankAccount();
  ProcessAmount(ba);
}
```

The `ProcessAmount()` performs a few operations, including invoking the `AccumulateInterest()` method. The cast of `ba` to a `SavingsAccount` is necessary because `ba` is declared to be a `BankAccount`. The program compiles properly because all type conversions are via explicit cast.

All goes well with the first call to `ProcessAmount()` from within `Test()`. The `SavingsAccount` object `sa` is passed to the `ProcessAmount()` method. The cast from `BankAccount` to `SavingsAccount` causes no problem because the `ba` object was originally a `SavingsAccount` anyway.

The second call to `ProcessAmount()` is not so lucky, however. The cast to `SavingsAccount` cannot be allowed. The `ba` object does not have an `AccumulateInterest()` method.

An incorrect conversion generates an error during the execution of the program (a so-called *run-time error*). Run-time errors are much more difficult to find and fix than compile time errors.

Avoiding invalid conversions using the `is` keyword

The `ProcessAmount()` function would be okay if it could ensure that the object passed to it is actually a `SavingsAccount` object before performing the conversion. C# provides the `is` keyword for this purpose.

The `is` operator accepts an object on the left and a type on the right. The `is` operator returns a `true` if the run-time type of the object on the left is compatible with the type on the right.

You can modify the previous example to avoid the run-time error by using the `is` operator:

```
public static void ProcessAmount(BankAccount bankAccount)
{
  // deposit a large sum to the account
  bankAccount.Deposit(10000.00);
  // if the object is a SavingsAccount . . .
  if (bankAccount is SavingsAccount)
  {
    // ...then collect interest now
    SavingsAccount savingsAccount = (SavingsAccount)bankAccount;
    savingsAccount.AccumulateInterest();
  }
}
public static void TestCast()
{
  SavingsAccount sa = new SavingsAccount();
  ProcessAmount(sa);
  BankAccount ba = new BankAccount();
  ProcessAmount(ba);
}
```

The added `if` statement checks the `bankAccount` object to ensure that it's actually of class `SavingsAccount`. The `is` operator returns a `true` when `ProcessAmount()` is called the first time. When passed a `BankAccount` object in the second call, however, the `is` operator returns a `false`, avoiding the illegal cast. This version of the program does not generate a run-time error.

On the one hand, I strongly recommend that you protect all upcasts with the `is` operator to avoid the possibility of a run-time error. On the other hand, you should avoid upcasts altogether, if possible.

The `object` class

Consider the following related classes:

```
public class MyBaseClass {}
public class MySubClass : MyBaseClass {}
```

The relationship between the two classes enables the programmer to make the following run-time test:

```
public class Test
{
  public static void GenericFunction(MyBaseClass mc)
  {
    // if the object truly is a subclass . . .
    if (mc is MySubClass)
    {
```

```
        // ...then handle as a subclass
        MySubClass msc = (MySubClass)mc;

        // . . . continue . . .
      }
    }
  }
```

In this case, the function `GenericFunction()` differentiates between subclasses of `MyBaseClass` using the `is` keyword.

How do you differentiate between seemingly unrelated classes using the same `is` operator? C# extends all classes from the common base class `object`. That is, any class that does not specifically inherit from another class inherits from the class `object`. Thus, the following two declarations are identical:

```
class MyClass1 : object {}
class MyClass2 {}
```

`MyClass1` and `MyClass2` share a common base class of `object`. This allows the following generic function:

```
public class Test
{
  public static void GenericFunction(object o)
  {
    if (o is MyClass1)
    {
      MyClass1 mc1 = (MyClass1)o;
      // . . .
    }
  }
}
```

`GenericFunction()` can be invoked with any type of object. The `is` keyword will dig the `MyClass1` pearls from the `object` oysters.

Inheritance and the Constructor

The `InheritanceExample` program from earlier in this chapter relies upon those awful `Init...` functions to initialize the `BankAccount` and `SavingsAccount` objects to a valid state. Outfitting these classes with constructors is definitely the right way to go, but it does introduce a little complexity.

Invoking the default base class constructor

The default base class constructor is invoked any time a subclass is constructed. The constructor for the subclass automatically invokes the constructor for the base class, as the following simple program demonstrates:

```
// InheritingAConstructor - demonstrate that the base
//                          class constructor is invoked
//                          automatically
using System;
namespace InheritingAConstructor
{
  public class Class1
  {
    public static int Main(string[] args)
    {
      Console.WriteLine("Creating a BaseClass object");
      BaseClass bc = new BaseClass();
      Console.WriteLine("\nNow creating a SubClass object");
      SubClass sc = new SubClass();
      // wait for user to acknowledge
      Console.WriteLine("Press Enter to terminate...");
      Console.Read();
      return 0;
    }
  }
  public class BaseClass
  {
    public BaseClass()
    {
      Console.WriteLine("Constructing BaseClass");
    }
  }
  public class SubClass : BaseClass
  {
    public SubClass()
    {
      Console.WriteLine("Constructing SubClass");
    }
  }
}
```

The constructors for BaseClass and SubClass do nothing more than output a message to the command line. Creating the BaseClass object invokes the default BaseClass constructor. Creating a SubClass object invokes the BaseClass constructor before invoking its own constructor.

The output from this program is as follows:

```
Creating a BaseClass object
Constructing BaseClass

Now creating a SubClass object
Constructing BaseClass
Constructing SubClass
Press Enter to terminate...
```

A hierarchy of inherited classes is much like the floors of a building. Each class is built upon the classes that it extends. There's a clear reason for this: Each class is responsible for itself. A subclass should not be held responsible for initializing the members of the base class, any more than some outside function. The BaseClass must be given the opportunity to construct its members before the SubClass members are given a chance to access them.

Passing arguments to the base class constructor — mama sing base

The subclass invokes the default constructor of the base class, unless specified otherwise — even from a subclass constructor other than the default. The following, slightly updated example demonstrates this feature:

```
using System
namespace Example
{
  public class Class1
  {
    public static int Main(string[] args)
    {
      Console.WriteLine("Invoking SubClass()");
      SubClass sc1 = new SubClass();
      Console.WriteLine("\nInvoking SubClass(int)");
      SubClass sc2 = new SubClass(0);
      // wait for user to acknowledge
      Console.WriteLine("Press Enter to terminate...");
      Console.Read();
      return 0;
    }
  }
  public class BaseClass
  {
    public BaseClass()
    {
      Console.WriteLine("Constructing BaseClass (default)");
    }
    public BaseClass(int i)
    {
      Console.WriteLine("Constructing BaseClass (int)");
    }
  }
  public class SubClass : BaseClass
  {
    public SubClass()
    {
      Console.WriteLine("Constructing SubClass (default)");
    }
    public SubClass(int i)
    {
      Console.WriteLine("Constructing SubClass (int)");
    }
  }
}
```

Executing this program generates the following results:

```
Invoking SubClass()
Constructing BaseClass (default)
Constructing SubClass (default)

Invoking SubClass(int)
Constructing BaseClass (default)
Constructing SubClass (int)
Press Enter to terminate...
```

The program first creates a default object. As expected, C# invokes the default `SubClass` constructor, which first passes control to the default `BaseClass` constructor. The program then creates an object, passing an integer argument. Again as expected, C# invokes the `SubClass(int)`. This constructor invokes the default `BaseClass` constructor, just as in the earlier example, because it has no data to pass.

A subclass constructor can invoke a specific base class constructor using the keyword `base`.

This feature is very similar to the way that one constructor invokes another within the same class using the `this` keyword. See Chapter 11 for the inside scoop on constructors and `this`.

For example, consider the following small program, `InvokeBaseConstructor`:

```csharp
// InvokeBaseConstructor - demonstrate how a subclass can
//                         invoke the base class constructor of its
//                         choice using the base keyword
using System;
namespace InvokeBaseConstructor
{
  public class BaseClass
  {
    public BaseClass()
    {
      Console.WriteLine("Constructing BaseClass (default)");
    }
    public BaseClass(int i)
    {
      Console.WriteLine("Constructing BaseClass({0})", i);
    }
  }
  public class SubClass : BaseClass
  {
    public SubClass()
    {
      Console.WriteLine("Constructing SubClass (default)");
    }
    public SubClass(int i1, int i2) : base(i1)
    {
      Console.WriteLine("Constructing SubClass({0}, {1})",
                                               i1, i2);
    }
  }
```

```
public class Class1
{
  public static int Main(string[] args)
  {
    Console.WriteLine("Invoking SubClass()");
    SubClass sc1 = new SubClass();
    Console.WriteLine("\nInvoking SubClass(1, 2)");
    SubClass sc2 = new SubClass(1, 2);
    // wait for user to acknowledge
    Console.WriteLine("Press Enter to terminate...");
    Console.Read();
    return 0;
  }
}
}
```

The output from this program is as follows:

```
Invoking SubClass()
Constructing BaseClass (default)
Constructing SubClass (default)

Invoking SubClass(1, 2)
Constructing BaseClass(1)
Constructing SubClass(1, 2)
Press Enter to terminate...
```

This version begins the same as the previous examples, by creating a default
SubClass object using the default constructor of both BaseClass and
SubClass.

The second object is created with the expression new SubClass(1, 2). C#
invokes the SubClass(int, int) constructor, which uses the base keyword
to pass one of the values on to the BaseClass(int) constructor. Presumably,
SubClass passes the first argument to the base class for processing and continues on using the second value itself.

The Updated BankAccount *Class*

The program ConstructorSavingsAccount found on the enclosed CD-ROM
is an updated version of the SimpleBankAccount program. In this version,
however, the SavingsAccount constructor can pass information back up to
the BankAccount constructors. Only Main() and the constructors themselves are shown here:

```
// ConstructorSavingsAccount - implement a SavingsAccount
//                             as a form of BankAccount; don't
//                             use any virtual methods but do
//                             implement the constructors
//                             properly
using System;
namespace ConstructorSavingsAccount
{
  // BankAccount - simulate a bank account each of which
```

```
//                 carries an account id (which is assigned
//                 upon creation) and a balance
public class BankAccount
{
  // bank accounts start at 1000 and increase sequentially
  // from there
  public static int nNextAccountNumber = 1000;
  // maintain the account number and balance for each object
  public int nAccountNumber;
  public decimal mBalance;
  // Constructors
  public BankAccount():this(0)
  {
  }

  public BankAccount(decimal mInitialBalance)
  {

    nAccountNumber = ++nNextAccountNumber;
    mBalance = mInitialBalance;
  }
  // . . . same stuff here . . .
}
// SavingsAccount - a bank account that draws interest
public class SavingsAccount : BankAccount
{
  public decimal mInterestRate;
  // InitSavingsAccount - input the rate expressed as a
  //                      rate between 0 and 100
  public SavingsAccount(decimal mInterestRate) : this(0, mInterestRate)
  {
  }
  public SavingsAccount(decimal mInitial,
                        decimal mInterestRate) : base(mInitial)
  {
    this.mInterestRate = mInterestRate / 100;
  }
  // . . . same stuff here . . .
}
public class Class1
{
  // DirectDeposit - deposit my paycheck automatically
  public static void DirectDeposit(BankAccount ba,
                                   decimal mPay)
  {
    ba.Deposit(mPay);
  }
  public static int Main(string[] args)
  {
    // create a bank account and display it
    BankAccount ba = new BankAccount(100);
    DirectDeposit(ba, 100);
    Console.WriteLine("Account {0}", ba.ToBankAccountString());
    // now a savings account
    SavingsAccount sa = new SavingsAccount(12.5M);
    DirectDeposit(sa, 100);
    sa.AccumulateInterest();
    Console.WriteLine("Account {0}", sa.ToSavingsAccountString());
    // wait for user to acknowledge the results
    Console.WriteLine("Press Enter to terminate...");
    Console.Read();
    return 0;
  }
}
```

BankAccount defines two constructors: one that accepts an initial account balance, and the default constructor, which does not. In order to avoid duplicating any code within the constructor, the default constructor invokes the BankAccount(initial balance) constructor using the this keyword.

The SavingsAccount class provides two constructors, as well. The SavingsAccount(interest rate) constructor invokes the SavingsAccount (interest rate, initial balance) constructor, passing an initial balance of 0. This most general constructor passes the initial balance to the BankAccount(initial balance) constructor using the base keyword, as shown graphically in Figure 12-1.

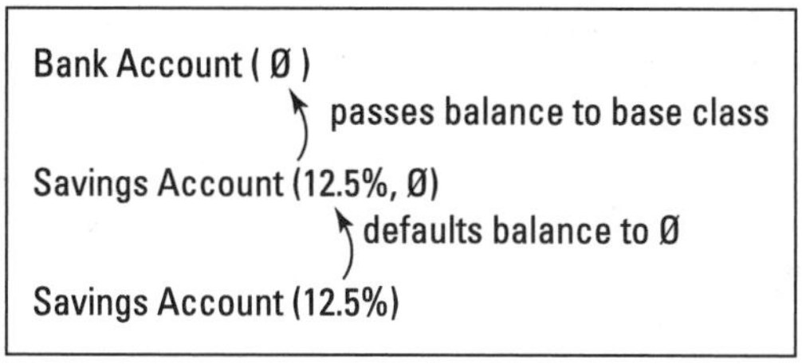

Figure 12-1:
The path taken when constructing a Savings-Account object using the default constructor.

Bank Account (Ø)

↖) passes balance to base class

Savings Account (12.5%, Ø)

↖) defaults balance to Ø

Savings Account (12.5%)

I've modified Main()to get rid of those infernal Init...() functions, replacing them with constructors instead. The output from this program is the same:

```
Account 1001 - $200.00
Account 1002 - $112.50 (12.5%)
Press Enter to terminate...
```

The Destructor

C# also provides a method that's inverse to the constructor, called the destructor. The destructor carries the name of the class with a tilde (~) in front. For example, the ~BaseClass method is the destructor for BaseClass.

C# invokes the destructor when it is no longer using the object. The default destructor is the only destructor that can be created because the destructor cannot be invoked directly. In addition, the destructor is always virtual.

When an inheritance ladder of classes is involved, the destructors are invoked in the reverse order of the constructors. That is, the destructor for the subclass is invoked before the destructor for the base class.

Garbage collection and the C# destructor

The destructor method in C# is much less useful than it is in some other object-oriented languages, such as C++, because C# has what's known as nondeterministic destruction.

The memory for an object is removed from the heap when the program executes the new command. This block of memory remains reserved as long as any valid references to that memory are running around.

The memory is said to be "unreachable" when the last reference goes out of scope. In other words, no one can access that block of memory after there are no more references to it.

C# doesn't do anything in particular when a memory block first becomes unreachable. A low-priority task executes in the background, looking for unreachable memory blocks. The so-called garbage collector executes at low priority in order to avoid negatively affecting program performance. As the garbage collector finds unreachable memory blocks, it returns them to the heap.

Normally, the garbage collector operates silently in the background. The garbage collector only takes over control of the program for a short period when heap memory begins to run out.

The C# destructor is nondeterministic because it is not invoked until the object is garbage collected, and that could occur long after the object is no longer being used. In fact, if the program terminates before the object is found and returned to the heap, the destructor is not invoked at all.

The net effect is that C# programmers cannot rely on the destructor to operate automatically as they can in languages such as C++.

Chapter 13

Poly-what-ism?

In This Chapter

▶ Deciding whether to hide or override a base class method — So many choices!

▶ Building abstract classes — Are you for real?

▶ Declaring a method and the class that contains it to be abstract

▶ Starting a new hierarchy on top of an existing one

▶ Sealing a class from being subclassed

*I*nheritance allows one class to "adopt" the members of another. Thus, I can create a class `SavingsAccount` that inherits data members like `account id` and methods like `Deposit()` from a base class `BankAccount`. That's nice, but this definition of inheritance is not sufficient to mimic what's going on out there in the trenches.

Drop back 10 yards to Chapter 12 if you don't remember much about class inheritance.

A microwave oven is a type of oven, not because it looks like an oven, but because it performs the same functions as an oven. A microwave oven may perform additional functions, but at the least, it performs the base oven functions — most importantly, heating up my nachos when I say, "StartCooking." (I rely on my object of class `Refrigerator` to cool down the beer.) I don't particularly care what the oven must do internally to make that happen, any more than I care what type of oven it is, who made it, or whether it was on sale when my wife bought it . . . Hey, wait, I do care about that last one.

From our human vantage point, relationship between a microwave oven and a conventional oven doesn't seem like such a big deal, but consider the problem from the oven's point of view. The steps a conventional oven performs internally are completely different from those that a microwave oven might take (not to mention those that a convection oven performs).

The power of inheritance lies in the fact that a subclass doesn't *have* to inherit every single method from the base class just the way it's written. A subclass can inherit the essence of the base class method while implementing the details differently.

Overloading an Inherited Method

Two or more functions can have the same name as long as the number and/or types of the arguments differ.

It's a simple case of function overloading

Giving two functions the same name is called *overloading*, as in "Keeping them straight is overloading my brain."

The arguments of a function become a part of its extended name, as the following example demonstrates:

```
public class MyClass
{
  public static void AFunction()
  {
    // do something
  }
  public static void AFunction(int)
  {
    // do something else
  }
  public static void AFunction(double d)
  {
    // do something even different
  }
  public static void Main(string[] args)
  {
    AFunction();
    AFunction(1);
    AFunction(2.0);
  }
}
```

C# can differentiate the methods by their arguments. Each of the calls within `Main()` accesses a different function.

The return type is not part of the extended name. You can have two functions that differ only in their return type.

Different class, different method

Not surprisingly, the class to which a function or method belongs is also a part of its extended name. Consider the following code segment:

```
public class MyClass
{
  public static void AFunction();
  public static void AMethod();
}
```

```
public UrClass
{
  public static void AFunction();
  public static void AMethod();
public class Class1
{
  public static void Main(string[] args)
  {
    UrClass.AFunction();
    // invoke the MyClass.AMethod() member function
    MyClass mcObject = new MyClass();
    mcObject.AMethod();
  }
}
```

The name of the class is a part of the extended name of the function. The
function MyClass.AFunction() has about as much to do with UrClass.
AFunction() as your YourCar.StartOnAColdMorning() and MyCar.
StartOnAColdMorning() — at least yours works.

Peek-a-boo — Hiding a base class method

Okay, so a method in one class can overload another method in its own class
by having different arguments. As it turns out, a method can also overload a
method in its base class. Overloading a base class method is known as *hiding*
the method.

Suppose my bank adopts a policy that makes savings account withdrawals
different from other types of withdrawals. Suppose, just for the sake of argument, that withdrawing from a savings account costs $1.50.

Taking the functional approach, you could implement this policy by setting a
flag in the class to indicate whether the object is a SavingsAccount or just a
simple BankAccount. Then, the withdrawal method would have to check the
flag to decide whether it needs to charge the $1.50:

```
public BankAccount(int nAccountType)
{
  private decimal mBalance;
  private bool isSavingsAccount;
  // indicate the initial balance and whether the
  // account that you're creating is a savings
  // account or not
  public BankAccount(decimal mInitialBalance,
                     bool isSavingsAccount)
  {
    mBalance = mInitialBalance;
    this.isSavingsAccount = isSavingsAccount;
  }
  public decimal Withdraw(decimal mAmount)
  {
    // if the account is a savings account . . .
    if (isSavingsAccount)
    {
```

```
      // ...then skim off $1.50
      mBalance -= 1.50M;
    }
    // continue on with the same withdraw code:
    if (mAmountToWithdraw > mBalance)
    {
      mAmountToWithdraw = mBalance;
    }
    mBalance -= mAmountToWithdraw;
    return mAmountToWithdraw;
  }
}
class MyClass
{
  public void SomeFunction()
  {
    // I wanna create me a savings account:
    BankAccount ba = new BankAccount(0, true);
  }
}
```

My function must tell the BankAccount whether it's a SavingsAccount in the constructor by passing a flag. The constructor saves off that flag and uses it in the Withdraw() method to decide whether to charge the extra $1.50.

The more object-oriented approach hides the method Withdraw() in the base class BankAccount, with a new method of the same name, height, and hair color in the SavingsAccount class:

```
// HidingWithdrawal - hide the withdraw method in the
//                    base class with a method in the
//                    subclass of the same name
using System;
namespace HidingWithdrawal
{
  // BankAccount - a very basic bank account
  public class BankAccount
  {
    protected decimal mBalance;
    public BankAccount(decimal mInitialBalance)
    {
      mBalance = mInitialBalance;
    }
    public decimal Balance
    {
      get { return mBalance; }
    }
    public decimal Withdraw(decimal mAmount)
    {
      decimal mAmountToWithdraw = mAmount;
      if (mAmountToWithdraw > mBalance)
      {
        mAmountToWithdraw = mBalance;
      }
      mBalance -= mAmountToWithdraw;
      return mAmountToWithdraw;
    }
  }
  // SavingsAccount - a bank account that draws interest
  public class SavingsAccount : BankAccount
```

```
{
  public decimal mInterestRate;
  // SavingsAccount — input the rate expressed as a
  //              rate between 0 and 100
  public SavingsAccount(decimal mInitialBalance,
                        decimal mInterestRate)
    : base(mInitialBalance)
  {
    this.mInterestRate = mInterestRate / 100;
  }
  // AccumulateInterest — invoke once per period
  public void AccumulateInterest()
  {
    mBalance = mBalance + (mBalance * mInterestRate);
  }
  // Withdraw — you can withdraw any amount up to the
  //            balance; return the amount withdrawn
  public decimal Withdraw(decimal mWithdrawal)
  {
    // take our $1.50 off the top
    base.Withdraw(1.5M);
    // now you can withdraw from what's left
    return base.Withdraw(mWithdrawal);
  }
}
public class Class1
{
  public static void MakeAWithdrawal(BankAccount ba,
                                     decimal mAmount)
  {
    ba.Withdraw(mAmount);
  }
  public static int Main(string[] args)
  {
    BankAccount ba;
    SavingsAccount sa;
    // create a bank account, withdraw $100, and
    // display the results
    ba = new BankAccount(200M);
    ba.Withdraw(100M);
    // try the same trick with a savings account
    sa = new SavingsAccount(200M, 12);
    sa.Withdraw(100M);
    // display the resulting balance
    Console.WriteLine("When invoked directly:");
    Console.WriteLine("BankAccount balance is {0:C}",
                      ba.Balance);
    Console.WriteLine("SavingsAccount balance is {0:C}",
                      sa.Balance);
    // wait for user to acknowledge the results
    Console.WriteLine("Press Enter to terminate...");
    Console.Read();
    return 0;
  }
}
}
```

The `Main()` in this case creates a `BankAccount` object with an initial balance of $200 and then withdraws $100. `Main()` repeats the trick with a `SavingsAccount` object. When `Main()` withdraws money from the base class, `BankAccount.Withdraw()` performs the withdraw function with great aplomb. When `Main()` then withdraws $100 from the savings account, the method `SavingsAccount.Withdraw()` tacks on the extra $1.50.

Notice that the `SavingsAccount.Withdraw` class uses `BankAccount.Withdraw()` rather than manipulate the balance directly. If possible, let the base class maintain its own data members.

What makes the hiding approach better than adding a simple test?

On the surface, adding a flag to the `BankAcount.Withdraw()` method may seem simpler than all this method-hiding stuff. After all, it's just four little lines of code, two of which are nothing more than braces.

The problems are manifold — I've been waiting all these chapters to use that word. One problem is that the `BankAccount` class has no business worrying about the details of `SavingsAccount`. That would break our "Render unto Caesar" rule. That leads to the real problem: Suppose my bank subsequently decides to add a `CheckingAccount` or a `CDAccount` or a `TBillAccount`? Those are all likely additions, and they all have different withdrawal policies, each requiring its own flag. After three or four different types of accounts, our old `Withdraw()` method starts looking pretty complicated. Each of those types of classes should worry about its own withdrawal policies and leave our poor old `BankAccount.Withdraw()` alone.

What about accidentally hiding a base class method?

I could accidentally hide a base class method. For example, I might have a `Vehicle.TakeOff()` method that starts the vehicle rolling. Later, someone else extends my `Vehicle` class with an `Airplane` class. Its `TakeOff()` method is entirely different. Clearly, this is a case of mistaken identity — the two methods have no similarity other than their identical name.

Fortunately for us, C# detects this problem.

C# generates an ominous looking warning when it compiles the earlier example `HidingWithdraw()` program. The text of the warning message is long, but here's the important part:

```
'SavingsAccount.Withdraw(double)' hides inherited member
            'BankAccount.Withdraw(double)'.
```

C# is trying to tell you that you've written a method in a subclass with the same name as a method in the base class. Is that what you really meant to do?

This message is just a warning. You don't even notice it unless you switch over to the Output window to take a look. But, it's very important to sort out and fix all warnings. In almost every case, a warning is telling you about something that could bite you if you don't fix it.

The descriptor `new` tells C# that the hiding of methods is intentional and not the result of some oversight:

```
// no withdraw() pains now
new public decimal Withdraw(decimal dWithdrawal)
{
  // . . . no change internally . . .
}
```

This use of the keyword new has nothing to do with the same word new used to create an object.

Let me go on record right now that this is one thing about C# (and C++ before it) that irks me: Do what you will with my methods, but don't overload my keywords. When I say new, I want to create an object. They could have used another keyword to indicate intentional overloading.

Calling back to base

Return to the SavingsAccount.Withdraw() method in the example earlier in this chapter. The call to BankAccount.Withdraw() from within this new method includes the new keyword base.

The following version of the function without this new keyword does not work:

```
new public double Withdraw(double dWithdrawal)
{
  double dAmountWithdrawn = Withdraw(dWithdrawal);
  if (++nNumberOfWithdrawalsThisPeriod > 1)
  {
    dAmountWithdrawn += Withdraw(1.5);
  }
  return dAmountWithdrawn;
}
```

This call has the same problem as the following one:

```
void fn()
{
  fn(); // call yourself
}
```

The call to fn() from within fn() ends up calling itself over and over. Similarly, a call to Withdraw() from within the function calls itself in a loop, chasing its tail until the program eventually crashes.

Somehow, you need to indicate to C# that the call from within SavingsAccount.Withdraw() is meant to invoke the base class BankAccount.Withdraw() method. One approach is to cast the this pointer into an object of class BankAccount before making the call:

```
// Withdraw - this version accesses the hidden method in the base
//            class by explicitly recasting the this object
new public double Withdraw(double dWithdrawal)
{
```

```
// cast the this pointer into an object of class BankAccount
BankAccount ba = (BankAccount)this;
// invoking the Withdraw() using this BankAccount object
// calls the function BankAccount.Withdraw()
double dAmountWithdrawn = ba.Withdraw(dWithdrawal);
if (++nNumberOfWithdrawalsThisPeriod > 1)
{
  dAmountWithdrawn += ba.Withdraw(1.5);
}
return dAmountWithdrawn;
}
```

This solution does work: The call `ba.Withdraw()` now invokes the `BankAccount` method, just as intended. The problem with this approach is the explicit reference to `BankAccount`. A future change to the program might rearrange the inheritance hierarchy so that `SavingsAccount` no longer inherits directly from `BankAccount`. Such a rearrangement breaks this function in a way that future programmer may not easily find. Heck, I would never be able to find a bug like that.

You need a way to tell C# to call the `Withdraw()` function from "the class immediately above" in the hierarchy without naming it explicitly. That would be the class that `SavingsAccount` extends. C# provides the keyword `base` for this purpose.

This is the same keyword `base` that a constructor uses to pass arguments to its base class constructor.

The C# keyword `base` is the same thing as `this` but recast to the base class no matter what that class might be:

```
// Withdraw - you can withdraw any amount up to the
//            balance; return the amount withdrawn
new public decimal Withdraw(decimal mWithdrawal)
{
  // take our $1.50 off the top
  base.Withdraw(1.5M);
  // now you can withdraw from what's left
  return base.Withdraw(mWithdrawal);
}
```

The call `base.Withdraw()` now invokes the `BankAccount.Withdraw()` method, thereby avoiding the "invoking itself" problem. In addition, this solution will not break if the inheritance hierarchy is changed.

Polymorphism

You can overload a method in a base class with a method in the subclass. As simple as this sounds, it introduces considerable capability, and with capability comes danger.

Here's a thought experiment: Should the decision to call `BankAccount.Withdraw` or `SavingsAccount.Withdraw()` be made at compile time or run time?

To understand the difference, I'll change the previous `HidingWithdrawal` program in a seemingly innocuous way. I call this new version `HidingWithdrawalPolymorphically`. (I've streamlined the listing by leaving out the stuff that doesn't change.)

```
public class Class1
{
    public static void MakeAWithdrawal(BankAccount ba,
                                       decimal mAmount)
    {
        ba.Withdraw(mAmount);
    }
    public static int Main(string[] args)
    {
        BankAccount ba;
        SavingsAccount sa;
        ba = new BankAccount(200M);
        MakeAWithdrawal(ba, 100M);
        sa = new SavingsAccount(200M, 12);
        MakeAWithdrawal(sa, 100M);
        // display the resulting balance
        Console.WriteLine("\nWhen invoked through intermediary");
        Console.WriteLine("BankAccount balance is {0:C}", ba.Balance);
        Console.WriteLine("SavingsAccount balance is {0:C}", sa.Balance);
        // wait for user to acknowledge the results
        Console.WriteLine("Press Enter to terminate...");
        Console.Read();
        return 0;
    }
}
```

The output from this program may or may not be confusing, depending upon what you expected:

```
When invoked through intermediary
BankAccount balance is $100.00
SavingsAccount balance is $100.00
Press Enter to terminate...
```

This time, rather than performing a withdrawal in `Main()`, the program passes the bank account object to the function `MakeAWithdrawal()`.

The first question is fairly straightforward: Why does the `MakeAWithdrawal()` function even accept a `SavingsAccount` object when it clearly states that it is looking for a `BankAccount`? The answer is obvious: "Because a `SavingsAccount` IS_A `BankAccount`."

The second question is subtle. When passed a `BankAccount` object, `MakeAWithdrawal()` invokes `BankAccount.Withdraw()` — that's clear enough. But when passed a `SavingsAccount` object, `MakeAWithdrawal()` calls the same method. Shouldn't it invoke the `Withdraw()` method in the subclass?

The prosecution intends to show that the call `ba.Withdraw()` should invoke the method `BankAccount.Withdraw()`. Clearly, the `ba` object is a `BankAccount`. To do anything else would merely confuse the state. The defense has witnesses back in `Main()` to prove that although the `ba` object is declared `BankAccount`, it is, in fact, a `SavingsAccount`. The jury is dead-locked. Both arguments are equally valid.

In this case, C# comes down on the side of the prosecution. The safer of the two possibilities is to go with the declared type because it avoids any mis-communication. The object is declared to be a `BankAccount`, and that's that.

What's wrong with using the declared type every time?

In some cases, you don't want to go with the declared type. "What you want, what you really, really want . . ." is to make the call based upon the *real type* — that is, the run-time type, as opposed to the declared type. This capability to decide at run time is called *polymorphism* or *late binding*. Going with the declared type every time is called *early binding* because that sounds like the opposite of late binding.

The ridiculous term *polymorphism* comes from the Greek: *poly* meaning more than one, *morph* meaning action, and *ism* meaning some ridiculous Greek term.

Polymorphism and late binding are not exactly the same. The difference is subtle, however. *Polymorphism* refers to the capability of deciding which method to invoke at run time. *Late binding* refers to the way a language implements polymorphism.

Polymorphism is key to the power of object-oriented programming. It's so important that languages that don't support polymorphism can't advertise themselves as OO languages. (I think it's an FDA regulation: You can't label a language that doesn't support OO unless you add a disclaimer from the surgeon general, or something like that.)

Languages that support classes but not polymorphism are called object-based languages. Ada is an example of such a language.

Without polymorphism, inheritance has little meaning. Let me spring yet another example on you to show why. Suppose I had written this really boffo program that used some class called, just to pick a name out of the air, `Student`. After months of design, coding, and testing, I release this application to rave reviews from colleagues and critics alike. (There's even talk of starting a new Nobel Prize category for software, but I modestly brush such talk aside.)

Time passes, and my boss asks me to add to this program the capability of handling graduate students, who are similar but not identical to normal students. (The graduate students probably claim that they're not similar at all.) Suppose that the formula for calculating the tuition for a graduate student is completely different from that for a simple student. Now, my boss doesn't know or care that deep within the program, there are numerous calls to the member function calcTuition(). (There's a lot that he doesn't know or care about, by the way.)

```
void SomeFunction(Student s)
{
  // . . . whatever it might do . . .
  s.CalcTuition();
  // . . . continues on . . .
}
```

If C# didn't support late binding, I would need to edit someFunction() to check whether the student object passed to it is a GraduateStudent or a Student. The program would call Student.CalcTuition() when s is a Student and GraduateStudent.CalcTuition() when it's a graduate student.

That doesn't seem so bad, except for three things. First, this is only one function. Suppose that calcTuition() is called from many places. Also, suppose that calcTuition() is not the only difference between the two classes. The chances are not good that I will find all the places that need to be changed.

With polymorphism, I can let C# decide which method to call.

Accessing a hidden method polymorphically using is

How can I make my program polymorphic? C# provides one approach to solving the problem manually in a brand new keyword: is. The expression ba is SavingsAccount returns a true or a false depending upon the run-time class of the object. The declared type might be BankAccount, but what type is it really?

```
public class Class1
{
  public static void MakeAWithdrawal(BankAccount ba,
                                     decimal mAmount)
  {
    if ba is SavingsAccount
    {
      SavingsAccount sa = (SavingsAccount)ba;
      sa.Withdraw(mAmount);
    } else
    {
      ba.Withdraw(mAmount);
    }
  }
}
```

Now, when `Main()` passes the function a `SavingsAccount` object, `MakeAWithdrawal()` checks the run-time type of the `ba` object and invokes `SavingsAccount.Withdraw()`.

Just as an aside, the programmer could have performed the cast and the call in a single line: `((SavingsAccount)ba).Withdraw(mAmount);`. I mention this only because you see it a lot in programs written by showoffs.

Actually, the "is" approach works but it's a really bad idea. The `is` approach requires `SomeFunction()` to be aware of all the different types of students and which of them are represented by different classes. That puts too much responsibility on poor old `SomeFunction()`. Right now, my application handles only two types of bank accounts, but suppose my boss asks me to implement a new account type, `CheckingAccount`, and this new account has different `Withdraw()` requirements. My program won't work properly if I don't search out and find every function that checks the run-time type of its argument. Doh!

Declaring a method virtual

As the author of `SomeFunction()`, I don't want to know about all the different types of accounts. I want to leave it up to the programmers that use `SomeFunction()` to know about their account types and leave me alone. I want C# to make decisions about which methods to invoke based on the run-time type of the object.

I tell C# to make the run-time decision of which version of `Withdrawal()` by marking the base class function with the keyword `virtual` and each subclass with the keyword `override`.

I've rewritten the previous example program using polymorphism. I have added output statements to the `Withdraw()` methods to prove that the proper methods are indeed being invoked. (I've cut out the duplicated stuff to avoid boring you any more than you already are.) Here's the `PolymorphicInheritance` program:

```
// PolymorphicInheritance — hide a method in the
//                          base class polymorphically
using System;
namespace PolymorphicInheritance
{
  // BankAccount — a very basic bank account
  public class BankAccount
  {
    // . . . the same stuff here . . .
    public virtual decimal Withdraw(decimal mAmount)
    {
      decimal mAmountToWithdraw = mAmount;
      if (mAmountToWithdraw > mBalance)
```

```
        {
           mAmountToWithdraw = mBalance;
        }
        mBalance -= mAmountToWithdraw;
        return mAmountToWithdraw;
      }
    }
    // SavingsAccount - a bank account that draws interest
    public class SavingsAccount : BankAccount
    {
      // . . . same stuff here, too . . .
      // Withdraw - you can withdraw any amount up to the
      //           balance; return the amount withdrawn
      override public decimal Withdraw(decimal mWithdrawal)
      {
        // take our $1.50 off the top
        base.Withdraw(1.5M);
        // now you can withdraw from what's left
        return base.Withdraw(mWithdrawal);
      }
    }
    public class Class1
    {
      public static void MakeAWithdrawal(BankAccount ba,
                                         decimal mAmount)
      {
        ba.Withdraw(mAmount);
      }
      public static void Main(string[] args)
      {
        // . .. nope, no change here either . . .
      }
    }
}
```

The output from executing this program is as follows:

```
When invoked through intermediary
BankAccount balance is $100.00
SavingsAccount balance is $98.50
Press Enter to terminate...
```

The `Withdraw()` method is flagged as `virtual` in the base class `BankAccount`, while the `Withdraw()` method in the subclass is flagged with the keyword `override`. The `MakeAWithdrawal()` method is unchanged and yet the output of the program is different because the call `ba.Withdraw()` is resolved based upon `ba`'s real time type.

To get a good feel for how this works, you really need to step through the program in the Visual Studio debugger. Just build the program as normal and then repeatedly press the F11 key to watch the program go through its paces. It's impressive to watch the same call end up in two different methods at two different times.

C# During Its Abstract Period

A duck is a type of bird, I think. So are a cardinal and a hummingbird. In fact, every bird out there is actually some subtype of bird. The flip side of that argument is that no bird exists that isn't some subtype of bird. That doesn't sound too profound, but in a way, it is. The software equivalent of that statement is that all `bird` objects are instances of some subclass of `Bird` — there's no instance of class `Bird`.

Different types of birds share many properties (otherwise, they wouldn't be birds), but no two types share every property. If they did, they wouldn't be different types. To pick a particularly gross example, not all birds `Fly()` the same way. Ducks have one style. The cardinal's style is similar but not identical. The hummingbird's style is completely different. Don't even get me started about emus and ostriches.

But if birds don't all fly the same, and there's no such thing as a bird, then what the heck is `Bird.Fly()`? The subject of this section, that's what.

Class factoring

People generate taxonomies of objects by factoring out commonalities. To see how factoring works, consider two classes, `HighSchool` and `University`, as shown in Figure 13-1. This figure uses the Unified Modeling Language (UML), a graphical language to describe a class along with the relationship of that class to others.

A Car IS_A Vehicle but a Car HAS_A Motor.

You can see in Figure 13-1 that high schools and universities have several similar properties — actually many more than you might think. Both schools offer a publicly available `Enroll()` method for adding `Student` objects to the school. In addition, both classes offer a private member `numStudents` that indicates the number of students attending the school. One final common feature is the relationship between students: One school can have any number of students — a student can attend only a single school at one time. Even high schools and most universities offer more than I've described, but one of each type of member is all I need.

In addition to the features of a high school, the university contains a method `GetGrant()` and a data member `nAvgSAT`. High schools don't have an SAT entrance requirement, and they don't get federal grants — unless I went to the wrong high schools.

Figure 13-1 is fine, as far as it goes, but lots of information is duplicated. You could reduce the duplication by allowing the more complex class `University` to inherit from the simpler `HighSchool` class, as shown in Figure 13-2.

UML Lite

The Unified Modeling Language (UML) is an expressive language capable of clearly defining a great deal about the relationships of objects within a program. One advantage of UML is that you can ignore the more specific language features without losing the meaning entirely.

The most basic features of UML are as follows:

✔ Classes are represented by a box divided vertically into three sections. The name of the class appears in the upper-most section.

✔ The data members of the class appear in the middle section, and the methods of the class in the bottom. You can omit either the middle or bottom section if the class has no data members or methods.

✔ Members with a '+' in front are public; those with a '−' are private. UML doesn't have a symbol to describe protected and internal visibility.

A private member is only accessible from other members of the same class. A public member is accessible to all classes.

✔ The '{abstract}' next to the name indicates an abstract class or method.

UML actually uses a different symbol for abstract method, but let's keep it simple.

✔ An arrow between two classes represents a relationship between two classes. A number above the line expresses cardinality. The '*' symbol means *any number*. If no number is present, the cardinality is assumed to be 1. Thus, in Figure 13-1, you can see that a single university has any number of students.

✔ A line with a large, open arrow expresses the IS_A relationship (inheritance). Other types of relationships include the HAS_A relationship.

Figure 13-1:
A UML description of the `HighSchool` and `University` classes.

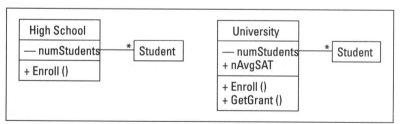

The `HighSchool` class is left unchanged, but the `University` class is easier to describe. We say that "a `University` is a `HighSchool` that also has an `nAvgSAT` and a `GetGrant()` method." But this solution has a fundamental problem: A university is not a high school that . . . anything.

You say, "So what? Inheriting works, and it saves effort." True, but my reservations are more than stylistic trivialities. My reservations are at some of the best restaurants in town — at least, that's what all the truckers say. Such misrepresentations are confusing to the programmer, both now and in the future. Someday, a programmer unfamiliar with my programming tricks will have to read and understand what my code does. Misleading representations are difficult to reconcile and understand.

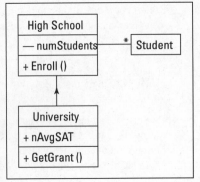

Figure 13-2: Inheriting High-School simplifies the University class, but it introduces problems.

In addition, such misrepresentations can lead to problems down the road. Suppose the high school decides to name a "favorite" student at the prom — not that I would know anything about that sort of thing. The clever programmer adds the NameFavorite() method to the HighSchool class, which the application invokes to name the favorite Student object.

But now I have a problem. Most universities don't name a favorite anything, other than price. However, as long as University inherits from HighSchool, it inherits the NameFavorite() method. One extra method may not seem like a big deal. "Just ignore it," you say.

One extra method isn't a big deal, but it's just one more brick in the wall of confusion. Extra methods and properties accumulate over time, until the University class is carrying lots of extra baggage. Pity the poor software developer that has to understand which methods are "real" and which are not.

"Inheritances of convenience" lead to another problem. The way it's written, Figure 13-2 implies that a University and a HighSchool have the same enrollment procedure. As unlikely as that sounds, assume it's true. The program is developed, packaged up, and shipped off to the unwitting public — of course, I've embedded the requisite number of bugs so they'll want to upgrade to Version 2 with all the bug fixes for a small fee, of course.

Months pass before the school district decides to modify the enrollment procedure. It won't be obvious to anyone that by modifying the high school enrollment procedure, they've also modified the sign-up procedure at the local college.

How can you avoid these problems? Don't go to school is one way, but another would be to fix the source of the problem: A university is not a particular type of high school. A relationship exists between the two, but IS_A is not the right one. Instead, both high schools and universities are special types of schools.

Figure 13-3 describes this relationship. The newly defined class School contains the common properties of both types of schools, including the relationship they both have with Student objects. School even contains the common Enroll() method, although it's abstract because HighSchool and University don't implement Enroll() the same.

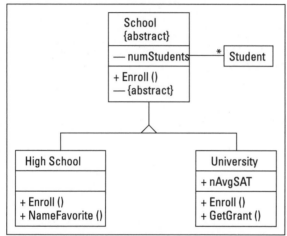

Figure 13-3:
Both High-
School
and
Univer-
sity
should be
based on a
common
School
class.

The classes HighSchool and University now inherit from a common base class. Each contains its unique members: NameFavorite() in the case of HighSchool, and GetGrant() for the University. In addition, both classes override the Enroll() method with a version that describes how that type of school enrolls students.

The introduction of the School class has at least two big advantages. One advantage is that it corresponds with reality. A University is a School, but it is not a HighSchool. Matching reality is nice but not conclusive. The second advantage is that it isolates one class from changes or additions to the other. When my boss comes along later, as will undoubtedly happen, and asks that I introduce the commencement exercise to the university, I can add the CommencementSpeech() method to the University class without impacting HighSchool.

This process of culling out common properties from similar classes is called *factoring*. This is an important feature of object-oriented languages for the reasons described so far plus one more: reduction in redundancy. Let me repeat, redundancy is bad, there is no place for redundancy; said another way . . .

Factoring is legitimate only if the inheritance relationship corresponds to reality. Factoring together a class `Mouse` and `Joystick` because they're both hardware pointing devices is legitimate. Factoring together a class `Mouse` and `Display` because they both make low-level operating system calls is not.

Factoring can and usually does result in multiple levels of abstraction. For example, a program written for a more developed school hierarchy may have a class structure more like that shown in Figure 13-4.

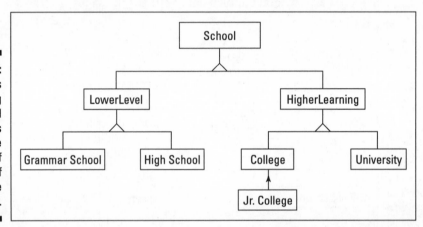

Figure 13-4: Class factoring can and usually does result in the addition of layers of inheritance hierarchy.

You can see that I have inserted a pair of new classes in between `University` and `School`: `HigherLearning`. I've subdivided this new class into `College` and `University`. This type of multitiered class hierarchy is common and desirable when factoring out relationships. They correspond to reality and they can teach you sometimes subtle features of your solution.

Note, however, that there's no Unified Factoring Theory for any given set of classes. The relationship in Figure 13-4 seems natural, but suppose that an application cared more about differentiating types of schools that are administered by local politicians from those that aren't. This relationship, shown in Figure 13-5, is a more natural fit for that type of problem.

I'm left with nothing but a concept — the abstract class

As intellectually satisfying as factoring is, it introduces a problem of its own. Return one more time to `BankAccount`. Think for a minute about how you might go about defining the different member functions defined in `BankAccount`.

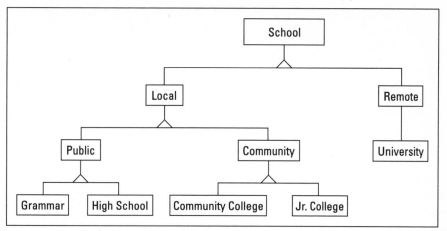

Figure 13-5:
There's no "correct" factoring. The proper way to break down the classes is partially a function of the problem being solved.

Most BankAccount member functions are no problem because both account types implement them in the same way. You should implement those common functions with BankAccount. Withdraw() is different, however. The rules for withdrawing from a savings account differ from those for withdrawing from a checking account. You'll have to implement SavingsAccount.Withdrawal() differently from CheckingAccount.Withdraw(). But how are you supposed to implement BankAccount.Withdrawal()?

Ask the bank manager for help. I imagine the conversation going something like the following:

"What are the rules for making a withdrawal from an account?" you ask, expectantly.

"What type of account? Savings or checking?" comes the reply.

"From an account," you say. "Just an account."

Blank look. (One might say a "blank bank look" . . . Then again, maybe not.)

The problem is that the question doesn't make sense. There's no such thing as "just an account." All accounts (in this example) are either checking accounts or savings accounts. The concept of an account is an abstract one that factors out properties common to the two concrete classes. It is incomplete, because it lacks the critical property Withdraw(). (After you get further into the details, you may find other properties that a simple account lacks.)

The concept of a BankAccount is abstract.

How do you use an abstract class?

Abstract classes are used to describe abstract concepts.

An *abstract class* is a class with one or more abstract methods. Oh, great! That helps a lot. Okay, an abstract method is a method marked `abstract`. We're really moving now. Let me try again: An abstract method has no implementation — now you're really confused.

Consider the following stripped-down demonstration program:

```
// AbstractInheritance - the BankAccount class is actually
//                       abstract because there is no single
//                       implementation for Withdraw
namespace AbstractInheritance
{
  using System;
  // AbstractBaseClass - create an abstract base class with nothing
  //                     but an Output() method
  abstract public class AbstractBaseClass
  {
    // Output - abstract class output that outputs a string
    abstract public void Output(string sOutputString);
  }
  // SubClass1 - one concrete implementation of AbstractBaseClass
  public class SubClass1 : AbstractBaseClass
  {
    override public void Output(string sSource)
    {
      string s = sSource.ToUpper();
      Console.WriteLine("Call to SubClass1.Output() from within {0}", s);
    }
  }
  // SubClass2 - another concrete implementation of AbstractBaseClass
  public class SubClass2 : AbstractBaseClass
  {
    override public void Output(string sSource)
    {
      string s = sSource.ToLower();
      Console.WriteLine("Call to SubClass2.Output() from within {0}", s);
    }
  }
  class Class1
  {
    public static void Test(AbstractBaseClass ba)
    {
      ba.Output("Test");
    }
    public static void Main(string[] strings)
    {
      /*
       * You can't create an AbstractBaseClass object because it's
       * abstract - duh. C# generates a compile time error if you
       * uncomment the following line
       */
      // AbstractBaseClass ba = new AbstractBaseClass();
      // now repeat the experiment with Subclass1
      Console.WriteLine("Creating a SubClass1 object");
      SubClass1 sc1 = new SubClass1();
```

```
      Test(sc1);
      // and finally a Subclass2 object
      Console.WriteLine("\nCreating a SubClass2 object");
      SubClass2 sc2 = new SubClass2();
      Test(sc2);
      // wait for user to acknowledge
      Console.WriteLine("Press Enter to terminate...");
      Console.Read();
    }
  }
}
```

The program first defines the class AbstractBaseClass with a single abstract Output() method. Because it is declared abstract, Output() has no implementation.

Two classes inherit from AbstractBaseClass: SubClass1 and SubClass2. Both are concrete classes because they override the Output() method with "real" methods.

A class can be declared abstract whether it has abstract members or not; however, a class can only be concrete when all its abstract methods have been hidden with real methods.

The two subclass Output() methods differ in a trivial way. Both accept an input string, which they regurgitate back to the user. However, one coverts the string to all caps before output and the other to all lowercase.

The output from this program demonstrates the polymorphic nature of AbstractBaseClass:

```
Creating a SubClass1 object
Call to SubClass1.Output() from within TEST

Creating a SubClass2 object
Call to SubClass2.Output() from within test
Press Enter to terminate...
```

An abstract class is automatically virtual.

Creating an abstract object — Not!

Notice something about the AbstractInheritance program: It is not legal to create an AbstractBaseClass object, but the argument to Test() is declared to be an object of class AbstractBaseClass or one of its subclasses. It's the subclasses clause that's critical here. The SubClass1 and SubClass2 objects can be passed because they are both concrete subclasses of AbstractBaseClass.

Restarting a Class Hierarchy

The `virtual` keyword can also be used to start a new inheritance hierarchy. Consider the class hierarchy demonstrated in the `InheritanceTest` program:

ON THE CD

```
// InheritanceTest - examine the way that the virtual

//                    keyword can be used to start a
//                    new inheritance ladder
namespace InheritanceTest
{
  using System;
  public class Class1
  {
    public static int Main(string[] strings)
    {
      Console.WriteLine("\nPassing a BankAccount");
      BankAccount ba = new BankAccount();
      Test1(ba);

      Console.WriteLine("\nPassing a SavingsAccount");
      SavingsAccount sa = new SavingsAccount();
      Test1(sa);
      Test2(sa);

      Console.WriteLine("\nPassing a SpecialSaleAccount");
      SpecialSaleAccount ssa = new SpecialSaleAccount();
      Test1(ssa);
      Test2(ssa);
      Test3(ssa);

      Console.WriteLine("\nPassing a SaleSpecialCustomer");
      SaleSpecialCustomer ssc = new SaleSpecialCustomer();
      Test1(ssc);
      Test2(ssc);
      Test3(ssc);
      Test4(ssc);

      // wait for user to acknowledge
      Console.WriteLine();
      Console.WriteLine("Hit Press Enter to terminate...");
      Console.Read();
      return 0;
    }

    public static void Test1(BankAccount account)
    {
      Console.WriteLine("  to Test(BankAccount)");
      account.Withdraw(100);
    }

    public static void Test2(SavingsAccount account)
    {
      Console.WriteLine("  to Test(SavingsAccount)");
      account.Withdraw(100);
    }

    public static void Test3(SpecialSaleAccount account)
    {
      Console.WriteLine("  to Test(SpecialSaleAccount)");
```

```
            account.Withdraw(100);
        }

        public static void Test4(SaleSpecialCustomer account)
        {
            Console.WriteLine("  to Test(SaleSpecialCustomer)");
            account.Withdraw(100);
        }
    }
    // BankAccount - simulate a bank account each of which
    //                carries an account id (which is assigned
    //                upon creation) and a balance
    public class BankAccount
    {
        // Withdrawal - you can withdraw any amount up to the
        //              balance; return the amount withdrawn
        virtual public void Withdraw(double dWithdraw)
        {
            Console.WriteLine("    calls BankAccount.Withdraw()");
        }
    }
    // SavingsAccount - a bank account that draws interest
    public class SavingsAccount : BankAccount
    {
        override public void Withdraw(double dWithdrawal)
        {
            Console.WriteLine("    calls SavingsAccount.Withdraw()");
        }
    }

    // SpecialSaleAccount - account used only during a sale
    public class SpecialSaleAccount : SavingsAccount
    {
        new virtual public void Withdraw(double dWithdrawal)
        {
            Console.WriteLine("    calls SpecialSaleAccount.Withdraw()");
        }
    }

    // SaleSpecialCustomer - account used for special customers
    //                       during the sale period
    public class SaleSpecialCustomer : SpecialSaleAccount
    {
        override public void Withdraw(double dWithdrawal)
        {
            Console.WriteLine
                ("    calls SaleSpecialCustomer.Withdraw()");
        }
    }
}   }
}
```

Each of these classes extends the class above it. Notice, however, that the SpecialSaleAccount.Withdraw() has been flagged as virtual, effectively breaking the inheritance ladder at that point. When viewed from the perspective of BankAccount, the SpecialSaleAccount and SaleSpecialCustomer classes look exactly like a SavingsAccount. It is only when viewed from the perspective of a SpecialSaleAccount that the new versions of Withdraw() become available.

Creating a new hierarchy

Why does C# support creating a new inheritance hierarchy? Isn't polymorphism complicated enough already?

C# was created to be a "netable" language in the sense that classes which a program executes, even subclasses, may be distributed across the Internet. That is, a program I'm writing can directly utilize classes from standard repositories located on other computers via the Internet.

I can extend a class that I load over the Internet. Overriding the methods of a standard, tested hierarchy of classes may have unintended effects. Establishing a new hierarchy of classes enables my program to enjoy the benefits of polymorphism without any danger of breaking the existing code.

This is demonstrated with the small program. The function `Main()` invokes a series of `Test()` methods, each designed to accept a different subclass. Each of these versions of `Test()` calls `Withdraw()` from the perspective of a different class of object.

The output from this program is as follows:

```
Passing a BankAccount
  to Test(BankAccount)
    calls BankAccount.Withdraw()
Passing a SavingsAccount
  to Test(BankAccount)
    calls SavingsAccount.Withdraw()
  to Test(SavingsAccount)
    calls SavingsAccount.Withdraw()
Passing a SpecialSaleAccount
  to Test(BankAccount)
    calls SavingsAccount.Withdraw()
  to Test(SavingsAccount)
    calls SavingsAccount.Withdraw()
  to Test(SpecialSaleAccount)
    calls SpecialSaleAccount.Withdraw()
Passing a SaleSpecialCustomer
  to Test(BankAccount)
    calls SavingsAccount.Withdraw()
  to Test(SavingsAccount)
    calls SavingsAccount.Withdraw()
  to Test(SpecialSaleAccount)
    calls SaleSpecialCustomer.Withdraw()
  to Test(SaleSpecialCustomer)
    calls SaleSpecialCustomer.Withdraw()
```

Press Enter to terminate...I have bolded the calls of special interest. The `BankAccount` and `SavingsAccount` classes operate exactly as you would expect. However, when calling `Test(SavingsAccount)`, both the `SpecialSalesAccount` and `SaleSpecialCustomer` pass themselves off as a `SavingsAccount`. It's only when looking at the next lower level that the new `SaleSpecialCustomer` hierarchy can be used in lieu of a `SpecialSaleAccount`.

Sealing a Class

You may decide that you don't want future generations of programmers to be able to extend a particular class. You can lock the class using the keyword `sealed`. A sealed class cannot be used as the base class for any other class.

Consider the following code snippet:

```
using System;
public class BankAccount
{
  // Withdrawal — you can withdraw any amount up to the
  //              balance; return the amount withdrawn
  virtual public void Withdraw(double dWithdraw)
  {
    Console.WriteLine("invokes BankAccount.Withdraw()");
  }
}
public sealed class SavingsAccount : BankAccount
{
  override public void Withdraw(double dWithdrawal)
  {
    Console.WriteLine("invokes SavingsAccount.Withdraw()");
  }
}
public class SpecialSaleAccount : SavingsAccount
{
  override public void Withdraw(double dWithdrawal)
  {
    Console.WriteLine("invokes SpecialSaleAccount.Withdraw()");
  }
}
```

This snippet generates the following compiler error:

```
'SpecialSaleAccount' : cannot inherit from sealed class 'SavingsAccount'
```

The `sealed` keyword enables you to protect your class from the prying methods of some subclass. For example, allowing programmers to extend a class that implements system security would enable someone to create a security back door.

Sealing a class prevents another program, possibly on the Internet somewhere, from using a modified version of your class. The remote program can use the class as is, or not, but it can't inherit bits and pieces of your class while overriding the rest.

Chapter 14

When a Class Isn't a Class — the Interface and the Structure

. . . .

In This Chapter

▶ Investigating the CAN_BE_USED_AS relationship

▶ Defining an interface

▶ Using the interface to perform common operations

▶ Defining a structure

▶ Using the structure to unify classes, interfaces, and intrinsic value types into one

. . . .

A class can contain a reference to another class. This is the simple HAS_A relationship. One class can extend another class through the marvel of inheritance. That's the IS_A relationship. The C# interface implements another, equally important association: the CAN_BE_USED_AS relationship.

What Is CAN_BE_USED_AS?

If I want to jot down a note, I might scribble it on a piece of paper with a pen, stroke it into my personal digital assistant (PDA), or type it on my laptop.

Thus, I can say that all three objects — the pen, the PDA and the laptop — implement the TakeANote operation. Using the magic of inheritance, I could implement this in C# as follows:

```
abstract class ThingsThatRecord
{
  abstract public void TakeANote(string sNote);
}
public class Pen : ThingsThatRecord
{
  override public void TakeANote(String sNote)
  {
    // . . . scribble a note with a pen . . .
  }
}
```

```
public class PDA : ThingsThatRecord
{
  override public void TakeANote(String sNote)
  {
    // . . . stroke a note on the PDA . . .
  }
}
public class Laptop : ThingsThatRecord
{
  override public void TakeANote(String sNote)
  {
    // . . . whatever . . .
  }
}
```

If the term abstract has you stumped, drop back one pace to Chapter 13. If this whole concept of inheritance is a mystery, you need to spend more time Chapter 12.

This inheritance solution seems to work fine as far as the TakeANote() operation is concerned. A function such as RecordTask() can use the TakeANote() method to write down a shopping list without regard for the type of device supplied:

```
void RecordTask(ThingsThatRecord things)
{
  // this abstract method is implemented in all classes
  // that inherit ThingsThatRecord
  things.TakeANote("Shopping list");
  // . . . and so on . . .
}
```

However, this solution suffers from two very big problems. The first is fundamental: You can't really claim that the pen, the PDA, and the laptop have any type of IS_A relationship. Knowing how a pen works and how it takes notes gives me no information as to what a laptop is or how it records information. The name ThingsThatRecord is more of a description than a base class.

The second problem is purely technical. You might better describe Laptop as some subclass of Computer. Although you could reasonably extend PDA off of the same Computer base class, the same cannot be said of Pen. You would have to characterize a pen as some type of MechanicalWritingDevice or DeviceThatStainsYourShirt. However, a C# class cannot inherit from two different classes at the same time — a C# class can be only one type of thing.

Returning to the initial three classes, the only thing that the classes Pen, PDA, and Laptop have in common for our purposes is that they can all be used to record something. The CAN_BE_USED_AS Recordable relationship enables us to communicate their serviceability for a particular purpose without implying any inherent relationship between the three classes.

What Is an Interface?

An interface description looks much like a data-less class in which all the methods are abstract. The interface description for "things that record" might look like the following:

```
interface IRecordable
{
  void TakeANote(String sNote);
}
```

Notice the keyword `interface` where `class` might have gone. Within the braces of an interface appear a list of abstract methods. Interfaces do not contain definitions for any data members.

The method `TakeANote()` is written without an implementation. The keywords `public` and `virtual` or `abstract` are not necessary. All methods in an interface are public, and an interface is not involved in normal inheritance.

By convention, begin the names of interfaces with the letter *I*. In addition, use adjectives for the names of interfaces. As always, these are only suggestions, and I bear no legal responsibility nor are these suggestions suitable for any particular . . . . In other words, C# doesn't care.

The following declaration indicates that the class `PDA` implements the `IRecordable` interface:

```
public class PDA : IRecordable
{
  public void TakeANote(string sNote)
  {
    // . . . do something to record the note . . .
  }
}
```

There's no difference in the syntax of a declaration that inherits a base class `ThingsThatRecord` and a declaration that implements an interface `IRecordable`.

This is the main reason for the naming convention used for interface names: so you can tell an interface from a class.

The bottom line is that an interface describes a capability, like `Swim Safety Training` or `Class A Driver's License`. As a class, I earn my `IRecordable` badge when I implement the `TakeANote` ability.

Can 1 Get a Short Example?

A class implements an interface by providing a definition for every method of the interface:

```
public class Pen : IRecordable
{
  public void TakeANote(string sNote)
  {
    // . . . record the note with a pen . . .
  }
}
public class PDA : ElectronicDevice, IRecordable
{
  public void TakeANote(string sNote)
  {
    // . . . graffiti write the note . . .
  }
}
public class Laptop : Computer, IRecordable
{
  public void TakeANote(string sNote)
  {
    // . . . type in the note . . .
  }
}
```

Each of these three classes inherits a different base class but implements the same IRecordable interface.

Notice the distinction in terminology. You *inherit* or *extend* a base class while you *implement* an interface. Don't look at me; I don't why these terms were picked, but the terminology does help to keep them separate — it sure helps you understand what the heck someone is saying.

The IRecordable interface indicates that each of the three classes can be used to jot down a note using the TakeANote() method. To see how this might be useful, consider the following function:

```
public class Class1
{
  static public void RecordShoppingList(IRecordable recordObject)
  {
    // create a shopping list
    string sList = GenerateShoppingList();
    // now jot it down
    recordObject.TakeANote(sList);
  }
  public static void Main(string[] args)
  {
    PDA pda = new PDA();
    RecordShoppingList(pda);
  }
```

In effect, this code snippet says that the function RecordShoppingList() will accept as its argument any object that implements the TakeANote()

method — in human terms, "any object that can record a note." `RecordShoppingList()` does not make any assumptions about the exact type of `recordObject`. The fact that the object is actually a `PDA` or that it is a type of `ElectronicDevice` is not important, as long as it can take a note.

Can I See a Program that CAN_BE_USED_AS an Example?

The following `SortInterface` program is a special offer. These capabilities brought to you by two different interfaces cannot be matched in any inheritance relationship, anywhere. Interface implementations are standing by.

However, I want to break the `SortInterface` program up into sections to demonstrate various principles — pfft! As if I had principles. I just want to make sure you can see exactly how the program works.

Creating your own interface at home in your spare time

The following `IDisplayable` interface is satisfied by any class that contains a `GetString()` method. `GetString()` returns a `string` representation of the object that can be displayed using `WriteLine()`:

```
// IDisplayable - an object that implements the
//                GetString() method
interface IDisplayable
{
  // return description of yourself
  string GetString();
}
```

The following `Student` class implements `IDisplayable`:

```
class Student : IDisplayable
{
  private string sName;
  private double dGrade = 0.0;
  // access read-only methods
  public string Name
  {
    get
    {
      return sName;
    }
  }
  public double Grade
  {
    get
```

```
    {
      return dGrade;
    }
}
// GetString - return a representation of the student
public string GetString()
{
    string sPadName = Name.PadRight(9);
    string s = String.Format("{0}:{1:N0}",
                              sPadName, Grade);

    return s;
}
}
```

The call to PadRight() makes sure the field where the name goes will be at least nine characters wide. Any extra space after the name is padded with spaces. Padding a string to a standard length makes rows of objects line up nicely. The {1:N0} says, "Display the grade with commas (or dots, depending on what country you're in) every three digits." The 0 part means round off any fractional part.

Given this declaration, I can now write the following program fragment (the entire program appears in the "Putting it all together" section, later in this chapter):

```
// DisplayArray - display an array of objects that
//                implement the IDisplayable interface
public static void DisplayArray
                  (IDisplayable[] displayables)
{
    int length = displayables.Length;
    for(int index = 0; index < length; index++)
    {
      IDisplayable displayable = displayables[index];
      Console.WriteLine("{0}", displayable.GetString());
    }
}
```

This DisplayArray() method can display any type of array, as long as the members of the array define a GetString() method. The following is an example of the output from DisplayArray():

```
Homer     :0
Marge     :85
Bart      :50
Lisa      :100
Maggie    :30
```

Whooeee! See how nicely the grades line up with the names all padded out to a common length?

Predefined interfaces

Likewise, you'll find more interfaces built into the standard C# library than gun racks at an NRA convention. For example, the IComparable interface is defined as follows:

```
interface IComparable
{
  // compare the current object to the object 'o'; return
  // a 1 if larger, -1 if smaller, and 0 otherwise
  int CompareTo(object o);
}
```

A class implements the IComparable interface by implementing a CompareTo() method. For example, String() implements this method by comparing two strings. If the strings are identical, it returns a 0. If they are not, it returns either a 1 or a –1, depending upon which one is "greater."

If you want all the details of how one string is "greater" than another, see Chapter 9.

It seems a little Darwinian, but you could say that one Student object is "greater than" another Student object if his grade point average is greater. He's either a better student or a better apple polisher — it doesn't really matter.

Implementing the CompareTo() method implies that the objects have a sorting order. If one student is "greater than" another, you must be able to sort the students from "least" to "greatest." In fact, the Array class implements the following method already:

```
Array.Sort(IComparable[] objects);
```

This method sorts an array of objects that implements the IComparable interface. Which class doesn't even matter. For example, they could even be Student objects. The Array class could even sort the following version of Student:

```
// Student - description of a student with name and grade
class Student : IComparable
{
  private double dGrade;
  // access read-only methods
  public double Grade
  {
    get
    {
      return dGrade;
    }
```

```
     }
     // CompareTo - compare one student to another;
     //             one student is "better" than another
     //             if his grades are better
     public int CompareTo(object rightObject)
     {
       Student leftStudent = this;
       Student rightStudent = (Student)rightObject;
       // now generate a -1, 0, or 1 based upon the
       // sort criteria (the student's grade)
       if (rightStudent.Grade < leftStudent.Grade)
       {
         return -1;
       }
       if (rightStudent.Grade > leftStudent.Grade)
       {
         return 1;
       }
       return 0;
     }
   }
```

Sorting an array of Students is reduced to a single call:

```
void MyFunction(Student[] students)
{
  // sort the array of IComparable objects
  Array.Sort(students);
}
```

You provide the comparator, and Array does all the work.

Compare this example to the sorting algorithm in Chapter 6. Implementing that algorithm was really painful and took lots of code. By the way, you have no assurances that Array.Sort() is any better or faster than that algorithm, just easier.

Putting it all together

This is the moment you've all been waiting for: the complete SortInterface program utilizing features described earlier in this chapter:

```
// SortInterface - the SortInterface program demonstrates how
//                 the interface concept can be used to provide
//                 an enhanced degree of flexibility in factoring
//                 and implementing classes
using System;
namespace SortInterface
{
  // IDisplayable - an object that can convert itself into
  //                a displayable string format
  interface IDisplayable
  {
    // GetString - return a string representation of yourself
    string GetString();
  }
```

```
class Class1
{
  public static void Main(string[] args)
  {
    // Sort students by grade...
    Console.WriteLine("Sorting the list of students");
    // get an unsorted array of students
    Student[] students = Student.CreateStudentList();
    // utilize the IComparable interface to sort the
    // array
    IComparable[] comparableObjects = (IComparable[])students;
    Array.Sort(comparableObjects);
    // now the IDisplayable interface to display the results
    IDisplayable[] displayableObjects = (IDisplayable[])students;
    DisplayArray(displayableObjects);
    // Now sort an array of birds by name using
    // the same routines even though the class Bird and
    // Student have no common base class
    Console.WriteLine("\nSorting the list of birds");
    Bird[] birds = Bird.CreateBirdList();
    // notice that it's not really necessary to cast the
    // objects explicitly...
    Array.Sort(birds);
    DisplayArray(birds);
    // wait for user to acknowledge the results
    Console.WriteLine("Press Enter to terminate...");
    Console.Read();
  }
  // DisplayArray - display an array of objects that
  //                implement the IDisplayable interface
  public static void DisplayArray
    (IDisplayable[] displayables)
  {
    int length = displayables.Length;
    for(int index = 0; index < length; index++)
    {
      IDisplayable displayable = displayables[index];
      Console.WriteLine("{0}", displayable.GetString());
    }
  }
}
// ---------- Students - sort students by grade -------
// Student - description of a student with name and grade
class Student : IComparable, IDisplayable
{
  private string sName;
  private double dGrade = 0.0;
  // Constructor - initialize a new student object
  public Student(string sName, double dGrade)
  {
    // save off the object's data
    this.sName = sName;
    this.dGrade = dGrade;
  }
  // CreateStudentList - to save space, just create
  //                a fixed list of students
  static string[] sNames =
        {"Homer", "Marge", "Bart", "Lisa", "Maggie"};
  static double[] dGrades =
        {0, 85, 50, 100, 30};
  public static Student[] CreateStudentList()
  {
```

```
      Student[] sArray = new Student[sNames.Length];
      for (int i = 0; i < sNames.Length; i++)
      {
        sArray[i] = new Student(sNames[i], dGrades[i]);
      }
      return sArray;
    }
    // access read-only methods
    public string Name
    {
      get
      {
        return sName;
      }
    }
    public double Grade
    {
      get
      {
        return dGrade;
      }
    }
    // implement the IComparable interface:
    // CompareTo — compare another object (in this case,
    //             Student objects) and decide which
    //             one comes after the other in the
    //             sorted array
    public int CompareTo(object rightObject)
    {
      // compare the current Student (let's call her
      // 'left') against the other student (we'll call
      // her 'right') — generate an error if both
      // left and right are not Student objects
      Student leftStudent = this;
      if (!(rightObject is Student))
      {
        Console.WriteLine
          ("Compare method passed a nonStudent");
        return 0;
      }
      Student rightStudent = (Student)rightObject;
      // now generate a -1, 0, or 1 based upon the
      // sort criteria (the student's grade)
      // (the Double class has a CompareTo() method
      // we could have used instead)
      if (rightStudent.Grade < leftStudent.Grade)
      {
        return -1;
      }
      if (rightStudent.Grade > leftStudent.Grade)
      {
        return 1;
      }
      return 0;
    }
    // implement the IDisplayable interface:
    // GetString — return a representation of the student
    public string GetString()
    {
      string sPadName = Name.PadRight(9);
      string s = String.Format("{0}:{1:N0}",
                               sPadName, Grade);
```

```
      return s;
   }
}
// ----------Birds — sort birds by their names--------
// Bird — just an array of bird names
class Bird : IComparable, IDisplayable
{
   private string sName;
   // Constructor — initialize a new student object
   public Bird(string sName)
   {
      this.sName = sName;
   }
   // CreateBirdList — return a list of birds to the caller;
   //                  use a canned list to save time
   static string[] sBirdNames =
      { "Oriole", "Hawk", "Robin", "Cardinal",
        "Bluejay", "Finch", "Sparrow"};
   public static Bird[] CreateBirdList()
   {
      Bird[] birds = new Bird[sBirdNames.Length];
      for(int i = 0; i < birds.Length; i++)
      {
         birds[i] = new Bird(sBirdNames[i]);
      }
      return birds;
   }
   // access read-only methods
   public string Name
   {
      get
      {
         return sName;
      }
   }
   // implement the IComparable interface:
   // CompareTo — compare the birds by name; use the
   //             built-in String class compare method
   public int CompareTo(object rightObject)
   {
      // we'll compare the "current" bird to the
      // "right-hand object" bird
      Bird leftBird = this;
      Bird rightBird = (Bird)rightObject;
      return String.Compare(leftBird.Name, rightBird.Name);
   }
   // implement the IDisplayable interface:
   // GetString — returns the name of the bird
   public string GetString()
   {
      return Name;
   }
}
}
```

The `Student` class (it's about in the middle of the program listing) implements the `IComparable` and `IDisplayable` interfaces as described earlier.
The `CompareTo()` compares the students by grade, which results in the students being sorted by grade. The `GetString()` returns the name and grade
of the student.

The other methods of Student include the read-only Name and Grade properties, a simple constructor, and a CreateStudentList() method. This list method just returns a fixed list of students. (Originally, I thought about enabling the user to enter the student names from the keyboard, but the listing got so big that it wasted paper and obscured the point of the program.)

The Bird class at the bottom of the listing also implements the IComparable and IDisplayable interfaces. It implements CompareTo() by comparing the names of the birds using the similar method built into the String class. So, one bird is greater than another if its name is greater. This method results in the birds being sorted in alphabetical order. The GetName() method just returns the name of the bird.

Now we're set up for the good part back in Main(). The CreateStudent List() method is used to return an unsorted list, which is stored in the array students.

Name collections of objects, such as an array, using a plural noun.

This array of students is first cast into an array of comparableObjects. This differs from the arrays used in other chapters (most notably the arrays in Chapter 6). Those are arrays of objects of a particular class, like an array of Student objects, while comparableObjects is an array of objects that implement the IComparable interface, irrespective of what class they might be.

The comparableObjects array is passed to the built-in Array.Sort() method, which sorts them by grade.

The sorted array of Student objects is then passed to the locally defined DisplayArray() method. DisplayArray() iterates through an array of objects that implement GetString(). It uses the Array.Length property to know how many objects are in the array. It then calls GetString() on each object and displays the result to the console using WriteLine().

The program back in Main() continues by sorting and displaying birds! I think we can agree that birds have nothing to do with students. However, the class Bird implements the IComparable interface by comparing the names of the birds and the IDisplayable interface by returning the name of the bird.

Notice that Main() does not recast the array of birds this time. There's no need. This is similar to the following:

```
class BaseClass {}
class SubClass : BaseClass {}
class Class1
{
  public static void SomeFunction(BaseClass bc) {}
  public static void AnotherFunction()
  {
```

```
    SubClass sc = new SubClass();
    SomeFunction(sc);
  }
}
```

Here, an object of class `SubClass` can be passed in lieu of a `BaseClass` object because a `SubClass` IS_A `BaseClass`.

Similarly, an array of `Bird` objects can be passed to a method expecting an array of `IComparable` objects because `Bird` implements that interface. The very next call to `DisplayArray()` passes the `birds` array, again without a cast because `Bird` implements the `IDisplayable` interface.

The output from the program appears as follows:

```
Sorting the list of students
Lisa    :100
Marge   :85
Bart    :50
Maggie  :30
Homer   :0

Sorting the list of birds
Bluejay
Cardinal
Finch
Hawk
Oriole
Robin
Sparrow
Press Enter to terminate...
```

The students and birds are sorted, each according to its kind.

Inheriting an Interface

An interface can "inherit" the methods of another interface. I use quotes around the word *inherit* because it's not true inheritance no matter how it may appear:

```
// ICompare — an interface that can both compare itself
//            and display its own value
public interface ICompare : IComparable
{
    // GetValue — returns the value of itself as an int
    int GetValue();
}
```

The `ICompare` interface inherits the requirement to implement the `CompareTo()` method from `IComparable`. To that, it adds the requirement to implement `GetValue()`. An `ICompare` object can be used as an `IComparable` object because, by definition, the former implements the requirements of the latter. However, this is not complete inheritance in the object-oriented, C# meaning of the word. Polymorphism is not possible. In addition, constructor relationships don't apply.

I demonstrate interface inheritance in the `AbstractInterface` program in the following section.

Facing an Abstract Interface

A class must override every method of an interface in order to implement the interface. However, a class may override the method of an interface with an abstract method (such a class is abstract, of course):

```
// AbstractInterface - demonstrate that an interface
//                     can be implemented with an
//                     abstract class
using System;
namespace AbstractInterface
{
  // ICompare - an interface that can both compare itself
  //            and display its own value
  public interface ICompare : IComparable
  {
    // GetValue - returns the value of itself as an int
    int GetValue();
  }
  // BaseClass - implement the ICompare interface by
  //             providing a concrete GetValue() method and
  //             an abstract CompareTo()
  abstract public class BaseClass : ICompare
  {
    int nValue;
    public BaseClass(int nInitialValue)
    {
      nValue = nInitialValue;
    }
    // implement the ICompare interface:
    // first with a concrete method
    public int GetValue()
    {
      return nValue;
    }
    // complete the ICompare interface with an abstract method
    abstract public int CompareTo(object rightObject);
  }
  // SubClass - complete the base class by overriding the
  //            abstract CompareTo() method
  public class SubClass: BaseClass
  {
    // pass the value passed to the constructor up to the
    // base class constructor
    public SubClass(int nInitialValue) : base(nInitialValue)
    {
```

```
      }
      // CompareTo - implement the IComparable interface; return
      //             an indication of whether a subclass object is
      //             greater than another
      override public int CompareTo(object rightObject)
      {
        BaseClass bc = (BaseClass)rightObject;
        return GetValue().CompareTo(bc.GetValue());
      }
    }
    public class Class1
    {
      public static int Main(string[] strings)
      {
        SubClass sc1 = new SubClass(10);
        SubClass sc2 = new SubClass(20);
        MyFunc(sc1, sc2);
        // wait for user to acknowledge the results
        Console.WriteLine("Press Enter to terminate...");
        Console.Read();
        return 0;
      }
      // MyFunc - use the methods provided by the ICompare interface
      //          to display the value of two objects and then an
      //          indication of which is greater (according to the
      //          object itself)
      public static void MyFunc(ICompare ic1, ICompare ic2)
      {
        Console.WriteLine("The value of ic1 is {0} and ic2 is {1}",
                      ic1.GetValue(), ic2.GetValue());
        string s;
        switch (ic1.CompareTo(ic2))
        {
          case 0:
            s = "is equal to";
            break;
          case -1:
            s = "is less than";
            break;
          case 1:
            s = "is greater than";
            break;
          default:
            s = "something messed up";
            break;
        }
        Console.WriteLine(
            "The objects themselves think that ic1 {0} ic2", s);
      }
    }
}
```

AbstractInterface is another one of those large but relatively simple programs.

The ICompare interface describes a class that can compare two objects and fetch their value. ICompare inherits the CompareTo() requirement from the IComparable interface. To that, ICompare adds GetValue(), which returns the value of the objects as an int.

Even though it may return the value of the object as an `int`, `GetValue()` says nothing about the internals of the class. Generating an `int` value may involve a complex calculation, for all I know.

The class `BaseClass` implements the `ICompare` interface — the concrete `GetValue()` method returns the data member `nValue`. However, the `CompareTo()` method, which is also required by the `ICompare` interface, is declared `abstract`.

Declaring a class `abstract` means that it is an incomplete concept lacking an implementation of one or more properties — in this case, the method `CompareTo()`.

`SubClass` provides the `CompareTo()` method necessary to become concrete.

Notice that `SubClass` automatically implements the `ICompare` interface, even though it doesn't explicitly say so. `BaseClass` promised to implement the methods of `Icompare`, and `SubClass` IS_A `BaseClass`. By inheriting these methods, `SubClass` automatically implements `ICompare`.

`Main()` creates two objects of class `SubClass` with different values. It then passes those objects to `MyFunc()`. The `MyFunc()` method expects to receive two objects of interface `ICompare`. `MyFunc()` uses the `CompareTo()` method to decide which object is greater and then uses `GetValue()` to display the "value" of the two objects.

The output from this program is short and sweet:

```
The value of ic1 is 10 and ic2 is 20
The objects themselves think that ic1 is less than ic2
Press Enter to terminate...
```

The C# `struct` *has no Class*

C# appears to have a dichotomy in the way you declare variables. You declare and initialize value type variables such as `int` and `double` one way:

```
int n;
n = 1;
```

However, you declare and initialize references to objects in a completely different way:

```
public class MyClass
{
    public int n;
}
MyClass mc;
mc = new MyClass();
```

The `class` variable `mc` is known as a *reference type* because the variable `mc` refers to potentially distant memory. Intrinsic variables like `int` or `double` are known as *value type variables*.

If you examine `n` and `mc` more closely, however, you see that the only real difference is that C# allocates the memory for the value type variable automatically while you have to allocate the memory for the class object. `int` is from Venus; `MyClass` is from Mars. Is there nothing that can tie the two together into a Unified Class Theory?

The C# structure

C# defines a third variable type called a *structure* that bridges the gap between the reference types and the value types.

The syntax of a structure declaration looks like that of a class:

```
public struct MyStruct
{
  public int n;
  public double d;
}
public class MyClass
{
  public int n;
  public double d;
}
```

A structure object is accessed like a class object but allocated like a value type:

```
// declaring and accessing a simple value type
int n;
n = 1;
// declaring a struct is much like declaring a simple int
MyStruct ms;
ms.n = 3;       // access the members the same as a class object
ms.d = 3.0;
// a class object must be allocated out of a separate
// memory area
MyClass mc = new MyClass;
mc.n = 2;
mc.d = 2.0;
```

A `struct` object is stored like an intrinsic variable in memory. The variable `ms` is not a reference to some external memory block allocated off a separate memory area.

The "special memory area" from whence class objects come is called the *heap*. Don't ask me why. No, really, don't ask me why.

The `ms` object occupies the same local memory that the variable `n` occupies, as shown in Figure 14-1.

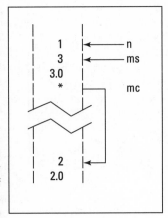

The distinction between reference and value types is even more obvious in the following example. Allocating an array of 100 reference objects requires the program to invoke new 101 times (once for the array and once for each object):

```
MyClass[] mc = new MyClass[100];
for(int i = 0; i < ms.Length; i++)
{
  mc[i] = new MyClass();
}
mc[0].n = 0;
```

This array also involves a considerable amount of overhead, both in space and time. First, each element in the mc array must be large enough to contain a reference to an object. In addition, each MyClass object has unseen overhead above and beyond the single data member n. Finally, there's the time the program takes to go through the motions of whittling off a tiny chunk of memory 100 times.

The memory for the structure objects is allocated as part of the array:

```
// declaring an array of simple int value types
int[] integers = new int[100];
integers[0] = 0;
// declaring an array of structs is just as easy
MyStruct[] ms = new MyStruct[100];
ms[0].n = 0;
```

The structure constructor

Interestingly, a structure can be initialized using a class-like syntax:

```
public struct MyStruct
{
  public int n;
  public double d;
}
MyStruct ms = new MyStruct();
```

Despite appearances, this does not allocate a block of memory off of the heap. It just initializes n and d to zero.

You can construct a nondefault constructor of your own that actually does something:

```
public struct Test
{
  private int n;
  public Test(int n)
  {
    this.n = n;
  }
}
public class Class1
{
  public static void Main(string[] args)
  {
    Test test = new Test(10);
  }
}
```

Despite its appearance the declaration test = new Test(10); does not allocate memory — it only initializes the value type memory that's already there.

The wily methods of a structure

A structure can have instance members, including methods and properties. A structure can have static members. The static members of a structure may have initializers, but the nonstatic (instance) members may not. Normally, a structure object is passed to a function by value, but it may be passed by reference if this is specifically indicated in the function call. A structure cannot inherit a class (other than Object, as described in the section "'Oh, the Value and the Reference Can Be Friends . . .' — Unifying the Type System," later in this chapter) and it cannot be inherited by some other class. A structure can implement an interface.

See Chapter 8 if you don't remember the difference between a static and an instance member. See Chapter 7 for a review of pass by value and pass by reference. Chapter 12 discusses inheritance. Check out Chapter 14 if you don't know what an interface . . . . Wait, that's this chapter.

All classes inherit from Object whether they specifically say so or not. You can override the methods of Object. In practical terms, the only method you may want to override is ToString(). ToString() allows the object to create a displayable representation of itself.

Putting a struct through its paces in an example

The following example program demonstrates the different features of a structure:

```
// StructureExample - demonstrate the various properties
//                    of a struct object
using System;
using System.Collections;
namespace StructureExample
{
  public interface IDisplayable
  {
    string ToString();
  }
  public struct Test : IDisplayable
  {
    // a struct can have both object and
    // class (static) data members;
    // static members may have initializers
    private int n;
    private static double d = 20.0;
    // a constructor can be used to initialize
    // the data members of a struct
    public Test(int n)
    {
      this.n = n;
    }
    // a struct may have both object and class
    // (static) properties
    public int N
    {
      get { return n;}
      set { n = value; }
    }
    public static double D
    {
      get { return d; }
      set { d = value; }
    }
    // a struct may have a method
    public void ChangeMethod(int nNewValue, double dNewValue)
    {
```

```
      n = nNewValue;
      d = dNewValue;
    }
    // ToString — overrides the ToString method in object
    override public string ToString()
    {
      return string.Format("({0:N}, {1:N})", n, d);
    }
  }
  public class Class1
  {
    public static int Main(string[] args)
    {
      // create a Test object
      Test test = new Test(10);
      Console.WriteLine("Initial value of test");
      OutputFunction(test);
      // try to modify the test object by passing it
      // as an argument
      ChangeValueFunction(test, 100, 200.0);
      Console.WriteLine("Value of test after calling" +
                        " ChangeValueFunction(100, 200.0)");
      OutputFunction(test);
      // try to modify the test object by passing it
      // as an argument
      ChangeReferenceFunction(ref test, 100, 200.0);
      Console.WriteLine("Value of test after calling" +
                        " ChangeReferenceFunction(100, 200.0)");
      OutputFunction(test);
      // a method can modify the object
      test.ChangeMethod(1000, 2000.0);
      Console.WriteLine("Value of test after calling" +
                        " ChangeMethod(1000, 2000.0)");
      OutputFunction(test);
      // wait for user to acknowledge the results
      Console.WriteLine("Press Enter to terminate...");
      Console.Read();
      return 0;
    }
    // ChangeValueFunction — pass the struct by reference
    public static void ChangeValueFunction(Test t,
                           int newValue, double dNewValue)
    {
      t.N = newValue;
      Test.D = dNewValue;
    }
    // ChangeReferenceFunction — pass the struct by reference
    public static void ChangeReferenceFunction(ref Test t,
                           int newValue, double dNewValue)
    {
      t.N = newValue;
      Test.D = dNewValue;
    }
    // OutputFunction — outputs any method that implements
    //                  ToString()
    public static void OutputFunction(IDisplayable id)
    {
      Console.WriteLine("id = {0}", id.ToString());
    }
  }
}
```

The `StructureExample` program first defines an interface, `IDisplayable`, and then a simple structure, `Test`, which implements that interface. `Test` also defines two members: an instance member, `n`, and a static member, `d`. A static initializer sets the member `d` to 20; however, an initializer for the instance member `n` is not allowed.

The `Test` structure defines a constructor, an instance property `N`, and a static property `D`.

`Test` defines a method of its own — `ChangeMethod()` — as well as overriding the `ToString()` method. In providing `ToString()`, `Test` implements the `IDisplayable` interface.

The `Main()` function puts `Test` through it paces. First, it creates an object `test` out of local memory and uses the constructor to initialize that space. `Main()` then calls `OutputFunction()` to display the object.

`Main()` next calls the function `ChangeValueFunction()`, passing `test` along with two numeric constants. `ChangeValueFunction()` assigns these two numbers to the `Test` members `n` and `d`. Upon return from the function, the `OutputFunction()` reveals that `d` has been changed while `n` has not.

The call to `ChangeValueFunction()` passes the `struct` object `test` by value. The object `t` within that function is a copy of the original `test` and not the object itself. Thus, the assignment to `t.N` changes the local copy but has no effect on `test` back in `Main()`. However, all objects of class `Test` share the same static member `d`. Thus, the assignment to `Test.D` changes `d` for all objects, including `test`.

The next call is to the function `ChangeReferenceFunction()`. This function appears the same as its `ChangeValueFunction()` except for the addition of the keyword `ref` to the argument list. `test` is now passed by reference, so the argument `t` refers to the original object `test` and not some newly created copy.

The final call in `Main()` is to the method `ChangeMethod()`. Calls to methods always pass the current object by reference, so the changes made in this method are retained back in `Main()`.

The output from the program appears as follows:

```
Initial value of test
id = (10.00, 20.00)
Value of test after calling ChangeValueFunction(100, 200.0)
id = (10.00, 200.00)
Value of test after calling ChangeReferenceFunction(100, 200.0)
id = (100.00, 200.00)
Value of test after calling ChangeMethod(1000, 2000.0)
id = (1,000.00, 2,000.00)
Press Enter to terminate...
```

"Oh, the Value and the Reference Can Be Friends . . ." — Unifying the Type System

Structures and classes do have one striking similarity: They both derive from `Object`. In fact, all classes and structures, whether they say so or not, derive from `Object`. This fact unifies the different variable types.

This unification of variable types is foreign to other C-derived languages like C++ and Java. In fact, the dichotomy of reference versus value type objects in Java can be a real pain. Everything's a pain in C++, so one more is hardly noticed.

Predefined structure types

The similarity between structures and simple value types is more than skin deep. In fact, a simple value type is a structure. For example, `int` is another name for the structure `Int32`, while `double` is another name for the structure `Double`, and so forth. Table 14-1 shows the full list of types and their corresponding `struct` names.

Table 14-1	The `struct` Names for the Intrinsic Variable Types
Type Name	`struct` *Name*
bool	Boolean
byte	Byte
sbyte	SByte
char	Char
decimal	Decimal
double	Double
float	Single
int	Int32
uint	UInt32
long	Int64
ulong	UInt64

(continued)

Table 14-1 *(continued)*

Type Name	struct *Name*
object	Object
short	Int16
ushort	UInt16

So, how do common structures unify the type system? An example

An int is another name for Int32. Because all structs derive from Object, int must derive from Object as well. This leads to some fascinating results, as the following program demonstrates:

```
// TypeUnification — demonstrate how int and Int32
//                   are actually the same thing and
//                   how they all derive from object
using System;
namespace TypeUnification
{
  public class Class1
  {
    public static int Main(string[] args)
    {
      // create an int and initialize it to zero
      int i = new int();
      // assign it a value and output it via the
      // IFormattable interface
      i = 1;
      OutputFunction(i);
      // the constant 2 implements the same interface
      OutputFunction(2);
      // in fact, you can use the same object directly
      Console.WriteLine("Output directly = {0}", 3.ToString());
      // this can be truly useful; you can pick an int out of
      // a list:
      Console.WriteLine("\nPick the integers out of a list");
      object[] objects = new object[5];
      objects[0] = "this is a string";
      objects[1] = 2;
      objects[2] = new Class1();
      objects[3] = 4;
      objects[4] = 5.5;
      for(int index = 0; index < objects.Length; index++)
      {
        if (objects[index] is int)
        {
          int n = (int)objects[index];
          Console.WriteLine("the {0}th element is a {1}",
                            index, n);
        }
      }
```

```
     // another use for the type unity
     Console.WriteLine("\nDisplay all the objects in the list");
     int nCount = 0;
     foreach(object o in objects)
     {
       Console.WriteLine("Objects[{0}] is <{1}>",
         nCount++, o.ToString());
     }
     // wait for user to acknowledge the results
     Console.WriteLine("Press Enter to terminate...");
     Console.Read();
     return 0;
   }
   // OutputFunction - outputs any method that implements
   //                  ToString()
   public static void OutputFunction(IFormattable id)
   {
     Console.WriteLine("Value from OutputFunction = {0}",
                       id.ToString());
   }
   // ToString - provide a simple string function
   override public string ToString()
   {
     return "StructureExample program Class1";
   }
 }
}
```

This program puts the Int32 struct through its paces.

Main() begins by creating an int object i. Main() uses the Int32() default constructor (or you could say the int() constructor) to initialize i to zero. The program continues by assigning a value to i. Admittedly, this differs slightly from the format you would use for a structure that you might create.

Main() passes the variable i to OutputFunction(), which is declared to accept an object that implements the IFormattable interface. The IFormattable interface is the same as the IDisplayable interface that I define in other programs — the only method in IFormattable is ToString. All classes and structures inherit the IFormattable interface from Object.

OutputFunction() tells the IFormattable object to display itself — the Int32 variable has no problem at all because it has its own ToString() method. This is demonstrated even more graphically in the call Output Function(2). Being of type Int32, the constant 2 also implements IFormattable. Finally, just to shove your nose in it, Main() invokes 3.ToString() directly. That output from this first section of Main() is

```
Value from OutputFunction = 1
Value from OutputFunction = 2
Output directly = 3
```

The program now enters a unique section. Main() declares an array of objects of type Object. It stores a string in the first element, an int in the second, an instance of Class1 in the third, and so on. This is allowed because String, Int32, and Class1 all derive from Object.

The program then loops through the objects in the array. Main() is able to pick out the integers by asking each object whether it IS_A Int32 using the is keyword. The output from this portion of the program is as follows:

```
Pick the integers out of a list
the 1th element is a 2
the 3th element is a 4
```

The program completes its showing off by again using the Object lineage. All subclasses of Object — that would be all classes — implement ToString(). Therefore, if we just want to display the members of the object array, we really don't need to worry about their type. The final section of Main() loops through the object array again, this time asking each object to format itself using its ToString() method. The results appear as follows:

```
Display all the objects in the list
Objects[0] is <this is a string>
Objects[1] is <2>
Objects[2] is <StructureExample program Class1>
Objects[3] is <4>
Objects[4] is <5.5>
Press Enter to terminate...
```

Like animals coming off of Noah's Arc, each object displays itself as one of its kind. I implemented a trivial ToString() for Class1 just to show that it knows how to play nice with all the other classes.

In fact, this ToString() property is undoubtedly how Console.Write() can perform its magic. I haven't looked into the source code, but I would bet that Write() accepts its arguments as objects. It can then simply invoke ToString() on the object to convert it into displayable format (Other than the first argument, which might contain {n} format controls).

Chapter 15

Some Exceptional Exceptions

I know it's difficult to accept, but occasionally a method (or function) doesn't do what it's supposed to do. Even the ones I write — especially the ones I write — don't always do what they're supposed to. Users are notoriously unreliable, as well. No sooner do you ask for an int than some user inputs a character string. Sometimes, the method goes merrily along, blissfully ignorant of the fact that it is spewing out garbage. However, good programmers write their functions to anticipate problems and report them as they occur.

I'm talking about run time errors, not compile time errors, which C# spits out when you try to build your program.

The *exception mechanism* is a means for reporting these errors in a way that the calling function can best understand and handle the problem.

Handling an Error the Old-Fashioned Way — (Re)Turn It

Not reporting run time errors is never a good idea. And I mean *never*. If you don't intend to debug your programs, and you don't care whether they work, it's probably an okay idea.

The following FactorialError program demonstrates what happens when errors go undetected. This program calculates and reports the factorial function for numerous values, some of them even legal.

The factorial of a number N is equal to N * N – 1 * N – 2 * . . . * 1. For example, factorial 4 is 4 * 3 * 2 * 1, or 24. The factorial function is only valid for positive, whole numbers.

```
// FactorialWithError - create and exercise a factorial
//                      function that has no error checks
//                      at all
using System;
namespace FactorialWithError
{
  // MyMathFunctions - a collection of mathematical functions
  //                   I created (it's not much to look at yet)
  public class MyMathFunctions
  {
    // Factorial - return the factorial of a value
    //             provided
    public static double Factorial(double dValue)
    {
      // begin with an "accumulator" of 1
      double dFactorial = 1.0;
      // loop from nValue down to one, each time
      // multiplying the previous accumulator value
      // by the result
      do
      {
        dFactorial *= dValue;
        dValue -= 1.0;
      } while(dValue > 1);
      // return the accumulated value
      return dFactorial;
    }
  }
  public class Class1
  {
    public static void Main(string[] args)
    {
      // call factorial in a loop from 6 down to -6.
      for (int i = 6; i > -6; i--)
      {
        // display the result of each pass
        Console.WriteLine("i = {0}, factorial = {1}",
                          i, MyMathFunctions.Factorial(i));
      }
      // wait for user to acknowledge
      Console.WriteLine("Press Enter to terminate...");
      Console.Read();
    }
  }
}
```

The Factorial() function begins by initializing an accumulator variable to 1. The function then enters a loop, multiplying the accumulator by successively smaller values for nValue until nValue reaches 1. The resulting accumulator value is returned to the caller.

The Factorial() algorithm sounds pretty good until you see how it's called. Main() enters a loop starting at a reasonable value for a factorial and counting down toward 1. Rather than stop, however, Main() just keeps on going until it reaches –6. I know that –6 is a strange value, but you gotta stop somewhere.

Executing the function generates the following output:

```
i = 6, factorial = 720
i = 5, factorial = 120
i = 4, factorial = 24
i = 3, factorial = 6
i = 2, factorial = 2
i = 1, factorial = 1
i = 0, factorial = 0
i = -1, factorial = -1
i = -2, factorial = -2
i = -3, factorial = -3
i = -4, factorial = -4
i = -5, factorial = -5
Press Enter to terminate...
```

Just a glance by one wise in the way of the factorial can see that these results don't make sense. First of all, the result of a factorial cannot be negative. Second, notice how the negative values don't grow at the same rate as the positive values. Clearly, something is wrong.

The incorrect results returned here are subtle compared to what could have happened. Had the loop within `Factorial()` been written as `do {...} while (dValue != 0)`, the program would have crashed when passed a negative number. Of course, I never would have written a check like `while(dValue != 0)` because approximation errors might have caused the test for zero to fail, anyway.

Returning an error indication

Although simple enough, the `Factorial()` function lacks critical error checks: The factorial of a negative number is not defined. The factorial of a noninteger value also is undefined. The `Factorial()` function should include a test for these conditions.

But, what is the `Factorial()` function to do with an error condition, should one arise? It knows the problem but not how it came to be. The best that `Factorial()` can do is report the error to the calling function — maybe the caller knows where the problem originated.

The classic way to indicate an error in a function is to return some value that the function can't otherwise return. For example, the returned value from factorial can't be negative. Thus, the factorial function could return a –1 if passed a negative number, a –2 for a noninteger, and so on, for each possible error. The calling function can check the returned value: If it's a negative, the calling function knows an error occurred. By checking the actual value of the return, the caller can tell the nature of the problem.

The following `FactorialErrorReturn` **program makes the necessary adjustments:**

ON THE CD

```
// FactorialErrorReturn — create a factorial program that
//                        returns an error indication when
//                        something goes wrong
using System;
namespace FactorialErrorReturn
{
  // MyMathFunctions — a collection of mathematical functions
  //                   I created (it's not much to look at yet)
  public class MyMathFunctions
  {
    // the following represent illegal values
    public const int NEGATIVE_NUMBER = -1;
    public const int NON_INTEGER_VALUE = -2;
    // Factorial — return the factorial of a value
    //             provided
    public static double Factorial(double dValue)
    {
      // don't allow negative numbers
      if (dValue < 0)
      {
        return NEGATIVE_NUMBER;
      }
      // check for non-integer
      int nValue = (int)dValue;
      if (nValue != dValue)
      {
        return NON_INTEGER_VALUE;
      }
      // begin with an "accumulator" of 1
      double dFactorial = 1.0;
      // loop from nValue down to one, each time
      // multiplying the previous accumulator value
      // by the result
      do
      {
        dFactorial *= dValue;
        dValue -= 1.0;
      } while(dValue > 1);
      // return the accumulated value
      return dFactorial;
    }
  }
  public class Class1
  {
    public static void Main(string[] args)
    {
      // call factorial in a loop from 6 down to -6.
      for (int i = 6; i > -6; i--)
      {
        // calculate the factorial of the number
        double dFactorial = MyMathFunctions.Factorial(i);
        if (dFactorial == MyMathFunctions.NEGATIVE_NUMBER)
        {
          Console.WriteLine
                  ("Factorial() passed a negative number");
          break;
        }
        if (dFactorial == MyMathFunctions.NON_INTEGER_VALUE)
        {
```

```
            Console.WriteLine
                    ("Factorial() passed a non-integer number");
            break;
        }
        // display the result of each pass
        Console.WriteLine("i = {0}, factorial = {1}",
                          i, MyMathFunctions.Factorial(i));
    }
    // wait for user to acknowledge
    Console.WriteLine("Press Enter to terminate...");
    Console.Read();
    }
  }
}
```

Factorial() now performs a series of tests before it starts. The first test is for a negative number — 0 is allowed in this test because it generates a reasonable result. If this test passes, the function immediately returns with an error indication. The argument is then compared with an integer version of itself: If they are equal, the fractional part of the argument must be zero.

Main() checks the results returned from the Factorial() program for indication of a detected error. However, values like –1 and –2 have little meaning to any programmer that either uses or maintains this code. To give the error returns a little more life, the MyMathFunctions class defines a couple of integer constants. The const NEGATIVE_NUMBER is set to the value –1, and NON_INTEGER_VALUE to –2. That doesn't change anything, but the constants make the program, especially the calling function Main(), much more readable.

The Southern Naming Convention assigns constants names with all capital letters, and words separated by an underscore. Some more liberal programmers are withholding their tithes, but the convention isn't likely to change.

These constant error values are accessed through the class, as in MyMathClass.NEGATIVE_NUMBER. A const variable is automatically static, making it a class property shared by all objects.

The Factorial() function now reports that a negative value is being passed as an argument and reports the problem back to Main(), which exits, stage right, with an appropriate error message:

```
i = 6, factorial = 720
i = 5, factorial = 120
i = 4, factorial = 24
i = 3, factorial = 6
i = 2, factorial = 2
i = 1, factorial = 1
i = 0, factorial = 0
Factorial() passed a negative number
Press Enter to terminate...
```

Indicating an error condition via a return value from a function is how error processing has been done ever since the early days of FORTRAN. Why change it now?

I'm here to report, that seems fine to me

What's wrong with returning error codes? It was good enough for FORTRAN! Yeah, but so were vacuum tube computers. Unfortunately, the error code approach has several problems.

First, this solution relies upon the ability to return some otherwise illegal value, but functions exist for which all possible return values are legal. Not all functions are lucky enough to return only positive values. You can't take the log of a negative number, but logarithms can be either negative or positive.

Although you can circumvent this problem by using the return value of the function to return error status and return any data via an `out` argument type, this solution is less intuitive and loses some of the expressive power of a function. In any case, after you've seen how exceptions work, you'll throw this idea away faster than you get rid of knives and forks at a fried chicken picnic.

Second, there's only so much information you can store in an integer. `Factorial()` returns a −1 if the argument is negative. Identifying the problem might be easier if we knew exactly what the negative value was, but there's no place to return that type of information.

Third, the processing of error returns is optional. You don't gain much by having `Factorial()` return an error code that the calling function doesn't check. Sure, as lead programmer, I can make all kinds of menacing threats like, "You will check your error returns, or else." I remember reading all the programming books with the dire threats of banishment from the programmers' union if anyone found out, but all good FORTRAN programmers knew that the language can't force anyone to check anything, and very often, those checks didn't happen.

Often, even if I do check the error return from `Factorial()` or any other function, all my function can do is report the error up the line. The problem is that the calling function is compelled to check all the possible error returns from all the functions it calls. Pretty soon, all code begins to have the following appearance:

```
// call SomeFunction, check the error return, handle it,
// and return
errRtn = someFunc();
if (errRtn == SF_ERROR1)
{
  Console.WriteLine("Error type 1 call to someFunc()");
  return MY_ERROR_1;
}
```

```
if (errRtn == SF_ERROR2)
{
  Console.WriteLine("Error type 2 in call to someFunc()");
  return My_ERROR_2;
}
// call SomeOtherFunctions, check its error returns and so forth
errRtn = someOtherFunc();
if (errRtn == SOF_ERROR1)
{
  Console.WriteLine("Error type 1 call to someFunc()");
  return MY_ERROR_3;
}
if (errRtn == SOF_ERROR2)
{
  Console.WriteLine("Error type 1 call to someFunc()");
  return MY_ERROR_4;
}
```

This mechanism has several problems:

- It's highly repetitive.
- It forces the user to invent and keep track of numerous error return indications.
- It mixes the error handling code into the normal code flow, thereby obscuring the normal, nonerror path.

These problems don't seem so bad in this simple example, but they become increasingly worse as the calling code becomes more complex. The result is that error handling code doesn't get written to handle all the conditions that it should.

Fortunately, the exception error reporting mechanism solves these problems.

Using an Exceptional Error Reporting Mechanism

C# introduces a totally new mechanism for capturing and handling errors called exceptions. This mechanism is based on the keywords try, catch, throw, and final. In outline form, it works like this: A function will try to get through a piece of code. If a piece of code detects a problem, it will throw an error indication, which the functions can catch, and no matter what happens, it finally executes a special block of code at the end:

```
public class MyClass
{
  public void SomeFunction()
  {
    // set up to catch an error
    try
```

```
    {
      // call a function
      SomeOtherFunction();
      // . . . make whatever other calls you want . . .
    }
    catch(Exception e)
    {
      // control passes here in the event of an
      // error anywhere within the try block and
      // any function it calls;
      // the Exception object describes the error
    }
  }
  public void SomeOtherFunction()
  {
    // . . . error occurs somewhere within the function . . .
    throw new Exception("Description of error");
    // . . . function continues . . .
  }
}
```

The `SomeFunction()` function surrounds some section of code in a block labeled with the keyword `try`. Any function called within that block or any function that it calls or . . . is considered within the `try` block.

A `try` block is followed immediately by the keyword `catch`, which is followed by a block to which control passes in the event of an error anywhere within the `try` block. The argument to the `catch` block is an object of class `Exception` or some subclass of `Exception`.

Somewhere deep in the bowels of `SomeOtherFunction()`, an error occurs. Always at the ready, the function reports a runtime error with the `throw` of an `Exception` object back to the first block to `catch` it.

Can I Get an Example?

The following `FactorialException` program demonstrates the key elements of the exception mechanism:

```
// FactorialException - create a factorial program that
//                      reports illegal arguments to Factorial()
//                      using an Exception
using System;
namespace FactorialException
{
  // MyMathFunctions - a collection of mathematical functions
  //                   I created (it's not much to look at yet)
  public class MyMathFunctions
  {
    // Factorial - return the factorial of a value
    //             provided
    public static double Factorial(int nValue)
    {
```

```
      // don't allow negative numbers
      if (nValue < 0)
      {
        // report negative argument
        string s = String.Format(
            "Illegal negative argument to Factorial {0}",
            nValue);
        throw new Exception(s);
      }
      // begin with an "accumulator" of 1
      double dFactorial = 1.0;
      // loop from nValue down to one, each time
      // multiplying the previous accumulator value
      // by the result
      do
      {
        dFactorial *= nValue;
      } while(--nValue > 1);
      // return the accumulated value
      return dFactorial;
    }
  }
  public class Class1
  {
    public static void Main(string[] args)
    {
      try
      {
        // call factorial in a loop from 6 down to -6.
        for (int i = 6; i > -6; i--)
        {
          // calculate the factorial of the number
          double dFactorial = MyMathFunctions.Factorial(i);
          // display the result of each pass
          Console.WriteLine("i = {0}, factorial = {1}",
                            i, MyMathFunctions.Factorial(i));
        }
      }
      catch(Exception e)
      {
        Console.WriteLine("Fatal error:");
        Console.WriteLine(e.ToString());
      }
      // wait for user to acknowledge
      Console.WriteLine("Press Enter to terminate...");
      Console.Read();
    }
  }
}
```

This "exceptional" version of Main() wraps almost its entire contents in a try block.

Always sandwich the contents of Main() in a try block, because Main() is the starting point for the program. Any exception not caught somewhere else will percolate up to Main(). This is your last opportunity to grab the error before it ends up back in Windows, where the error message will be much harder to interpret.

The catch block at the end of Main() catches the Exception object and uses its ToString() method to display most of the error information contained within the exception object in a single string.

TIP

The more conservative Exception.Message property returns a more readable, but less descriptive subset of the error information.

This version of the Factorial() function includes the same check for a negative argument as the previous version. If the argument is negative, Factorial() formats an error message that describes the problem, including the value that it found to be so offensive. Factorial() then bundles this information into a newly created Exception object, which it throws back to the calling function.

The output from this program appears as follows (I've trimmed up the error messages a bit to make them more readable):

```
i = 6, factorial = 720
i = 5, factorial = 120
i = 4, factorial = 24
i = 3, factorial = 6
i = 2, factorial = 2
i = 1, factorial = 1
i = 0, factorial = 0
Fatal error:
System.Exception: Illegal negative argument to Factorial -1
    at Factorial(Int32 nValue) in c:\c#program\Factorial\class1.cs:line 23
    at FactorialException.Class1.Main(String[] args) in
                c:\c#program\Factorial\class1.cs:line 52
Press Enter to terminate...
```

The first few lines display the actual factorial of the numbers 6 through 0. The factorial of –1 generates the message starting with Fatal error — wooo, that don't sound good.

The first line in the error message was formatted back in Factorial() itself. This line describes the nature of the problem, including the offending value of –1.

The remainder of the output is what is known as a *stack trace*. The first line of the stack trace describes where the exception was thrown. In this case, the exception was thrown in Factorial(int) — more specifically, line 23 within the source file Class1.cs. Factorial() was invoked in the function Main(string[]) or link 52 within the same file. The stack trace stops with Main() because that's the module in which the exception was caught.

TIP

The stack trace is available in one of the Visual Studio debugger windows. I describe it in Chapter 16.

You have to admit that this is pretty impressive. The message describes the problem and identifies the offending argument. The stack trace tells you where the exception was thrown and how the program got there. With that information, you should be drawn to the problem like a tornado to a trailer park.

Creating Your Own Exception Class

The standard, off-the-shelf Exception class provided in the C# class library can provide more information than a top executive whistle blower on *60 Minutes*. You can ask the exception object where it was thrown, along with any string that the reporting function wants to communicate across the great divide. In some cases, however, the standard ol' Exception class just doesn't cut it. You may have too much information to squeeze into a single string. For example, an application function may want to pass along the offending object for analysis.

A locally defined class can inherit the Exception class as it would any other class:

```
// CustomException - add a reference to MyClass to the standard
//                   exception class
public class CustomException : Exception
{
  private MyClasss myobject;
  CustomException(string sMsg, MyClass mo) : base(sMsg)
  {
    myobject = mo;
  }
  // give outside classes access to an informative class
  public MyClass MyCustomObject{ get {return myobject;}}
}
```

This CustomException class is custom-made for reporting in software that deals with the infamous MyClass. This subclass of Exception stores off the same string as the original, but adds the ability to store a reference to the miscreant within the exception.

The following example catches the CustomException class and puts its MyClass information to use:

```
public class Class1
{
  public void SomeFunction()
  {
    try
    {
      // . . . processing before the example function
      SomeOtherFunction();
      // . . . whatever continued processing . . .
    }
    catch(MyException me)
    {
```

```
      // you still have access to the Exception methods
      string s = me.ToString();
      // but you also have access to any properties or methods
      // unique to your custom exception class
      MyClass mo = me.MyCustomObject;
      // for example, ask the MyClass object to display itself
      string s = mo.GetDescription();
    }
  }
  public void SomeOtherFunction()
  {
    // create myobject
    MyClass myobject = new MyClass();
    // . . . report some error involving myobject . . .
    throw new MyException("Error withis MyClass object", myobject);
    // . . . remainder of function . . .
  }
}
```

In this code snippet, SomeFunction() invokes SomeOtherFunction() from
within an all-inclusive try block. SomeOtherFunction() creates and uses a
myobject. Somewhere within SomeOtherFunction(), an error-checking
function prepares to throw an exception to report an error condition that has
just arisen. Rather than create a simple Exception, SomeFunction() avails
itself of the hot and new exception for the new millennium, MyException, to
report not only an error message, but also the miscreant myobject.

The catch phrase back in Main() specifies that it is looking for a MyException
object. Once caught, the application code can still query any properties of an
Exception, as in the call to ToString(). This catch can also invoke methods
the miscreant MyClass object stored with the throw.

Assigning Multiple Catch Blocks

The code snippet in the previous section describes the throwing and catching of a locally defined MyException object. However, consider again the
catch phrase used in that example:

```
public void SomeFunction()
{
  try
  {
    SomeOtherFunction();
  }
  catch(MyException me)
  {
  }
}
```

What if SomeOtherFunction() had thrown a simple Exception or some
other non-MyException type of exception? It would be like trying to catch

a football with a baseball glove — the catch doesn't match the throw. Fortunately, C# enables the program to define numerous `catch` phrases, each designed for a different type of exception:

The `catch` phrases must be lined up nose to tail after the `try` block. They should be arranged from the more specific to the more general. C# checks each `catch` block, sequentially comparing the object thrown with the `catch` phrase's argument type:

```
public void SomeFunction()
{
  try
  {
    SomeOtherFunction();
  }
  catch(MyException me)
  {
    // all MyException objects are caught here
  }
  catch(Exception e)
  {
    // all otherwise uncaught exceptions are caught here
  }
}
```

Were `SomeOtherFunction()` to throw an `Exception` object, it would pass over the `catch(MyException)` because an `Exception` is not a type of `MyException`. It would be caught by the next `catch` phrase: the `catch(Exception)`.

Any class that inherits `MyException` IS_A `MyException`:

```
class MySpecialException : MyException
{
  // . . . whatever . . .
}
```

Given the chance, `MyException` catch will grab a `MySpecialException` object.

Always line up the `catch` phrases from most specific to most general. Never place the more general `catch` phrase first:

```
public void SomeFunction()
{
  try
  {
    SomeOtherFunction();
  }
  catch(Exception me)
  {
    // all MyException objects are caught here
  }
  catch(MyException e)
  {
```

```
      // no exception ever gets this far because it's
      // caught by the more general catch phrase
    }
  }
```

The more general `catch` phrase starves the `catch` phrase that follows by intercepting any `throw`.

Letting some throws slip through your fingers

What if C# goes down the line looking for a `catch` phrase in the calling function to match the current exception object and finds none that match? What if the calling function has no `catch` phrases at all? What do we do now, Auntie Em, Auntie Em?

Consider the following simple chain of function calls:

```
// MyException - demonstrate how a new exception class can be
//                created and to demonstrate how functions can
//                catch just the requirements that they're prepared
//                to handle
using System;
namespace MyException
{
  // introduce some type of 'MyClass'
  public class MyClass{}
  // MyException - - add a reference to MyClass to the standard
  //                exception class
  public class MyException : Exception
  {
    private MyClass myobject;

    public MyException(string sMsg, MyClass mo) : base(sMsg)
    {
      myobject = mo;
    }

    // give outside classes access to an informative class
    public MyClass MyCustomObject{ get {return myobject;}}
  }

  public class Class1
  {
    // f1 - - catch generic exception object
    public void f1(bool bExceptionType)
    {
      try
      {
        f2(bExceptionType);
      }
      catch(Exception e)
      {
```

```
      Console.WriteLine("Caught a generic exception in f1()");
      Console.WriteLine(e.Message);
    }
  }

  // f2 -  - be prepared to catch a MyException
  public void f2(bool bExceptionType)
  {
    try
    {
      f3(bExceptionType);
    }
    catch(MyException me)
    {
      Console.WriteLine("Caught a MyException in f2()");
      Console.WriteLine(me.Message);
    }
  }

  // f3 -  - don't bother to catch any error exceptions
  public void f3(bool bExceptionType)
  {
    f4(bExceptionType);
  }

  // f4 -  - throw one of two types of exceptions
  public void f4(bool bExceptionType)
  {
    // we're working with some local object
    MyClass mc = new MyClass();
    if(bExceptionType)
    {
      // error occurs - throw the object with the exception
      throw new MyException("MyException thrown in f4()",
                             mc);
    }
    throw new Exception("Generic Exception thrown in f4()");
  }

  public static void Main(string[] args)
  {
    // throw a generic exception first
    Console.WriteLine("Throw a generic exception first");
    new Class1().f1(false);
    // now throw one of my exceptions
    Console.WriteLine("\nThrow a specific exception first");
    new Class1().f1(true);

    // wait for user to acknowledge
    Console.WriteLine("Hit Press Enter to terminate...");
    Console.Read();
  }
 }
}
```

Main() creates a Class1 object and immediately uses it to invoke the f1()
method. This method calls f2(), which calls f3(), which calls f4(). The
f4() function performs incredibly sophisticated error checking which drives
it to throw either a MyException or a generic Exception object, depending
upon the bool argument. At first, the exception is passed back to f3().

There, C# finds no catch phrases, so control continues up the chain to f2(), which catches the MyException derivative. This does not match the generic Exception object thrown initially, so control continues to roll its way upstream. Finally, f1() contains a catch that matches the object thrown.

The second call from Main() causes f4() to throw a MyException object, which is caught in f2(). This exception is not sent on to f1() because it was caught and handled in f2().

The output from this program appears as follows:

```
Throw a generic exception first
Caught a generic exception in f1()
Generic Exception thrown in f4()

Throw a specific exception first
Caught a MyException in f2()
MyException thrown in f4()
Press Enter to terminate...
```

A function like f3(), which contains no catch phrases at all, is not uncommon. I might go so far as to say that most functions have no catch phrases — but then again, I might not. A function need not catch an exception if it is not prepared to handle the error in a meaningful way. What about some math function ComputeX() which happens to call Factorial() as part of its internal calculation? Assuming that its internal code is correct, if Factorial() throws an exception, it's because the caller passed some incorrect data. ComputerX() may or may not have any idea as to what data was wrong. In any case, it certainly can't fix the problem.

A function like f2() catches only one type of exception. f2() is looking for a certain class of error. For example, MyException might be an exception type defined for a brilliant library of classes that I've just written — in fact, I call it the BrilliantLibrary. The functions that make up the BrilliantLibrary throw and catch MyException exceptions like the infield of a baseball team warming up.

However, the BrilliantLibrary functions also call functions out of the generic System library. The Brilliant functions might not understand how to handle generic System exceptions, especially if they're caused by erroneous input.

If you don't know what to do with an exception, let it pass on through to the caller. However, be fair with yourself. Don't let an exception pass on by just because you're too lazy to write the necessary error handler.

Rethrowing an object

In some cases, a method cannot completely handle the error but doesn't want to let the exception just fly by without putting in its two cents. It's like a math function that calls Factorial() when it blows up. Even though the problem's ultimate cause may be incorrect input, the math routine may be able offer some extra evidence as to what happened.

A catch block can partially digest the error thrown and then throw the rest up — this is not a pretty image I'm getting.

Intercepting an error exception is most common for methods that allocate assets. For example, consider a method F() that opens a file upon entry with the intention of closing the file before returning. Somewhere in the middle of its processing, F() invokes G(). An exception thrown from G() would go breezing back straight through F() without giving it a chance to close its file. This leaves the file hanging open until the program eventually terminates. An ideal solution is for F() to include a catch block that closes any open files. F() is free to pass the exception on after it has completed cleaning up.

There are two ways to rethrow an error. One approach is to throw a second exception with additional or, at least, the same information:

```
public void f1()
{
  try
  {
    f2();
  }
  // catch an error . . .
  catch(MyException me)
  {
    // ... work off part of the error . . .
    Console.WriteLine("Caught a MyException in f1()");
    // . . . . now generate a new exception to pass
    //  back up the call chain
    throw new Exception("Error thrown from f1()");
  }
}
```

Throwing a new exception object enables a class to reformulate a new error message with extra information while tying up any loose ends that the exception may have left hanging. Passing a generic Exception object in lieu of the limited distribution MyException object ensures that the exception is handled at levels above f1().

Throwing a new exception has the disadvantage that the stack trace starts over again from the point of the new throw. The source of the original error is lost unless f1() takes special precautions to save it.

Including a `throw` command by itself with no argument rethrows the same exception object:

```
public void f1()
{
  try
  {
    f2();
  }
  // catch an error . . .
  catch(Exception e)
  {
    // . . . work off part of the error . . .
    Console.WriteLine("Caught an Exception in f1()");
    // . . . now continue the same exception exception on its way
    throw;
  }
}
```

Rethrowing the same exception object offers an advantage and a disadvantage. (Isn't it always the way?) Rethrows enable intermediate functions to catch exceptions to release or close allocated assets while enabling the final consumer of the exception object to follow the stack trace all the way back to its source. However, the intermediate function cannot (or should not) add any extra information by modifying the exception before rethrowing it.

Overriding the Exception Class

The following user-defined exception class can save off extra information that isn't possible in a conventional `Exception` object:

```
// MyException — add a reference to MyClass to the standard
//               exception class
public class MyException : Exception
{
  private MyClasss myobject;
  MyException(string sMsg, MyClass mo) : base(sMsg)
  {
    myobject = mo;
  }
  // give outside classes access to an informative class
  public MyClass MyObject{ get {return myobject;}}
}
```

Consider again my `BrilliantLibrary` of functions. These functions know how to populate and fetch these new members of the `MyException` class, thereby providing just the information necessary to track every known error and a few that have yet to be discovered. The problem with this approach is that only `BrilliantLibrary` functions glean any benefit from the new members in `MyException`.

Overriding the methods already present in the `Exception` class can give existing functions outside of `BrilliantLibrary` access to new data. Consider the exception class defined in the following `CustomException` program:

```
// CustomException - create a custom exception that
//                   displays the information we want
//                   in a more friendly format
using System;
namespace CustomException
{
  public class CustomException : Exception
  {
    private MathClass mathobject;
    private string sMessage;
    public CustomException(string sMsg, MathClass mo)
    {
      mathobject = mo;
      sMessage =  sMsg;
    }
    override public string Message
    {
      get{return String.Format("Message is <{0}>, Object is {1}",
                              sMessage, mathobject.ToString());}
    }
    override public string ToString()
    {
      string s = Message;
      s += "\nException thrown from ";
      s += TargetSite;
      return s;
    }
  }
  // MathClass - a collection of mathematical functions
  //             I created (it's not much to look at yet)
  public class MathClass
  {
    private int nValueOfObject;
    private string sObjectDescription;
    public MathClass(string sDescription, int nValue)
    {
      nValueOfObject = nValue;
      sObjectDescription = sDescription;
    }
    public int Value {get {return nValueOfObject;}}
    // Message - display the message with the value of the
    //           attached of the MathClass object
    public string Message
    {
      get
      {
        return String.Format("({0} = {1})",
          sObjectDescription,
          nValueOfObject);
      }
    }
    // ToString - prepend the custom Message with the
    //            standard Exception.ToString() message
    override public string ToString()
    {
```

```
          string s = Message + "\n";
          s += base.ToString();
          return s;
        }
        // Inverse - return 1/x
        public double Inverse()
        {
          if (nValueOfObject == 0)
          {
            throw new CustomException("Can't take inverse of 0", this);
          }
          return 1.0 / (double)nValueOfObject;
        }
    }
    public class Class1
    {
      public static void Main(string[] args)
      {
        try
        {
          // take the inverse of 0
          MathClass mathObject = new MathClass("Value", 0);
          Console.WriteLine("The inverse of d.Value is {0}",
                            mathObject.Inverse());
        }
        catch(Exception e)
        {
          Console.WriteLine("\nUnknown fatal error:\n{0}",
                            e.ToString());
        }

        // wait for user to acknowledge
        Console.WriteLine("Press Enter to terminate...");
        Console.Read();
      }
    }
}
```

Let me break in here for a commercial announcement from the author. This
CustomException class ain't so great. It stores off a message and an object,
just like MyException. However, rather than provide new methods for
accessing these data elements, it overrides the existing property Message
that returns the error message contained by the exception, and the method
ToString() that returns the message plus the stack trace.

Overriding these functions means that even functions designed to catch the
generic Exception class have limited access to the new data members.

Beginning with Main(), the program creates a MathClass object whose value
is 0 and then cleverly attempts to take the inverse. I don't know about you,
but I haven't seen too many inverses of 0 running around, and were my function to return some number, I would start to get suspicious.

Actually the Intel processor does return a value for 1.0/0.0: `Infinity`. Several special floating point values exist to handle such cases rather than throw an exception because not all languages are prepared to handle exceptions. These special values include positive and negative Infinity and positive and negative NaN (Not_a_Number).

Under normal circumstances, the `Inverse()` method returns the obvious. When passed a zero, however, the far-sighted method throws a `CustomException`, passing an explanatory string along with the erroneous object.

Working backward, `Main()` catches the exception. `Main()` outputs a short message meant to explain where the program is in its processing: "Unknown fatal error" probably means that the program is about to close up shop and go home. `Main()` then gives the exception a chance to explain itself by invoking its `ToString()` method. (See the sidebar titled "The class business card: ToString()," in this chapter.)

Because the exception object in this case is actually a `CustomException`, control passes to `CustomException.ToString()`. This `ToString()` method displays the exception message with the original target method and line number attached.

`Message()` is a virtual method in `Exception`, which custom exceptions should inherit.

Rather than assume too much, `Message()` allows the `MathClass` object to display itself as well using its `ToString()` method. The `MathClass.ToString()` returns a string containing the object's description and value.

Don't assume any more than you have to. Rely upon an object's `ToString()` method to create a `string` version of the object rather than reaching into the object itself and pulling out values for display.

The output from the `CustomException` program is

```
Unknown fatal error:
Message is <Can't take inverse of 0>, Object is (Value = 0)
CustomException.MathClass
Exception thrown from Double Inverse()
Press Enter to terminate...
```

To review just a second: The message `Unknown fatal error:` comes from `Main()`. The string `Message is <Can't take inversion of 0>, Object is <~~>` comes from `CustomException`. The message `Value = 0` comes from the `MathClass` object itself. The final line, `Exception thrown from Double Inverse`, comes from `CustomException`.

The class business card: ToString()

All classes inherit from a common base class that carries the clever name Object. I explore this unifying property of all classes in Chapter 17, however, it is worth mentioning here that Object includes a method, ToString(), which converts the contents of the object into a string. The idea here is that each class should override the ToString() method to display itself in a meaningful way. I use the method GetString() in earlier chapters because I don't want to get into inheritance issues; however, the principle is the same. For example, a Student.ToString() method might display the student's name and student id.

Most functions, even those built into the C# library, use the ToString() method to display objects. Thus, overriding ToString() has the very useful side effect that the object will be displayed in its own unique format, no matter who does the displaying.

As Bill Gates would say, "Cool."

Chapter 16

Handling Files in C#

● ●

In This Chapter

▶ Managing multiple source files in a single program

▶ Reading and writing data files

● ●

*F*ile access can mean two different things in C#. The most obvious meaning is the storage and retrieval of data on the disk. A second meaning, however, involves the way that C# source code is grouped into source files.

Functions enable you to divide a long string of code into separate, maintainable units. The class structure enables you to group both data and functions in meaningful ways to further reduce the complexity of the program. C# provides yet another level of grouping: C# enables you to group similar classes into a separate library.

Dividing a Single Program into Multiple Source Files

The programs in this book are only for demonstration purposes. Each program is no more than a few dozen lines long and contains no more than a couple of classes. An industrial-strength program, complete with all the necessary bells and whistles, can include hundreds of thousands of lines of code, spread over a hundred or more classes.

Storing all these classes into a single module quickly becomes impractical. First, you have the problem of keeping the classes straight. Second, the work of creating large programs usually is spread among numerous programmers. Two programmers can't edit the same file at the same time — each programmer needs her own source file or files. Finally, compiling a large module may take a considerable amount of time — you can draw out a coffee break for only so long before the boss starts getting suspicious. Compiling a module just because a single line in one class has changed becomes intolerable.

For these reasons, the smart C# programmer divides a program up into multiple .CS source files, which are compiled and built together into a single executable.

Consider an airline ticketing system: You have the interface to the reservations agent that you call on the phone, another interface to the person behind the gate counter, the Internet, not to mention the part that controls aircraft seat inventory, plus the part that calculates fares (including taxes) — it just goes on and on. A program like that gets huge before it's all over.

To put all those classes into one big `Class1.cs` source file is more unreasonable than the settlement proposed by my ex-wife, for the following reasons:

- ✔ Only one person can edit a given source file at one time. You may have 20 or 30 programmers working on a large project at one time. One file would limit 24 programmers to one hour of editing a day, and that would be around the clock. If you break the program up into 24 files, it would be possible, though difficult, for each programmer to edit at the same time. Break the program up so that each class has its own file, and orchestrating the same 24 programmers is much easier.

- ✔ A single source file can get extremely difficult to understand. It's much easier to get a grip on modules like `ResAgentInterface.cs`, `GateAgentInterface.cs`, `ResAgent.cs`, `GateAgent.cs`, `Fare.cs`, and `Aircraft.cs`.

- ✔ Rebuilding a large program like an airline reservation system can take a long time. You certainly wouldn't want to rebuild all the instructions that make up the system just because some programmer changed a single line. Visual Studio can rebuild the single modified file in a multifile program and then stack all the object files back together.

A *project file* contains the instructions about which files go together and how they are combined.

You can combine project files to generate combinations of programs that depend on the same user-defined classes. For example, you may want to couple a write program with the corresponding read program. That way, if one changes, the other gets rebuilt automatically. One project would describe the write program while another describes the read program. A set of project files is known as a *solution*.

Visual C# programmers use the Visual Studio Explorer to combine C# source files into projects within the Visual Studio environment. I describe the Visual Studio Explorer in Bonus Chapter 2, on the CD-ROM that comes with this book.

Collecting Source Files into Namespaces

You combine common classes into a space with an assigned meaningful name. For example, you may compile all math-related routines into a `MathRoutines` namespace.

It is possible, but very unlikely, to divide a single file into multiple namespaces. More commonly, you group multiple files. For example, the file `Point.cs` might contain the class `Point` and the class `ThreeDSpace.cs` to describe the properties of a Euclidean space. You could combine `Point.cs`, `ThreeDSpace.cs`, and other C# source files into the `MathRoutines` namespace.

The namespace serves several purposes. A namespace represents a loose coupling of classes. As an application programmer, you can reasonably assume that the classes that make up the `MathRoutines` namespace are all math-related. By the same token, when looking for just the perfect math function, you would look in the classes that make up the `MathRoutines` namespace first.

Namespaces avoid the possibility of name conflicts. For example, a file input/output library may contain a class `Convert` which converts the representation in one file type to that of another. At the same time, a translation library may contain a class of the same name. Assigning the namespaces `FileIO` and `TranslationLibrary` to the two sets of classes avoids the problem: `FileIO.Convert` clearly differs from the class `TranslationLibrary.Convert`.

Declaring a namespace

You declare a namespace using the keyword `namespace` followed by a name and an open and closed parentheses block. The classes within that block are part of the namespace:

```
namespace MyStuff
{
  class MyClass {}
  class UrClass {}
}
```

In this example, both `MyClass` and `UrClass` are part of the `MyStuff` namespace.

The Visual Studio Application Wizard puts each class it creates in a namespace with the same name as that of the directory that it creates. Look at any of the programs in this book, each of which was created by the Application Wizard. For example, the `AlignOutput` program is created in the `AlignOutput` folder. The name of the source file is `Class1.cs`, which matches the name of the default class. The name of the namespace within `Class1.cs` is the same as that of the folder: `AlignOutput`.

If you don't specify a namespace designation, C# puts your class in the global namespace. This is the base namespace for all other namespaces.

Accessing modules in the same namespace

The namespace of a class is a part of the extended class name. Consider the following example:

```
namespace MathRoutines
{
  class Sort
  {
    public void SomeFunction(){}
  }
}
namespace Paint
{
  public class PaintColor
  {
    public PaintColor(int nRed, int nGreen, int nBlue) {}
    public void Paint() {}
    public static void StaticPaint() {}
  }
}
namespace MathRoutines
{
  public class Test
  {
    static public void Main(string[] args)
    {
      // create an object of type Sort in the same namespace
      // as we are and invoke some function
      Sort obj = new Sort();
      obj.SomeFunction();
      // create an object in another namespace - notice that the
      // namespace name must be included explicitly in every
      // class reference
      Paint.PaintColor black = new Paint.PaintColor(0, 0, 0);
      black.Paint();
      Paint.PaintColor.StaticPaint();
    }
  }
}
```

In this case, the two classes Sort and Test are contained within the same namespace, MathRoutines, even though they appear in different declarations within the module.

Normally, Sort and Test would be in different C# source modules that you build together into one program. See Bonus Chapter 2 on the CD-ROM for a description of how to break a program up into multiple C# source files.

The function Test.Main() can reference the Sort class without specifying the namespace because the two classes are in the same namespace. However,

Main() must specify the Paint namespace when referring to PaintColor, as in the call to Paint.PaintColor.StaticPaint(). Notice that you do not need to take any special steps when referring to black.Paint() because the class of the black object is known, namespace and all.

using *a namespace*

Referring to a class name by its fully qualified name can become a distraction. C# enables you to avoid this tedium with the keyword using. The using command adds the specified namespace to a list of default namespaces that C# searches when trying to resolve a class name. The following example program compiles without even a whimper of complaint:

```
namespace Paint
{
  public class PaintColor
  {
    public PaintColor(int nRed, int nGreen, int nBlue) {}
    public void Paint() {}
    public static void StaticPaint() {}
  }
}
namespace MathRoutines
{
  // add Paint to the namespaces that are searched
  // automatically
  using Paint;
  public class Test
  {
    static public void Main(string[] args)
    {
      // create an object in another namespace - the
      // namespace name does not need to be included because
      // the namespace is included in a "using" phrase
      PaintColor black = new PaintColor(0, 0, 0);
      black.Paint();
      PaintColor.StaticPaint();
    }
  }
}
```

The using command says, "If you can't find the class specified in the current namespace, look in that namespace to see if you can find it there." You can specify as many namespaces as you like, but all using commands must appear in a row at the very beginning of the program.

All programs include the command using System;. This command gives the program automatic access to the functions included in the system library, such as WriteLine().

Controlling class access with namespaces

Namespaces allow a certain level of independence among sets of largely unre-lated classes. For example, if you were working on a set of mathematical classes, you might use a container class to store off sets of values.

The level of independence is called the *level of coupling*. A class that accesses the internal members of another class is said to be *tightly coupled*. Classes that access each other only through the public methods are said to be *loosely coupled*.

Chapter 11 demonstrates how the public, protected, and private descrip-tors uncouple classes within a single namespace. The addition of keyword internal specifies that an object is accessible from within the namespace but not to external classes. Members flagged internal protected are accessible both to classes within the same namespace and to subclasses.

The following example AccessControl program demonstrates how the com-plete set of access controls works:

```
// AccessControl - demonstrate the various forms of
//                 access control
namespace AccessControl
{
  using System;
  using AccessControlLib;
  public class Class1 : Class2
  {
    public static int Main(string[] strings)
    {
      Class1 class1 = new Class1();
      Class2 class2 = new Class2();
      Class3 class3 = new Class3();
      // public methods are accessible from other classes
      // in other namespaces
      class2.A_public();
      // protected methods are accessible through the
      // inheritance hierarchy
      class1.B_protected();
      //class3.B_protected();
      // private methods are only accessible from the same
      // class
      //class2.C_private();
      class1.C_private();
      // internal methods are only accessible from a
      // class in the same namespace
      //class2.D_internal();
      class3.D_internal();
      // protected internal methods are accessible
      // either via the inheritance hierarchy or from
      // any class within the same namespace
      class1.E_internalprotected();
      class3.E_internalprotected();
      // wait for user to acknowledge the results
```

```
      Console.WriteLine("Press Enter to terminate...");
      Console.Read();
      return 0;
    }
  public void C_private()
  {
    Console.WriteLine("Class1.C_private");
  }
}
// Class3 - an internal class is accessible to other
//          classes within the same namespace but
//          not to external classes that use that
//          namespace
internal class Class3
{
  // declaring a class internal forces all public
  // methods to be internal as well
  public void A_public()
  {
    Console.WriteLine("Class3.A_public");
  }
  protected void B_protected()
  {
    Console.WriteLine("Class3.B_protected");
  }
  internal void D_internal()
  {
    Console.WriteLine("Class3.D_internal");
  }
  public void E_internalprotected()
  {
    Console.WriteLine("Class3.E_internalprotected");
  }
 }
}
```

```
namespace AccessControlLib
{
  using System;
  public class Class2
  {
    public void A_public()
    {
      Console.WriteLine("Class2.A_public");
    }
    protected void B_protected()
    {
      Console.WriteLine("Class2.B_protected");
    }
    private void C_private()
    {
      Console.WriteLine("Class2.C_private");
    }
    internal void D_internal()
    {
      Console.WriteLine("Class2.D_internal");
    }
    internal protected void E_internalprotected()
    {
      Console.WriteLine("Class2.E_internalprotected");
    }
  }
}
```

The program `AccessControl` is made up of `Class1` and `Class3`, which are contained in the namespace `AccessControl`, and the class `Class2` in the namespace `AccessControlLib`. The method calls within `Class1.Main()` demonstrate each access type:

✔ Methods declared `public` are accessible to all methods in all name-spaces. Thus, `Class1` can invoke `Class2.A_public()` directly.

✔ Methods declared `protected` are accessible from the class `Class2` and any class that inherits from `Class1`. The call `class1.B_protected()` is allowed because `Class1` inherits from `Class2`. The call `class3.B_protected()` is illegal.

✔ Methods declared `private` are only accessible to other members of the same class. Thus, the call `class2.C_private()` is not allowed, while the call `class1.C_private()` is okay.

✔ A method declared `internal` is accessible to all classes within the same namespace. Thus, the call `class2.D_internal()` is not allowed. The call `class3.C_internal()` is allowed because `Class3` is a part of the `AccessControl` namespace.

✔ The keyword `internal protected` combines the `internal` and the `protected` accesses. Thus, the call `class1.E_internalprotected()` is allowed because `Class1` extends `Class2` (this is the `protected` part). The call `class3.E_internalprotected()` is also allowed because `Class1` and `Class3` are part of the same namespace (this is the `internal` part).

✔ Declaring `Class3 internal` has the effect of reducing the access to `internal` or less. Thus, `public` methods become `internal`, while `protected` methods become `internal protected`.

The output from this program is as follows:

```
Class2.A_public
Class2.B_protected
Class1.C_private
Class3.D_internal
Class2.E_internalprotected
Class3.E_internalprotected
Press Enter to terminate...
```

Declare methods with the most restricted access possible. A private method may be modified at will without worrying what effect that may have on other classes. An internal class or method within `MathRoutines` is used in support of other math classes. See Chapter 11 if you aren't convinced about the wisdom of loose coupling between classes.

Collecting Data into Files

The console application programs in this book mostly take their input from and send their output to the console. Programs outside this section have better — or at least different — things to bore you with than file manipulation I don't want to confuse their message with the extra baggage of involved input/output (I/O). However, console applications that don't perform any file I/O at all are about as common as Sierra Club banners at a paper mill.

The I/O classes are described in the System.IO namespace. The basic file I/O class is the FileStream. In days past, the programmer would open a file. The open command would prepare the file and return a handle. Usually, this handle was nothing more than a number like the one they give you when you place an order at a Burger Whop. Every time you wanted to read or write to the file, you presented this ID.

C# uses a more intuitive approach. C# associates each file with an object of class FileStream. The constructor for FileStream opens the file. The methods of FileStream perform the file I/O.

FileStream is not the only class that can perform file I/O. However, it does represent your good ol', basic file which covers 90% of your file I/O needs. This is the root class described in this section. If it's good enough for C#, it's good enough for me.

FileStream is a very basic class. Open a file, close a file, read a block, and write a block, and that's just about all you've got. Fortunately, the System.IO namespace contains a set of classes that wrap around FileStream to give you easier access and that warm fuzzy feeling:

- ✔ ReadBinary/WriteBinary: A pair of stream classes that contain methods for reading and writing each of the value types: ReadChar(), WriteChar(), ReadByte(), WriteByte(), and so on. This class is useful for writing an object out in binary (nonhuman-readable) format.

- ✔ TextReader/TextWriter: A pair of classes for reading characters (text). This class comes in two flavors: StringReader/StringWriter and StreamReader/StreamWriter.

- ✔ StringReader/StringWriter: A simple stream class that's limited to just reading and writing strings.

- ✔ StreamReader/StreamWriter: A more sophisticated text reader and writer for the more discriminating palette.

This section provides the following programs, which demonstrate ways to use these classes: FileWrite and FileRead.

Asynchronous I/O: Is it worth waiting for?

Normally, a program waits for a file I/O request to complete before continuing. Call a `read()` method, and you generally don't get control back until the file data is safely in the boat. This is known as *synchronous I/O*.

The C# `System.IO` classes also support asynchronous I/O. Using asynchronous I/O, the `read()` call returns immediately to allow the program to continue doing something else while the I/O request is completed in the background. The program can check a "done" flag at its leisure to decide when the I/O has completed.

This is sort of like cooking hamburgers. Using synchronous I/O, you would put the meat in the pan on the stovetop and stand there watching it until the meat has completed cooking before you go off and start cutting the onions that go on the burgers.

Using asynchronous I/O, you can start cutting up the onions while the hamburger patties are cooking. Every once in awhile, you peek over to see if the meat is done. When it is, you stop cutting, take the meat off the stovetop and slap it on the buns.

Asynchronous I/O can substantially improve performance of the program, but it adds another level of complexity.

Using `StreamWriter` *and wronger*

Programs generate two kinds of output. Some programs write blocks of data in pure binary format. This type of output is useful for storing off objects in an efficient way.

Many, if not most, programs read and write human-readable, string text. The `StreamWriter` and `StreamReader` are the most flexible of the human friendly stream classes.

Human-readable data was formerly known as ASCII or, slightly later, ANSI strings. These two monikers refer to the standards organization that defined them. However, ANSI encoding does not provide for the alphabets east of Austria and west of Hawaii; it can only handle Roman letters. It has no characters for Cyrillic, Hebrew, Arabic, Hindi, or any other language. The more flexible Unicode file format is backward compatible with ANSI characters but still provides for a large number of other alphabets. Unicode comes in several formats; however, UTF8 is the default format for C#.

The following `FileWrite` program reads lines of data from the console and writes them to a file of the user's choosing.

```
// FileWrite - write input from the Console into
//              a text file
using System;
using System.IO;
namespace FileWrite
{
  public class Class1
  {
    public static void Main(string[] args)
    {
      // create the filename object - the while loop allows
      // us to keep trying with different filenames until
      // we succeed
      StreamWriter sw = null;
      string sFileName = "";
      while(true)
      {
        try
        {
          // enter output filename (simply Press Enter to quit)
          Console.Write("Enter filename "
                     + "(Enter blank filename to quit):");
          sFileName = Console.ReadLine();
          if (sFileName.Length == 0)
          {
            // no filename - this jumps beyond the while
            // loop to safety
            break;
          }
          // open file for writing; throw an exception if the
          // file already exists:
          //    FileMode.CreateNew to create a file if it
          //                       doesn't already exist or throw
          //                       an exception if file exists
          //    FileMode.Append to create a new file or append
          //                    to an existing file
          //    FileMode.Create to create a new file or
          //                    truncate an existing file
          //    FileAccess possibilities are:
          //                    FileAccess.Read,
          //                    FileAccess.Write,
          //                    FileAccess.ReadWrite
          FileStream fs = File.Open(sFileName,
                                 FileMode.CreateNew,
                                 FileAccess.Write);
          // generate a file stream with UTF8 characters
          sw = new StreamWriter(fs, System.Text.Encoding.UTF8);
          // read one string at a time, outputting each to the
          // FileStream open for writing
          Console.WriteLine("Enter text; enter blank line to stop");
          while(true)
          {
            // read next line from Console;
            // quit if line file is blank
            string sInput = Console.ReadLine();
            if (sInput.Length == 0)
            {
              break;
```

```
        }
        // write the line just read to output file
        sw.WriteLine(sInput);
    }
    // close the file we just created
    sw.Close();
    sw = null;
}
catch(IOException fe)
{
    // whoops -- an error occurred somewhere during
    // the processing of the file - tell the user
    // what the full name of the file is:
    // tack the name of the default directory
    // onto the filename
    string sDir = Directory.GetCurrentDirectory();
    string s = Path.Combine(sDir, sFileName);
    Console.WriteLine("Error on file {0}", s);
    // now output the error message in the exception
    Console.WriteLine(fe.Message);
}
}
// wait for user to acknowledge the results
Console.WriteLine("Press Enter to terminate...");
Console.Read();
}
}
}
```

`FileWrite` uses the `System.IO` namespace as well as `System`. `System.IO` contains the file I/O functions.

The program starts in `Main()` with a `while` loop containing a `try` block. This is not uncommon for a file manipulation program. (The section on the `StreamReader` uses a slightly different approach to achieve the same end.)

Encase all file I/O functions in a `try` block with a `catch` which generates an appropriate error message. It's generally considered bad form to generate an inappropriate error message.

The `while` loop serves two functions. First, it allows the program to go back and retry in the event of an I/O failure. For example, if the program can't find a file that the user wants to read, the program can ask for the filename again to make sure before blowing off the user. Second, executing a `break` command from within the program breezes you right past the `try` block and dumps you off at the end of the loop. This is a convenient mechanism for exiting a function or program.

The `FileWrite` program reads the name of the file to create from the console. The program terminates by breaking out of the `while` loop if the user enters a null filename. The key to the program occurs in the next two lines.

First, the program creates a `FileStream` object that represents the output file on the disk. The `FileStream` constructor used here takes three arguments:

✔ **The filename:** This is pretty clearly the name of the file to open. A simple name like `filename.txt` is assumed to be in the current directory. A filename that starts with a back slash, like `\some directory\filename.txt`, is assumed to be the full path on the local machine. Filenames that start with two slashes — for example, `\\your machine\some directory\some file.txt` — are resident on other machines. The filename encoding gets rapidly more complicated from here.

✔ **The file mode:** This argument specifies what you want to do to the file. The basic write modes are create (`CreateNew`), append (`Append`) and overwrite (`Create`). `CreateNew` creates a new file. `CreateNew` throws an `IOException` if the file already exists. The simple `Create` mode creates the file if it doesn't exist but overwrites the file if it does exist. Just like it sounds, `Append` creates a file if it doesn't exist but adds to the end of an existing file.

✔ **The access type:** A file can be opened for reading, writing, or both.

`FileStream` has numerous constructors, each of which defaults one or both of the mode and access arguments. However, in my humble opinion, you should specify these arguments explicitly because they have a strong effect on the program.

In the next line, the program wraps the newly opened `FileStream` object in a `StreamWriter` object, `sw`. The `StreamWriter` class wraps around the `FileStream` object to provide a set of text friendly methods. The first argument to the `StreamWriter` constructor is the `FileStream` object. The second argument specifies the encoding to use. The default encoding is UTF8.

You don't need to specify the encoding when reading a file. `StreamWriter` writes out the encoding type in the first three bytes of the file. The `StreamReader` reads these three bytes when the file is opened, to determine the encoding.

The `FileWrite` program then begins reading lines of string input from the console. The program quits reading when the user enters a blank line, but until then, it gobbles up whatever it's given and spits it into the `StreamWriter` `sw` using the `WriteLine()` method.

The similarity between the `StreamWriter.WriteLine()` and `Console.WriteLine()` is more than just a coincidence.

Finally, the file is closed with the `sw.Close()` expression.

Notice that the program nulls out the `sw` reference upon closing the file. A file object is pretty useless after the file has been closed. It is good programming practice to null out a reference after it becomes invalid so you won't try to use it again in the future.

The `catch` block following the file close is like a soccer goalie: It's there to catch any file error that may have occurred anywhere in the program. The catch outputs an error message, including the name of the errant file. But it doesn't output just a simple filename — it outputs the entire filename, including the path, for your reading pleasure. It does this by tacking the current directory name onto the front of the filename you entered, using the `Path.Combine()` method. (`Path` is a class designed to manipulate path information.)

The *path* is the full name of the file folder. In the made-up filename `c:\user\temp directory\text.txt`, the path would be the `c:\user\temp directory` part.

The `Combine()` method is smart enough to realize that a file like `c:\test.txt, Path()` is not in the current directory.

Upon encountering the end of the `while` loop, either by completing the `try` block or by being vectored through the `catch`, the program returns to the top to allow the user to write to another file.

A sample run of the program appears as follows. My input is bolded:

```
Enter filename (Enter blank filename to quit):TestFile1.txt
Enter text; enter blank line to stop
This is some stuff
So is this
As is this

Enter filename (Enter blank filename to quit):TestFile1.txt
Error on file C:\C#Programs\FileWrite\bin\Debug\TestFile1.txt
The file exists.

Enter filename (Enter blank filename to quit):TestFile2.txt
Enter text; enter blank line to stop
I messed up back there. I should have called it
TestFile2.

Enter filename (Enter blank filename to quit):
Press Enter to terminate...
```

Everything goes smoothly when I enter some random text into `TestFile1.txt`. When I try to open `TestFile1.txt` again, however, the program spits out the message `The file exists` with the filename attached. The path to the file is tortured because the "current directory" is the directory in which Visual Studio put the executable file. Correcting my mistake, I enter text into the correct filename — that would be `TestFile2.txt` — without complaint.

Improve your reading speed and comprehension through `StreamReader`

Writing to a file is pretty cool, but it's sort of worthless if you can't read the file back some day. The following `FileRead` program puts the *input* back into

the phrase *file I/O*. This program reads a text file like the ones created by
`FileWrite`:

```
// FileRead - read a text file and write it
//            out to the Console
using System;
using System.IO;
namespace FileRead
{
  public class Class1
  {
    public static void Main(string[] args)
    {
      // we'll need a file reader object
      StreamReader sr;
      string sFileName = "";
      // keep trying to get a real filename until we can find
      // one (the only way that the user has to quit is to
      // break the program by pressing Ctrl+C
      while(true)
      {
        try
        {
          // enter input filename
          Console.Write("Enter the name of a text file to read:");
          sFileName = Console.ReadLine();
          // user didn't enter anything; throw an error
          // to indicate that this is not acceptable
          if (sFileName.Length == 0)
          {
            throw new IOException("Null filename entered");
          }
          // open a file stream for reading; don't create the
          // file if it doesn't already exist
          FileStream fs = File.Open(sFileName,
            FileMode.Open,
            FileAccess.Read);
          // convert this into a StreamReader - this will use
          // the first three bytes of the file to indicate the
          // encoding used (but not the language)
          sr = new StreamReader(fs, true);
          break;
        }
          // error thrown - report the filename and the error
        catch(IOException fe)
        {
          Console.WriteLine("{0}\n\n", fe.Message);
        }
      }
      // read the contents of the file
      Console.WriteLine("\nContents of file:");
      try
      {
        // read one line at a time
        while(true)
        {
          // read a line
          string sInput = sr.ReadLine();
          // quit when we don't get anything back
          if (sInput == null)
          {
            break;
```

```
        }
        // write whatever we read to the console
        Console.WriteLine(sInput);
      }
    }
    catch(IOException fe)
    {
      // snag any read/write errors and report them
      // (this also breaks us out of the loop)
      Console.Write(fe.Message);
    }
    // close the file now that we're done with it
    // (ignore any error)
    try
    {
      sr.Close();
    }
    catch {}
    // wait for user to acknowledge the results
    Console.WriteLine("Press Enter to terminate...");
    Console.Read();
  }
 }
}
```

FileRead takes a different approach to filenames. In this program, the user reads one and only one file. The user must enter a valid filename for the program to output. After the program has read the file, it quits. If the user wants to peek into a second file, she'll just have to run the program again.

The program starts out with a while loop, just like its FileWrite cousin. Within the loop, the program fetches the name of the file to read from the user. If the name of the file is nothing but a blank, the program throws its own error message: Null filename entered. If the filename is non-null, it's used to open a FileStream object in read mode. The File.Open() call here is the same as the one used in FileWrite:

✔ The first argument is the name of the file.

✔ The second argument is the file mode. The mode FileMode.Open says, "Open the file if it exists, and throw an exception if it doesn't." The other option is OpenNew, which creates a zero-length file if the file doesn't already exist. Personally, I never saw the need for that mode (who wants to read from an empty file?), but each to his own is what I say.

✔ The final argument indicates that I want to read from this FileStream. The other alternatives are Write and ReadWrite.

The resulting FileStream object fs is then wrapped in a StreamReader object sr to provide convenient methods for accessing the text file.

This whole file-open section is encased in a try block encased in a while loop wrapped within an enigma. This try block is strictly for the file open. If an error occurs during the open process, the exception is caught, an error is output, and the program loops back up to query the user for a filename again.

However, if the process ends in a healthy, strapping baby `StreamReader` object, the `break` command breaks out of the file-open logic and heads on down the path to the read section.

`FileRead` and `FileWrite` represent two different ways to handle file exceptions. You can either wrap the entire file-handling program in a single `try` block, as in `FileWrite`, or you can give the file-open section its own `try` block. Providing a separate `try` block is usually easier, and it enables you to generate a more specific error message.

The file-open process done, the `FileRead` program reads a line of text from the file using the `ReadLine()` call. The program outputs this line to the console with the ubiquitous `Console.WriteLine()` call before heading back up to the top of the loop to read another line of text. The `ReadLine()` call returns a `null` when the program reaches the end of the file. When this happens, the program breaks out of the read loop, closes the object, and terminates.

Notice how the `Close()` call is wrapped in its own little `try` block. A `catch` with no arguments catches anything. Any error thrown by the `Close()` is caught and ignored. The `catch` exists to keep the exception from propagating up the food chain and aborting the program. The error is ignored because the program can't do anything about an invalid `Close()` and it's going to terminate in the next line, anyway.

I included the null `catch` for demonstration purposes only. Providing a single call its own `try` block with a "catch anything" keeps a program from aborting over an unimportant error. However, only use this technique if an error would be truly, no fake, non-damaging.

Here's a sample run:

```
Enter the name of a text file to read:TestFilex.txt
Could not find file "C:\C#Programs\FileRead\TestFilex.txt".


Enter name of file to read:TestFile1.txt

Contents of file:
This is some stuff
So is this
As is this
Press Enter to terminate...
```

Unless I'm mistaken, this is the same input as the `TestFile1.txt` created in the `FileWrite` program.

It is not the same file, however. I had to copy the file created in `TestWrite` from the `TestWrite\bin\debug` directory to the `TestRead\bin\debug` directory. Provide a full pathname like `c:\test.txt` in both programs if you want the two files to be the same. (I would have done that in these test programs, but I didn't want to dirty up your root directory with my mess.)

Part V

Windows Programming with Visual Studio

The 5th Wave   By Rich Tennant

"We're here to clean the code."

In this part . . .

Understanding C# is one thing; figuring out how to write a full-blown Windows application with bows, tassels, buttons, and bells is quite another. Just for fun, Part V takes you step-by-step through the process of using C# together with the Visual Studio interface to create a "more than trivial" Windows application. You'll be proud of the result even if your kid doesn't call his friends over to see it.

Chapter 17

Creating a Windows Application — Appearances Count

In This Chapter

▶ Picking a problem to solve

▶ Designing a solution

▶ Beginning the solution by finger painting

*U*nderstanding C# does not mean figuring out how to write fully functional Windows applications. Before you take on Windows programming in C#, you must have a firm foundation in C# programming concepts — the kind that can only come from a few months of console application programming.

I'm willing to back off from that statement if you've already created Windows applications in a programming language such as C++.

However, you can familiarize yourself with Windows programming by going through the steps to build a simple application. This chapter takes you through the steps for painting an application using the Visual Studio Forms Designer. Chapter 18 goes through the steps for performing the operations suggested by the forms, menus, ribbons, buttons, and bells that you build in this chapter.

What's the Problem Here?

I thought long and hard (at least 15 minutes) to come up with a problem that would highlight the powerful features of C# without accentuating my hips. Here's the problem: Generate a `SimpleEditor` program. This barebones text editor will have the following features:

✔ Users can enter and delete text. (Otherwise, it wouldn't be much of an editor.)

✔ Users can cut and paste text both within `SimpleEditor` and between it and other applications, such as Microsoft Word.

✔ SimpleEditor supports fonts that are bold, italic, or both.

✔ Users can select a font size between 8 and 24 points. These limitations are arbitrary, but the point is not too many points.

✔ SimpleEditor should not allow you to exit without coaxing you to save an edited file. (However, you can exit without saving if the file has not changed.)

Laying Out the Problem

Anytime you're presented with a problem, you should first push yourself back from the keyboard and really think the obstacles through. In the case of a Windows application, this task involves three steps:

1. **Describe the problem in some detail.**

   These details are the requirements for the application. As you program along, you may be tempted to add a feature here or a tuck there. Resist. This tendency is known as feature-itis. As you go along, make note of possible improvements for a future release. However, adding features on the fly risks creating an application that starts out being one thing and ends up being quite another.

2. **Lay out the solution visually.**

   All programs should have a reasonable human interface; otherwise, reasonable humans won't interface with them. In the case of a Windows application, this means deciding what widgets to use and how to position them. Choosing the proper widgets is partially a matter of learning what widgets are available, partially a matter of having some artistic talents (leaves me out), and partially a matter of being willing to work on the solution. You can actually sit at the computer terminal to perform this function. The Windows Forms Designer is so flexible that you can use it as a drawing tool.

3. **Design the solution based upon the problem description and its appearance.**

   Large applications need to be designed in great detail. For example, I am currently working on a ticketing system for a major airline. The design effort for that program will take 15 people about 6 months. The entire coding and debugging effort is slated for another 12 months after that. However, a small Windows application tends to be driven by the interface. This is more or less the case with SimpleEditor.

Designing the layout

SimpleEditor is an editor — and it's simple. It must have a large window where the user can enter text. Because this window is the most important part of any editor, it should be in the middle and cover most of the display.

All Windows applications require a File menu item, followed immediately to the right with Edit. The rest of the menu items are application specific, except for Help, which appears as the last menu item.

Under File, we need a way to open a file (File⇨Open), a way to save a file (File⇨Save), and a way to get the heck out of Dodge City (File⇨Exit). The little close button on the window frame should have the same effect as File⇨Exit. We don't need a File⇨Close command — as neat as that would be, there's no requirement, so push on. File⇨Close can go into Version 2.

The Edit menu needs the "big three" edit options: Cut, Copy, and Paste. In addition, all editors understand the shortcut keys for those edit options: Ctrl+X, Ctrl+C, and Ctrl+V, respectively.

SimpleEditor also will need a Format menu, with Bold and Italics submenu items to control the boldness and the italicization of the text.

Providing real Help is a complicated task — much too complicated for a SimpleEditor. The Help menu for this application will have to get by with the absolute minimum: the About option.

One final requirement: We need a way to control the font size. Here is one place for a little flight of fancy. In addition to a simple window where the user can enter the desired size font, SimpleEditor will sport a little cursor-like slider bar called a TrackBar. Slide the thumb all the way to one end to get 8 points. Slide it to the other end, and you win with a total of 24 points of font. (I have an ulterior motive here: I want to show how you tie two I/O objects together so changes in one are reflected in the other.)

My solution

Given the parameters I describe in the preceding section, I came up with the solution shown in Figure 17-1 — your results may vary according to your tastes.

Figure 17-1:
My solution
to the
`Simple`
`Editor`
problem.

Painting the Solution

As you can well imagine, I had to complete numerous steps to get from nothing to that work of art shown in Figure 17-1. As I explain in the following sections, those steps aren't too bad if you take them one at a time.

Creating the Windows application framework

To create the framework for the Windows application:

1. **Choose File⇨New⇨Project.**

   Visual Studio pops up the familiar New Project window.

2. **Rather than taking the usual Console Application approach, click the Windows Application icon and enter the filename** SimpleEditor.

   The Location entry in the New Project window specifies the base directory for the `SimpleEditor` files. In other words, Visual Studio will root all the files I create in `C:\C#Programs\SimpleEditor`.

3. **Click OK.**

   Visual Studio thinks for awhile before generating the display shown in Figure 17-2.

   This curious display is known as the Windows Forms Designer. The box on the left is the Form, which will form the basis for the `SimpleEditor` program.

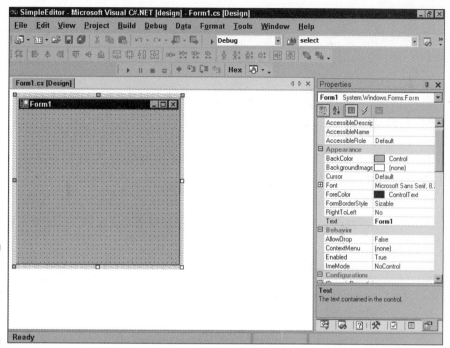

Figure 17-2:
The initial
display for
all Windows
applications.

A *form* is a window with the title bar across the top and the option of scroll bars. In C# talk, a *window* is nothing but a rectangular box into which you can store pictures or text. Windows don't have menus or labels or even those cute little minimize, maximize, and close widgets.

4. **Build the template program that Windows has created.**

Color me paranoid, but I like to make sure that any error that pops up later is really my problem and not some error introduced by Visual Studio. Sure enough, the solution builds. Executing the program reveals nothing but an empty form with the label Form1. Clicking the close button stops the program.

The area to the right of the display is known as the Properties. It isn't obvious at first, but there's a direct connection between the form on the left and its properties on the right. For example, notice that the Text property is Form1. Change it just for fun.

5. **Select this setting and change it to Simple Editor.**

As soon as you do, the label on the form changes from the ridiculous Form1 to Simple Editor.

6. **Rebuild the application and execute it.**

Sure enough, the form name has changed, as shown in Figure 17-3.

Figure 17-3:
Changing
the form's
Text
property
changes its
name in the
title bar.

Ignore the man behind the curtain

Before I go any further, I want to take a peek at the C# code generated by the Windows Forms Designer — I have to see what's going on here. The Solution Explorer shows that the source file for this program is contained in a file called Form1.cs. That matches the name at the top of the Windows Forms Designer window.

Choose View⇨Code to reveal a new window containing the C# source for Forms1.cs shown here:

```
using System;
using System.Drawing;
using System.Collections;
using System.ComponentModel;
using System.Windows.Forms;
using System.Data;
namespace SimpleEditor
{
  /// <summary>
  /// Summary description for Form1.
  /// </summary>
  public class Form1 : System.Windows.Forms.Form
  {
    /// <summary>
    /// Required designer variable.
    /// </summary>
    private System.ComponentModel.Container components = null;
    public Form1()
    {
      //
      // Required for Windows Form Designer support
      //
      InitializeComponent();
      //
      // TODO: Add any constructor code after InitializeComponent call
      //
    }
    /// <summary>
    /// Clean up any resources being used.
    /// </summary>
```

```
protected override void Dispose( bool disposing )
{
  if( disposing )
  {
    if (components != null)
    {
      components.Dispose();
    }
  }
  base.Dispose( disposing );
}
#region Windows Form Designer generated code
/// <summary>
/// Required method for Designer support - do not modify
/// the contents of this method with the code editor.
/// </summary>
private void InitializeComponent()
{
  //
  // Form1
  //
  this.AutoScaleBaseSize = new System.Drawing.Size(5, 13);
  this.ClientSize = new System.Drawing.Size(292, 273);
  this.Name = "Form1";
  this.Text = "Simple Editor";
}
#endregion
/// <summary>
/// The main entry point for the application.
/// </summary>
[STAThread]
static void Main()
{
  Application.Run(new Form1());
}
```

I know the program must start with `static Main()`, which is all the way at the bottom of the listing. The comment substantiates my conviction that this is the place to start. The only statement within `Main()` creates a `Form1()` object and passes it to a method `Application.Run()`. I'm not sure what the `Run()` is all about, but I strongly suspect that the `Form1` class is the same Form1 window that I saw back in the Forms Designer.

 Actually, the `Application.Run()` is starting the `Form` object in its own execution thread. The original thread dies as soon as the new `Form1` is created. The `Form1` thread lives on until it is specifically stopped. The `SimpleEditor` program itself continues to execute as long as any user-defined threads are active.

The constructor for `Form1` invokes a method `InitializeComponent()`. Any user initialization code should go after that call — or at least that's what the comment says.

The `InitializeComponent` method is where the Windows components are created. The special comment immediately before this function says, in effect,

"Keep your mitts off this section of code because this is where I, the Forms Designer, do my thing." In fact, the Forms Designer generates the code between the #region and the #endregion comments as a result of my painting.

In this simple case, the application starts by setting the AutoScaleBaseSize member of the this object. I'm not too sure what that property is. Thankfully, I don't have to know because the Forms Designer takes care of it for me, but I know that this is the Form object itself. Looking down to the last line in InitializeComponent, I can see this.Text is set to "Simple Editor."

Consider this point carefully for a moment because this is the key to the Forms Designer. The Designer displays the properties of the form. One of those properties is Text. I changed the value of Text to "Simple Editor." The Designer added a line of code that set the form's Text property appropriately.

The Dispose method is invoked when Form1 is closed. This method is not particularly interesting in this case, because closing the form terminates the editor.

Editing the edit window

The most pronounced property of SimpleEditor is the edit window:

1. **Open the toolbox by choosing View⇨Toolbox.**

   The toolbox is a series of C# drawing objects, sometimes also known as *components*. The toolbox contains several different sets of widgets, including a set called Windows Forms, which contains the widgets needed to build SimpleEditor.

   The term *component* is not limited to drawing objects, but all drawing objects are components, so the term works for this discussion.

   The Data widgets are used to link up easily with external databases. The Components widgets support multitasking. The General section is where you can add widgets of your own making. All these topics are interesting but, you guessed it, beyond the scope of this book.

   Scrolling up and down reveals a plethora, no, a cornucopia of components. There are labels, buttons, textboxes, menus, and a host of other drawing objects. Surely one of these is just what is needed for the edit window. You might think that a TextBox is just the thing; however, textboxes are more suited to simple (usually one-line) text input. For example, you'll use a textbox to let the user enter a single integer number for the font size.

   In fact, the best choice for the edit window is a RichTextBox. A RichTextBox inputs and outputs text in what is known as Rich Text Format, or RTF. An RTF file is like a Microsoft Word .DOC file, except that RTF is something of a standard. RTF has all the properties we need: It

supports italics, bold, and different font sizes, and it's supported by
most Windows word processors, including Microsoft Word, and word
processors written for other operating systems, such as Unix.

2. **To create the editing surface, click the** `RichTextBox` **symbol in the
toolbox. Then, move the cursor out near the upper left-hand corner of
the Simple Editor form and drag it down and to the right, creating a
window such as that shown in Figure 17-4.**

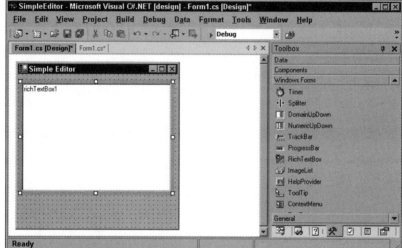

Figure 17-4:
The
`RichText`
`Box` is
where the
user edits
text in the
`Simple`
`Editor.`

Don't fret too much about the exact sizing or placement of the
`RichTextBox`. You can always move it and resize it, as necessary.

3. **I don't like the initial** `richTextBox1` **text. To change it, open up the
Properties window and set the** `Text` **to "nothing." That is, delete whatever's there, leaving a blank field.**

The text within the `RichTextBox` disappears.

Two components may interpret the same property in different ways. The
`Text` property is the best example of this point. The text field of a `Form`
is the label in the header; text for a `TextBox` is the contents; and the text
of a button is the label on the button. Even though each component
interprets the `Text` property differently, the property makes sense in
the context of each component.

4. **To see how far you've come already, rebuild and execute the
application.**

`SimpleEditor` pops up with the textbox in the middle. You can type,
move the cursor about to insert text, and you can even select text. Of
course, you can't do anything with the text, but `SimpleEditor` has
come a long way already.

Building the menus

The order of these next steps doesn't really matter, but I decided to add the menu options next. For this, you need a `MainMenu` component:

1. **Click the `MainMenu` component in the toolbox. Then, click at the location of the left-most main menu item.**

   A small window opens with the enticing contents `Type Here`.

2. **Follow the simple instructions the Windows Forms Designer presents: Click the phrase `Type Here` and then type the name of your first menu item:** File.

   The Forms Designer responds by opening a `Type Here` prompt below and a second one to the right of the original menu item, as shown in Figure 17-5. I'm so excited I don't know which one to type in first.

Figure 17-5:
The
`MainMenu`
component
entices me
with the
option of
typing both
main menu
and
submenu
entries.

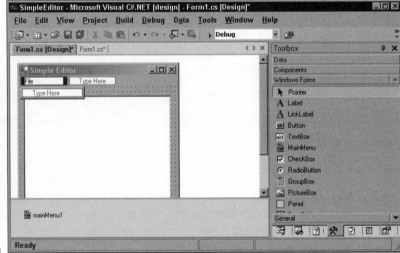

3. **Click the `Type Here` prompt below File and then enter the three submenu items for the File menu:** Open, Save, **and** Exit.

4. **That done, click the `Type Here` to the right of File and then enter** Edit **and its options:** Cut, Copy, **and** Paste.

5. **Moving out to the right again, add** Format **and its submenu options:** Bold **and** Italics.

6. **Finally, add** Help **to the menu bar.**

Notice the window the Windows Forms Designer has opened below the drawing area with the entry `mainMenu1`. You can click this object to set the properties of the menu as a whole. You also use this area to contain objects that aren't normally visible — for example, a pop-up dialog box.

Click one of the menu items and then skim down the list of properties. Sure enough, there's a `Text` property again — this time, it's the menu label. Another field of interest is the `Shortcut` property shown in Figure 17-6. Clicking this property opens a drop-down list showing all the possible special shortcut keys you can use to select this item.

Pressing a shortcut key performs the same function as choosing the associated menu option. For example, pressing Ctrl+C is the same as choosing Edit⇨Copy, and a lot faster.

7. **Going through the list, assign CtrlO to File⇨Open, as shown in Figure 17-6. Repeating the process, assign control keys as shown in Table 17-1.**

Table 17-1	Menu Items and Corresponding Shortcut Keys
Menu Item	*Shortcut*
File⇨Open	Ctrl+O
File⇨Save	Ctrl+S
File⇨Exit	Ctrl+Q
Edit⇨Cut	Ctrl+X
Edit⇨Copy	Ctrl+C
Edit⇨Paste	Ctrl+V
Format⇨Bold	Ctrl+B
Format⇨Italics	Ctrl+I
Help	F1

8. **As always, rebuild the program and try it out.**

You can type into the text window and you can slap menu items open and closed. Of course, so far, `SimpleEditor` is more than just simple — it's a sham. Choosing File⇨Exit has no effect at all. You have to add code behind each of these menu items to make them do something. That's the subject of Chapter 18.

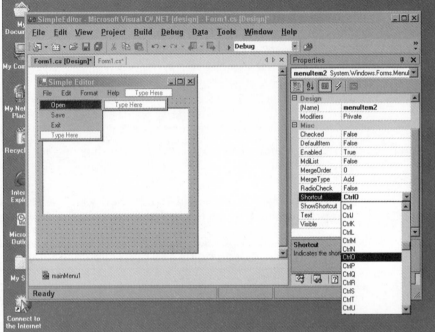

Figure 17-6:
The
Shortcut
property
specifies
which
shortcut key
you want to
assign to
the menu
item.

Adding the font adjustment controls

SimpleEditor also requires the ability to change the font within some arbitrary limits. In this section, you add a TextBox into which the user can type the new font size. SimpleEditor also will sport an analog control known as a TrackBar, which the user can drag from one end to the other to increase and decrease the font size.

Besides making SimpleEditor easier to use, this feature also demonstrates how you can tie two controls together.

1. **Open the toolbox and drag a** TextBox **to the bottom of the** SimpleEditor **window. The default size is a little too large for two digits, so downsize it horizontally.**

   (I've been downsized before, but not horizontally — I was able to walk out standing up.) In addition, I'm not really fond of the default font size. I would prefer something a little jazzier and a lot bigger.

   Lots of stuff goes into the Font property: the size and the font itself, plus properties like bold, italics, and strikethrough. For this reason, a little plus sign appears to the left of the Font property. Click the plus sign, and Font explodes like a balloon into various font-type properties, as shown in Figure 17-7. (The plus sign also becomes a minus — click that, and the Font property shrinks back to its former minute glory.)

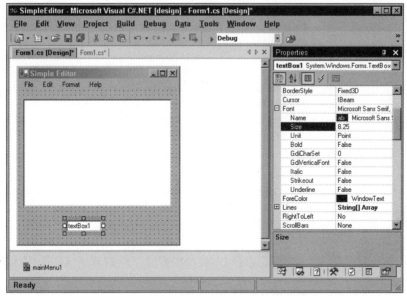

Figure 17-7:
Some properties, such as Font, actually consist of various subproperties, which you must set individually.

2. **In the** `Font` **property window, set the font size to 12 and the font to Bold Arial, my favorite.**

3. **Grab the lower-right corner of the textbox to resize it to fit two digits plus a little more — you don't want the digits to appear squeezed.**

4. **Set the** `TextAlign` **property to** `Center`, **zero out the** `Text`, **and you're all set.**

In case you aren't sure what you can do with any given component, the list of properties is there in the Properties window for all to see. Just select the component and scan up and down in the Properties window to set whatever properties strike your fancy. You can't hurt anything: If you don't like it, you can always set the property back. If you get things too far out of whack, just select the component, press the Delete key, and poof — it's gone.

One final trick: You need to center the textbox within the form. You could eyeball it, moving it a little to the left, a little to the right — sort of like when my wife has me move furniture. However, you don't really need to.

5. **Select the** `TextBox` **and choose Format⇨Center in Form⇨Horizontally, and the object moves over to the proper spot.**

I only wish my couch had a Center Horizontally option.

6. **Now comes the** `TrackBar`. **Select the** `TrackBar` **component from the ToolBox and position it properly at the very bottom of the** `SimpleEditor` **form.**

The vertical size of a TrackBar is fixed, but you can stretch the TrackBar from left to right until it reaches a comfortable size. Once again "reasonable" is personal preference, and you can change the size again after you see how it looks in practice.

The TrackBar has several Behavior properties of interest. In operation, SimpleEditor will need to query the TrackBar for its current value. This raises the question, "What are the values when the thumb is all the way to the left or the right?" You control this by setting the Minimum and Maximum properties, respectively. You want font sizes between 8 and 24 points.

7. **Select the TrackBar (if it isn't already). Set the Minimum property to 8 and the Maximum property to 24. Set the Value property to 12.**

8. **Center the TrackBar by choosing Format⇨Center in Form⇨ Horizontal, and it's done.**

Slap a coat of paint on it and we're done

The Font size components are in position and ready to go, but they're still a bit antisocial. You and I know the Font size information goes there, but nobody else will. SimpleEditor needs some labels to describe the purpose of the different fields.

1. **To fix the problem, place a Label component to the left of the font TextBox and set its Text property to "Font Size". A Font of 10 point, Arial Bold will match the TextBox font nicely.**

2. **Now add a label on the left-hand side of the TrackBar. Set its Font to the same 10 point, Arial Bold. This time, set the Text to 8, to match the minimum value of the TrackBar.**

3. **Repeat the process for a Label on the right-hand side of the TrackBar. Set the text of this Label to 24, to match the maximum TrackBar value.**

In Chapter 18, I demonstrate how the values of these labels can be set automatically to match the TrackBar values, but for now I just hard-code them.

4. **Once again, build the SimpleEditor to make sure all is well in the world.**

No one could be happier with the result shown in Figure 17-8.

Resizing the form

Users like resizable windows. To be more specific, users may want to resize the SimpleEditor form. By default, forms are resizable, but the objects contained in them generally are not resizable. You can correct this, but the solution isn't trivial.

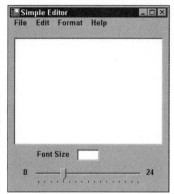

Figure 17-8:
Simple
Editor is
ready for
the ball.

For the easiest fix, simply don't allow users to resize the form. It isn't exactly obvious but resizability is a function of the border. Setting the FormBorderStyle property to Fixed3D takes care of any prying mouse pointers:

1. **Select the Form. Look for the** FormBorderStyle **property. The property is** Sizable **by default. Click on this property to reveal a drop-down list of possible settings. Select** Fixed3D **and nix to resizing.**

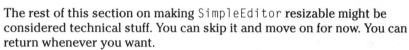

   The rest of this section on making SimpleEditor resizable might be considered technical stuff. You can skip it and move on for now. You can return whenever you want.

   The problem with resizing the form is instructing the components within the Form as to how they should respond. By default, most components are not resizable. Resize the form, and these components stay where they are, as shown in Figure 17-9.

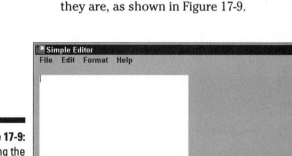

Figure 17-9:
Leaving the
components
untouched
as the form
resizes is
probably
not what
the user
expects.

If `SimpleEditor` is to be resizable, the components need to know what to do. For example, as things gets taller, the `TrackBar` should move right along with the bottom edge of the `Form`. That is, the `TrackBar` is *anchored* to the bottom of the form. As the `Form` grows vertically, the `TrackBar` hangs onto the bottom edge.

In addition, the `TrackBar` should expand horizontally between the left and right edges of the `Form`. Anchoring the `TrackBar` to both the left and right edges generates this effect. No matter how wide the `Form` might become, the `TrackBar` will never get further away from either the left or right edges of the `Form`.

In total, the `TrackBar` should be anchored to the `Bottom`, `Left`, and `Right` edges.

2. **To set the anchor property, select the** `TrackBar` **and click** `Anchor`.

The current anchor properties appear on the right, along with a small drop-down arrow.

3. **Click the arrow.**

A small window appears with four arms, each in a different direction. The colored arms represent the anchor. You can see that the default anchor is the upper-left corner of the form (which explains why the `TrackBar` didn't move as the `Form` resized).

4. **Click the upper arm off, and the left, right, and bottom arms on.**

Figure 17-10 shows the result.

Figure 17-10:
Clicking the arms of the anchor box to on (darkened) or off (white) sets the anchor property automatically.

You can type in **Bottom**, **Top**, **Left**, or **Right** into the `Anchor` field without using the visual aid, if you prefer.

5. **Anchor each of the components separately.**

Table 17-2 lists the proper anchoring for each component.

Table 17-2	The Proper Anchors for the Components
Component	*Anchors*
RichTextBox	Top, Bottom, Left, Right
"Font Size" TextBox	Bottom
"Font Size" Label	Bottom
TrackBar	Bottom, Left, Right
Left TrackBar Label	Bottom, Left
Right TrackBar Label	Bottom, Right

When you rebuild SimpleEditor, resizing works as expected, as shown by the "small SimpleEditor" in Figure 17-11 and the "big SimpleEditor" in Figure 17-12.

Figure 17-11:
The small
Simple
Editor.

Figure 17-12:
The
anchored
components
that make
up the
Simple
Editor
track
properly as
the editor
resizes.

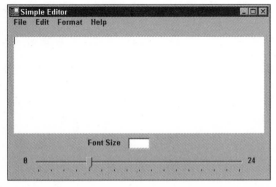

What Hath We Wrought?

The following listing shows a subset of the `InitializeComponent()` method that the Forms Designer has created. The method is very large now, so I have cut out only a small section:

```
namespace SimpleEditor
{
  /// <summary>
  /// Summary description for Form1.
  /// </summary>
  public class Form1 : System.Windows.Forms.Form
  {
    private System.Windows.Forms.RichTextBox richTextBox1;
    private System.Windows.Forms.MainMenu mainMenu1;
    private System.Windows.Forms.MenuItem menuItem1;
    //...
    #region Windows Form Designer generated code
    private void InitializeComponent()
    {
      this.mainMenu1 = new System.Windows.Forms.MainMenu();
      this.menuItem1 = new System.Windows.Forms.MenuItem();
      this.trackBar1 = new System.Windows.Forms.TrackBar();
      //....
      //
      // mainMenu1
      //
      this.mainMenu1.MenuItems.AddRange(new System.Windows.Forms.MenuItem[] {

              this.menuItem1,

              this.menuItem5,

              this.menuItem9,

              this.menuItem12});
      //
      // trackBar1
      //
      this.trackBar1.Anchor = ((System.Windows.Forms.AnchorStyles.Bottom |
              System.Windows.Forms.AnchorStyles.Left)
        | System.Windows.Forms.AnchorStyles.Right);
      this.trackBar1.Location = new System.Drawing.Point(40, 248);
      this.trackBar1.Maximum = 24;
      this.trackBar1.Minimum = 8;
      this.trackBar1.Name = "trackBar1";
      this.trackBar1.Size = new System.Drawing.Size(208, 42);
      this.trackBar1.TabIndex = 2;
      this.trackBar1.Value = 12;
    }
    #endregion
  }
}
```

I have deleted all but the sections dealing with the `MainMenu`, one of the `Menu` options, and the `TrackBar`. Each of these objects is a data member of the `Form1` class. The Forms Designer created the names of these data members by concatenating the type of the object with a counting number.

I could have had you set the names to something more meaningful within the Properties window, but I didn't bother. For large programs, assigning your own names can make the resulting code much easier to read.

The `InitializeComponent()` method begins by creating an object of each type.

Don't be confused by the fact that the Windows Forms Designer provides the full name for each class, including its namespace, `System.Windows.Forms`

In a subsequent section, `InitializeComponent()` assigns each of these objects the properties you set in the Properties window.

The properties you didn't change are the default properties of the object and, hence, don't appear in the code. For example, you can see that `trackBar1` is anchored on the `AnchorStyles.Bottom`, `AnchorStyles.Left`, and `AnchorStyles.Right`. In addition, the `Maximum` and `Minimum` properties are set to 24 and 8, and the initial `Value` property is set to 12.

The rest of `InitializeComponents()` is long but follows the same pattern of assigning a value to each property I changed.

How Do You Learn About Components?

One question new C# Windows programmers ask is, "How do you know what components are available and what each one does?" One approach is to play with them: Grab a component, drag it out into the form, select it, and then start scanning the properties.

A second aid is to look up the component in the Visual Studio Help. The name of the class is the same as that which appears in the toolbox. Thus, if you want to know how to use a `RadioButton`, you can start by entering **RadioButton** in the Help Index. Visual Studio Help pops up a window containing an explanation of the component and example code, on occasion.

Finally, for every example you can find, scan through the InitializeComponents() method until you understand what the Forms Designer is doing. This strategy will introduce you to new components and their properties and give you some idea as to their purpose.

Experience makes the job of finding the right component easier and easier.

What Comes Next?

Remember that the SimpleEditor created in this chapter is very simple. It looks nice, but it's so simple that it doesn't actually do anything at all. Chapter 18 adds the code necessary to turn SimpleEditor into a real editor.

Chapter 18

Completing Your Windows Application — Lights, Camera, Action!

• •

In This Chapter

▶ Implementing the menu items

▶ Copying data to and from the clipboard

▶ Performing simple manipulations on fonts

▶ Tying two different controls together so changes to one are reflected in the other

▶ Reading and saving the editor's contents

▶ Using dialog boxes

• •

C hapter 17 creates a nice-looking `SimpleEditor` application. Unfortunately, the `SimpleEditor` in Chapter 17 doesn't actually do anything. Close, but no cigar. This chapter adds the layers necessary to make it work. In this chapter, you transform `SimpleEditor` into something useful: an editor capable of reading and writing text files, bolding and italicizing text, changing font size, reading and writing to the clipboard, and resizing at will.

The complete `SimpleEditor` is on the enclosed CD-ROM.

Adding Action

The Forms Designer simplifies the job of creating a Windows-oriented application. The program opens up a toolbox of thingies such as buttons, textboxes, and labels. (These thingies are more formally known as *components*.) You simply grab a component out of the toolbox and drop it on the form. Then, you can customize the component by adjusting any number of properties in the cleverly named Properties window.

The Properties window lists two fundamentally different types of properties. One set, which I'll call the *static properties*, includes the font, the shape, the background color, and the initial text. These properties correspond to C# properties. (See Chapter 11 for a description of the C# Property construct.)

The Properties window offers a completely different set of properties that more accurately correspond to methods. I'll call these *active properties*.

Active properties actually correspond to something known as a *delegate*. (No, not someone wearing a donkey pin or an elephant pin on their lapel and waving a campaign sign.) A delegate is a reference to an object/method pair. The object in this case is the selected component, and the method portion is the "property" within the active properties menu.

Dynamic properties are more commonly known as *events*. A method that's invoked when the event occurs is known as an *event handler*. However, I want to stay away from unnecessary complexity.

The active properties of an object are the methods C# invokes when certain predefined circumstances occur. For example, the `Button.Click` property is invoked when the user clicks a button. However, these active properties provide much finer control than that. For example, you have a property for depressing the button and another for releasing the button, should you choose to differentiate between the two. Another property gets triggered when the mouse is over the button, whether clicked or not, and yet another property comes into play when the mouse goes somewhere else. (This is usually used to change the color of the button when the mouse is properly positioned.)

To access the active properties, select the component and then click the little lightning bolt at the top of the Properties window. Figure 18-1 shows a subset of the active properties for a `TextBox`.

You need to assign one or more active properties to each component in the `SimpleEditor` if this application is to do its job adequately. Suddenly, `SimpleEditor` doesn't seem so simple.

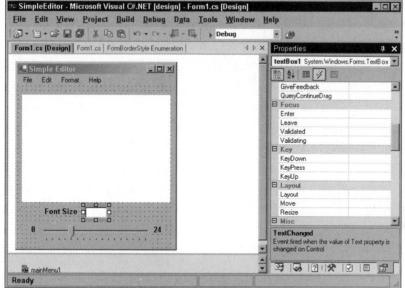

Figure 18-1:
Even the
lowly
TextBox
offers
dozens of
active
properties.

A Sure-Fire Menu for Editing the Edit Menu

There's no particular reason to start with one component or another, so why not start with the easiest and work your way up? One of the more difficult features in earlier versions of Windows was the clipboard; however, the C# library makes copying to and from the clipboard a breeze.

The clipboard is a background section in Windows where material that has been copied or cut is stored until it is later pasted. The clipboard must be maintained in Windows because users may clip an object such as text in one application and paste it into another.

The SetDataObject method of the Clipboard class writes a DataObject to the clipboard. A DataObject consists of the data to store and a description of the object's type.

Identifying the type of data is very important. For example, the user may try to cut a spreadsheet and paste it into the SimpleEditor window. Without some way of filtering that out, SimpleEditor would end up displaying a large string of garbage (at best).

The following function stores a string of text identified as type RTF (Rich Text Format) to the clipboard:

```
private void WriteClipboard(string rtfText)
{
  DataObject data = new DataObject();
  data.SetData(DataFormats.Rtf, rtfText);
  Clipboard.SetDataObject(data, true);
}
```

The method WriteClipboard() accepts a string of text to be copied to the clipboard. It begins by creating a DataObject() into which it stores the string and an indication that the text is actually a series of RTF commands and not a spreadsheet or a database object. The DataFormats class is really nothing more than a set of descriptors of different data formats, DataFormats.Rtf being the one we want. The SetDataObject() method copies the RTF string onto the clipboard.

Reading data off of the clipboard is the same process in reverse. However, you must add several extra tests to make sure the read request is ignored if the clipboard doesn't contain string data:

```
private string ReadClipboard()
{
  // get whatever's on the clipboard
  IDataObject data = Clipboard.GetDataObject();
  if (data == null)
  {
    return null;
  }
  // get the data out, but make sure that's it
  // RTF data
  object o = data.GetData(DataFormats.Rtf, true);
  if (o == null)
  {
    return null;
  }
  // OK, we got something; make absolutely sure
  // that it's a string
  if ((o is string) == false)
  {
    return null;
  }
  // that's it - we got something
  return (string)o;
}
```

ReadClipboard() starts by trying to retrieve an object off of the clipboard. If it doesn't find anything there, it returns nothing. It then tries to read an RTF string from the object. Once again, if the clipboard object is not an RTF string, it returns a null. Finally, if something's on the clipboard and if it's an RTF string, ReadClipboard() returns the string to the caller.

1. **Double-click** Form1.cs **in the Solution Explorer window to display the C# source code.**

2. **Type in the `WriteClipboard()` and `ReadClipboard()` methods.**

   Edit⇨Cut, Edit⇨Copy, and Edit⇨Paste are now relatively simple operations.

3. **Select the Edit⇨Paste menu item in the Forms Designer.**

4. **Select the little lightning bolt to display the active properties. Now select the active property `Click`.**

5. **Enter a meaningful name of a function in the text window. I chose `EditPaste` to match the menu selection.**

   The Forms Designer creates an empty method, which it links into the menu item in such a way that this method is invoked when the user clicks it.

6. **Repeat Steps 3 through 5 for the Cut and Copy menu items. I called these methods `EditCut` and `EditCopy`.**

7. **You must add the contents of the functions by hand (darn!). Edit the three edit methods as follows:**

```
private void EditCut(object sender, System.EventArgs e)
{
  string rtfText = richTextBox1.SelectedRtf;
  WriteClipboard(rtfText);

  // now wipe out what's already there
  richTextBox1.SelectedRtf = "";
}

private void EditCopy(object sender, System.EventArgs e)
{
  string rtfText = richTextBox1.SelectedRtf;
  WriteClipboard(rtfText);
}

private void EditPaste(object sender, System.EventArgs e)
{
  string s = ReadClipboard();
  if (s != null)
  {
    richTextBox1.SelectedRtf = s;
  }
}
```

The `SelectedRtf` property is equal to the text that is currently selected. The `EditCopy()` method passes this property to the `WriteClipboard()`. The `EditCut()` method does the same but then wipes out the selected text by setting it to an empty string. The `EditPaste()` method reads an RTF string off of the clipboard and then overwrites the currently selected text (or inserts the text at the current cursor position if no text is selected).

Double-clicking the property name within the Properties window takes you directly to the function. This can save a lot of time.

8. **Rebuild the** `SimpleEditor` **program, resulting in a program that can actually cut and paste.**

9. **Run the program by choosing Debug⇨Start.**

10. **Type in a few lines of text in the edit window.**

11. **Select a bit of text, choose Edit⇨Cut (or press the Ctrl+X key combination), move the cursor, choose Edit⇨Paste (or press Ctrl+V), and voila! The text has moved.**

Even more impressive, `SimpleEditor` can cut and paste from other applications, such as Microsoft Word. Figure 18-2 shows a section cut from a Word document and pasted into the `SimpleEditor`. The RTF format can retain the formatting information: One line is in Heading Level 1 format, the next in Normal format, and the last in Code format.

Figure 18-2: Selections pasted out of Word retain their formatting.

The `RichTextBox` does all the formatting work that you previously had to do yourself with great difficulty.

Go Boldly Forth and Italicize

The `SimpleEditor` can now cut and paste formatted data, but it still can't change fonts on its own. For that, you need the Format menu and the Font size controls.

Changing font style and size

Setting the font, bold, and italicize functions are actually very similar. Therefore, you can save some effort by creating a single function capable of handling all three operations, such as the following:

```
//----------------Format & Font size--------------
bool isBolded = false;
bool isItalics = false;
float fontSize = 12.0F;
private void SetFont()
{
  FontStyle fs = FontStyle.Regular;
  if (isBolded)
  {
    fs |= FontStyle.Bold;
  }
  if (isItalics)
  {
    fs |= FontStyle.Italic;
  }
  Font font = new Font(richTextBox1.Font.FontFamily, fontSize, fs);
  richTextBox1.SelectionFont = font;
}
```

The key to this function is the `Font()` constructor. Many versions of the `Font` constructor exist. However, this particular version accepts the arguments we're looking for: the current font, the new font size, and the new font style. The `FontStyle` is a bit pattern made up of such properties as bold, italics, strikethrough, and underline. Start with `FontStyle.Regular` and add whichever of these style-properties using the C# OR (`||`) operator. Two flags, `isBolded` and `isItalics`, maintain the bold or italics state of the system.

The first argument to the constructor specifies the actual font. (The ability to change fonts was not a requirement for `SimpleEditor`.) The `richTextBox1.Font` command returns a description of the current font in use. `FontFamily` property returns the font type. For example, it might return "Arial" or "Times New Roman." Thus, the constructor creates a new font object with the same font but a new size and new boldness and italics properties.

The final assignment changes the font of the selected text or the text typed from here forward.

The expression `richTextBox1.Font = font;` changes the font of all the text in the box at once.

Implementing the Format menu items

The following steps implement the Format menu items:

1. **Select the Format⇨Bold menu option.**

2. **Select the `Click` active property and enter the name** FormatBold.

3. **Repeat the process for the Format⇨Italics menu option. Use the name** FormatItalics.

4. **Edit the new functions as follows:**

```
private void FormatBold(object sender, System.EventArgs e)
{
  isBolded = !isBolded;
  menuItem10.Checked = isBolded;
  SetFont();
}

private void FormatItalics(object sender, System.EventArgs e)
{
  isItalics = !isItalics;
  menuItem11.Checked = isItalics;
  SetFont();
}
```

Both functions toggle the respective flag and invoke `SetFont()` to update the font accordingly.

`FormatBold()` and `FormatItalics()` set the `menuItem10.Checked` flag to `true` or `false` to create a little check box in front of the menu item to show that the item is in effect. (`menuItem10` is the Format⇨Bold menu item, while `menuItem11` is Format⇨Italics).

The names of your menu items might differ if you added them in a different order than I did. To find out the name of a particular component, select the component in the Forms Designer. The name and type of the component appear at the top of the Properties window.

You really don't have to put up with the Forms Designer assigned names. You can change the `Name` property when you first create the object. In this way, you can assign more meaningful names that are easier to remember.

5. **Just to be on the safe side, add a call to** `SetFont()` **in the constructor to set the initial font properly:**

```
public Form1()
{
  //
  // Required for Windows Form Designer support
  //
  InitializeComponent();

  //
  // TODO: Add any constructor code after InitializeComponent call
  //
  // set font to the default size and style
  SetFont();
}
```

6. **Build the program and execute it.**

7. **Enter some text and select it with the mouse.**

8. **Choose Format⇨Bold and Format⇨Italics in any order.**

Figure 18-3 shows the results of bolding and italicizing some text within the `SimpleEditor` window. Notice also that the currently enabled options appear with a small check. Thus, you can see from the Format menu that both Bold and Italics are enabled. This is a result of setting the `Checked` property.

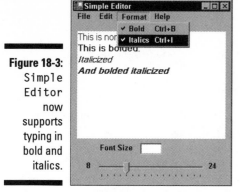

Figure 18-3:
`Simple`
`Editor`
now
supports
typing in
bold and
italics.

Setting the Font Size

Setting the font size uses the same `SetFont()` function, but it's a little trickier because it can be controlled with two different components.

Changing font size via the `TrackBar`

Changing the font size via the `TrackBar` is straightforward:

1. **Select the track bar in the Forms Designer.**

2. **Select the active property** `Scroll`. **Type in the function name**
   FontSizeControl.

3. **Switch over to the** `Form1.cs` **source code and edit the new functions
   as follows:**

```
// invoked when the user moves the font size TrackBar
private void FontSizeControl(object sender, System.EventArgs e)
{
    // read the new font size directly out of the TrackBar
    fontSize = trackBar1.Value;

    // convert it into a string and copy that into the
    // TextBox so that the two match up
    textBox1.Text = String.Format("{0}", fontSize);

    // now adjust the font
    SetFont();
}
```

`FontSizeControl()` is invoked whenever the user moves the track bar.
The function reads the new value out of the `TrackBar` control. This
value is an integer number between 8 and 24. The function uses the
`String.Format()` method to convert that number into a text string,

which it then copies into the Font Size `TextBox`. That done, `FontSizeControl()` invokes `SetFont()` to update the font being used in the edit window.

I describe `SetFont()` in the section "Changing font style and size," earlier in this chapter.

4. **Build the program. Execute the program.**

5. **Enter some text into the text window and select it with the mouse.**

6. **Grab the track bar and move it left and right.**

Figure 18-4 shows the results. You can't tell from a static picture, but the numbers in the `TextBox` update rapidly to match the `TrackBar` setting as the thumb is moved back and forth. The area of text selected grows and shrinks with the movement of the `TrackBar` as well.

Figure 18-4: By coupling the two together, the numeric font size in the `TextBox` changes to match the setting of the `TrackBar`.

Changing font size via the TextBox

The user can also enter a font directly into the Font Size `TextBox` — otherwise, the `TextBox` wouldn't be of much use. This function has to work in the opposite direction from the `FontSizeControl()` function. In addition, this function is a little more complicated because it must deal with all the garbage that a user might input. However, in the end, `FontSizeEntered()` must perform the same operation: Read the new value, update the font size, and update the `TrackBar` to match.

1. **Select the Font Size `TextBox` object.**

2. **Select the `TextChanged` active property and enter the name** FontSizeEntered.

C# will invoke this method when the user types a new value into the Font Size `TextBox`.

3. Edit the newly created function as follows:

```
// invoked when the user types into the TextBox used
// for font size entry
private void FontSizeEntered(object sender, System.EventArgs e)
{
  // read out the contents of the TextBox
  string sText = textBox1.Text;

  // ignore any conversion error that might take place
  try
  {

    // if there's anything there...
    //if (sText.Length > 0)
    // ...convert it into an integer
    int nFontSize = Int32.Parse(sText);

    // if the value is within proper range...
    if (nFontSize >= trackBar1.Minimum && nFontSize <= trackBar1.Maximum)
    {
      // ...update the trackbar and...
      trackBar1.Value = nFontSize;

      // ...update the font (SetFont() reads its font
      // size directly out of the TrackBar
      SetFont();
    }
  }
  catch {}:
}
```

This method is invoked on every keystroke and not just the last. For example, entering **24** generates two calls: one with the value 2 and the second with a value of 24. In this application, that doesn't matter, but just be aware.

`FontSizeEntered()` first reads the contents of the `TextBox`. It then enters a `try` block. The `Int32.Parse()` function converts the contents of the `TextBox` into an `int` value. This conversion function throws an exception if the string found there cannot be converted into a valid integer. The universal `catch` at the bottom of the function block snags but ignores the exception without modifying the font size. Likewise, if the string entered by the user can be converted into a number but the number is outside the legal range of 8 to 24 points, it is ignored.

If the font size is legal, `FontSizeEntered()` updates the `TrackBar` to match the new value by setting its `Value` property. For example, suppose the `TrackBar` is sitting at 12. As soon as the user enters the string 22, the `TrackBar` thumb snaps from the left side over to the 22 setting on the right.

The `Font()` function updates the font to be used for subsequent input.

4. Build and execute the program.

5. Enter some text and select it.

6. **Type in a font size between 8 and 24.**

Notice that the font size changes and the track bar moves to the corresponding location.

Saving Off the User's Data

Without the ability to read and write files, the `SimpleEditor` is not much more than a game.

Reading the name of the file

To read a file, you have to know which file to read. C# provides a special dialog box known as the `OpenFileDialog` just for this purpose. Eventually, the user will want to save the edited text back out to disk. You guessed it: For this purpose, you need the `SaveFileDialog`. Slap those two dialog boxes around the file read and write skills from Chapter 16, and you have a complete editor.

Adding an `OpenFileDialog` is as easy as spitting in the sea — assuming, of course, that you're near the shore:

1. **Drag an `OpenFileDialog` component from the toolbox to the area beneath the edit window. You can drop it next to the `mainMenu1` icon.**

2. **Repeat the process for the `SaveFileDialog`.**

The result should look like Figure 18-5.

The `OpenFileDialog` component really has only one static property of interest. When an open file appears, it usually appears with a list of different file types. For example, Notepad starts by looking for *.txt files. Word begins looking for *.doc files when it first opens. These are called *filters*. The last option in the list of filters is always *.*, which means *all files*.

The filters for the open dialog are stored in the `Filter` property. The language of this field is obtuse: The input is in the form of name/filter pairs, each separated by a | character. Each pair also is separated by a |.

3. **Set the `Filter` property to the string "RTF Files|*.rtf|All files|*.*".**

This initializes the `OpenFileDialog` to look only for RTF files, but offers the option of looking at all files.

"All files|*.*" should always be the last entry in the filter list. This is the selection of last resort for the user.

4. **Repeat the process for the `Filter` property of the `SaveFileDialog`.**

Figure 18-5:
Dropping an
`OpenFile`
`Dialog`
and
`SaveFile`
`Dialog`
from
the toolbox
onto the
`Simple`
`Editor`
produces
most of the
chit-chat
dialog for
opening and
saving files.

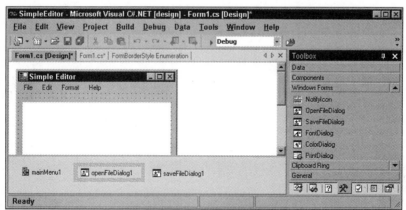

Reading from an RTF file

The `OpenFileDialog` is amazingly easy to use. The `ShowDialog()` method opens the dialog box. The `SimpleEditor` doesn't need to do anything while the user scrolls about trying to find just the right file to open. After the user is finished, she clicks either OK or Cancel. Only then does control return. The return value from `ShowDialog()` is `DialogResult.OK` if the user clicked the OK button. If not, we don't really care what it is.

The `OpenFile()` method returns either a valid `IO.Stream` with which to read the file or a `null` if the specified file can't be read for some reason. These two methods are combined into the following `OpenAndReadFile()` function:

```
// read the file specified by the user into the RichTextBox
// (return a true if the RichTextBox is changed)
private bool OpenAndReadFile()
{
  bool bReturnValue = false;
  try
  {
    // get the filename from the user
    if (openFileDialog1.ShowDialog() == DialogResult.OK)
    {
      // open the file
      System.IO.Stream strInput = openFileDialog1.OpenFile();
      if (strInput != null)
      {
        // if the file was opened successfully, associate
        // a stream reader
```

```
        System.IO.StreamReader strRdr =
                new System.IO.StreamReader(strInput);
        // read the entire file contents
        string sContents = strRdr.ReadToEnd();
        richTextBox1.Rtf = sContents;
        // OK - we've changed the text window
        bReturnValue = true;
        // make sure we close the file so that others
        // can read it
        strRdr.Close();
      }
    }
  }

    catch(Exception e)
  {
    // output the error message in the text window itself
    richTextBox1.Text = "Can't read file\n";
    richTextBox1.Text += e.Message;
    bReturnValue = true;
  }
  return bReturnValue;
}
```

The function begins by popping up an `OpenFileDialog`. If the dialog box returns an OK, the function attempts to open the selected file using the convenient `OpenFile()` method. If that method returns a valid `Stream` object, `OpenAndReadFile()` wraps the `Stream` object in a more convenient `StreamReader`. It then reads the entire contents of the file. It copies this buffer into the `RichTextBox` by assigning it to the `Rtf` property. Finally, `OpenAndReadFile()` closes the file.

Editors that read the entire file into memory are much easier to write than those that leave the majority of the file on disk. In any case, C# does not limit its `RichTextBox` to the frustratingly small 64KB buffer that Notepad uses.

If a file I/O error occurs, `OpenAndReadFile()` writes the error message out to the `RichTextBox` itself.

The `OpenFileDialog` was added to the `SimpleReader` application earlier by dragging it out of the toolbox.

Writing to an RTF file

The `SaveFileDialog` class provides methods that are just as convenient as the open versions:

```
// save file off to disk; return a true if successful
// (this time don't bother to catch an exception - I wouldn't
// know what to do with it anyway)
private bool SaveSpecifiedFile()
{
  bool bReturnValue = false;
  // this code follows the exact same format as OpenAndReadFile()
```

```
if (saveFileDialog1.ShowDialog() == DialogResult.OK)
{
  System.IO.Stream strOutput = saveFileDialog1.OpenFile();
  if (strOutput != null)
  {
    System.IO.StreamWriter strWtr =
                  new System.IO.StreamWriter(strOutput);
    strWtr.Write(richTextBox1.Rtf);
    strWtr.Close();
    bReturnValue = true;
  }
}
return bReturnValue;
}
```

This function follows the exact same path as the earlier OpenAndReadFile() method. First, it opens the SaveFileDialog and waits for an OK to come back. If it does, the program tries to open the file. If possible, the program writes out the entire contents of the RichTextBox as returned by the Rtf property.

The SaveFileDialog was added to the SimpleReader application earlier by dragging it out of the toolbox. No assembly required.

Putting Read and Write in a box and slapping a menu on it

The neat little OpenAndReadFile() and SaveSpecifiedFile() methods are nice but useless until they have been tied to a menu option.

Use the following steps to implement the File⇨Open and File⇨Save menu items:

1. **Create the** OpenAndReadFile() **and** SaveSpecifiedFile() **methods described in the previous sections.**

2. **Select the File⇨Save menu item in the Forms Designer.**

3. **Select the** Click **active property. Type in the function name** FileSave, **as shown in Figure 18-6.**

4. **Repeat the process for the File⇨Open menu item. Use the function name** FileOpen.

5. **Edit the** FileOpen() **and** FileSave() **methods as follows:**

```
private void FileOpen(object sender, System.EventArgs e)
{
  OpenAndReadFile();
}

private void FileSave(object sender, System.EventArgs e)
{
  SaveSpecifiedFile();
}
```

These two simple functions give `SimpleEditor` the right to be called a real editor — it can now read and write files. For example, although you can't tell it, the text shown in Figure 18-7 was actually written by Microsoft Word (saved in RTF format, of course) and read using the File⇨Open command.

Figure 18-6:
Typing in the name `FileSave` in the `Click` property of the Save submenu generates a new function, which is invoked whenever the user chooses File⇨Save.

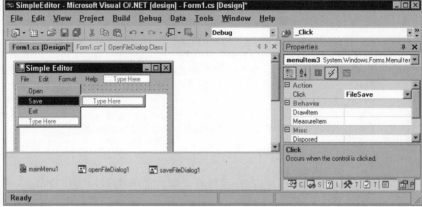

Figure 18-7:
`Simple Editor` is a real editor now, able to read tall RTF files in a single bound.

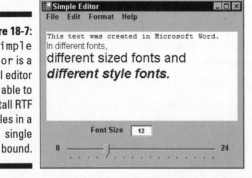

Don't Throw Away My Changes on Exit!

Implementing the File⇨Exit command is easy:

1. Select the File⇨Exit menu item.

2. Select the `Click` **property and enter the function name** FileExit.

3. Edit the newly created `FileExit()` **method as follows:**

```
private void FileExit(object sender, System.EventArgs e)
{
    Application.Exit();
}
```

The `Application` class controls the overall program. Its `Exit()` method exits stage right, just like it sounds. The problem with this approach is that exiting the program without performing a File⇨Save first means loss of your work. That's bad.

Fortunately, the read and write methods give us what we need to avoid this catastrophe. `SaveSpecifiedFile()` returns a `bool` indicating whether the data has been saved off successfully. What we need is a "dirty" flag, indicating whether something in the `RichTextBox` needs to be saved. We would set the flag to `false` when a file was first read — nothing has changed. Typing, cutting, or pasting into the textbox would set the flag to `true`. Saving the data off to disk would then reset the flag to `false`. Let's call the flag `bTextChanged`.

Of course, the user could always exit from the program even if the latest and greatest had not been saved off; however, the user must make a conscious decision to do so — that means clicking the OK button in a warning window.

The following `IsChangeOK()` method will do nicely:

```
// the following method makes sure the user does not
// inadvertently lose edits by popping open a message
// box if the RichTextBox is "dirty"
bool bTextChanged = false;
private bool IsChangeOK()
{
    // it's always OK to exit the program
    // if nothing has changed
    if (bTextChanged == false)
    {
        return true;
    }
    // but something has changed; check to see what the user
    // wants to do about it
    DialogResult dr = MessageBox.Show("Text changed. "
                        + "Click OK to throw away changes.",
                            "Text Modified",
                            MessageBoxButtons.YesNo);
    return dr == DialogResult.Yes;
}
```

The `IsChangeOK()` returns a `true` if it is okay to lose the current contents of the `RichTextBox`. First of all, if the changed flag is set to `false`, nothing has changed since the last File⇨Save, so there's nothing to lose.

If something has changed, the function pops open a `MessageBox` to ask what the user wants to do: continue and lose any changes, or cancel and retain them. The MessageBox class is as simple as the dialog boxes. The Show() method opens up a box with the specified message and specified title. The YesNo property says, "Make it one of those message boxes with just a Yes and a No button." If the MessageBox returns a DialogResult.Yes, then user is saying it's okay to wipe out any unsaved changes.

The following updates to FileOpen(), FileSave(), and FileExit() should do the trick:

```
private void FileOpen(object sender, System.EventArgs e)
{
  // don't open a new file and overwrite the old one
  if (IsChangeOK() == false)
  {
    return;
  }
  // it's OK, he says
  OpenAndReadFile();
  // the text box is now in the unchanged state
  bTextChanged = false;
}
private void FileSave(object sender, System.EventArgs e)
{
  // set the changed flag to false if the save
  // worked
  if (SaveSpecifiedFile())
  {
    bTextChanged = false;
  }
}
private void FileExit(object sender, System.EventArgs e)
{
  // don't exit unless the data has been saved already
  // or the user says it's OK
  if (IsChangeOK() == false)
  {
    return;
  }
  // go ahead and bail out
  Application.Exit();
}
```

In each case, the IsChangeOK() method is invoked before performing an operation that would result in the loss of a change.

There's still one piece missing: Something needs to set the bTextChanged flag to true when the textbox changes. The RichTextBox provides just the ticket: a dynamic property TextChanged(), which is invoked whenever anything happens to change the contents of the text box. Select the RichTextBox yet one more time and enter the method name TextChanged in the TextChanged property. The method consists of nothing more than setting the dirty flag:

```
// this method is called when something changes
private void TextChanged(object sender, System.EventArgs e)
{
  bTextChanged = true;
}
```

So, it's time to give it a try:

1. **Read in some text from an existing RTF file.**

2. **Type a new line below the original.**

3. **Choose File⇨Exit.**

   Breathe a sigh of relief as the warning shown in Figure 18-8 appears.

4. **Click Yes, and the program exits.**

5. **Repeat the process starting with Step 1. Click No, and the program continues on as if nothing had happened.**

Figure 18-8:
Simple
Editor
pops open
a warning
when the
user tries
to do
something
that would
result in the
loss of data.

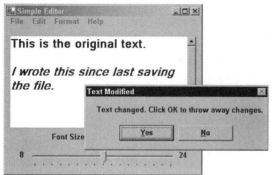

Implementing the Close Window Button

One small problem remains. It is still possible to exit the application by closing the window:

1. **Select the entire window frame.**

2. **Select the** Closing **active property.**

3. **Enter the function name** ApplicationWindowClosing.

   C# invokes the Closing property when the user clicks the Close Window gadget (the small x) in the upper-right corner of the Form header. Attaching a method to that property is not a problem. The problem is what to do when control gets there. The answer lies in a facet of the property methods, which I have ignored up until now.

   When C# calls a method as a result of some button being clicked or some value being typed, it passes two arguments. The first is known as the sender. This object is the component that originated the stimulus.

The methods that we generated could only be invoked from one source. However, differentiating senders can be useful in reducing the amount of code to be written, and I'm always in favor of reducing the amount of code I have to write. For example, a single method could be used to handle a large number of separate radio buttons — the sender would indicate which radio button was clicked.

The second argument contains other event information tied to the reason for calling the method. However, the CancelEventArgs class passed to our method as a result of clicking the Window close method contains a Cancel property. This property defaults to false. However, if you set that flag to true, the Window-closing operation is halted in its tracks.

4. **Update the ApplicationWindowClosing() method with the same "don't lose data" logic utilized with such success in File⇨Exit:**

```
private void ApplicationWindowClosing(object sender,
        System.ComponentModel.CancelEventArgs e)
{
  if (!IsChangeOK())
  {
    e.Cancel = true;
  }
}
```

5. **Build the program and run it.**

6. **Enter some text and click the little window close button.**

Notice the same warning message as that produced by File⇨Exit.

Building Your Own Windows Applications

Creating the SimpleEditor program requires lots of steps, and it's a relatively simple application. However, it is, in fact, much easier to create a Windows application using Visual Studio .NET than with earlier tools. Four or five years ago, even small tricks like opening a message box were difficult. Back in the days of Windows 3.1, these same operations were pure torture.

Don't be discouraged, however. Think about what you want your application to look like and how you want it to work. Write it down. Only then use the Forms Designer to paint the components that make up your application. Use the Properties window to search through the properties you want to set, both static and dynamic, to make the application operate just the way you want it to.

Part VI
The Part of Tens

In this part . . .

What Dummies book would be complete without a Part of Tens? C# is great at finding errors in your programs when you try to build them — you've probably noticed that. However, the error messages it generates can be cryptic — you've probably noted that, as well. Chapter 19 reviews the ten most common build-time error messages and what they most likely mean. Knowledge is power, so Chapter 19 also suggests fixes for the problems being reported.

Many readers will have come to C# through the most common of all object-oriented languages, C++. Chapter 20 quickly reviews the differences between the two languages.

Chapter 19

The Ten Most Common Build Errors (And How to Fix Them)

- -

In This Chapter

▶ The name 'memberName' does not exist in the class or namespace 'className'

▶ Cannot implicitly convert type 'x' into 'y'

▶ 'className.memberName' is inaccessible due to its protection level

▶ Use of unassigned local variable 'n'

▶ The file 'programName.exe' cannot be copied into the run directory. The process cannot...;

▶ The keyword new is required on 'subclassName.methodName' because it hides 'baseclassName.methodName'

▶ 'subclassName' : cannot inherit from sealed class 'baseclassName'

▶ 'className' does not implement interface member 'methodName'

▶ 'methodName' : not all code paths return a value

▶ } expected

- -

C# makes the ol' college try at finding errors in your C# code. In fact, C# homes in on syntax errors like a tornado heading for a double-wide. Other than really stupid mistakes like trying to compile your shopping list, the same complaints seem to pop up, over and over.

This chapter describes 10 common build-time error messages. A few warnings are in order, however. First, C# can get awfully long-winded. I have whittled down some of the error messages so the message can fit on one page, let alone one line. In addition, an error message has places to insert the name of an errant data member or an obnoxious class. In place of these specific names, I have inserted `variableName`, `memberName`, or `className`.

Finally, C# doesn't simply spit out the name of the class. It prefers to tack on the full namespace name — just in case the entire error message would have been visible without scrolling over to your neighbor's house.

The name 'memberName' does not exist in the class or namespace 'className'

This error message could mean that you forgot to declare a variable, as in the following example:

```
for(index = 0; index < 10; index++)
{
  // . . . whatever . . .
}
```

The variable index is not defined anywhere. (See Chapter 3 for instructions on declaring variables.) This example should have been written as follows:

```
for(int index = 0; index < 10; index++)
{
  // . . . whatever . . .
}
```

The same applies to data members of a class. (See Chapter 6.)

A more likely possibility is that you misspelled a variable name. The following is a good example:

```
class Student
{
  public string sStudentName;
  public int nID;
}
class MyClass
{
  static public void MyFunction(Student s)
  {
    Console.WriteLine("Student name = " + s.sStudentName);
    Console.WriteLine("Student Id = " + s.nId);
  }
}
```

The problem here is that MyFunction() references a data member nId rather than the actual data member nID. Although you see the similarity, C# does not. The programmer wrote down nId, but there's no nId, and that's all there is to it. The fact that nID is lurking around the corner, alphabetically speaking, is irrelevant.

Less popular but still way up on the Top 10 play list is the possibility that the variable was declared in a different scope:

```
class MyClass
{
  static public void AverageInput()
  {
    int nCount = 0;
```

```
    while(true)
    {
      // read in a number
      string s = Console.ReadLine();
      int n = Int32.Parse(s);
      // quit when the user enters a negative number
      if (n < 0)
      {
        break;
      }
      // accumulate the value entered
      nSum += n;
      nCount++;
    }
    // now output the results
    Console.WriteLine("The total is " + nSum);
    Console.WriteLine("The average is " + nSum / nCount);
    // this generates a build time error message
    Console.WriteLine("The terminating value was " + s);
  }
}
```

The last line in this function is incorrect. The problem is that a variable is limited to the scope in which it is defined. The variable s is not defined outside of the while() loop.

Cannot implicitly convert type 'x' into 'y'

This error usually indicates that you are trying to use two different variable types in the same expression — for example:

```
int nAge = 10;
// generates an error message
int nFactoredAge = 2.0 * nAge;
```

The problem here is that 2.0 is a variable of type double. The int nAge multiplied by the double 2.0 results in a double value. C# will not automatically store a double into the int variable nFactoredAge because information might be lost — most notably, any fractional value that the double may possess.

Some conversions are not at all obvious, as in the following example:

```
class MyClass
{
  static public float FloatTimes2(float f)
  {
    // this generates a build time error
    float fResult = 2.0 * f;
    return fResult;
  }
}
```

You might think that doubling a float would be okay, but that's sort of the problem. 2.0 is not a float but of type double. A double times a float is a double. C# will not store a double value back into a float variable due to — you guessed it — possible loss of data, in this case, several digits of accuracy.

Implicit conversions can further confuse the casual reader (that's me on a good day). The following version of FloatTimes2() works just fine:

```
class MyClass
{
  static public float FloatTimes2(float f)
  {
    // this works fine
    float fResult = 2 * f;
    return fResult;
  }
}
```

The constant 2 is of type int. An int times a float is a float, which can be stored off in the float variable fResult.

The implicit conversion error message can also arise when performing operations on "unnatural" types. For example, you cannot add two char variables, but C# can convert char variables into int values for you when necessary to get the job done. This leads to the following:

```
class MyClass
{
  static public void SomeFunction()
  {
    char c1 = 'a';
    char c2 = 'b';
    // I don't know what this even means, but it's illegal anyway - not for the
    // reason you think
    char c3 = c1 + c2;
  }
}
```

Adding two characters together makes no sense, but C# tries anyway. Because addition isn't defined for type char, it converts c1 and c2 into int values and then performs the addition. Unfortunately, the resulting int value cannot be converted back down into a char without some help.

Most, but not all, conversions are okay with an explicit cast. Thus, the following function works without complaint:

```
class MyClass
{
  static public float FloatTimes2(float f)
  {
    // this works OK with the explicit cast
    float fResult = (float)(2.0 * f);
    return fResult;
  }
}
```

The result of 2.0 * f is still of type double, but the programmer has indicated that she specifically wants the result down-converted to a float even in the unlikely event that it results in the loss of data.

A second approach would be to make sure that all constants are of the same type:

```
class MyClass
{
  static public float FloatTimes2(float f)
  {
    // this works OK because 2.0F is a float constant
    float fResult = 2.0F * f;
    return fResult;
  }
}
```

This version of the function uses a constant 2.0 of type `float` rather than the default `double`. A `float` times a `float` is a `float`.

'className.memberName' is inaccessible due to its protection level

This error indicates that a function is trying to access a member to which it does not have access. For example, a method in one class may be trying to access a private member in another class (see Chapter 11):

```
public class MyClass
{
  public void SomeFunction()
  {
    YourClass uc = new YourClass();
    // this doesn't work properly because MyClass can't access the private
            member
    uc.nPrivateMember = 1;
  }
}
public class YourClass
{
  private int nPrivateMember = 0;
}
```

Usually, the error is not so blatant. Often, you've simply left the descriptor off of either the member object or the class itself. By default, a member of a class is `private` while a class is `internal`. Thus, `nPrivateMember` is still private in the following example:

```
class MyClass
{
  public void SomeFunction()
  {
    YourClass uc = new YourClass();
    // this doesn't work properly because MyClass can't access the private
              member
    uc.nPrivateMember = 1;
  }
}
```

```
}
public class YourClass
{
   int nPrivateMember = 0;      // this member is still private
}
```

In addition, even though SomeFunction() is declared public, it still can't be accessed from classes in other modules because MyClass itself is internal.

The moral of the story is: "Always specify the protection level of your classes and their members." A lemma is: "Don't declare public members in a class which itself is internal — it doesn't do any good and it's just confusing."

Use of unassigned local variable 'n'

Just like it says, this message indicates that you declared a variable but didn't give it an initial value. This is usually an oversight, but it can occur when you really meant to pass a variable as an out argument to a function:

```
public class MyClass
{
   public void SomeFunction()
   {
     int n;
     // this is OK because C# only returns a value in n; it does not
     // pass a value into the function
     SomeOtherFunction(out n);
   }
   public void SomeOtherFunction(out int n)
   {
     n = 1;
   }
}
```

In this case, n is not assigned a value inside of SomeFunction(), but it is in SomeOtherFunction(). SomeOtherFunction() ignores the value of an out argument as if it didn't exist, which it doesn't in this case.

The file 'programName.exe' cannot be copied into the run directory. The process cannot...;

Usually, this message repeats multiple times. In almost every case, it means you forgot to terminate the program before you rebuilt it. In other words, you did the following:

1. You successfully built your program (let's assume it's a console application, though it can happen to any C# output).

2. You got to the message "Press Enter to terminate," but in your haste, you didn't. So, your program is still executing. Instead, you switched back to Visual Studio to edit the file.

3. You tried to build the program again with the new updates. At this point, you get this error message.

An executable .EXE file is locked by Windows until the program actually quits. Visual C# cannot overwrite the old .EXE executable with the new version until the program terminates.

Switch over to the application and terminate it. In the case of a console application just press the Enter key to terminate the program. You also can terminate the program from within Visual Studio by choosing Debug⇨Stop Debugging.

After the older program has terminated, rebuild the application.

If you can't get rid of the error by terminating the program, there's an outside chance that the directory is messed up. Close the solution, exit Visual Studio, reboot, and then reopen the solution. If that doesn't work, I'm sorry — punt.

The keyword new is required on 'subclassName.methodName' because it hides 'baseclassName.methodName'

With this message, C# is telling you that you've overloaded a method in a base class without overriding it. (See Chapter 13 for details.) Consider the following example:

```
public class BaseClass
{
  public void Function()
  {
  }
}
public class SubClass : BaseClass
{
  public void Function()
  {
  }
}
public class MyClass
{
  public void Test()
  {
```

```
    SubClass sb = new SubClass();
    sb.Function();
  }
}
```

The function `Test()` cannot get at the method `BaseClass.Function()` from the subclass object `sb` because it is hidden by `SubClass.Function()`. You intended to do one of the following:

🗸 You really did intend to hide the base class method. In that case, add the `new` keyword to the `SubClass` definition, as in the following example:

```
public class SubClass : BaseClass
{
  new public void Function()
  {
  }
}
```

🗸 You really meant to inherit the base class polymorphically, in which case you should have declared the two classes as follows:

```
public class BaseClass
{
  public virtual void Function()
  {
  }
}

public class SubClass : BaseClass
{
  public overrides void Function()
  {
  }
}
```

See Chapter 13 for details.

This is not an error — just a warning in the task list window.

'subclassName' : cannot inherit from sealed class 'baseclassName'

This message indicates that someone has sealed the class so you can't inherit from it or change any of its properties. Typically, only library classes are sealed. There's nothing you can do about this one.

'className' does not implement interface member 'methodName'

Implementing an interface represents a promise to provide a definition for all the methods of that interface. This message says you broke that promise by not implementing the method named. Several possible reasons exist:

✔ Your dog ate your homework. Basically, you just forgot or were unaware of the method. Be more careful next time.

✔ You misspelled the method or gave the wrong arguments.

Consider the following example:

```
Interface Me
{
    void aFunction(float);
}
public class MyClass : Me
{
    public void aFunction(double d)
    {
    }
}
```

The class `MyClass` does not implement the interface function `aFunction(float)`. The function `aFunction(double)` doesn't count because the arguments don't match.

Go back to the drawing board and eat all your methods until the interface has been completely fulfilled.

Not fully implementing an interface is essentially the same thing as trying to create a concrete class from an abstract one without hiding all the abstract methods.

'methodName' : not all code paths return a value

With this message, C# is telling you that your method was declared non-void and one or more paths don't return anything. This can happen in either of two ways:

✔ You have an `if` statement that has a return without a value specified.

✔ (more likely) You calculated a value and never returned it.

Both of these possibilities are demonstrated in the following class:

```
public class MyClass
{
  public string ConvertToString(int n)
  {
    // convert the int n into a string s
    string s = n.ToString();
  }
  public string ConvertPositiveNumbers(int n)
  {
    // only positive numbers are valid for conversion
    if (n > 0)
    {
      string s = n.ToString();
      return s;
    }
              Console.WriteLine("the argument {0} is invalid", n);
  }
}
```

ConvertToString() calculates a string to return, but never returns it. Just add a return s; at the bottom of the method.

The ConvertPositiveNumbers() returns the string version of the int argument n when n is positive. In addition, it correctly generates an error message when n is not positive. But even if n is not positive, the function still has to return *something*. Return either a null or an empty string "" in these cases — which one works best depends on the application.

} expected

This error indicates that C# was expecting another close brace when the program listing just stopped. Somewhere along the way, you forgot to close a class definition, a function, or an if block. Go back through the listing, matching the open and closed braces, until you find the culprit.

This error message is often the last in a whole series of often nonsensical error messages. Don't bother worrying about addressing the other error messages until you've fixed this one.

Chapter 20

The Ten Most Significant Differences between C# and C++

In This Chapter

▶ No global data or functions

▶ All objects are allocated off of the heap

▶ No more pointer variables allowed

▶ Sell me a few of your properties

▶ I'll never include a file again

▶ Don't construct — initialize

▶ Define your variable types well, my child

▶ No multiple inheriting

▶ Projecting a good interface

▶ The unified type system

*T*he C# language is more than a little bit based on the C++ programming language. This is hardly surprising because Microsoft built Visual C++, the most successful hard-core programming language for the Windows environment. All of your best geeks were working in Visual C++. But C++ has been showing its age for awhile now.

However, C# is not just a coat of paint over a rusty language. C# offers numerous improvements, both by adding features and by replacing good features with better ones. Here are the Top Ten best improvements — I took these straight from the Letterman show.

No Global Data or Functions

C++ passes itself off as an object-oriented language, and it is, in the sense that you can program in an object-oriented fashion using C++. You can also sidestep class objects by just throwing data and functions out there in some global space, open to the elements and any programmer with a keyboard.

C# makes its programmers declare their allegiance: All functions and all data members must join up with a class. You want to access that function or data? You have to go through the author of that class — no exceptions.

All Objects Are Allocated Off of the Heap

C/C++ allows memory to be allocated in three different ways, each with its own disadvantages:

- **Global objects exist throughout the life of the program.** A program can easily allocate multiple pointers to the same global object. Change one, and they all change, whether they're ready or not.

- **Stack objects are unique to individual functions (that's good), but they are deallocated when the function returns.** Any pointer to a deallocated memory object becomes invalid. That would be fine if anyone told the pointer; however, the pointer still thinks it's pointing to a valid object, and so does its programmer.

- **Heap objects are allocated as needed.** These objects are unique to a particular execution thread.

The problem is that it's too easy to forget what type of memory a pointer refers to. Heap objects must be returned when you're done with them. Forget to do so, and your program will progressively lose memory until it can no longer function. On the other hand, if you release the same block of heap more than once and "return" a block of global or stack memory, your program is headed for a long nap — maybe Ctrl+Alt+Del can wake it up.

C# solves this problem by allocating all objects off of the heap. Even better than that, C# returns memory to the heap for you. No more blue screen of death because you sent the wrong memory block to the heap.

No More Pointer Variables Allowed

The introduction of pointers to C ensured the success of that language. Pointer manipulation was a powerful feature. Old-hand machine language programmers could still pull the programming shenanigans they were used to. C++ retained the pointer and heap features from C without modification.

Unfortunately, neither the programmer nor the program can differentiate a good pointer from a bad one. Read memory from an uninitialized pointer, and your program crashes, if you're lucky. If you're not lucky, the program cranks right along, treating some random block of memory as if it were a valid object.

Pointer problems are often difficult to pin down. An invalid pointer program usually reacts differently every time you run it.

Fortunately for all concerned, C# manages to sidestep pointer problems by doing away with them altogether. The references that it uses instead are type-safe and cannot be manipulated by the user into something that can kill the program.

Sell Me a Few of Your Properties

Every good programmer knows that access to data members should be carefully controlled through a `get()` method to return its value and an optional `set()` method to set the value. Every programmer who has worked with `get()` and `set()` functions realizes how unnatural that feels:

```
using System;
public class Student
{
  private string sName;
  public void set(string sName)
  {
    this.sName = sName;
  }
  public string get()
  {
    // return a copy of the name
    return String.Copy(sName);
  }
}
class MyClass
{
  public void AddLastName(Student student)
  {
    student.set(student.get() + " Kringle");
  }
}
```

The C# Property feature implements `get()` and `set()` functions in a manner that's completely natural to the application program:

```
using System;
public class Student
{
  private string sName;
  public string Name
  {
    set { sName = value;}
    get { return String.Copy(sName); }
  }
}
class MyClass
{
```

```
public void AddLastName(Student student)
{
  student.Name = student.Name + "Kringle";
}
}
```

I'll Never Include a File Again

C++ enforces strict type checking — that's a good thing. It does so by compelling you to declare your functions and classes in so-called include files, which are then used by modules. However, getting all the include files set up in just the right order for your module to compile can get very complicated.

C# does away with that nonsense. Instead, C# searches out and finds the class definitions on its own. If you invoke a `Student` class, C# finds the class definition on its own to make sure you're using it properly. C# doesn't need any hints.

Don't Construct — Initialize

I could see the usefulness of constructors the first time I laid eyes on them. Provide a special function to make sure that all the data members were set up correctly? What an idea! The only problem is that I ended up adding trivial constructors for every class I wrote:

```
public class Account
{
  private double balance;
  private int numChecksProcessed;
  private CheckBook checkBook;
  public Account()
  {
    balance = 0.0;
    numChecksProcessed = 0;
    checkBook = new CheckBook();
  }
}
```

Why can't I just initialize the data members directly and let the language generate the constructor for me? C++ asked why; C# answers why not? C# does away with unnecessary constructors by allowing direct initialization:

```
public class Account
{
  private double balance = 0.0;
  private int numChecksProcessed = 0;
  private CheckBook checkBook = new CheckBook();
}
```

Define Your Variable Types Well, My Child

C++ is very politically correct. It doesn't want to step on any computer's toes by requiring that a particular type of variable be limited to any particular range of values. It specifies that an `int` is about "so big" and a `long` is "bigger." This indecisiveness leads to obscure errors when trying to move a program from one type of processor to another.

C# doesn't beat around the bush. It says, an `int` is 32 bits and a `long` is 64 bits, and that's the way it's going to be. As a programmer, you can take that information to the bank or to another computer without unexpected errors popping up.

No Multiple Inheriting

C++ allows a single class to inherit from more than one base class. For example, a `SleeperSofa` can inherit from both class `Bed` and class `Sofa`. This sounds really neat and, in fact, it can be very useful. The only problem is that inheriting from multiple base classes can cause some of the most difficult-to-find programming problems in the business.

C# drops back and avoids the increased number of errors by taking multiple inheritance away. However, that wouldn't have been possible had C# not replaced multiple inheritance with a new feature: the interface.

Projecting a Good Interface

When people stepped back and looked at the multiple inheritance nightmare that they had gotten themselves into, they realized that over 90 percent of the time, the second base class existed merely to describe the subclass. For example, a perfectly ordinary class might inherit an abstract class `Persistable` with an abstract method `read()` and another `write()`. This forced the subclass to implement the `read()` and `write()` methods and told the rest of the world that those methods were available for use.

Programmers then realized that the more light-weight interface could do the same thing. A class that implements an interface like the following example is promising to C# and country that it provides the `read()` and `write()` capability:

```
interface IPersistable
{
  void read();
  void write();
}
```

Unified Type System

The C++ class is a nice feature. It allows data and their associated functions to be bundled up into neat little packages that just happen to mimic the way that people think of things in the world. The only problem is that any language must provide room for simple variable types like integer and floating point numbers. This need resulted in a caste system. Class objects lived on one side of the tracks, while value-type variables like int and float lived on the other. Sure, value types and object types were allowed to play in the same program, but the programmer had to keep them separate in his mind.

C# breaks down the Berlin Wall that divides value types from object types. For every value type, there is a corresponding "value type class" called a *structure*. These low-cost structures can mix freely with class objects, enabling the programmer to make statements like the following:

```
MyClass myObject = new MyClass();
Console.WriteLine(myObject.ToString());// display a "myObject" in string format
int i = 5;
Console.WriteLine(i.ToString());        // display an int in string format
Console.WriteLine(5.ToString());        // display the constant 5 in string
                 format
```

Not only can I invoke the same method on int as I do on a MyClass object, but I can also do it to a constant like '5'. This scandalous mixing of variable types is a powerful feature of C#.

Appendix

About the CD-ROM

*T*he CD-ROM that comes tucked away inside the back cover of *C# For Dummies* contains lots of goodies. First, there's the source code from the numerous program examples you find throughout the book. In addition, I've included a couple of utilities that can make your programming life easier. However, your machine must meet a few minimum system requirements before you can make much use of them.

System Requirements

The main System Requirement is that **you must have Visual Studio .NET installed on your computer before you can build and execute the example programs on the CD**. Visual Studio .NET is a separately available product from Microsoft, Inc. Visual Studio .NET is not supplied with this book.

The hardware requirements for using the CD that comes with this book are the same as those for Visual Studio .NET. Refer to the Visual Studio System Requirements for details. However, for adequate performance, you will need

✔ At least a 500MHz Pentium II processor. (You can get by with less but the response time may become intolerable.)

✔ At least 256MB of RAM — more if you can get it. Visual Studio .NET has a large appetite for memory.

✔ 2GB of free disk storage. Visual Studio .NET seems much less sensitive to available disk space. The example programs contained on the enclosed CD-ROM take up a minimal amount of space.

✔ A CD-ROM drive.

Using the CD

To install the example programs found on the enclosed CD-ROM, follow these steps:

1. **Install Visual Studio .NET.**

   You will find the installation instructions with your Visual Studio .NET package. Visual Studio .NET is not supplied with this book.

2. **Insert the CD-ROM into your computer's CD-ROM drive.**

   Give your computer a moment to take a look at the CD.

   You'll know it's done when the light on the front of the CD-ROM drive goes out.

3. **Double-click the My Computer icon. (It's probably located in the upper-left corner of your desktop.)**

   This action opens the My Computer window, which displays all the drives attached to your computer along with the Control Panel, a folder of printers, and other handy things like that.

4. **Double-click the icon for your CD-ROM drive.**

   Another window opens up, showing the directory name C#Programs, the License.txt agreement, and the Readme.txt file.

5. **Double-click License.txt.**

   This file contains the end-user license that you agreed to when you broke the seal and removed the CD-ROM from the plastic pocket. When you are finished reading the license, close the program that displayed the file, most likely NotePad.

6. **Double-click Readme.txt.**

   This file contains any late-breaking information.

7. **Drag the C#Programs folder to your hard drive.**

   To complete this step, click the C#Programs icon with the left mouse button. While still holding the button down, move the mouse over to the hard disk icon in the My Computer window you opened in Step 3. Let go of the mouse button.

   This step copies all the example programs from the CD-ROM to a folder called C#Programs on your hard disk. You can rename this folder, or you can copy it somewhere else on your hard disk, but I don't recommend it. If you do, make a mental note of the new directory name. You will need to use that name instead of C#Programs wherever it appears in the book.

I provided the source files in C#Programs to save you needless typing. When you create a project, Visual Studio creates a folder of the same name. Visual Studio will not create a project if a folder of the same name already exists. For example, you cannot create a project VirtualInheritance in the C#Programs folder because that name is already taken. You can use a directory name other than C#Programs (for example, MyC#Programs), or you may name your project VirtualInheritance2. You can then copy the VirtualInheritance\Class1.cs C# source file into your project folder.

What You'll Find

This CD-ROM contains a number of wonderful gifts.

The C# programs

The first thing you'll find on the CD are the C# source files for the programs from throughout this book. These source files are organized into directories by program name. Each directory contains all the files that go with a single example program and nothing more.

Two bonus chapters

The *C# For Dummies* CD-ROM also includes two bonus chapters.

Bonus Chapter 1 demonstrates how to handle large amounts of data. It goes through the more complex issues such as manipulating directories, maintaining containers, and building and tearing down linked lists.

Bonus Chapter 2 shows you some of the Ins and Outs of the Visual Studio .NET interface. This chapter describes what some of the not-very-obvious buttons do. It also shows you how to use the Visual Studio integrated debugger.

The bonus CD-ROM chapters are in Adobe PDF (Portable Document Format) files. The CD includes a copy of the free Adobe Acrobat Reader software. You need to install the Acrobat Reader if you don't already have it on your computer before you can read these nifty bonus chapters.

To install the Acrobat Reader software, just double-click the Adobe icon and follow the instructions. You'll need to read and accept the license agreement. From there, just accept the defaults and you'll be fine.

After you install Adobe Acrobat Reader, just double-click the chapter names to read them. You can also print the chapter material from Adobe Acrobat Reader.

SharpDevelop

Visual Studio .NET is a power packed user interface, but all that power comes at a price. Visual Studio can be very slow to start up on computers with just the minimum specifications.

SharpDevelop is a nice, light-weight editor for C#. It offers a File⇨New capability for creating template C# files. It uses the same type of color coding to make C# listings easier to read. It supports all the common editing commands. Best of all, you can build your programs directly from Sharp Developer.

You must have Visual Studio .NET installed on your machine in order for Sharp Developer to work. Sharp Developer is not a complete C# development environment. It's just a C# editor that's much quicker to start up and get going.

The installation instructions for SharpDevelop say

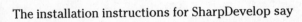

- ✔ Install the .NET SDK.
- ✔ Copy the SharpDevelop distribution to a directory of your choice.
- ✔ Run SharpDevelop.exe in the installation\bin directory.
- ✔ You can make your own link to SharpDevelop on your desktop.

Here's what that really means:

- ✔ Copy the SharpDevelop distribution to a directory of your choice on your hard disk. I suggest `C:\Program Files\SharpDevelop`.
- ✔ Execute SharpDevelop by double-clicking `\Program Files\ SharpDevelop\SharpDevelop.exe`.

You can make it much more convenient to execute SharpDevelop by creating a link on your desktop, as follows:

1. **Right-click SharpDevelop.exe.**

2. **Choose Create Shortcut.**

   A file with the name `Shortcut to SharpDevelop.exe` appears.

3. **Drag the shortcut file to the desktop.**

   You can now simply double-click the shortcut file to execute SharpDevelop.

WithClass 2000 Trial Version

The *C# For Dummies* CD-ROM also includes a trial version of WithClass 2000 from MicroGold Software.

A good program of any size, be it written in C# or some other language, must be properly designed and thought out. No tool can help you with the "thought out" part, but the Unified Modeling Language (UML) is the *lingua franca* for capturing your design. Chapter 13 touches on UML "just a little bit" in its discussion of class factoring; however, there's much more to UML than is dreamt of in that chapter. You can write out UML designs with a crayon and a Big Chief notepad if you want; however, a large-scale operation requires a powerful UML editor. Unfortunately, powerful UML editors carry a powerful price tag.

Full-featured, commercial UML editors cost many thousands of dollars and require a cast of thousands to support them. WithClass 2000 is a UML editor designed for home use.

WithClass 2000 is not cheap. You can buy a new computer for the asking price of this puppy. I'm not kidding — I just did. Check out WithClass 2000 for yourself with this 30-day trial version. If it's right for you and your situation, then consider buying it.

WithClass2000 does not install properly on Windows 2000. I suspect that it does not work for other variations of NT (including Windows XP).

You can install the Enterprise edition by executing the file `WithClass 2000\Enterprise\wc200demo.exe` directly from the CDROM. The Pro edition contained in the `WithClass 2000\Pro` directory has slightly fewer features.

WithClass 2000 is a powerful, professional-grade design package. It comes with a correspondingly professional price tag. This is a 30-day trial version only. Read the `ReadMe First.txt` file for a description of any limitations.

If You've Got Problems (Of the CD Kind)

I tried my best to recompile the programs contained on this CD-ROM on a computer with the minimum system requirements. Alas, your computer may differ, and some programs may not work for some reason, or they may work but very slowly.

The most likely problem is that you do not have the .NET environment installed. Programs created in C# require a set of .NET libraries, which you must have installed on your computer. As of the time of this writing, these libraries did not come preinstalled, though versions of Windows after

Windows 2000 were purported to do so. If you have installed Visual Studio on your computer, you definitely have the necessary .NET libraries. Otherwise, you may be able to download them from `www.microsoft.com`.

Another possible problem is that your computer does not have enough memory (RAM). Visual Studio itself is very memory hungry, though the programs that it generates are not.

If you get an error message such as `Not enough memory` or `Setup cannot continue`, try one or more of the following suggestions and then try using the software again:

- ✓ **Close unnecessary running programs.** The more programs you have running, the less memory you have to execute Visual Studio.

- ✓ **Have your local computer store add more RAM to your computer.** This is admittedly a drastic and potentially expensive step. However, the more memory that you can throw at Visual Studio the better, especially when using Windows NT, Windows 2000 or later.

If you still have trouble installing the items from the CD, please call the Hungry Minds, Inc. Customer Service phone number at 800-762-2974 (outside the U.S.: 317-572-3994) or send e-mail to `techsupdum@hungryminds.com`. If you run into problems with the C# source code on this CD, check out the list of common problems and solutions on my Web site: `www.stephendavis.com`.

Index

• Q •

• R •

Hungry Minds, Inc.
End-User License Agreement

5. Limited Warranty.

(a) HMI warrants that the Software and Software Media are free from defects in materials and workmanship under normal use for a period of sixty (60) days from the date of purchase of this Book. If HMI receives notification within the warranty period of defects in materials or workmanship, HMI will replace the defective Software Media.

(b) **HMI AND THE AUTHOR OF THE BOOK DISCLAIM ALL OTHER WARRANTIES, EXPRESS OR IMPLIED, INCLUDING WITHOUT LIMITATION IMPLIED WARRANTIES OF MERCHANTABILITY AND FITNESS FOR A PARTICULAR PURPOSE, WITH RESPECT TO THE SOFTWARE, THE PROGRAMS, THE SOURCE CODE CONTAINED THEREIN, AND/OR THE TECHNIQUES DESCRIBED IN THIS BOOK. HMI DOES NOT WARRANT THAT THE FUNCTIONS CONTAINED IN THE SOFTWARE WILL MEET YOUR REQUIRE- MENTS OR THAT THE OPERATION OF THE SOFTWARE WILL BE ERROR FREE.**

(c) This limited warranty gives you specific legal rights, and you may have other rights that vary from jurisdiction to jurisdiction.

6. Remedies.

(a) HMI's entire liability and your exclusive remedy for defects in materials and workman- ship shall be limited to replacement of the Software Media, which may be returned to HMI with a copy of your receipt at the following address: Software Media Fulfillment Department, Attn.: *C# For Dummies*, Hungry Minds, Inc., 10475 Crosspoint Blvd., Indianapolis, IN 46256, or call 1-800-762-2974. Please allow four to six weeks for delivery. This Limited Warranty is void if failure of the Software Media has resulted from accident, abuse, or misapplication. Any replacement Software Media will be warranted for the remainder of the original warranty period or thirty (30) days, whichever is longer.

(b) In no event shall HMI or the author be liable for any damages whatsoever (including without limitation damages for loss of business profits, business interruption, loss of business information, or any other pecuniary loss) arising from the use of or inability to use the Book or the Software, even if HMI has been advised of the possibility of such damages.

(c) Because some jurisdictions do not allow the exclusion or limitation of liability for conse- quential or incidental damages, the above limitation or exclusion may not apply to you.

7. U.S. Government Restricted Rights.
Use, duplication, or disclosure of the Software for or on behalf of the United States of America, its agencies and/or instrumentalities (the "U.S. Government") is subject to restrictions as stated in paragraph (c)(1)(ii) of the Rights in Technical Data and Computer Software clause of DFARS 252.227-7013, or subparagraphs (c) (1) and (2) of the Commercial Computer Software - Restricted Rights clause at FAR 52.227-19, and in similar clauses in the NASA FAR supplement, as applicable.

8. General.
This Agreement constitutes the entire understanding of the parties and revokes and supersedes all prior agreements, oral or written, between them and may not be modified or amended except in a writing signed by both parties hereto that specifically refers to this Agreement. This Agreement shall take precedence over any other documents that may be in conflict herewith. If any one or more provisions contained in this Agreement are held by any court or tribunal to be invalid, illegal, or otherwise unenforceable, each and every other pro- vision shall remain in full force and effect.

GNU General Public License

Version 2, June 1991

Preamble

The licenses for most software are designed to take away your freedom to share and change it. By contrast, the GNU General Public License is intended to guarantee your freedom to share and change free software — to make sure the software is free for all its users. This General Public License applies to most of the Free Software Foundation's software and to any other program whose authors commit to using it. (Some other Free Software Foundation software is covered by the GNU Library General Public License instead.) You can apply it to your programs, too.

When we speak of free software, we are referring to freedom, not price. Our General Public Licenses are designed to make sure that you have the freedom to distribute copies of free software (and charge for this service if you wish), that you receive source code or can get it if you want it, that you can change the software or use pieces of it in new free programs; and that you know you can do these things.

To protect your rights, we need to make restrictions that forbid anyone to deny you these rights or to ask you to surrender the rights. These restrictions translate to certain responsibilities for you if you distribute copies of the software, or if you modify it.

For example, if you distribute copies of such a program, whether gratis or for a fee, you must give the recipients all the rights that you have. You must make sure that they, too, receive or can get the source code. And you must show them these terms so they know their rights.

We protect your rights with two steps: (1) copyright the software, and (2) offer you this license which gives you legal permission to copy, distribute and/or modify the software.

Also, for each author's protection and ours, we want to make certain that everyone understands that there is no warranty for this free software. If the software is modified by someone else and passed on, we want its recipients to know that what they have is not the original, so that any problems introduced by others will not reflect on the original authors' reputations.

Finally, any free program is threatened constantly by software patents. We wish to avoid the danger that redistributors of a free program will individually obtain patent licenses, in effect making the program proprietary. To prevent this, we have made it clear that any patent must be licensed for everyone's free use or not licensed at all.

The precise terms and conditions for copying, distribution and modification follow.

TERMS AND CONDITIONS FOR COPYING, DISTRIBUTION AND MODIFICATION

0. This License applies to any program or other work which contains a notice placed by the copyright holder saying it may be distributed under the terms of this General Public License. The "Program", below, refers to any such program or work, and a "work based on the Program" means either the Program or any derivative work under copyright law: that is to say, a work containing the Program or a portion of it, either verbatim or with modifications and/or translated into another language. (Hereinafter, translation is included without limitation in the term "modification".) Each licensee is addressed as "you".

   Activities other than copying, distribution and modification are not covered by this License; they are outside its scope. The act of running the Program is not restricted, and the output from the Program is covered only if its contents constitute a work based on the Program (independent of having been made by running the Program). Whether that is true depends on what the Program does.

1. You may copy and distribute verbatim copies of the Program's source code as you receive it, in any medium, provided that you conspicuously and appropriately publish on each copy an appropriate copyright notice and disclaimer of warranty; keep intact all the notices that refer to this License and to the absence of any warranty; and give any other recipients of the Program a copy of this License along with the Program.

   You may charge a fee for the physical act of transferring a copy, and you may at your option offer warranty protection in exchange for a fee.

2. You may modify your copy or copies of the Program or any portion of it, thus forming a work based on the Program, and copy and distribute such modifications or work under the terms of Section 1 above, provided that you also meet all of these conditions:

   a) You must cause the modified files to carry prominent notices stating that you changed the files and the date of any change.

   b) You must cause any work that you distribute or publish, that in whole or in part contains or is derived from the Program or any part thereof, to be licensed as a whole at no charge to all third parties under the terms of this License.

   c) If the modified program normally reads commands interactively when run, you must cause it, when started running for such interactive use in the most ordinary way, to print or display an announcement including an appropriate copyright notice and a notice that there is no warranty (or else, saying that you provide a warranty) and that users may redistribute the program under these conditions, and telling the user how to view a copy of this License. (Exception: if the Program itself is interactive but does not normally print such an announcement, your work based on the Program is not required to print an announcement.)

   These requirements apply to the modified work as a whole. If identifiable sections of that work are not derived from the Program, and can be reasonably considered independent and separate works in themselves, then this License, and its terms, do not apply to those sections when you distribute them as separate works. But when you distribute the same sections as part of a whole which is a work based on the Program, the distribution of the whole must be on the terms of this License, whose permissions for other licensees extend to the entire whole, and thus to each and every part regardless of who wrote it.

   Thus, it is not the intent of this section to claim rights or contest your rights to work written entirely by you; rather, the intent is to exercise the right to control the distribution of derivative or collective works based on the Program.

In addition, mere aggregation of another work not based on the Program with the Program (or with a work based on the Program) on a volume of a storage or distribution medium does not bring the other work under the scope of this License.

3. You may copy and distribute the Program (or a work based on it, under Section 2) in object code or executable form under the terms of Sections 1 and 2 above provided that you also do one of the following:

   a) Accompany it with the complete corresponding machine-readable source code, which must be distributed under the terms of Sections 1 and 2 above on a medium customarily used for software interchange; or,

   b) Accompany it with a written offer, valid for at least three years, to give any third party, for a charge no more than your cost of physically performing source distribution, a complete machine-readable copy of the corresponding source code, to be distributed under the terms of Sections 1 and 2 above on a medium customarily used for software interchange; or,

   c) Accompany it with the information you received as to the offer to distribute corresponding source code. (This alternative is allowed only for noncommercial distribution and only if you received the program in object code or executable form with such an offer, in accord with Subsection b above.)

   The source code for a work means the preferred form of the work for making modifications to it. For an executable work, complete source code means all the source code for all modules it contains, plus any associated interface definition files, plus the scripts used to control compilation and installation of the executable. However, as a special exception, the source code distributed need not include anything that is normally distributed (in either source or binary form) with the major components (compiler, kernel, and so on) of the operating system on which the executable runs, unless that component itself accompanies the executable.

   If distribution of executable or object code is made by offering access to copy from a designated place, then offering equivalent access to copy the source code from the same place counts as distribution of the source code, even though third parties are not compelled to copy the source along with the object code.

4. You may not copy, modify, sublicense, or distribute the Program except as expressly provided under this License. Any attempt otherwise to copy, modify, sublicense or distribute the Program is void, and will automatically terminate your rights under this License. However, parties who have received copies, or rights, from you under this License will not have their licenses terminated so long as such parties remain in full compliance.

5. You are not required to accept this License, since you have not signed it. However, nothing else grants you permission to modify or distribute the Program or its derivative works. These actions are prohibited by law if you do not accept this License. Therefore, by modifying or distributing the Program (or any work based on the Program), you indicate your acceptance of this License to do so, and all its terms and conditions for copying, distributing or modifying the Program or works based on it.

6. Each time you redistribute the Program (or any work based on the Program), the recipient automatically receives a license from the original licensor to copy, distribute or modify the Program subject to these terms and conditions. You may not impose any further restrictions on the recipients' exercise of the rights granted herein. You are not responsible for enforcing compliance by third parties to this License.

7. If, as a consequence of a court judgment or allegation of patent infringement or for any other reason (not limited to patent issues), conditions are imposed on you (whether by court order, agreement or otherwise) that contradict the conditions of this License, they do not excuse you from the conditions of this License. If you cannot distribute so as to satisfy simultaneously your obligations under this License and any other pertinent obligations, then as a consequence you may not distribute the Program at all. For example, if a patent license would not permit royalty-free redistribution of the Program by all those who receive copies directly or indirectly through you, then the only way you could satisfy both it and this License would be to refrain entirely from distribution of the Program.

If any portion of this section is held invalid or unenforceable under any particular circumstance, the balance of the section is intended to apply and the section as a whole is intended to apply in other circumstances.

It is not the purpose of this section to induce you to infringe any patents or other property right claims or to contest validity of any such claims; this section has the sole purpose of protecting the integrity of the free software distribution system, which is implemented by public license practices. Many people have made generous contributions to the wide range of software distributed through that system in reliance on consistent application of that system; it is up to the author/donor to decide if he or she is willing to distribute software through any other system and a licensee cannot impose that choice.

This section is intended to make thoroughly clear what is believed to be a consequence of the rest of this License.

8. If the distribution and/or use of the Program is restricted in certain countries either by patents or by copyrighted interfaces, the original copyright holder who places the Program under this License may add an explicit geographical distribution limitation excluding those countries, so that distribution is permitted only in or among countries not thus excluded. In such case, this License incorporates the limitation as if written in the body of this License.

9. The Free Software Foundation may publish revised and/or new versions of the General Public License from time to time. Such new versions will be similar in spirit to the present version, but may differ in detail to address new problems or concerns.

Each version is given a distinguishing version number. If the Program specifies a version number of this License which applies to it and "any later version", you have the option of following the terms and conditions either of that version or of any later version published by the Free Software Foundation. If the Program does not specify a version number of this License, you may choose any version ever published by the Free Software Foundation.

10. If you wish to incorporate parts of the Program into other free programs whose distribution conditions are different, write to the author to ask for permission. For software which is copyrighted by the Free Software Foundation, write to the Free Software Foundation; we sometimes make exceptions for this. Our decision will be guided by the two goals of preserving the free status of all derivatives of our free software and of promoting the sharing and reuse of software generally.

NO WARRANTY

11. BECAUSE THE PROGRAM IS LICENSED FREE OF CHARGE, THERE IS NO WARRANTY FOR THE PROGRAM, TO THE EXTENT PERMITTED BY APPLICABLE LAW. EXCEPT WHEN OTHERWISE STATED IN WRITING THE COPYRIGHT HOLDERS AND/OR OTHER PARTIES PROVIDE THE PROGRAM "AS IS" WITHOUT WARRANTY OF ANY KIND, EITHER EXPRESSED OR IMPLIED, INCLUDING, BUT NOT LIMITED TO, THE IMPLIED WARRANTIES OF MERCHANTABILITY AND FITNESS FOR A PARTICULAR PURPOSE. THE ENTIRE RISK AS TO THE QUALITY AND PERFORMANCE OF THE PROGRAM IS WITH YOU. SHOULD THE PROGRAM PROVE DEFECTIVE, YOU ASSUME THE COST OF ALL NECESSARY SERVICING, REPAIR OR CORRECTION.

12. IN NO EVENT UNLESS REQUIRED BY APPLICABLE LAW OR AGREED TO IN WRITING WILL ANY COPYRIGHT HOLDER, OR ANY OTHER PARTY WHO MAY MODIFY AND/OR REDISTRIBUTE THE PROGRAM AS PERMITTED ABOVE, BE LIABLE TO YOU FOR DAMAGES, INCLUDING ANY GENERAL, SPECIAL, INCIDENTAL OR CONSEQUENTIAL DAMAGES ARISING OUT OF THE USE OR INABILITY TO USE THE PROGRAM (INCLUDING BUT NOT LIMITED TO LOSS OF DATA OR DATA BEING RENDERED INACCURATE OR LOSSES SUSTAINED BY YOU OR THIRD PARTIES OR A FAILURE OF THE PROGRAM TO OPERATE WITH ANY OTHER PROGRAMS), EVEN IF SUCH HOLDER OR OTHER PARTY HAS BEEN ADVISED OF THE POSSIBILITY OF SUCH DAMAGES.

END OF TERMS AND CONDITIONS

How to Apply These Terms to Your New Programs

If you develop a new program, and you want it to be of the greatest possible use to the public, the best way to achieve this is to make it free software which everyone can redistribute and change under these terms.

To do so, attach the following notices to the program. It is safest to attach them to the start of each source file to most effectively convey the exclusion of warranty; and each file should have at least the "copyright" line and a pointer to where the full notice is found.

```
one line to give the program's name and an idea of what it does.
                Copyright (C) yyyy  name of author

This program is free software; you can redistribute it and/or
modify it under the terms of the GNU General Public License
as published by the Free Software Foundation; either version 2
of the License, or (at your option) any later version.

This program is distributed in the hope that it will be useful,
but WITHOUT ANY WARRANTY; without even the implied warranty of
MERCHANTABILITY or FITNESS FOR A PARTICULAR PURPOSE.  See the
GNU General Public License for more details.

You should have received a copy of the GNU General Public License
along with this program; if not, write to the Free Software
Foundation, Inc., 59 Temple Place - Suite 330, Boston, MA 02111-1307, USA.
Also add information on how to contact you by electronic and paper mail.
If the program is interactive, make it output a short notice like this
when it starts in an interactive mode:
Gnomovision version 69, Copyright (C) yyyy name of author
Gnomovision comes with ABSOLUTELY NO WARRANTY; for details type `show w'.
This is free software, and you are welcome to redistribute it under
certain conditions; type `show c' for details.
```

The hypothetical commands show w and show c should show the appropriate parts of the General Public License. Of course, the commands you use may be called something other than show w and show c; they could even be mouse-clicks or menu items — whatever suits your program.

You should also get your employer (if you work as a programmer) or your school, if any, to sign a "copyright disclaimer" for the program, if necessary. Here is a sample; alter the names:

```
Yoyodyne, Inc., hereby disclaims all copyright
interest in the program `Gnomovision'
(which makes passes at compilers) written
by James Hacker.

signature of Ty Coon, 1 April 1989
Ty Coon, President of Vice
```

This General Public License does not permit incorporating your program into proprietary programs. If your program is a subroutine library, you may consider it more useful to permit linking proprietary applications with the library. If this is what you want to do, use the GNU Library General Public License instead of this License.

Installation Instructions

To install the example programs found on the enclosed CD-ROM, follow these steps:

1. **Install Visual Studio .NET.**

   Visual Studio .NET is not supplied with this book.

2. **Insert the CD-ROM into your computer's CD-ROM drive.**

3. **Double-click the My Computer icon.**

4. **In the My Computer window, double-click the icon for your CD-ROM drive.**

5. **In the resulting window, double-click License.txt.**

   This file contains the end-user license that you agreed to when you broke the seal and removed the CD-ROM from the plastic pocket. When you are finished reading the license, close the program that displayed the file, most likely NotePad.

6. **Double-click Readme.txt.**

   This file contains any late-breaking information.

7. **Click and drag the** C#Programs **folder to your hard drive, copying all the example programs from the CD-ROM to a folder called** C#Programs **on your hard disk.**

   You can rename this folder, or you can copy it somewhere else on your hard disk, but I don't recommend it. If you do, make a mental note of the new directory name. You will need to use that name instead of C#Programs wherever it appears in the book.

I provided the source files in C#Programs to save you needless typing. When you create a project, Visual Studio creates a folder of the same name. Visual Studio will not create a project if a folder of the same name already exists. For example, you cannot create a project VirtualInheritance in the C#Programs folder because that name is already taken. You can use a directory name other than C#Programs (for example, MyC#Programs), or you may name your project VirtualInheritance2. You can then copy the VirtualInheritance\Class1.cs C# source file into your project folder.

For more details, see the "About the CD-ROM" appendix.